LATE AND POST-SOVIET RUSSIAN LITERATURE
A Reader

Book 2

The Thaw and Stagnation

CULTURAL SYLLABUS

Series Editor: Mark LIPOVETSKY (*University of Colorado-Boulder*)

ACADEMIC
STUDIES
PRESS

LATE AND POST-SOVIET RUSSIAN LITERATURE

A Reader

Book 2

The Thaw and Stagnation

Edited by
Mark Lipovetsky
and Lisa Ryoko Wakamiya

BOSTON / 2015

Library of Congress Cataloging-in-Publication Data:
A catalog record for this book as available from the Library of Congress.

The book is supported by Mikhail Prokhorov Foundation
(translation program TRANSCRIPT).

ISBN 978-1-61811-432-7 (hardback)
ISBN 978-1-61811-433-4 (electronic)
ISBN 978-1-61811-434-1 (paperback)

Book design by Ivan Grave
On the cover: *The Horizon*, by Erik Bulatov (1971/1972)

Published by Academic Studies Press in 2015
28 Montfern Avenue
Brighton, MA 02135, USA
press@academicstudiespress.com
www.academicstudiespress.com

CONTENTS

PART II: LITERATURE OF THE STAGNATION

Acknowledgments

We are very grateful to The Mikhail Prokhorov Foundation
for the support of both volumes of this project through the
"Transcript" grant program. This support was essential to the
completion of this project.

This project also received support from the Text and Academic
Authors Association. Our special thanks for the generosity of
the following people and institutions who provided copyright
permissions without charge:

Alexander Genis and Elvira Vayl; Copyright © 2003 for
Pyotr Vail' and Alexander Genis, "60-e: Mir sovetskogo
cheloveka," *Izbrannoe. In 2 vols.* Vol. 1. Ekaterinburg:
U-Faktoriia, 2003. P. 611–620; 699–713.

Robert Porter; Copyright © 2007 for Robert Porter,
Solzhenitsyn's One Day in the Life of Ivan Denisovich.
Bristol: Bristol Classical Press, 2007. P. 40–49.

Zoya Boguslavskaya; Copyright © 1967 for Andrei
Voznesensky, *AntiWorlds*. London: Oxford University
Press, 1967. P. 40–41, 49–50, 51, 66–68.

The Trustees of the Liddell Hart Centre for Military Archives
and Lianne Smith, Archives Services Manager at King's
College London. Copyright © 1987 for "Interview with
Evgeny Evtushenko."

Aleksandr Daniel and Irina Uvarova; Copyright © 1967 for
Yuli Daniel, *This is Moscow Speaking*. Trans. Stuart Hood,
Harold Shukman, John Richardson. London: Collins and
Harvill, 1968. P. 20–66.

Natalia Tendryakova and Maria Tendryakova; Copyright © 1995 for Vladimir Tenrdryakov's "Bread for a Dog."

Valentina Brougher and Frank Miller; Copyright © 2011 for the translations and annotations of Vladimir Tendryakov's "Bread for a Dog," Varlam Shalamov's "Eulogy," and Yurii Dombrovsky's "Little Arm, Leg, Cucumber," published in: *50 Writers: An Anthology of 20th Century Russian Short Stories.* Boston: Academic Studies Press, 2011. Selected, with an Introduction by Mark Lipovetsky and Valentina Brougher. Translated and annotated by Valentina Brougher and Frank Miller. P. 365–379; 466–86; 505–522.

FTM Literary Agency (Moscow); Copyright © for Varlam Shalamov's "On Prose" and "Eulogy."

Alena Galich (heir) and Maria Bloshteyn (translation); Copyright © 2008 for Alexander Galich, *Dress Rehearsal.* Bloomington: Slavica, 2008. P. 169–92.

Maria Rozanova (heir) and Maria-Regina Kecht (translation); Copyright ©1982 for Andrey Sinyavsky, "Dissent as a Personal Experience," *Yearbook of Comparative and General Literature* 31 (1982): 21–29.

Sem' dnei Publishing House (Moscow); Copyright © 2009 for Vasilii Aksenov, *Tainstvennaia strast'.* Moscow: Sem' dnei, 2009. P. 82–86, 88–95, 96–100, 105–107, 119–133.

Alexei Yurchak; Copyright © 2006 for Alexei Yurchak. *Everything Was Forever, Until It Was No More: The Last Soviet Generation.* Princeton and Oxford: Princeton University Press, 2006. P. 126–155.

Aleksei Losev (heir) and Henry Pickford (translation); Copyright © 2014, Translation copyright © 2014 Henry W. Pickford; for Lev Losev's poems from *Selected Early Poems by Lev Loseff,* edited, translated, and with introduction by Henry Pickford. Spuyten Duyvil Publishing; Bilingual edition, 2013.

Olga Kushlina (heir); Copyright © Viktor Krivulin; permission to translate and publish Viktor Krivulin's poems.

The Estate of Yevgeny Kharitonov and Arch Tait (translation); Copyright © 1998 for Yevgeny Kharitonov, *Under House Arrest*. Trans. Arch Tait. London: Serpent's Tail, 1997. P. 149–57; 184–7.

Olga Sedakova; Copyright © 1991; "Vspominaia Venedikta Erofeeva," *Teatr* 9 (1991): 98–104.

Mikhail Epshtein; Copyright © 1999. Epstein, Mikhail. "Charms of Entropy and New Sentimentality: The Myth of Venedikt Erofeev," in Alexander Genis, Mikhail Epstein, and Slobodanka Vladiv-Glover, *Russian Postmodernism: New Perspectives on Post-Soviet Culture*. Edited and translated by Slobodanka Vladiv-Glover. Oxford and New York: Berghahn Books, 1999. P. 427–42.

Nadezhda Burova (heir), Valentina Polukhina, Robert Reed and Joe Andre (translators); Copyright © 1995 for Dmitry Prigov. *Texts of Our Life: Bilingual Selected Poems*. Edited and introduced by Valentina Polukhina. Keele: Essays in Poetics Publications, 1995. P. 16–33.

Vladimir Shinkarev; Copyright © Vladimir Shinkarev, "Mit'ki," in *Mit'ki: Vybrannoe*. Ed. Pavel Krusanov. St. Petersburg: Kanon, 1999. P. 11–16, 43–50.

We deeply appreciate the cooperation of the following publishing companies for the paid permission to reprint:

Harper Collins Publishers: for Chapters 10 [P. 386–92] and 12 [P. 402–18] (11,200 words) from *The Gulag Archipelago 1918–1956* by Aleksandr I. Solzhenitsyn. Authorized Abridgement with a New Introduction by Edward E. Ericson, Jr. Copyright © 1985 by The Russian Social Fund. Reprinted by permission of Harper Collins Publishers.

Harper Collins Publishers: for excerpt from P. 141–66 (8,712 words) from *Forever Flowing: A Novel By Vasily Grossman*. Translated by Thomas P. Whitney. Copyright © 1997 by Possev-Verlag. English translation copyright © 1972 by Thomas P. Whitney. Reprinted by permission of Harper Collins Publishers.

Farrar, Straus, and Giroux, LLC: for "Letters to a Roman Friend," "May 24, 1980," "The Hawk's Cry in Autumn," from *Selected Poems* by Joseph Brodsky, *Selected Poems in English*. Translated by or with the author. Edited by Ann Kjellberg. New York: Farrar, Straus and Giroux, 2002. P. 58–60, 211, 49–52. Reprinted by permission of Farrar, Straus and Giroux, LLC.

Farrar, Straus, and Giroux, LLC: for "Less Than One" from *Less Than One* by Joseph Brodsky. Joseph Brodsky, *Less Than One: Selected Essays*. New York: Farrar, Straus, and Giroux, 1987. P. 3–33. Copyright © 1986 by Joseph Brodsky. Reprinted by permission of Farrar, Straus and Giroux, LLC.

Farrar, Straus, and Giroux, LLC: for "No, not one face, but two . . . ," "Someone's crying all night . . . ," "We don't get to choose our century . . . ," "As at every doorstep grow rowan and maple . . . ," "Pan," "Memoirs," and "Before the War: Recollections," from *Apollo In The Snow: Selected Poems* by Aleksandr Kushner. Translated by Paul Graves and Carol Ueland. New York: Farrar, Straus, and Giroux, 1992. P. 6, 21, 36–37, 41, 61–62, 80–81. Translation copyright © 1988, 1989, 1991 by Paul Graves and Carol Ueland. Reprinted by permission of Farrar, Straus and Giroux, LLC.

Farrar, Straus, and Giroux, LLC: for an excerpt from Andrei Bitov, *Pushkin House*. Translated by Susan Brownsberger. New York: Farrar, Straus, and Giroux, 1987. P. 351–55. Translation copyright © 1987 by Susan Brownsberger. Reprinted by the permission of Farrar, Straus and Giroux, LLC.

W. W. Norton: "Bathhouse Blues" by Vladimir Vysotsky, "Cigarette Butt" by Yuz Aleshkovsky, "Dialogue" by Vladimir Vysotsky, "Lesbian Song" by Yuz Aleshkovsky, "Monkey" by Genrikh Sapgir, "Parody of A Bad Detective Story" by Vladimir Vysotsky, "Personal Meeting" by Yuz Aleshkovsky, "Radioblab" by Genrikh Sapgir, "A Voice" by Genrikh Sapgir, "Wolf Hunt" by Vladimir Vysotsky, translated by H. William Tjalsma, from *Metropol: A Literary Almanac,* edited by Vassily Aksyonov, Viktor Yerofeyev, Fazil Iskander, Andrei Bitov, and Yevgeny Popov. Copyright © 1982 by ARDIS/RLT. Copyright © 1979 by Metropol. Used by permission of W. W. Norton & Company, Inc.

Bloodaxe Books: for the reprint of the following poems from Elena Shvarts, *Paradise: Selected Poems.* Translated by Michael Molnar and Catriona Kelly; "The Dump" (P. 25), "Elegy on the X-Ray Photo of My Skull" (P. 69), "I was born with an unlined palm" (P. 77), "Orpheus" (P. 89).

Counterpoint: Copyright © Sergei Dovlatov, 1982, from *The Zone* by Sergei Dovlatov. Reprinted by permission of Counterpoint. Translated by Anne Frydman © 1982. Reprinted by permission of Counterpoint.

Viktor Erofeev; Copyright © 1991 for "Vremia 'Metropolia,'" *Antologiia Samizdata,* edited by Mark Barbaladze. http://antology.igrunov.ru/after_75/periodicals/metropol/1087390559.html

Permission requests sent to Yevgeny Yevtushenko and his publishers remained unanswered at the time this book went to press. We will be happy to remit all necessary fees for the reprint of Yevtushenko's poems from: Yevgeny Yevtushenko, *The Collected Poems, 1952–1990.* Edited by Albert C. Todd with the author and James Ragan. New York: Henry Holt, 1991. P. 102–104, 113–14, 165–170.

No less deserving of acknowledgment are the translators whose efforts enabled many works to appear here in English for the first time: Rebecca Pyatkevich, Sibelan Forrester, Brian R. Johnson, and Sarah H. Kapp.

Special thanks go to Igor and Kira Nemirovsky and Meghan Vicks at Academic Studies Press for bringing this project to completion.

Part I

LITERATURE OF THE THAW

INTRODUCTION

Typically, the post-Stalin cultural history of Russia is divided according to the following political periodization: the Thaw (1954–1968), Stagnation (1968–86), Perestroika (1987–1991), and the post-Soviet period (1991–present). The chronological borders for some of these periods are debatable (1968 or 1965? or 1964? 1987 or 1986? or even 1985?). Others are less ambiguous (1954 and 1991). However, the question remains: why do some political changes directly correspond to cultural shifts? Why did political reforms following Stalin's death in 1953 lead to the introduction of the Thaw, why did the ousting of Stalin's successor Nikita Khrushchev in 1964 shift the literary and cultural landscape into Stagnation culture, and why did Gorbachev's *perestroika* and especially the policies of *glasnost'* (openness) have such a dramatic effect on the entire cultural edifice?

The answer to these questions lies in the structure of Soviet society. A strict system of political censorship over all forms of cultural production, but especially literature and film, was established as early as the 1920s, but this is only partially responsible for the correlation between politics and culture. After all, underground and non-conformist literature did not disappear even in the harshest periods of Soviet history, such as the Great Terror of the 1930s (Anna Akhmatova's "Requiem," Lidia Chukovskaya's *Sofia Petrovna*, Osip Mandelstam's *Voronezh Notebooks*, and Andrei Platonov's *The Foundation Pit* attest to this). Certainly, back then and for many decades afterward, these texts were known only to a confined circle of readers, and their circulation was a dangerous enterprise for both their authors and the texts' "distributors." In the 1960s and 1970s, the production and circulation of uncensored literary texts developed into an entire system of *samizdat* (the self-publication of works reproduced in multiple copies by hand or typewriter) and *tamizdat* (when works were published "there," i.e., abroad, then smuggled into the USSR). However, the coexistence of "official" and "non-official" (non-conformist, uncensored) literatures is a phenomenon that permeates all of Soviet history, resulting not so much in a dialectic of opposing forces, but a plurality of opinions. What is significant is not only the quantitative growth of parallel literary production since the early 1960s, but the fact that this cultural realm included, in addition to politically charged texts that undermined state ideology and official versions of history, a range of modernist, avant-garde, and postmodern works that did not fit into realist aesthetics, let alone into the official doctrine of Socialist Realism.

In other words, Soviet culture — taken as whole, in all its "official" and "non-official" iterations — contributes to an ongoing and contentious debate about the nature of the communist experiment, its results, achievements, and crimes. This includes debates about the relationship between neo-traditionalist and modern visions of society, modernist and avant-garde approaches to culture. This latter debate traverses the borders dividing official and non-conformist cultural realms over the course of Soviet cultural history: works that criticized the Soviet regime for its destruction of traditional culture could only circulate underground (Solzhenitsyn's writings are the best-known example), while "formalism" — a term used to describe all forms of modernist and avant-garde art — was repressed as well.

Perhaps the reason for this paradox can be found in the inherent contradiction of the Stalinist social and cultural project (as well as in other totalitarian regimes): the creation of modern society by anti-modern, neo-traditionalist systems of social homogenization. These systems exhibit the quasi-religious character of Soviet ideology and evince, among other characteristics, the creation of a pantheon of heroes and leaders with a god-like leader at the top of the pyramid; elaborate social rituals, from celebratory demonstrations to show trials; promote nationalism and xenophobia; the solidification of the cultural canon; and the persecution of "others," a social spectrum that ranged from political dissidents labeled as "enemies of the people" to homosexuals, hipsters (*stiliagi*), Jews, "bourgeois individualists," "cosmopolitans," and still more "others."

However, the balance between striving toward modernization and systems of neo-traditionalism frequently changed in the course of Soviet history. The historical milestones associated with 1953 (Stalin's death), 1968 (the Soviet invasion of Czechoslovakia and the destruction of the dream of "socialism with a human face"), and 1987 (the introduction of *glasnost'*) signify the most dramatic moments of these shifts. Since the economic (state control over the economy) and political (one-party state) foundations of the Soviet regime remained unshaken since NEP and until *perestroika*, the majority of political changes affected the field of ideology; in other words, they affected the sphere of values and doctrines, which, in turn, is inseparable from the realm of culture. This is to say that every political change first and foremost affected culture, and only through the latter, the social fabric as a whole. It is no wonder that each of these political shifts immediately affected the balance of cultural forces: those who were persecuted yesterday would become celebrated today, and vice versa.

The period of the Thaw (named after Ilya Ehrenburg's novella of the same name) marked one of the most radical changes in this respect since the early 1930s. Khrushchev's "Secret Speech," delivered at the Twentieth Congress of the Communist Party in 1956, had a profound effect on Soviet society precisely because it exploded the neo-traditionalist order in an attempt to both preserve and modernize the Soviet political and economic regime. In a way, Khrushchev employed the mechanism of instantly converting a former hero or leader into an "enemy of the people," a tactic that was developed in Stalin's time. He did this, once again following Stalin's model, in order to consolidate his own power, neutralize the "old Stalinist guard," and disarm the all-powerful state security forces (former NKVD, then MGB, and finally the KGB) that had been the primary tool of Stalinist terror. But the fact that he used these methods against Stalin himself, the supreme leader, the axis of the Soviet quasi-religion, caused the ultimate crisis in Soviet civilization. Although Khrushchev, in this speech and afterward, tried to keep intact what seemed to be the foundations of the regime—faith in the communist utopia, the cult of Lenin that replaced the cult of Stalin, hostility to capitalism, and mantras about the supremacy of the first state founded by and for the victorious proletariat—the damage was irreparable, and the ideological and cultural transformations that ensued were unstoppable.

Khrushchev asked: "Why did we not do something earlier, during Stalin's life, in order to prevent the loss of innocent lives?" Toward answering this question, Khrushchev in part blamed Soviet writers, filmmakers, and scientists for mythologizing Stalin's abilities as a leader. "When we look at many of our novels, films and historical-scientific studies . . . the Soviet Army, supposedly thanks only to Stalin's genius, turned to the offensive and subdued the enemy. The epic victory gained . . . through our heroic people, is ascribed in this type of novel, film and 'scientific study' as being completely due to the strategic genius of Stalin."

Khrushchev's denouncement of Stalin (but not Stalinism), allowed for the publication of works such as Aleksandr Solzhenitsyn's 1962 *One Day in the Life of Ivan Denisovich*, which transformed Soviet literature by depicting a "typical" day in a remote labor camp. However, censorship and other regulatory practices mandated by the state continued to restrict what and whom could be published. Indeed, even Khrushchev's "Secret Speech" itself could not be published in Russia until 1989, when the reforms of *perestroika* that would lead to the collapse of the Soviet Union were underway.

Histories of the Thaw period identify Khrushchev and Solzhenitsyn as initiators of cultural change. Khrushchev, as First Secretary of the Communist Party of the Soviet Union, was uniquely positioned to advocate for reform. Solzhenitsyn, as a former "enemy of the people" and literary unknown, was not. Their anti-Stalinism did not unite them in any way, nor were the outcomes of their work confined to the period of the Thaw. Khrushchev's reforms were largely intended to move the concentration of power away from a single individual and strengthen the stability of the Communist Party elite, a goal that was achieved during the rule of his successor Leonid Brezhnev. Solzhenitsyn's work sought to disempower not only Stalinism, but the Party and the Soviet regime as a whole, a vision that eventually came to pass with the collapse of the Soviet Union. Viewing the cultural changes of the late Soviet period from the standpoint of the present reveals a longer, comparative perspective on how individuals contribute to political and cultural change.

The struggle for self-identification and the search for meaning did not take place exclusively in the political sphere. For the writer Vassily Aksyonov, the Thaw was "a time with no fear." Aksyonov and his young colleagues felt that they were "the new generation, the one which would change things in our country." As a leading figure in the youth prose movement and self-proclaimed *stiliaga* (hipster), Aksyonov introduced slang, a cosmopolitan sensibility, and even new modes of dress into Soviet literature and life. Aksyonov's name became synonymous with a romanticized vision of the Thaw, in which the writer and reader shared a common language, sense of fashion, and love of American jazz. Although Aksyonov would later revise this portrait of his generation in his 2008 autobiographic novel *A Mysterious Passion*, the youthful idealism the *stiliagi* exuded in their life and art during the Thaw stands beside the publication of Solzhenitsyn's *One Day in the Life of Ivan Denisovich*, Khrushchev's "Secret Speech," and the emergence of the poets Andrei Voznesensky and Yevgeny Yevtushenko as among the most vivid indications that a new era had begun.

Growing conflict within society was the first radical effect of Khrushchev's exposure of Stalin's crimes. Due to the political changes discussed above, the Thaw was a period of heated culture wars between those who wanted to preserve the Soviet symbolic order, such as hardcore Stalinists or followers of Khrushchev's version of communist ideology "cleansed" of the "cult of [Stalin's] personality," and those who embraced opportunities offered by a new and large-scale wave of modernization, the movement from uniformity to heterogeneity in culture and lifestyle, and greater personal and intellectual freedom. These culture wars are responsible for the numerous internal contradictions of the Thaw period, when each new degree of freedom was earned by bitter political struggle— and could be reversed the very next day. The literary journal *New World* (*Novyi mir*) became a hub of literary innovation during the Thaw, but the publication of nearly every issue was delayed due to the resistance of censors. 1956 was the year of Khrushchev's "Secret Speech" and the beginning of the political campaign against Stalinism, but it was also the year that democratic anti-communist uprisings in Hungary were suppressed (Aksyonov's *A Mysterious Passion* depicts how these events affected the creative intelligentsia). In 1958, with the Thaw in full swing, Boris Pasternak was forced to renounce the Nobel Prize he was awarded for his novel *Doctor Zhivago* (banned in the USSR). In 1961 the Twenty-Second Party Congress demanded the removal of Stalin's embalmed body from the Lenin Mausoleum on Red Square; in the same year, Vasily Grossman's novel *Life and Fate* was "arrested" by the KGB. In 1962, Solzhenitsyn's *One Day in the Life of Ivan Denisovich* was published and even nominated for the Lenin Prize in Literature; in the same year a peaceful workers' demonstration against high food prices in Novocherkassk was suppressed by mass shooting.

The works of many writers who were victims of Stalinist terror, or who were banned in Stalin's time, were returned to circulation during the Thaw. Among them were Isaac Babel, Mikhail Zoshchenko, Andrei Platonov, Anna Akhmatova, Marina Tsvetaeva, Ivan Bunin, Osip Mandelstam, Ilya Il'f and Evgeny Petrov, Nikolai Zabolotsky, Daniil Kharms, and many others. However, not all of their works were "rehabilitated." Platonov's novels, Bulgakov's *Heart of a Dog*, *The Fatal Eggs*, and other novellas, Akhmatova's "Requiem," Kharms' writings for adults, Mandelstam's late poems, and many other works remained banned. Classics of twentieth-century Russian literature, such as Evgeny Zamyatin, Vladimir Nabokov, Konstantin Vaginov, and Alexander Vvedensky, were forced into "oblivion" and could only be circulated in *samizdat* and *tamizdat* until the reforms of the 1980s.

Such contradictions are visible on a broader scale as well. On the one hand, Soviet society experienced a strong push toward modernization, which stimulated a surge of creativity among the younger generation. Still enchanted by the idea of communism, the "generation of the sixties," as it was then called, was also creating new identities and ways of living. Pyotr Vail' and Alexander Genis, in their book *The Sixties: The World of the Soviet Man*, provide a broad overview of these innovations. Vassily Aksyonov's *A Mysterious Passion* depicts additional forms of cultural innovation, including sexual revolution as the ultimate manifestation of newly-discovered, private, individual, even hedonistic values—a far cry from the self-sacrificing asceticism demanded by Stalinist culture.

Accompanying these processes was a quest for new subjectivities based on a new sense of the self that was not defined by a sense of belonging to the "collective body" of the Soviet people. These subjectivities are important by virtue of the dissimilarity between them and the challenge of realizing them in all their various forms in everyday life. This quest for new subjectivities found its most vibrant embodiment in the poetry of the sixties, as represented by Yevgeny Yevtushenko, Andrei Voznesensky, Alexander Galich, and others. Their poems were political precisely because they were personal. Each of these poets in his own way tried to define his "I" in its complex relationship to the "we," an attitude distinct from the previous subjugation of the personal to the collective. The public need for such discourse was supported by the unprecedented popularity of poetry in the sixties: poetry readings in the 1960s filled stadiums; poets could be likened to rock stars.

At the same time, the reevaluation of Stalinism, initiated by Khrushchev's speech, launched the process that in similar conditions was defined (in relation to Nazism) as "working through the past." The tragic experiences of victims of the Soviet regime, previously completely excluded from public view, were slowly but steadily entering the collective consciousness. Former prisoners of the Gulag were released by Khrushchev and began to return to society. Their experiences required a new understanding of the Stalinist epoch, and consequently of the entire Soviet experiment. Aleksandr Solzhenitsyn's *One Day in the Life of Ivan Denisovich* produced the first breakthrough, which affected not only Soviet readerships but also the Western perception of communism. After the publication of Solzhenitsyn's novella, many other works exploring the Gulag as the deepest point of historical trauma—such as Varlam Shalamov's stories, Solzhenitsyn's later novels and his *Gulag Archipelago*—emerged in quick succession. Other works analyzed the traumatic social distortions produced by the Soviet experience. These include Alexander Galich's songs, Grossman's *Life and Fate* and *Everything Flows*, Vladimir Tendryakov's autobiographical depiction of the post-collectivization Holodomor (famine), Andrey Sinyavsky's (Abram Tertz) and Yulii Daniel's (Nikolai Arzhak) "fantastic tales," all of which, like Pasternak's *Doctor Zhivago*, could be published only in *samizdat* and *tamizdat*. The authors of these works were banned from Soviet magazines and presses. Sometimes they endured public shaming, as Pasternak did, or expulsion into exile as in the cases of Solzhenitsyn and Galich. In other cases, they underwent trial and imprisonment as Sinyavsky and Daniel did, or, like Shalamov, suffered extreme poverty and isolation.

Manuscripts could also be confiscated and "arrested" as Grossman's were. However, this was not the only path open to those attempting to "work through" the Soviet experience. The "legal" literature of the sixties developed an elaborate "Aesopian language," a system of hints and allusions that allowed readers to read seemingly innocent texts as political allegories. These tricks did not fully deceive censors, but the censors were also Soviet people, and they were also affected by the crisis of Soviet ideology. They were therefore sometimes inclined to close their eyes to political subversion in a text, so long as it kept the illusion of propriety.

The crumbling of the Soviet symbolic order, the growing heterogeneity of society, and, most importantly, the process of "working through the past" begun during the Thaw, generated at least two significant lines of additional cultural and ideological transformation. The first was obviated by the intelligentsia's reaction to the arrest of Sinyavsky and Daniel in 1965 for publishing their literary works abroad. Designed by the authorities as a symbolic end to the "liberties" of the Thaw, this trial revealed the opposite: the impossibility of a return to Stalinism in culture. Not only did

Sinyavsky and Daniel not admit their guilt, defending their artistic freedom against criminal charges, the intelligentsia, or rather its liberal segment, openly supported these "criminals" by writing protest letters to official organs and circulating them in *samizdat*. This trial, many historians agree, was the first step of the dissident movement's methodical political confrontation with the regime; they used *samizdat* and *tamizdat* and communicated with Western diplomats and journalists to systematically expose the authorities' past and present crimes. Solzhenitsyn and Andrei Sakharov, the physicist and creator of the hydrogen bomb, became the leaders of two major trends in the Soviet dissident movement, of nationalist and liberal-democratic inclinations, respectively. Even dissident discourse, then, was characterized by heterogeneity.

Another consequence was less obvious, although for literature it had a no less profound effect than the emergence of the dissident movement had for Soviet ideology. Sinyavsky's and Daniel's short stories and novellas reintroduced the grotesque, *skaz*, and ambivalence—modalities almost completely excluded from Soviet literature since the early 1930s. Shalamov's minimalist "new prose" (as he defines it) attempted to create non-literature, or rather, anti-literature that was the only mode adequate to articulate the non-human experience of the Gulag. These writers were not alone in their attempts to create new languages that transcended the limits of representative forms of writing, resurrecting modernist experimentation in new cultural conditions and, thus, bridging the gap between the present and the past of Russian culture created by Socialist Realism and political terror. In reference to this gap, Joseph Brodsky stated in his 1987 Nobel Prize lecture: "Looking back, I can say again that we were beginning in an empty—indeed, a terrifyingly wasted—place, and that, intuitively rather than consciously, we aspired precisely to the re-creation of the effect of culture's continuity, to the reconstruction of its forms and tropes, toward filling its few surviving, and often totally compromised, forms, with our own new, or appearing to us as new, contemporary content."

To sum up, the internal liberalization of society, coupled with the process of working through the historical trauma of the Soviet period, was prohibited in official culture, because its explosive potential, its power to undermine the legitimacy of the entire Soviet regime, was grasped by the political, ideological, and cultural establishment. However, this process could not be stopped entirely. It continued in the underground, and through strategies such as "Aesopian language" in official culture, thus preparing the collapse of the Soviet ideological and symbolic regime during *perestroika*.

Nikita Khrushchev

From "Speech to the 20th Congress of the CPSU"

Delivered February 24–25, 1956

[. . .] Stalin originated the concept "enemy of the people." This term automatically made it unnecessary that the ideological errors of a man or men engaged in a controversy be proven. It made possible the use of the cruelest repression, violating all norms of revolutionary legality, against anyone who in any way disagreed with Stalin, against those who were only suspected of hostile intent, against those who had bad reputations. The concept "enemy of the people" actually eliminated the possibility of any kind of ideological fight or the making of one's views known on this or that issue, even [issues] of a practical nature. On the whole, the only proof of guilt actually used, against all norms of current legal science, was the "confession" of the accused himself. As subsequent probing has proven, "confessions" were acquired through physical pressures against the accused. This led to glaring violations of revolutionary legality and to the fact that many entirely innocent individuals— [persons] who in the past had defended the Party line—became victims.

We must assert that, in regard to those persons who in their time had opposed the Party line, there were often no sufficiently serious reasons for their physical annihilation. The formula "enemy of the people" was specifically introduced for the purpose of physically annihilating such individuals.

It is a fact that many persons who were later annihilated as enemies of the Party and people had worked with Lenin during his life. Some of these persons had made errors during Lenin's life, but, despite this, Lenin benefited by their work; he corrected them and he did everything possible to retain them in the ranks of the Party; he induced them to follow him. [. . .]

Let us take the example of the Trotskyites. At present, after a sufficiently long historical period, we can speak about the fight with the Trotskyites with complete calm and can analyze this matter with sufficient objectivity. After all, around Trotsky were people whose origin cannot by any means be traced to bourgeois society. Part of them belonged to the Party intelligentsia and a certain part were recruited from among the workers. We can name many individuals who, in their time, joined the Trotskyites; however, these same individuals took an active part in the workers' movement before the Revolution, during the Socialist October Revolution itself, and also in the consolidation of the victory of this greatest of revolutions. Many of them broke with Trotskyism and returned to Leninist positions. Was it necessary to annihilate such people? We are deeply convinced that, had Lenin lived, such an extreme method would not have been used against any of them.

Such are only a few historical facts. But can it be said that Lenin did not decide to use even the most severe means against enemies of the Revolution when this was actually necessary? No; no one can say this. Vladimir Ilyich demanded uncompromising dealings with the enemies of the Revolution and of the working class and when necessary resorted ruthlessly to such methods. You will recall only V. I. Lenin's fight with the Socialist Revolutionary organizers of the anti-Soviet uprising, with the counterrevolutionary kulaks in 1918 and with others, when Lenin without hesitation used the most extreme methods against the enemies. Lenin used such methods, however, only against actual class enemies and not against those who blunder, who err, and whom it was possible to lead through ideological influence and even retain in the leadership. Lenin used severe methods only in the most necessary cases, when the exploiting classes were still in existence and were vigorously opposing the Revolution, when the struggle for survival was decidedly assuming the sharpest forms, even including a Civil War.

Stalin, on the other hand, used extreme methods and mass repressions at a time when the Revolution was already victorious, when the Soviet state was strengthened, when the exploiting classes were already liquidated and socialist relations were rooted solidly in all phases of national economy, when our Party was politically consolidated and had strengthened itself both numerically and ideologically.

It is clear that here Stalin showed in a whole series of cases his intolerance, his brutality and his abuse of power. Instead of proving his political correctness and mobilizing the masses, he often chose the path of repression and physical annihilation, not only against actual enemies, but also against individuals who had not committed any crimes against the Party and the Soviet Government. Here we see no wisdom but only a demonstration of the brutal force which had once so alarmed V. I. Lenin. [. . .]

An example of vile provocation, of odious falsification and of criminal violation of revolutionary legality is the case of the former candidate for the Central Committee Politburo, one of the most eminent workers of the Party and of the Soviet Government, Comrade [Robert] Eikhe, who had been a Party member since 1905.[1]

(Commotion in the audience.)

Comrade Eikhe was arrested on April 29, 1938 on the basis of slanderous materials, without the sanction of the [State] Prosecutor of the USSR. This was finally received 15 months after the arrest.

The investigation of Eikhe's case was made in a manner which most brutally violated Soviet legality and was accompanied by willfulness and falsification.

---

[1]   Robert Eikhe (1890–140)—a revolutionary and prominent Bolshevik Party functionary. Participated in the Civil War. Held various positions from the head of the Siberian regional Party committee to the minister of land and the candidate to Politburo. Khrushchev fails to mention that Eikhe was one of the organizers of Great Terror, being a member of one the first "Troika" (the tribunal of three judges) and personally responsible for the repression of almost 35,000 people in 1937 only! Arrested in 1938, after the arrest of his boss Ezhov, former Head of the NKVD, and accused in the organization of the Latvian fascist organization, tortured and executed. Rehabilitated in 1956.

Under torture, Eikhe was forced to sign a protocol of his confession prepared in advance by the investigative judges. In it, he and several other eminent Party workers were accused of anti-Soviet activity.

On October 1, 1939 Eikhe sent his declaration to Stalin in which he categorically denied his guilt and asked for an examination of his case. In the declaration he wrote: "There is no more bitter misery than to sit in the jail of a government for which I have always fought."

A second declaration of Eikhe has been preserved, which he sent to Stalin on October 27, 1939. In it [Eikhe] cited facts very convincingly and countered the slanderous accusations made against him, arguing that this provocatory accusation was on one hand the work of real Trotskyites whose arrests he had sanctioned as First Secretary of the West Siberian Regional Party Committee and who conspired in order to take revenge on him, and, on the other hand, the result of the base falsification of materials by the investigative judges.

Eikhe wrote in his declaration:

> ... On October 25 of this year I was informed that the investigation in my case has been concluded and I was given access to the materials of this investigation. Had I been guilty of only one hundredth of the crimes with which I am charged, I would not have dared to send you this pre-execution declaration. However I have not been guilty of even one of the things with which I am charged and my heart is clean of even the shadow of baseness. I have never in my life told you a word of falsehood, and now, finding both feet in the grave, I am still not lying. My whole case is a typical example of provocation, slander and violation of the elementary basis of revolutionary legality. . . .
>
> . . . The confessions which were made part of my file are not only absurd but contain slander toward the Central Committee of the All-Union Communist Party (Bolsheviks) and toward the Council of People's Commissars. [This is] because correct resolutions of the Central Committee of the All-Union Communist Party (Bolsheviks) and of the Council of People's Commissars which were not made on my initiative and [were promulgated] without my participation are presented as hostile acts of counterrevolutionary organizations made at my suggestion.

I am now alluding to the most disgraceful part of my life and to my really grave guilt against the Party and against you. This is my confession of counterrevolutionary activity. . . . The case is as follows: Not being able to suffer the tortures to which I was submitted by [Z.] Ushakov and Nikolayev—especially by the former, who utilized the knowledge that my broken ribs have not properly mended and have caused me great pain—I have been forced to accuse myself and others.

The majority of my confession has been suggested or dictated by Ushakov. The rest is my reconstruction of NKVD materials from Western Siberia for which I assumed all responsibility. If some part of the story which Ushakov fabricated and which I signed did not properly hang together, I was forced to sign another variation. The same thing was done to [Moisey] Rukhimovich, who was at first designated as a member of the reserve net and whose name later was removed without telling me anything about it. The same also was done with the leader of the reserve net, supposedly created by Bukharin in 1935. At first I wrote my [own] name in, and then I was instructed to insert [Valery] Mezhlauk's. There were other similar incidents.

. . . I am asking and begging you that you again examine my case, and this not for the purpose of sparing me but in order to unmask the vile provocation which, like a snake, wound itself around many persons in a great degree due to my meanness and criminal slander. I have never betrayed you or the Party. I know that I perish because of vile and mean work of enemies of the Party and of the people, who have fabricated the provocation against me.

It would appear that such an important declaration was worth an examination by the Central Committee. This, however, was not done. The declaration was transmitted to Beria while the terrible maltreatment of the Politburo candidate, Comrade Eikhe, continued.

On February 2, 1940, Eikhe was brought before the court. Here he did not confess any guilt and said as follows:

In all the so-called confessions of mine there is not one letter written by me with the exception of my signatures under the protocols, which were forced from me. I have made my confession under pressure from the investigative judge, who from the time of my arrest tormented me. After that I began to write all this nonsense. . . . The most important thing for me is to tell the court, the Party and Stalin that I am not guilty. I have never been guilty of any conspiracy. I will die believing in the truth of Party policy as I have believed in it during my whole life.

On February 4, Eikhe was shot.

(Indignation in the audience.) [. . .]

Facts prove that many abuses were made on Stalin's orders without reckoning with any norms of Party and Soviet legality. Stalin was a very distrustful man, sickly suspicious. We know this from our work with him. He could look at a man and say: "Why are your eyes so shifty today?" or "Why are you turning so much today and avoiding to look me directly in the eyes?" The sickly suspicion created in him a general distrust even toward eminent Party workers whom he had known for years. Everywhere and in everything he saw "enemies," "two-facers" and "spies." Possessing unlimited power, he indulged in great willfulness and stifled people morally as well as physically. A situation was created where one could not express one's own volition.

When Stalin said that one or another should be arrested, it was necessary to accept on faith that he was an "enemy of the people." Meanwhile, Beria's gang, which ran the organs of state security, outdid itself in proving the guilt of the arrested and the truth of materials which it falsified. And what proofs were offered? The confessions of the arrested, and the investigative judges accepted these "confessions." And how is it possible that a person confesses to crimes which he has not committed? Only in one way—because of the application of physical methods of pressuring him, tortures, bringing him to a state of unconsciousness, deprivation of his judgment, taking away of his human dignity. In this manner were "confessions" acquired. [. . .]

These and many other facts show that all norms of correct Party solution of problems were [in]validated and that everything was dependent upon the willfulness of one man.

The power accumulated in the hands of one person, Stalin, led to serious consequences during the Great Patriotic War.

When we look at many of our novels, films and historical-scientific studies, the role of Stalin in the Patriotic War appears to be entirely improbable. Stalin had foreseen everything. The Soviet Army, on the basis of a strategic plan prepared by Stalin long before, used the tactics of so-called "active defense," i.e., tactics which, as we know, allowed the Germans to come up to Moscow and Stalingrad. Using such tactics, the Soviet Army, supposedly thanks only to Stalin's genius, turned to the offensive and subdued the enemy. The epic victory gained through the armed might of the land of the Soviets, through our heroic people, is ascribed in this type of novel, film and "scientific study" as being completely due to the strategic genius of Stalin.

We have to analyze this matter carefully because it has a tremendous significance not only from the historical, but especially from the political, educational and practical points of view. What are the facts of this matter? [. . .]

The policy of large-scale repression against military cadres led also to undermined military discipline, because for several years officers of all ranks and even soldiers in Party and Komsomol cells were taught to "unmask" their superiors as hidden enemies.

(Movement in the audience.)

It is natural that this caused a negative influence on the state of military discipline in the initial stage of the war.

And, as you know, we had before the war excellent military cadres which were unquestionably loyal to the Party and to the Fatherland. Suffice it to say that those of them who managed to survive, despite severe tortures to which they were subjected in the prisons, have from the first war days shown themselves real patriots and heroically fought for the glory of the Fatherland. I have here in mind such [generals] as: [Konstantin] Rokossovsky (who, as you know, had been jailed); [Alexander] Gorbatov; [Kiril] Meretskov (who is a delegate at the present Congress); [K. P.] Podlas (he was an excellent commander who perished at the front); and many, many others. However, many such commanders perished in the camps and the jails and the Army saw them no more.

All this brought about a situation at the beginning of the war that was a great threat to our Fatherland.

It would be wrong to forget that, after [our] severe initial disaster[s] and defeat[s] at the front, Stalin thought that it was the end. In one of his [declarations] in those days he said: "Lenin left us a great legacy and we've lost it forever."

After this Stalin for a long time actually did not direct military operations and ceased to do anything whatsoever. He returned to active leadership only when a Politburo delegation visited him and told him that steps needed to be taken immediately so as to improve the situation at the front.

Therefore, the threatening danger which hung over our Fatherland in the initial period of the war was largely due to Stalin's very own faulty methods of directing the nation and the Party.

However, we speak not only about the moment when the war began, which led to our Army's serious disorganization and brought us severe losses. Even after the war began, the nervousness and hysteria which Stalin demonstrated while interfering with actual military operations caused our Army serious damage.

Stalin was very far from understanding the real situation that was developing at the front. This was natural because, during the whole Patriotic War, he never visited any section of the front or any liberated city except for one short ride on the Mozhaisk highway during a stabilized situation at the front. To this incident were dedicated many literary works full of fantasies of all sorts and so many paintings. Simultaneously, Stalin was interfering with operations and issuing orders which did not take into consideration the real situation at a given section of the front and which could not help but result in huge personnel losses.

I will allow myself in this connection to bring out one characteristic fact which illustrates how Stalin directed operations at the fronts. Present at this Congress is Marshal [Ivan] Bagramyan, who was once the head of operations in the Southwestern Front Headquarters and who can corroborate what I will tell you.

When an exceptionally serious situation for our Army developed in the Kharkov region in 1942, we correctly decided to drop an operation whose objective was to encircle [the city]. The real situation at that time would have threatened our Army with fatal consequences if this operation were continued.

We communicated this to Stalin, stating that the situation demanded changes in [our] operational plans so that the enemy would be prevented from liquidating a sizable concentration of our Army.

Contrary to common sense, Stalin rejected our suggestion. He issued the order to continue the encirclement of Kharkov, despite the fact that at this time many [of our own] Army concentrations actually were threatened with encirclement and liquidation.

I telephoned to [Marshal Alexander] Vasilevsky and begged him: "Alexander Mikhailovich, take a map" — Vasilevsky is present here — "and show Comrade Stalin the situation that has developed." We should note that Stalin planned operations on a globe.

(Animation in the audience.)

Yes, comrades, he used to take a globe and trace the front line on it. I said to Comrade Vasilevsky: "Show him the situation on a map. In the present situation we cannot continue the operation which was planned. The old decision must be changed for the good of the cause."

Vasilevsky replied, saying that Stalin had already studied this problem. He said that he, Vasilevsky, would not see Stalin further concerning this matter, because the latter didn't want to hear any arguments on the subject of this operation.

After my talk with Vasilevsky, I telephoned to Stalin at his *dacha*. But Stalin did not answer the phone and Malenkov was at the receiver. I told Comrade Malenkov that I was calling from the front and that I wanted to speak personally to Stalin. Stalin informed me through Malenkov that I should speak with Malenkov. I stated for the second time that I wished to inform Stalin personally about the grave situation which had arisen for us at the front. But Stalin did not consider it convenient to pick up the phone and again stated that I should speak to him through Malenkov, although he was only a few steps from the telephone.

After "listening" in this manner to our plea, Stalin said: "Let everything remain as it is!"

And what was the result of this? The worst we had expected. The Germans surrounded our Army concentrations and as a result [the Kharkov counterattack] lost hundreds of thousands of our soldiers. This is Stalin's military "genius." This is what it cost us.

(Movement in the audience.)

On one occasion after the war, during a meeting [between] Stalin [and] members of the Politburo, Anastas Ivanovich Mikoyan mentioned that Khrushchev must have been right when he telephoned concerning the Kharkov operation and that it was unfortunate that his suggestion had not been accepted.

You should have seen Stalin's fury! How could it be admitted that he, Stalin, had not been right! He is after all a "genius," and a genius cannot help but be right! Everyone can err, but Stalin considered that he never erred, that he was always right. He never acknowledged to anyone that he made any mistake, large or small, despite the fact that he made more than a few in matters of theory and in his practical activity. After the Party Congress we shall probably have to re-evaluate many [of our] wartime military operations and present them in their true light.

The tactics on which Stalin insisted—without knowing the basics of conducting battle operations—cost much blood until we succeeded in stopping the opponent and going over to the offensive.

The military knows that as late as the end of 1941, instead of great operational maneuvers flanking [our] opponent and penetrating behind his back, Stalin was demanding incessant frontal [counter-] attacks and the [re-]capture of one village after another.

Because of this, we paid with great losses—until our generals, upon whose shoulders the whole weight of conducting the war rested, succeeded in altering the situation and shifting to flexible-maneuver operations. [This] immediately brought serious changes at the front [that were] favorable to us.

All the more shameful was the fact that after our great victory over the enemy, which cost us so dearly, Stalin began to downgrade many of the commanders who had contributed so much to it. [This was] because Stalin ruled out any chance that services rendered at the front might be credited to anyone but himself.

Stalin was very much interested in assessments of Comrade [Grigory] Zhukov as a military leader. He asked me often for my opinion of Zhukov. I told him then, "I have known Zhukov for a long time. He is a good general and a good military leader."

After the war Stalin began to tell all kinds of nonsense about Zhukov. Among it [was] the following: "You praised Zhukov, but he does not deserve it. They say that before each operation at the front Zhukov used to behave as follows: He used to take a handful of earth, smell it and say, 'We can begin the attack,' or its opposite, 'The planned operation cannot be carried out.'" I stated at the time, "Comrade Stalin, I do not know who invented this, but it is not true."

It is possible that Stalin himself invented these things for the purpose of minimizing the role and military talents of Marshal Zhukov.

In this connection, Stalin very energetically popularized himself as a great leader. In various ways he tried to inculcate the notion that the victories gained by the Soviet nation during the Great Patriotic War were all due to the courage, daring, and genius of Stalin and of no one else. Just like [a] Kuzma Kryuchkov, he put one dress on seven people at the same time.

(Animation in the audience.)

In the same vein, let us take for instance our historical and military films and some [of our] literary creations. They make us feel sick. Their true objective is propagating the theme of praising Stalin as a military genius. Let us recall the film, *The Fall of Berlin.* Here only Stalin acts. He issues orders in a hall in which there are many empty chairs. Only one man approaches him to report something to him—it is [Alexander] Poskrebyshev, his loyal shield-bearer.

(Laughter in the audience.)

And where is the military command? Where is the Politburo? Where is the Government? What are they doing, and with what are they engaged? There is nothing about them in the film. Stalin acts for everybody, he does not reckon with anyone. He asks no one for advice. Everything is shown to the people in this false light. Why? To surround Stalin with glory—contrary to the facts and contrary to historical truth.

The question arises: Where is the military, on whose shoulders rested the burden of the war? It is not in the film. With Stalin's inclusion, there was no room left for it.

Not Stalin, but the Party as a whole, the Soviet Government, our heroic Army, its talented leaders and brave soldiers, the whole Soviet nation—these are the ones who assured victory in the Great Patriotic War.

(Tempestuous and prolonged applause.) [. . .]

Comrades, let us reach for some other facts. The Soviet Union justly is considered a model multinational state because we have assured in practice the equality and friendship of all [of the] peoples living in our great Fatherland.

All the more monstrous are those acts whose initiator was Stalin and which were rude violations of the basic Leninist principles [behind our] Soviet state's nationalities policies. We refer to the mass deportations of entire nations from their places of origin, together with all Communists and Komsomols without any exception. This deportation was not dictated by any military considerations.

Thus, at the end of 1943, when there already had been a permanent change of fortune at the front in favor of the Soviet Union, a decision concerning the deportation of all the Karachai from the lands on which they lived was taken and executed.

In the same period, at the end of December, 1943, the same lot befell the [Kalmyks] of the Kalmyk Autonomous Republic. In March, 1944, all the Chechens and Ingushi were deported and the Chechen-Ingush Autonomous Republic was liquidated. In April, 1944, all Balkars were deported from the territory of the Kabardino-

Balkar Autonomous Republic to faraway places and their Republic itself was renamed the Autonomous Kabardian Republic.

Ukrainians avoided meeting this fate only because there were too many of them and there was no place to which to deport them. Otherwise, [Stalin] would have deported them also.

(Laughter and animation in the audience.) [. . .]

Let us also recall the "affair of the doctor-plotters."

(Animation in the audience.)

Actually there was no "affair" outside of the declaration of the woman doctor [Lidiya] Timashuk, who was probably influenced or ordered by someone (after all, she was an unofficial collaborator of the organs of state security) to write Stalin a letter in which she declared that doctors were applying supposedly improper methods of medical treatment.

Such a letter was sufficient for Stalin to reach an immediate conclusion that there are doctor-plotters in the Soviet Union. He issued orders to arrest a group of eminent Soviet medical specialists. He personally issued advice on the conduct of the investigation and the method of interrogation of the arrested persons. He said that academician [V. N.] Vinogradov should be put in chains, and that another one [of the alleged plotters] should be beaten. The former Minister of State Security, Comrade [Semyon] Ignatiev, is present at this Congress as a delegate. Stalin told him curtly, "If you do not obtain confessions from the doctors we will shorten you by a head."

(Tumult in the audience.)

Stalin personally called the investigative judge, gave him instructions, and advised him on which investigative methods should be used. These methods were simple—beat, beat and, beat again.

Shortly after the doctors were arrested, we members of the Politburo received protocols with the doctors' confessions of guilt.

After distributing these protocols, Stalin told us, "You are blind like young kittens. What will happen without me? The country will perish because you do not know how to recognize enemies."

The case was presented so that no one could verify the facts on which the investigation was based. There was no possibility of trying to verify facts by contacting those who had made the confessions of guilt.

We felt, however, that the case of the arrested doctors was questionable. We knew some of these people personally because they had once treated us. When we examined this "case" after Stalin's death, we found it to have been fabricated from beginning to end.

This ignominious "case" was set up by Stalin. He did not, however, have the time in which to bring it to an end (as he conceived that end), and for this reason the doctors are still alive. All of them have been rehabilitated. They are working in the same places they were working before. They are treating top individuals, not excluding members of the Government. They have our full confidence; and they execute their duties honestly, as they did before.

In putting together various dirty and shameful cases, a very base role was played by a rabid enemy of our Party, an agent of a foreign intelligence service—Beria, who had stolen into Stalin's confidence. How could this provocateur have gained such a position in the Party and in the state, so as to become the First Deputy Chair of the Council of Ministers of the Soviet Union and a Politburo member? It has now been established that this villain climbed up the Government ladder over an untold number of corpses.

Were there any signs that Beria was an enemy of the Party? Yes, there were. Already in 1937, at a Central Committee Plenum, former People's Commissar of Health [Grigory] Kaminsky said that Beria worked for the Musavat intelligence service. But the Plenum had barely concluded when Kaminsky was arrested and then shot. Had Stalin examined Kaminsky's statement? No, because Stalin believed in Beria, and that was enough for him. And when Stalin believed in anyone or anything, then no one could say anything that was contrary to his opinion. Anyone daring to express opposition would have met the same fate as Kaminsky. [. . .]

During Stalin's life—thanks to known methods which I have mentioned, and quoting facts, for instance, from the *Short Biography* of Stalin—all events were explained as if Lenin played only a secondary role, even during the October Socialist Revolution. In many films and in many literary works the figure of Lenin was incorrectly presented and inadmissibly depreciated.

Stalin loved to see the film *The Unforgettable Year of 1919*, in which he was shown on the steps of an armored train and where he was practically vanquishing the foe with his own saber. Let Klimenty Yefremovich [Voroshilov], our dear friend, find the necessary courage and write the truth about Stalin; after all, he knows how Stalin had fought. It will be difficult for Comrade Voroshilov to undertake this, but it would be good if he did it. Everyone will approve of it, both the people and the Party. Even his grandsons will thank him.

(Prolonged applause.)

In speaking about the events of the October Revolution and about the Civil War, the impression was created that Stalin always played the main role, as if everywhere and always Stalin had suggested to Lenin what to do and how to do it. However, this is slander of Lenin.

(Prolonged applause.)

I will probably not sin against the truth when I say that 99 percent of the persons present here heard and knew very little about Stalin before the year 1924, while Lenin was known to all. He was known to the whole Party, to the whole nation, from children all the way up to old men.

(Tumultuous, prolonged applause.)

All this has to be thoroughly revised so that history, literature and the fine arts properly reflect V. I. Lenin's role and the great deeds of our Communist Party and of the Soviet people—a creative people.

(Applause.) [. . .]

One of the oldest members of our Party, Klimenty Yefremovich Voroshilov, found himself in an almost impossible situation. For several years he was actually deprived of the right of participation in Politburo sessions. Stalin forbade him to attend Politburo sessions and to receive documents. When the Politburo was in session and Comrade Voroshilov heard about it, he telephoned each time and asked whether he would be allowed to attend. Sometimes Stalin permitted it, but always showed his dissatisfaction.

Because of his extreme suspicion, Stalin toyed also with the absurd and ridiculous suspicion that Voroshilov was an English agent.

(Laughter in the audience.)

It's true—an English agent. A special tap was installed in his home to listen to what was said there.

(Indignation in the audience.) [. . .]

Stalin evidently had plans to finish off the older members of the Politburo. He often stated that Politburo members should be replaced by new ones. His proposal after the 19th Congress to elect 25 persons to the Central Committee Presidium was aimed at the removal of old Politburo members and at bringing in less experienced persons so that these would extol him in all sorts of ways.

We can assume that this was also a design for the future annihilation of the old Politburo members and, in this way, a cover for all shameful acts of Stalin, acts which we are now considering.

Comrades! So as not to repeat errors of the past, the Central Committee has declared itself resolutely against the cult of the individual. We consider that Stalin was extolled to excess. However, in the past Stalin undoubtedly performed great services to the Party, to the working class and to the international workers' movement.

This question is complicated by the fact that all this which we have just discussed was done during Stalin's life under his leadership and with his concurrence; here Stalin was convinced that this was necessary for the defense of the interests of the working classes against the plotting of enemies and against the attack of the imperialist camp.

He saw this from the position of the interest of the working class, of the interest of the laboring people, of the interest of the victory of socialism and communism. We cannot say that these were the deeds of a giddy despot. He considered that this should be done in the interest of the Party, of the working masses, in the name of the defense of the revolution's gains. In this lies the whole tragedy! [. . .]

Comrades! We must abolish the cult of the individual decisively, once and for all; we must draw the proper conclusions concerning both ideological-theoretical and practical work. It is necessary for this purpose:

First, in a Bolshevik manner to condemn and to eradicate the cult of the individual as alien to Marxism-Leninism and not consonant with the principles of Party leadership and the norms of Party life, and to fight inexorably all attempts at bringing back this practice in one form or another.

To return to and actually practice in all our ideological work the most important theses of Marxist-Leninist science about the people as the creator of history and as the creator of all material and spiritual good of humanity, about the decisive role of the Marxist Party in the revolutionary fight for the transformation of society, about the victory of communism.

In this connection we will be forced to do much work in order to examine critically from the Marxist-Leninist viewpoint and to correct the widely spread erroneous views connected with the cult of the individual in the spheres of history, philosophy, economy and of other sciences, as well as in literature and the fine arts. It is especially necessary that in the immediate future we compile a serious textbook of the history of our Party which will be edited in accordance with scientific Marxist objectivism, a textbook of the history of Soviet society, a book pertaining to the events of the Civil War and the Great Patriotic War.

Second, to continue systematically and consistently the work done by the Party's Central Committee during the last years, a work characterized by minute observation in all Party organizations, from the bottom to the top, of the Leninist principles of Party leadership, characterized, above all, by the main principle of collective leadership, characterized by the observance of the norms of Party life described in the statutes of our Party, and, finally, characterized by the wide practice of criticism and self-criticism.

Third, to restore completely the Leninist principles of Soviet socialist democracy, expressed in the Constitution of the Soviet Union, to fight willfulness of individuals abusing their power. The evil caused by acts violating revolutionary socialist legality which have accumulated during a long time as a result of the negative influence of the cult of the individual has to be completely corrected.

Comrades! The 20th Congress of the Communist Party of the Soviet Union has manifested with a new strength the unshakable unity of our Party, its cohesiveness around the Central Committee, its resolute will to accomplish the great task of building communism.

(Tumultuous applause.)

And the fact that we present in all their ramifications the basic problems of overcoming the cult of the individual which is alien to Marxism-Leninism, as well as the problem of liquidating its burdensome consequences, is evidence of the great moral and political strength of our Party.

(Prolonged applause.)

We are absolutely certain that our Party, armed with the historical resolutions of the 20th Congress, will lead the Soviet people along the Leninist path to new successes, to new victories.

(Tumultuous, prolonged applause.)

Long live the victorious banner of our Party—Leninism!

(Tumultuous, prolonged applause ending in ovation. All rise.)[2]

---

[2]   From: http://www.marxists.org/archive/khrushchev/1956/02/24.htm

Pyotr Vail' and Alexander Genis

Pyotr Vail' (1949, Riga, Latvia – 2009, Prague, Czech Republic). Graduated from Moscow Polygraph Institute as a literary editor, then worked in Riga. In 1977 immigrated to the United States. Worked as a journalist for several Russian newspapers in New York. Beginning in 1984 worked at the Russian Service of Radio Liberty as an anchor and author of program content. Lived in Prague after 1995. Co-authored six books of criticism and essays with Alexander Genis. In the 1990s became well known for his travelogues (*Genius Loci, The Map of the Motherland*).

Alexander Genis (b. 1953, Riazan'). Genis grew up in Riga, Latvia. Graduated from the School of Philology, University of Latvia, Riga. In 1977, immigrated to the United States. From 1983 worked at the Russian Service of Radio Liberty as an anchor and author of program content. Co-authored six books with Pyotr Vail'. Since the mid-1990s has worked alone. Author of numerous books of criticism, essays, and autobiographic prose.

FROM *THE SIXTIES: THE WORLD OF THE SOVIET MAN*[1]

Physicists and Lyricists. Science

From the moment that the country took aim at building communism, the question grew more and more urgent—who should be building it? To answer that question, the 60-ers needed to find their heroes. Not Pavka Korchagin, not Aleksandr Matrosov, not Aleksei Stakhanov. The old heroes had already done their duty. The future had to be built by someone untainted by the past.

The new, large, state-sponsored truth had to be built on a strong foundation not subject to political jolts. For this purpose, the twentieth century reasonably offered up science.

In the eyes of society, scientists had a decisive advantage—honesty. Also known as sincerity, decency, love of truth. The 60-ers rendered all these words synonymous and endowed them with the meaningfulness of a world outlook.

Two times two must equal four, regardless of the convictions of the person doing the counting. After the arbitrary Soviet past, the country badly needed an objective non-relativist present. The multiplication table had the quality of absolute truth. Hard sciences seemed to be the equivalent of moral clarity. An equals sign stood between honesty and mathematics.

---

[1]   Translated from Pyotr Vail' and Alexander Genis, "60–e: Mir sovetskogo cheloveka," *Izbrannoe. V 2–kh tt.* T.1 (Ekaterinburg: U-Faktoriia, 2003), 611–620; 699–713.

After it became clear that words lie, formulas seemed more trustworthy.

Scientists lived in the neighborhood, scientists were ordinary Soviet people. And yet—they were different. It wasn't for nothing that in the newspaper jargon of the time they were called the *priests of science*.

Society, slowly freeing itself from faith in the infallibility of Party and state, feverishly searched for a new cult. Science fit all the requirements. It combined the objectivity of truth with the incomprehensibility of its expression. Only those ordained into its mysteries could serve science in its temples—in the particle accelerators, for example.

Science seemed to be that long-awaited lever with which to overturn Soviet society and make it into a utopia built, naturally, on a foundation of indisputable truth.

It would be scientists, people of the future, rather than suspect party workers, who would bring the ancient hope of humanity into being. They, like soldiers or athletes, came to represent the nation's strength and health.

We didn't have to wait long for results. For the first time, Soviet physicists started receiving the Nobel Prize (1958, 1962, 1964). Cybernetics was rehabilitated. An audacious fight for genetics was taking place. New scientific centers appeared: Dubna, Academgorodok. In 1962 Mikhail Romm's film *Nine Days in One Year* spread with great success through the theaters. A new hero had been found.

Youth and talent suited the atmosphere of the time. Thanks to irony, it was possible to descend from heroic heights to the everyday. Small sins offset the pathos of the heroic deed. Meanwhile, mortal risk endowed everything else with a sense of importance. Of course, the hero had to be a physicist. That branch of science had fused the authority of abstract knowledge with practical results—for example, in the atom bomb.

The silently implied connection between war and physics gave the hero added importance. Because the frontlines passed through the accelerators and reactors, the physicists were always at the forefront. In the 60s the scientists took off their uniforms and replaced them with white robes. This masquerade did not alter the incomprehensible, but patriotic, inner content of the scientists' work. Moreover, it's worth remembering that Soviet physicists did not experience the moral torments of Hiroshima. The image of Frankenstein was foreign to the Russian imagination.

Unlike the heroes of earlier ages—revolutionaries, miners, or border guards—the nature of the scientists' heroic acts escaped understanding. The heroic deed was taken on faith.

Indeed, precisely because of the esoteric nature of science, extraneous details became crucial to the image of the scientist. For example: "The Good Physicist sings to guitar music, dances the Twist, drinks vodka, has a mistress, is bothered by various problems, dares, fights, professionally defeats in boxing the Bad Physicist, and in his spare time sacrifices himself for science."[2] Far from negating it, the parodic intensification here serves rather to underline the nature of the stereotype.

The scientific aura hung in the air of the 60s. It was the rare magazine that came out without an article under a pretty headline: "The Bread and Butter of Physics," "Stairway to the Sun," "The Citadel of the Peaceful Atom." Pathos poured out of them at will: "We wandered in the microcosm, as in an immense hall plunged into darkness."[3]

Even the caricatures of the 60s clothed their criticisms in the vocabulary of the era: "Rare earth elements: beryllium the bribe-taker, lithium the drunk, plutonium the thief."[4]

Probably the most prominent feature of the new hero's image was humor. Physicists did not merely joke; they had to joke if they

---

[2] Vladimir Vladin, "On scientists in general and young physicists in particular," *Fiziki prodolzhaiut shutit'* [*Physicists Keep Joking*] (Moscow, 1968), 308. If one considers that the first edition of this book, published in 1966, was called *Physicists Joke*, then the title of the second edition sounds like a manifesto. Characteristically, Valentin Turchin, a physics professor and the compiler of both volumes, became one of the most active and visible Soviet dissidents.

[3] *Ogonyok* (No. 51), 1964.

[4] *Ogonyok* (No. 16), 1964.

were to remain physicists. It was not the quality of the humor that caused delight, but the mere fact of its existence:

> Plasma—it's a tricky gas,
> Hardly ever hears us.
> Oh, you're good, kasha with butter,
> Oh, you're cold, plasma, I utter.[5]

What's significant here is the essentially folksy relation to the mysteries of nature. More importantly, humor raised scientists above the crowd. They were able to combine work and levity.

Pathos does not go well with laughter: laughter lowers pathos. Heroes can laugh, but only in the breaks between heroic deeds.

The scientists of the 60s, by contrast, were not disturbed by laughter. On the contrary, their laughter underscored that work did not burden them. The sacrifice that they brought to the altar of science was sweet and desired.

Tradition assigned a measure of martyrdom to heroic deeds. It insisted that the stars could only be reached via a road lined with thorns. But the new heroes emphasized not the results but the process: science was wonderful in and of itself, even without fame and money. The scientists were a privileged class; creative work was their privilege. The nation enviously watched these people who relished their work. The prophets of science bestowed joyful laughter on their cult.

Scientists became more than just heroes. Public opinion turned them into aristocrats of the soul. Only human frailties (the Twist) united them with the masses. Science became an institution that combined the means with the ends into a single creative impulse.

The kingdom of science seemed to be that very aluminum castle to which Chernyshevsky had summoned his readers.[6] The lucky ones who got to live there had already achieved Communism, which

---

[5]   *Ogonyok* (No. 38), 1963.

[6]   A reference to Nikolai Chernyshevsky's novel *What Is To De Done?* and its chapter "The Fourth Dream of Vera Pavlovna."

they built for themselves—without blood, victims, or demagoguery. While joking around.

"From each according to his ability, to each according to his needs," sighed respectful but distant admirers, seeing in the scientists a new type of personality—a personality freed from avarice and fear, a full, artistic, and harmonious personality (the Twist). That is, exactly the kind of personality that was described by the Ethics Code of the builder of Communism.

Like any myth, the myth of science, by portraying the desired as reality, did a lot to turn the real into the desired.

"The Russian cannot accept an empty heaven. Science cleared it of God, the saints and the angels. Science must populate it with new tenants: spaceships, sputniks and lunar crafts. If the Russian is to continue to believe in Communism, he must first of all believe in Soviet science."[7]

And he believed. Believed in the economy, which would create the abundance promised by Khrushchev; in cybernetics, which would put an end to bureaucracy; in genetics, which would fix the problems of bad heredity.

Scientists were to take the place of politicians. Hard sciences would replace the vagueness of ideology. A technocracy, rather than the partocracy, would lead the country into utopia, because it held the multiplication table in its hands.

It was natural that the myth of science was sustained and served, rendered more accessible and concrete, by science fiction novels. It was as if they had been created expressly for that purpose. It was not by accident that the genre became the most popular in the country. [. . .]

---

7   K. Pomerantsev, "Vo chto verit sovetskaia molodezh," [What do Soviet youth believe in] *Novyi zhurnal* (No. 78), 1965. In this collection of letters from the Soviet Union printed in an émigré journal, the myth of science is presented especially powerfully: "Only a scientist can be a truly free man . . . The evolution of our system will depend on science, on those discoveries still to come that undoubtedly will bring us closer to the west." It comes as no surprise that the publisher uses religious terminology to elaborate upon these pronouncements: "Not believing in God, and having lost faith in communism, Soviet man turned his faith and love toward science."

However naïve the postulates of this scientific religion might seem, they had enormous influence on the social ideals of the 60s. And in no small measure on the scientists themselves, who, naturally, were rather entertained by the indefatigable disciples of the new faith.

The scientists did, after all, work in science. Their work was, indeed, creative. What is more, scientists were in fact the freest constituent of Soviet society: "In order to work successfully and productively, research scientists need a lot more intellectual freedom and political rights than other social groups and classes of society."[8] In order to get ahead of the West in the number of bombs and yields of corn, scientists needed a certain amount of freedom. And they got it.

Robed in the trust of the party and the people, scientists could not help but feel their responsibility toward society. For them—the only ones in the country—science was not a myth, but reality. They saw in it a social lever and did not have the right to ignore the possibilities it gave them. The scientific intelligentsia clandestinely practiced constitutional freedoms forbidden to others. When in 1966 the Central Committee received a letter about the danger of Stalin's rehabilitation, it was signed by the nation's preeminent scientists—Pyotr Kapitsa, Lev Artsimovich, Mikhail Leontovich, Andrei Sakharov, Igor Tamm.

This is how the physicist Kapitsa expressed the position of the scientists: "In order to rule lawfully and democratically, each country absolutely must have independent institutions that can serve as arbiters in all constitutional problems. In the USA, the Supreme Court plays this role; in Britain it is the House of Lords. It seems that in the Soviet Union that moral function falls on the Academy of Sciences of the USSR."[9]

The knowledge that scientists possessed made them into an elite that was separate from politicians, the military, as well as the man in the street. The social pyramid had to be rebuilt in such

---

[8]   Zhores Medvedev, *Soviet Science* (New York: W. W. Norton & Co., 1978), 130.

[9]   Idem., 108.

a way that the aristocrats of the soul would find themselves atop it. The state's logic forced the scientists into the role of the shepherd. They knew what had to be done and could prove why things had to be handled in just that way. But they would prove it in their own tongue, the language of augurs, understandable only to them. The insensate crowd gazed up at the temple of science, while mysteries were performed inside it.

Scientists could not help but involve themselves in the business of society. But once they got involved, they became dissidents: their secret priestly activities became open knowledge. Once science spoke of morality, it debased its mysteries into universally understood theses, thus profaning its own cult.

The scientist dissolved the doors of the temple and became a member of the state apparatus or simply one of the crowd. By defrocking himself, the scientist turned into the citizen.

However, in Russia that position was already occupied by the poet. As everyone knew, it was the poet who "is obligated to be a citizen."[10] Logic, once translated into the idiom of state interests, by no means gained in convincibility: it lacked poetry. It was merely correct.

Scientists viewed science as a lever; the Party viewed it as a mode of blackmail. War, in which one side had logic and the other only brute force, turned out to be futile for both sides. The civic tendencies of Soviet science were eradicated together with science itself. (Zhores Medvedev remembers that after Soviet tanks invaded Prague, the theoretical department of the Institute of Atomic Energy in Obninsk was liquidated due to the politically incorrect attitudes of the scientists. There was nobody left who could do the work.[11])

The prophets, appointed by society to revel in the pleasures of pure science, could not resist temptation and came down to earth. Once there, they came to be seen as charlatans and were beaten with stones. Of course, there is nothing new in that story.

---

[10]   A quote from Nikolai Nekrasov's "The Poet and the Citizen."

[11]   Zhores Medvedev, *Soviet Science*, 134.

As soon as scientists decided to share responsibility for society with the state, state and society vindictively reminded them of the need for practical results. For example, corn, abundance, Communism, which was still just beyond the horizon.

When abstract knowledge was the sign of the times, it was tolerated. But when the scientists themselves, in order to engage in the dirty work of state-building, wanted to come down from the lofty heights, society saw them as equals. There was no need to watch oneself in front of an equal. Since scientists had chosen to condescend to reality, reality could hold its own against them. Once physicists stopped joking, they stopped being listened to.

All this meant that the fight between the physicists and the lyricists entered a new stage.

Poetry, which was learning how to rhyme elemental particles, was fed on scientific metaphors. Behind all of this stood the temple of extrasensory naked abstraction. The 60s interpreted science poetically, but only because science itself seemed like the citadel of sober prose.

When it became clear that the multiplication table could not handle Communism, it was found to be erroneous. Those who had only recently been cultural icons were labeled "pseudo-educated."[12] Russia reacted idealistically to the orgy of materialism. Lyricists extracted revenge on the physicists, and romantic ignorance danced on the ruins of the already unnecessary particle accelerators. The truth went into the soil.

However, interest in the religion of science did not pass for naught. The feeling of free creative work was too celebratory.[13] The

---

[12]   In Russian the word is "obrazovanshchina," a condescending term coined by Aleksandr Solzhenitsyn.

[13]   "Academgorodok was a remarkable place in the 60s, full of freedom, agony, proteins, and love for poetry . . . I came to it from neighboring Novosibirsk in 1962. The distance between them was 30 kilometers and a hundred light years. An enclave of the real Communist 'radiant future,' Academgorodok was something dreamed up by the Strugatsky brothers and their readers . . . Technocracy and cybernetics made everyone crazy in those years. The people were convinced that computers would take over the science of management and the fat-asses, apparatchiks and secretaries would vanish. One just needed to find an algorithm, load it in the

temples of science, with their displays of nonconformist art, their bearded bards singing, and previously unseen joyful customs, turned into museums. And it was there after all that the slightly self-assured, ironic elite had grown up.

The science of religion lost its disciples, and society lost faith in yet another myth. But the privileged scientific class remained. It remained in order to cherish its own privilege: remembering that two times two equals four. [. . .]

Laughter Without Cause. Humor

Posters, newspaper headlines, songs on the radio, slogans from the podiums—everything served to remind one of the 60s: life is wonderful! And it's wonderful first of all because it will be even more wonderful. Whereas the Stalin years postulated: *life has become better, life has become more joyful*—the 60s insisted on joys that were yet to come. It was one thing when the existence of happiness was announced off the official podium, it was another when each person understood it and awaited its arrival in his own way.

Since the victory of truth over deception was seen as the accomplishment of the period [the Thaw], pairs of irreconcilable enemies lined up, as in a retinue, behind these opposites. Pain and happiness, suffering and joy, tears and laughter, gloom and

---

computer's memory, then program the machine to achieve the common good. The state and Party cadres would watch open-mouthed and scratch their heads like a peasant behind the plow at the sight of a working tractor.

In this atmosphere people expressed the most uninhibited thoughts. They proudly declared that there were two hot spots on the planet: Vietnam and Academgorodok. *Samizdat* circulated freely and in mass quantities. Naturally, everyone wanted to look to the future and hope for glory and goodness. It seemed that Stalin's derailed train of socialism was back on track, and now it would charge forward, not stopping until it had reached Mars. Our slogan was 'Freedom on our own terms,' that is, we'll be free, and then there will be freedom" (from the émigré writer Izrail' Shamir's memoirs, generously made available in manuscript form to the authors by Konstantin Kuzminsky).

brightness, darkness and light, heaviness and lightness, stagnation and elation.

It was not enough to send a man into space; that man himself should be new and fresh. Gagarin himself brought almost more joy than his famous voyage: his open face, his blinding smile, his simple charm. For the first time, it seemed, the Soviet nation paid attention to the attractive packaging in which the good and useful item came:

> Handsome and graceful, he walked along the path to the podium toward the members of government; he was handsome as he stood on the Mausoleum. Imagine if, instead of Yuri Gagarin, a bear-like, coarse fellow had exited the plane and ambled over to the podium . . . Half of the charm of his accomplishment would have disappeared for us.[14]

The time of antitheses, oppositions, extremes gave birth to this style and this type of thinking: if he had "ambled," then it would have been better if he had not gone into space at all.

[. . .]

A coup took place as well in the country's color scheme. Posted advertisements began to gleam with color; shop windows livened up, neon signs lit up. Citizens, all dressed alike, as if in China, in blue Chinese raincoats, suddenly donned bright scarves, light-colored coats, and came out on to the beach in bright cotton robes. No one was embarrassed by the insane combination of bright red and bright green—"the Ryazan pattern."[15]

The interiors of apartments changed: painting the walls of one room different colors became all the rage. The most advanced ones dared to render their ceiling ultramarine and their bathroom scarlet. Specialists advised: "Single-color bedspreads should be augmented by pillows of two or three different colors. For example, grey-blue bedspreads and raspberry, yellow, and green pillows."[16]

---

[14]   *Estetika povedeniia* [The Aesthetics of Behavior], compiled and edited by Valentin Tolstykh (Moscow, 1965), 5, 7.

[15]   *Ogonyok* (No. 1), 1966.

[16]   T. Astrova, A. Koshchelev, B. Neshumov, "Delo vashikh ruk" [Your handiwork], *Iunost'*

The character of the furniture further underlined the dwelling's kindergarten-like appearance: low tables, foldout couches, the hybrid "bed-wardrobe." As a result, the house turned out to be not a castle but a doll's house.

The brightness of the 60s literally reflected itself on the face of the nation: in its makeup. Earlier, use of cosmetics had a corporate character: it was used by women who worked in the arts, or women attending a performance at the theater, or, finally, by women of loose morals. The widespread use of cosmetics became a protest against middle-class prudishness and a claim to the right to individualized beauty.

The energetic 60s influenced even the menus, as restaurants offered steak served with "Moderne" sauce and steamed veal cutlets called "Joy."[17]

Since even cutlets had entered the fray for the new, it was clear that literature, music, theater, and cinema also must answer with a joyful attitude, a fiery antagonism, and peals of laughter. Across the whole country discussions were held on the place of comedy in Soviet life, which necessarily came to the same optimistic conclusion: comedy has a right to exist! Radio and gramophone records uncontrollably poured forth songs that had no ideological, or for that matter any other, import:

> I walk to Sretenka across the Kuznetsky Bridge,
> Fellow Muscovites on my way I meet,
> And they are likely singing something sweet.

The key here is in the word "something." That, in its essence, was the ideology: the substance isn't important so long as it's entertaining.

The laughter revolution took place in the cinema. Conservatives complained about the preponderance of "laughter without any cause," but it was exactly the happy, loud, non-ideological laughter

(No. 2), 1963: 89. Color recommendations for remaining décor were no less garish: "For small and bright items, use more suitable, cheerful tones: orange, yellow, red" (85–86).

[17]   "A report from the Leningrad restaurant 'Neva,'" *Ogonyok* (No. 25), 1965.

that became the most effective illustration of the idea of sudden freedom. In the visual arts, this type of unpredictable looseness is known as eccentricity. [. . .]

In the depths of their souls the comedians of the 60s knew that they were dealing with something not quite legal, like pornography. After all, they also knew that laughter, because it is at its root destructive, was illicit. Even the "Youth Prose" movement, light-hearted to its core, knew its limits:

> "Guys, let's drink to friendship!" said Zelenin quietly, getting up.
> "Vivat!" cried everyone at once, and each thought that it was good of Sashka to come to the rescue and, without resorting to the smokescreen of humor, say what everyone else was thinking."[18]

In the fight against conservatives, the comedians demonstrated a tactical mastery of polemics. They enlisted the help of the authorities. Whether they suited the occasion or not, Marx's words were quoted ceaselessly: "This is needed in order for humanity to joyfully part with its past."[19] Marx turned out to be an inveterate man of the 60s.

Marx's formula went hand-in-hand with Lenin's famous laughter. The 60s imbued Ilyich with the simplicity of Bolshevism and the fighting spirit of the Komsomol. In this new interpretation, Lenin tirelessly uttered dirty and dumb jokes: "Here you have yet another beastly vibrating vacillation of the petit bourgeois"; "No, Gentlemen-Comrades, a lady with a child cannot be made innocent again!" Lenin was funny with a simplicity and inappropriateness that elicited tears:

> *Petrovsky*: . . . Right after the October Revolution an order abolishing the death penalty.
> *Kollontai*: Do you remember how Ilyich reacted to this? How he cracked up. I remember his words clearly! "How do you conduct a revolution without executions?"[20]

---

[18]   Vassily Aksyonov, "Kollegi" [Colleagues], *Iunost'* (No. 7), 1961: 181.

[19]   Karl Marx, Friedrich Engels, *Collected Works*, Vol. 1 (Moscow, 1955), 418.

[20]   Mikhail Shatrov, *1918. Plays* (Moscow, 1974), 28, 64, 145.

In the memoirs of the revolution published in those years, comical scenes were commonplace: "What a racket took place at the meeting of the Military Revolutionary Committee," "They were joyful, strong, mischievous," "And how much we laughed then!"[21]

Stalin's villainy appeared as a grim, grey, morose emptiness framed by the comic image of two comedians—Lenin and Khrushchev.

Khrushchev did in actuality like a laugh. Two dozen notes recording "laughter" and "merriment in the audience" accompany the Summary Report of the XXII Congress, even in the section "Getting Over the Consequences of the Personality Cult." The level of humor is the same as Lenin's. "Akulia-dear, why sew with your rear?" "No sowin', no reapin', just joyful tart-eatin'," "Beating determines consciousness."[22] The state laughter was transformed into an overwhelming all-USSR mirth. And once the head of the country rapped his shoe on the podium of the UN and promised to show the capitalists a thing or two, it became clear that an unbridled feeling of fun had overtaken the country.

Laughter came to be taken seriously. So much so that popular publications undertook scientific studies of the phenomenon: "Air, rhythmically pushing out through the small opening, produces those very discrete sounds (for example, ha-ha-ha), that uniquely characterize laughter."[23] This, in all seriousness.

No one doubted the beneficial role of laughter, entertainment, humor. In the course of many years, life's extremes—tragedy and laughter—had been truncated, warped, rendered false. Society, radically shaken by tragedy to a previously unknown level (the camps), choked and sought a fresh breath of air: true fun, which had been previously forbidden. Laughter became the synonym of truth.

Truth-laughter had two goals: the destruction of negative principles and the strengthening of positive ones. Satire, not very

---

[21]   E. Drabkina, "V kadre—ulybka . . ." [In the frame, a smile . . .]. *Iskusstvo kino* (No. 4), 1968: 9, 12, 13.

[22]   *Pravda*, 18 October, 1961.

[23]   *Nedelia*, 8–14 March, 1964.

different from the satire of previous years, handled the first goal wonderfully: with all the same exaggerated villains, the same belief in the immediate results of exposure.

What was new was the idea that only the joyful man could be a good man.[24] Laughter extolled freedom—in the sense that it was opposed to everything static, stagnant, constrained: that is, unfreedom. Belief in the beneficence of laughter reigned everywhere: from the popular joke "five minutes of laughter is like 200 grams of sour cream" to the direct declaration: "Life should be lived in good humor. If you make a person laugh, he will be incapable of any sort of villainy!"[25] [. . .]

Who Is to Blame? Dissidence

The phenomenon that later came to be called *dissidence* came into being inconspicuously. As a matter of fact, once the movement's participants received that foreign name, everything was over. Not for nothing did the dissidents use the term reluctantly, preferring instead the literal rendering—"otherwise-minded." That was, at least, warmer than the foreign sounds and hiss of "dissident." In Russian society, with its logocentricity, these nuances were important. Although the word "otherwise-minded," like any word with a negative or counter particle (anti-, contra-, etc.), also did not elicit very positive emotions. The name "rights advocates" worked better—in it one heard "rightness."

---

[24]   Cf. Fyodor Dostoevsky's *The Adolescent*, trans. Richard Pevear and Larissa Volokhonsky (New York: Vintage, 2003), 372: "'You, godless? No you're not godless,' the old man replied sedately, giving him an intent look. 'No, thank God!' he shook his head.
'You're a mirthful man.'
'And whoever is mirthful isn't godless?' the doctor observed ironically.
'That's a thought—in its own way!' Versilov observed, but not laughing at all."

[25]   From the comedy *Sem' nianek* [Seven Nannies], directed by Rolan Bykov (1962).

A paradox occurred: once designations, theories, and names appeared, the movement splintered into a series of factions with a multitude of organizational structures, ideological directions, tactical designs. One could speak of some sort of all-encompassing "dissidence" only when the dissidents themselves did not have any idea of who they were and what they were called. It was precisely, and only, during the early period of the movement, when there were no programs, no decrees, when the biggest insults were the words "party" and "organization," that the dissidents were a single entity—the party of decent people.

At issue here are not political but social facts. Dissidence did not have a history in the traditional sense: no founders, theorists, date of constituent assembly, or manifestos. It is impossible even to tell—especially at the earlier stages—who was a participant in the protest movement.

Earlier groups of the "otherwise-minded" were more easily defined, more traditional: Trotskyites, oppositioners, cosmopolitans, "killers in white robes." They always wanted something concrete: the abolition of kolkhozes, electrification, war-readiness, "take our blue-eyed sister Belorussia, dismember it, and give as ransom to the dictator of Cameroon."[26] The fantastical nature of the crimes paled in comparison with the mere fact of disagreement with the State.

Dissidents of the 60s did not suggest anything that had not already been proclaimed by the regime. The party called for frankness—they spoke the truth. Newspapers wrote about the reinstatement of "legal norms"—the dissidents followed the laws better than the prosecutors. The need for criticism was proclaimed from the podiums—that was what the dissidents were doing. The words "cult of personality" had become pejorative after Khrushchev's take-down of Stalin—and for many the road toward "otherwise-mindedness" came out of the fear of the appearance of a new cult of personality: "We saw that once again one name flashes

---

[26]   Venedikt Erofeev, "Val'purgieva noch', ili 'Shagi komandora'" [Walpurgis Night, or The Steps of the Commander], *Kontinent* (No. 45), 1985: 114.

from the newspapers and the posters, again the most banal and rude pronouncements of this person are presented as a revelation, as the quintessence of wisdom. . . ."[27]

What gave birth to otherwise-mindedness was the need for change in the genre and style of social systems. It was logical that the first steps of that movement were made by poets, artists, and writers. It made sense that out of the poetic readings at the monument to Mayakovsky, out of one group of friends, came such different leaders of dissident directions as Eduard Kuznetsov (roughly speaking—"Zionist"), Vladimir Osipov ("Slavophile"), Vladimir Bukovsky ("democrat").

Cultural opposition appeared before any other kind and developed with the utmost vigor.

The editorial rooms and publishing companies directed their excess stream of authors (Khrushchev announced that magazines received over 10,000 reminiscences on camp themes)[28] into *samizdat*.

In general, the term "otherwise-minded" is imprecise, because the most important thing in dissidence was not thinking otherwise but speaking otherwise. That is, the otherwise-minded, in the final analysis, countered the established style and language with their own style and their own language. The deep-seated, enduring triumphs and defeats of dissidence—as opposed to its episodic, specific triumphs and defeats—are connected first and foremost to this fact. In those cases when the protest movement used the language and style of its opponent, it lost. It was successful only when it acquired its own original methods.

In that sense, the evolution of the idea of rights advocacy is representative. Because it was concrete and clearly articulated, rights advocacy effectively harnessed the opposition: we should demand that the government adhere to its own laws. The idea, first put forth by Aleksandr Esenin-Vol'pin, had a tactical component:

---

[27] *Siniavskii i Daniel' na skam'e podsudimykh* [Sinyavsky and Daniel in the Court] (New York: Inter-Language Literary Associates, 1966), 41.

[28] Liudmila Alekseeva, *Istoriia inakomysliia v SSSR* [A History of Otherwise-Thinking in the USSR] (Benson, VT: Khronika, 1984), 245.

you can't demand too much at once. Let the government first learn to use its own laws, then afterwards it will become possible to proceed to change them.

Moreover, the rights advocacy movement had at its disposal a tool from the aesthetic sphere: the alternative to interpreting texts was to take them literally.

The legal literature quickly disappeared from stores and libraries. The "Penal Procedural Code" became a bestseller. Rights advocates fought on their opponent's territory, using their opponent's weapons—and the fact that that weapon was borrowed from the opponent was decisive. Once the newness passed, the central issue remained: the state knew the language with which the dissidents addressed it, and even if it lost in particular circumstances, it was nonetheless able to fully use its strategic advantages—it was, after all, the state.

Immersion into the specifics of the law made amateurs such as Vol'pin, Valery Chalidze, Julius Telesin, and Vladimir Al'brekht into professionals. But often the legal game closed in on itself, turning into a scholastic exercise. Answering the investigator's question: "Did you give your application # 3 to someone else to read, and if so, to whom?"—Julius answered, "Your question # 9 can be answered by my answer # 7"—so that by the end of the interrogation neither the investigator, nor Telesin, let alone the reader could tell what was the answer to what.[29]

The tactics of rights advocacy became the leading dissident approach. Andrei Amal'rik recalled: "I had an argument with the priest Sergei Zheludkov, and I argued that we can only turn to the government in cases of formal legal, but not ideological, questions: we can't discuss our ideas with those who put others in prison for these ideas. And I almost convinced him that I was right—only to come to doubt it myself."[30]

Only an idea (not tanks) can stand up to an idea. Questions of a "formal-legal nature" are fitting in a democratically developed

---

[29]   Andrei Amal'rik, *Zapiski dissidenta* [Notes of a Dissident] (Ann Arbor: Ardis, 1982), 56.

[30]   Ibid., 40.

society. Dissidents, by conducting themselves like free people in an unfree society, were ahead of their time. To put it simply—they lost. But that's only if the desired end was winning. The end was also the means—free conduct, creation of precedent, formation of public opinion. But that already adds up to an idea—the moral opposition.

In answering the eternal question of the Russian intelligentsia—who is to blame?—those members of the Soviet intelligentsia who were most consistent answered: we are. Repenting and offering themselves up as martyrs, dissidents were not calling for anything, but were making themselves into role models.

This is the essence and the meaning of one of the key events in the nation's moral life during that time—the letters of protest campaign. The *undersigned*, as they were uneuphonically called, were performing a sacral act, exorcising the "dark forces" using their own lives and fates. The rest took place according to well-known patterns, only instead of burning heretics there were party meetings, and public stoning was replaced with getting fired from one's job. It was characteristic of the Russian situation that the actions that led to catharsis were all writerly—the creation of a text; and after it, as a sign of authorship, a signature. At the start of the mass protest movement was the trial of two literary men—Andrey Sinyavsky and Yulii Daniel.[31] In court they acknowledged their authorship and defended the texts they had written. This was precisely what the participants of the petition campaigns did in defense of the two writers.

Dissidence as a creative act—this is how to interpret the motivational impulse that pushed many successful members of Soviet society to ruin their careers. If it's creativity, rather than fame, power or money, that is seen as the chief value, then it becomes clear "what it was that they still wanted"—these recognized scientists and famous writers.

---

[31]   "December 5, 1965 can be considered the birth of the human rights movement. On this day, on Pushkin Square in Moscow, the first demonstration took place, with the slogans 'We demand transparency in the Sinyavsky-Daniel trial!' and 'Respect the Soviet Constitution!'" (Alekseeva, *Istoriia inakomysliia v SSSR* [A History of Otherwise-Thinking in the USSR], 240, 251).

Soviet psychiatrists were generally correct when they insisted that these people were abnormal. They deviated from the psychological norm just as much as poets or religious ascetics. The creatively full life, which reaches its peak in the attractive martyrdom of heroic feats, is not and cannot be normal. "I waited for that court date as if it were a holiday"[32] — Vladimir Bukovsky. "That was the most awful moment of my life. But it was also my shining hour"[33] — Pyotr Grigorenko.

Loners with heightened creative potential defied Orwellian doublethink consciousness. It is interesting that Bukovsky defines even the very genesis of social protest in aesthetic terms. "Black is white, we're used to that already. Red is green, as they've convinced us. Blue is purple, we agreed on that ourselves, darn it! But now it turns out that navy is not navy, but yellow? Enough already!"[34]

Disagreement with the ugliness of the social scale demanded a reaction. The creative personality challenged the imperfect world with its values. And the highest of Russian values — friendship — became the basis of an emerging public opinion. What could be more exciting than badmouthing Soviet power in the company of witty, slightly drunk friends?

The attempt to prolong that exciting way of spending time is what turned into dissidence. It was not an accident that one of the more active participants of the movement was Valentin Turchin — not only a recognized scientist, but also the editor of the book *Physicists Joke*. Phrases overheard at KGB interrogations were exchanged like Arkady Raikin's witticisms: "Where did you get the Gospels?" " — From Matthew."[35] The tactic of the legal defense owes its popularity largely to the temptation of the game — the chance to deftly make a fool out of your opponent: "'If I were in your shoes I would claim

---

[32]   Vladimir Bukovsky, *I vozvrashchaetsia veter* [And the Wind Returns] (New York: Khronika, 1978), 267.

[33]   Petro Grigorenko, *V podpol'e mozhno vstretit' tol'ko krys* [You Only Meet Rats Underground] (New York: Detinets, 1981), 455.

[34]   Vladimir Bukovsky, *I vozvrashchaetsia veter*, 240.

[35]   Vladimir Al'brekht, *Kak byt' svidetelem* [How to Be a Witness] (Paris, 1981).

authorship,' says the investigator. 'If you continue to speak in this way, I'm afraid you will end up in my shoes,' say I."[36]

To be friends with witty, talented, and brave people was in itself an achievement and an honor. On an evening date, girls were taken, as the chief destination, to the places where famous dissidents lived. The ability to enter such an apartment was worth more than a ticket to the cinema. The element of friendship, meanwhile, forced one to keep up: "It was very difficult not to sign the letter: not signing meant admitting that I was afraid (doing so is always unpleasant for young people), or showed that I was not very concerned about the fate of my incarcerated friends."[37] For the high value of friendship, to fulfill the desire to prove that you're no worse than the others, one bartered a loss of comfort and even freedom: "They both (Vadim Delone and Evgenii Kushev) went to the demonstration not because they saw it as a personal necessity, but rather because 'declining was awkward,' 'it was hard to break a promise.'" Evgenii Kushev, who had been late to the demonstration, explained his actions in the following way when he was interrogated: "I felt bad that I hadn't been there, and so I decided to yell 'Down with dictatorship!'"[38]

Through all this thoughtless nobility one can see the marks of an upbringing predicated on putting moral values above material ones, collective consciousness over individual—as if Timur and his team,[39] those young Soviet do-gooders, had risen up against the regime.

In "An Open Letter to Sholokhov," Iurii Galanskov wrote: "The Soviet man did not succeed to the same degree that Soviet power did not succeed."[40] One can remove the negatives from the two

---

[36]   Ibid., 1981.

[37]   Andrei Al'marik, *Zapiski dissidenta*, 38.

[38]   Dina Kaminskaya, *Zapiski advokata* [A Lawyer's Notes] (New York: Khronika Press, 1984), 166.

[39]   Protagonist of Arkadii Gaidar's famous novella for children *Timur and His Team* (1940).

[40]   Dina Kaminskaya, Op.cit., 302.

parts of that phrase: the Soviet man succeeded to the same degree that Soviet power succeeded.

Like Timur and his team, the otherwise-minded took to doing out in the open what theoretically should have been in the open everywhere and with official sanction. The old woman who had been wearing out the threshold of the local village council to no avail suddenly found wood under her window, chopped by Timur's boys. In a similar manner, a laboratory assistant forced out his job because of his sympathies for Israel suddenly found himself provided with licensed legal help, a signed letter of protest, and the support of friends. Dissidents did what they had been taught to do in the Soviet school system: to be honest, principled, selfless, ready to help. The dissident movement became the best embodiment of the gospel of the triumph of spiritual ideals over material ones.

Dissidents were the "leading unit," even more leading than the Party. It is no accident that a significant number of the otherwise-minded was made up of a group who professed Leninist principles, and for whom doubts came down to the question: "Is it still possible and is it easier to fight for real Communism within the Party or outside it?"[41] For very different people the approach was the same. General Grigorenko: "Where we're going, what's going to happen to the country, to the cause of Communism . . . I start asking these questions and out of old habits turn to Lenin for answers . . ."[42] Anatoly Marchenko, a worker, "went digging in those 55 volume works in which the real Lenin had been hidden."[43] And even the young rebel Bukovsky "found reading Lenin to be of great benefit."[44]

The findings varied: some convinced themselves that the Party had corrupted Leninist teachings; others blamed the leader himself. But the inevitability of the result—protest against the surrounding

---

[41]   Raisa Orlova, *Vospominaniia o neproshedshem vremeni* [Memories of Time Not Yet Gone By] (Ann Arbor: Ardis, 1984), 195.

[42]   Petro Grigorenko, *V podpol'e mozhno vstretit' tol'ko krys*, 489–490.

[43]   Ibid., 633.

[44]   Vladimir Bukovsky, *I vozvrashchaetsia veter*, 92.

reality—gave birth to an unprecedented riot of mental malaise. The thinking part of Soviet society experienced an Oedipal complex epidemic. Acting deliberately, Russian Oedipi destroyed Laius-Lenin and Jocasta-Party with masochistic pleasure.

In substance, every dissident of the 60s is a separate drama, sometimes a tragedy. It was natural that these people were lifted up noticeably above the others. Thanks to Western radio stations, the names of leading dissidents became as well known as the names of pop artists. The otherwise-minded person became a public figure.

Characteristically, this happened while dissidence remained the localized acts of particular individuals, when its most developed organizational form was a fun group of friends who sang as one to the accompaniment of a guitar, drank, read poems and wrote letters of protest.

These fun gatherings changed the social climate in the country. The most important thing—the law of silence—had been broken. If earlier, the limit of civilian honesty was lack of participation, now the honest man was forced to speak.

If earlier public opinion expressed itself, at best, in a conspiracy of silence, now it found its voice.

The new principle—words rather than silence—became the main achievement of dissidence. Society could no longer be as it had been before: you can't unlearn how to speak.

Public opinion, based on the pronunciation of words, leaned, naturally, on those words that were pronounced by the leaders of the otherwise-minded movement. These were simple and clear words, whose theme came down to Solzhenitsyn's later commandment: "Live not by lies." The official ideology controlled the means of propaganda, but public opinion had control of peoples' minds. In this atmosphere, it is not surprising that "an article in *Izvestiia*[45] described Sinyavsky and Daniel as hypocrites who allegedly praised the Soviet government in the Soviet press, but surreptitiously bad-mouthed it abroad. It wasn't clear what disturbed the

---

[45]   A Soviet newspaper distributed throughout the Soviet Union.

article's author most—the words in praise of the government or the words against it."[46]

The retrospective view always produces distortion and bias, and "no doubt there's considerable fantasy, as always in such cases: the crew exaggerates its size and significance,"[47]—but it is still possible to speak confidently of the protest movement's wide-ranging influence, sometimes reported anecdotally—when well-known people among the otherwise-minded were approached with complaints about the building super or the local drunk. The dissidents' moral qualities set the tone of public life. The very fact that the academic Sakharov[48] existed inspired the provincial engineer to walk up to the podium at the party meeting. [. . .]

Life's logic led dissidents to the creation of organizations. This produced a certain effect (especially later, when the Helsinki groups,[49] with their clear sets of goals, came into existence), but it was not for nothing that the otherwise-minded were so afraid of organization.

That fear was double-edged: obviously, it was a fear of possible repression, but—and this is more important—it was also a fear of coming to resemble one's opponents. Bukovsky the young revolutionary could still treat the secret society like an entertaining game,[50] the better, having matured, to condemn that type of activity and announce: "Our only weapon was *glasnost'* . . . What was going on was not a political fight, but a fight of the living versus the

---

[46]   Vladimir Bukovsky, *I vozvrashchaetsia veter*, 231.

[47]   Fyodor Dostoevsky, *Demons*, trans. Richard Pevear and Larissa Volokhonsky (New York: Vintage, 1995), 270.

[48]   Andrei Sakharov (1921–1989) was a Soviet nuclear physicist, dissident and human rights activist. He was awarded the Nobel Peace Prize in 1975.

[49]   A reference to the Moscow Helsinki Group (also known as the Moscow Helsinki Watch Group), an NGO human rights monitoring group established in the Soviet Union in May 1976.

[50]   "At the words 'secret' and 'organization,' a joyful fire would light up in your interlocutor's eyes, and it was immediately apparent that he, like you, had long awaited vehicles armed with machine guns" (Bukovsky, Op.cit., 100).

dead, the natural versus the unnatural."[51] A talented literary man, Bukovsky names here not the phenomenon itself but its symptoms. Indeed, what was at issue was not a competition of forces but of styles.

In refusing to challenge the Party with a party, and an ideology with an ideology, dissidence avoided a direct, head-on collision with power and was attractive precisely because of its noble dissimilarity from it. Having gotten his fill of the surroundings, every Soviet person could repeat after Pyotr Grigorenko: "I'm full to the gills of the Party. Every kind of party is a coffin to living deeds."[52]

That is where the main contradiction insidiously lay. The Party, of course, is a coffin. But the absence of a program necessarily leads to the dissolution of the very idea of opposition: in whose name, what, and even—for whom? Stylistic difference implied the creation of a different form—but the search for that form kept coming up empty. More than that—a grandiose mess and darkness resulted. Here is general Grigorenko speaking in front of Crimean Tatars at the restaurant "Altai" in the capitol. His words, addressed to a people deprived of a homeland, are brave and direct: "Stop asking! Reclaim that which belongs to you by right!" The evening ends on a high note: "The room roared, went wild. We ended with 'The Internationale.' And it wasn't just the Crimean Tatars who sang it, but everyone who was in the restaurant at the time—the customers and the restaurant staff."[53] That's in 1967! The scene is overwhelming in its ambivalence, worthy of Orwell.

On the other hand, what should they have sung? The absence of slogans was a serious, even critical, problem. If one is to follow the moral imperative literally, the run-in with real life, which demands daily compromise, is inevitable. Moral truth, meanwhile, is by necessity absolute and uncompromising, and it is the rare individual who can live by its precepts. Moreover, truth is abstract: it does not take into account a particular society, having in mind

---

[51]   Vladimir Bukovsky, Op.cit., 248–249.

[52]   Petro Grigorenko, Op. cit., 523.

[53]   Ibid., 620–621.

instead a universal, generalized human being. That is, it does not give clear answers: how to be, what to do, who is to blame. As a result, the calls of the "live not by lies" type give birth to numerous theological debates—"What is a lie? What is truth?"—and get mired in these discussions. Moreover, the appeals to one's conscience suffer significantly from repetition, and a person can quickly outgrow moral postulates in the same way that fables became children's literature. An adult cannot get by purely on proverbs.

Dissidence experienced this as an underlying weakness. For public slogans it was forced to use the same set of ideas as any other revolution—equality, fairness, the rule of law. The same language.[54] The declarations of protest were essentially plagiarized from party documents—and marked with a negative sign.

[. . .] The only slogan with any force—"Follow your own laws!"—led only to what it was in its essence: a legal game that was useful only in specific cases.

The moral opposition was the business of individuals. No language could be found for slogans that appealed to a mass consciousness. The old words pushed away both orators and their listeners.

The problem of dissidence was decided, as is customary in Russia, on the level of literary studies. Andrey Sinyavsky talked at his trial about the "fantastical nature" of the Russian people, about "drunkenness as the other side of spirituality."[55] The judge, giving in to this out-of-place aestheticism, discussed with the defendant the color of the covers of his books.[56]

The aesthetic position of early dissidence flummoxed the powers-that-be because they did not know how to speak this language. But when the otherwise-minded movement began speaking with known and customary—that is, old—words, it

---

[54]   "I worked through my ideological writings in the summer of 1963 and came to the conclusion that it was necessary to fight the leadership of the Communist Party of the Soviet Union" (Ibid., 498).

[55]   *Siniavskii i Daniel' na skam'e podsudimykh* (New York, 1966), 78.

[56]   Ibid., 86.

became in full measure a way of thinking otherwise, rather than speaking otherwise. Immediately it became aligned with the usual enemies of the state. The Russian dictionary gained another noun of foreign extraction, such as "counter-revolutionary" and "cosmopolitan"—"dissidents."

However, the main achievement turned out to be outside the text: the appearance of public opinion in the Soviet Union. It was transmitted through folklore—songs, anecdotes, jokes, simple conversation. The company of friends became the medium: a public institution that actually had authority. That social phenomenon by definition did not have a goal, did not answer and was not called to answer the main questions: "what is to be done" and "who is to blame."

As it turned out, the means that produced dissidents turned out to be its ends.

Translated by Rebecca Pyatkevich

Aleksandr Solzhenitsyn
(1918, Kislovodsk — 2008, Moscow)

Graduated from the Department of Physics and Mathematics at Rostov State University in 1941. Also studied by correspondence at the Institute of History, Philosophy and Literature in Moscow. From 1941 to 1945, fought in WWII at the front as an officer. Arrested by the NKVD in February 1945 for the contents of his private correspondence with a former schoolmate. Sentenced to eight years of labor in the camps. Transferred in 1946, as a mathematician, to the scientific research institute of the MVD-MOB (Ministry of Internal Affairs, Ministry of State Security), the so-called *sharashka*, which he later depicted in *The First Circle*. In 1950 was sent to the newly established "Special Camps," intended exclusively for political prisoners. In such a camp, in the town of Ekibastuz in Kazakhstan (depicted in *One Day in the Life of Ivan Denisovich*), he worked as a miner and bricklayer. After serving his prison term was internally exiled from 1953 to 1956. During this period he worked as a schoolteacher in Riazan' and wrote prose. Was released and acquitted in 1956. In 1962, his novella *One Day in the Life of Ivan Denisovich* (written in 1959) was published by the prominent Moscow liberal literary journal *New World* (*Novyi mir*) and caused an international sensation. While his short stories were published, Solzhenitsyn's novels *The First Circle* and *The Cancer Ward* were banned by censors and circulated in *samizdat*, then published abroad. In the 1960s Solzhenitsyn became one of the leaders of the dissident movement. His political articles and statements were circulated in *samizdat*. In 1970 Solzhenitsyn was awarded the Nobel Prize in Literature. For an entire decade, he collected material for *The Gulag Archipelago*, the first volume of which was published in Paris in 1973. In 1974 Solzhenitsyn was detained, stripped of his Soviet citizenship and forcefully exiled from the USSR. From 1976 to 1996 he lived in the United States (Cavendish, Vermont), where he wrote a cycle of historical novels about the Russian revolution under the title *The Red Wheel*. From 1989 onward, Solzhenitsyn's works have been published in his homeland. After the fall of the Soviet regime, in 1994, Solzhenitsyn returned to Russia and settled in Moscow. He was inducted into the Russian Academy of Sciences and received the Russian State Prize for outstanding achievements in the humanities. Established a literary prize in his name in 1997. After his return to Russia, wrote several books of political journalism, memoirs, and a collection of short stories.

From *Solzhenitsyn's*
One Day in the Life of Ivan Denisovich[1]
Critical Responses in the West
Robert Porter

Not unsurprisingly, much of the initial Western critical response to *Ivan Denisovich* was, like the Soviet response, focused on the raw facts that the story depicted. Any substantive difference that there was resided in the fact that the story simply endorsed, in the eyes of many, what unsympathetic commentators on Soviet affairs had suspected or half-known all along. Such commentators were by no means as keen as Soviet critics were to see the work as an instrument to exorcise Stalinism once and for all, to reform the Soviet system, to return it to what any "loyal opposition" in the Soviet Union might call "Leninist norms."

One Western critic to argue that one of the work's chief merits lay in its straightforward depiction of a history hitherto unknown was Gleb Zekulin. Zekulin says that of the four stories Solzhenitsyn had thus far published (*Ivan Denisovich*, *Matryona's Home*, *An Incident at Krechetovka Station* [in Collected Works, *Incident at Kochetovka Station*], and *For the Good of the Cause*), the first two stand out "for their informative or cognitive value." Indeed, in his view, *Ivan Denisovich* is "a mine of information, much more so than the well-known 'Notes from the House of the Dead' by Dostoevsky, which treats in a not dissimilar artistic manner the same theme—

---

[1]   Published in: Robert Porter, *Solzhenitsyn's One Day in the Life of Ivan Denisovich* (Bristol: Bristol Classical Press, 2007), 40–49.

life in a prison camp—and to which it has often been compared." Zekulin tells us that from Solzhenitsyn's story we learn all about the daily routine in the camp, what the prisoners eat, the punishments they can expect, the layout of the camp and of the building site to which they are marched every day. Perhaps of more importance in Zekulin's view is the portrayal of the prisoners, classified roughly into good, hard-working individuals and the bad ones, who contrive to find themselves cushy jobs. The critic quickly goes on to point out the greater subtleties in this categorization "good," "better" and "not-so-good." He also notes—contentiously, it could be said, but none the less with some prescience of the debates that were eventually to emerge concerning Solzhenitsyn's nationalist tendencies—"the possibly unconscious unwillingness on the part of the author to put the non-Russians into the group of the 'better ones'; for instance, the two Estonians who work conscientiously, etc., etc., and possess in addition other moral and civic virtues, are nevertheless classified as 'not-so-good ones.' Is it that Solzhenitsyn, like his nineteenth-century predecessors, still views non-Russians as incapable of entirely pure, unselfish and noble motivations?"

Zekulin points out that the story also gives us information about the hard life of the free workers who live near the construction site and also about the very harsh conditions on the collective farms, with few able-bodied men remaining there to work, but rather earning big money by stenciling carpet patterns. Zekulin also detects in the work "a short survey of Soviet history from a peculiar though not unique angle: the generations of camp inmates" saying that the first waves of prisoners came in 1930 with the collectivization program, and they never diminished, being followed by the victims of the purges in the wake of Kirov's assassination in 1934, and of the great purge in 1937; and then came those—like Ivan—arrested after having escaped from the Germans during the war. Zekulin rounds off his discussion with remarks on the wall-building scene:

> At first glance this scene is the apotheosis of work, a song of praise to work (and, incidentally, the story's only "redemption" theme). But, seen more closely, it becomes quite plain that Shukhov and his brigade do not work for the work's sake but in order to erect as quickly as possible a shield against the killing

frost and to receive a bigger ration of bread. Their enthusiasm has no other basis. Among his mates Shukhov is the only one who pays any attention to the quality of the work (and even he slips a little towards the end of the scene), and the pride of work well done is a particular feature of his own character, not the general attitude.

There is much that one could take issue in Zekulin's remarks (for instance, that he makes no distinction between Ivan and Solzhenitsyn), but at the same time he offers some astute insights, concluding his survey of Solzhenitsyn's four stories with the assertion that the author "might be a great writer." His works are not just reproductions, more or less faithful, of certain characters or incidents. They are probes into human life and gauges of human behavior. As such, they necessarily preach, teach, and are, ultimately, moralistic.

Zekulin retains a degree of liberal neutrality in his assessment. But it needs to be borne in mind that Solzhenitsyn, on the strength of *Ivan Denisovich*, was granted membership of the Union of Soviet Writers, and was received by Khrushchev; in 1964, he was a candidate (unsuccessful, as it turned out) for the Lenin Prize for literature. It was natural then that Marxist intellectuals in the West (and elsewhere), as they watched the Soviet Union's attempts at reform (of which Solzhenitsyn was willy-nilly a part), should offer their own interpretation of the author's work. Eventually, nearly all shades of political opinion were to claim Solzhenitsyn's loyalties, and the same was true for particular religious groups. Whatever one's political or religious views may be, perhaps the ultimate test of a work of art's validity is that it defies categorization and is, if not "all things to all men," at least "many things to many men." It retains its appeal despite the ravages of time and the attempts of given interest groups to hijack it for their own ends. It is a measure of *Ivan Denisovich*'s power that, in addition to restoring to millions of semi-literate ex-prisoners a voice and some dignity, it compelled some of the world's leading intellectuals to reach for their pens. Whatever one might think about *Ivan Denisovich*, it is a story that is never going to appear as quaint, dated, abstruse and verbose as some of the comment it generated.

For this reason, if nothing else, the views of Georg Lukács (1885–1971) are worthy of attention. A Hungarian communist philosopher and literary critic, he lived in Russia during the 1930s and the war years, returning to his native Budapest in 1945. In 1956 he was Minister of Culture in the revolutionary government and after arrest and deportation by the Soviet government was allowed in 1957 to return to Hungary. Despite his ideological position he was held in high regard throughout the world for his scholarship. No doubt his attitude towards the Soviet government was as ambivalent as theirs was to him. Thus, Solzhenitsyn's books, artistic, truthful, and enjoying (at least temporarily) official Soviet approval, were a lifeline.

His essay on *Ivan Denisovich* of 1964 was combined with a study of *The First Circle* and *Cancer Ward* (1969) to produce a book which made a prophecy and celebrated the fulfillment of that prophecy. The novella frequently appears either as a precursor to a conquest of reality by the great epic and dramatic forms, or as a rearguard, a termination at the end of a period; that is, it appears either in the phase of a Not-Yet (*Nochnicht*) in the artistically universal mastery of the given social world, or in the phase of the No-Longer (*Nichtmehr*). Boccaccio precedes the period of the great bourgeois novels (Balzac, Stendhal), Maupassant rounds it off. One can say of contemporary and near-contemporary fiction that it often withdraws from the novel into the novella in its attempt to provide truth of man's moral stature, and he cites as examples Conrad's *Typhoon* or *The Shadow Line* and Hemingway's *The Old Man and the Sea*. In the case of Solzhenitsyn, he argues, it is a question of a beginning, "an exploration of the new reality, and not, as in the works of the important Bourgeois writers mentioned, the conclusion of a period."

Lukács informs us that Socialist Realism (represented by A. Tolstoy, Sholokhov and others) was at its best in the 1920s [before the theory was officially promulgated, R. P.], and degenerated under Stalin in the 1930s into what he calls "illustrating literature" which grew out of Party resolutions and produced puppet-like characters which were either positive heroes or parasites. *Ivan Denisovich* represents the rebirth of Socialist Realism, and is "a significant overture to this process of literary rediscovery of self in the socialist present." Solzhenitsyn's hero, like, in Lukács's view, the Socialist Realist heroes of the 1920s literature, grows out of the past and is thus as authentic as they were. "The world of socialism today stands on the eve of a renaissance of Marxism [. . .] it is also wrong to attempt to give Socialist Realism a premature burial." Lukács dwells on the routine in the camp, Solzhenitsyn's extremely economic descriptive method, and asserts that the work acquires a "symbolic totality." The critic makes some mention of the three other published stories, but regards *Ivan Denisovich* as the most successful. For our purposes it is sufficient to quote only the opening paragraph of the second part of his book:

> In the previous essay I argued the case that Solzhenitsyn's novellas represent a significant step in the renewal of the great traditions of Socialist Realism of the nineteen-twenties. The question of whether he himself would bring about the rebirth of Socialist Realism and its new growth into a significant world literature was one that I cautiously left open. I can now state with pleasure that I was far too cautious: Solzhenitsyn's two new novels represent a new high point in contemporary world literature.

A great many readers would be prepared to agree with the last sentence here. But it is difficult to see, with the benefit of hindsight, the arguments about the rebirth of Socialist Realism, Marxism and so on, as being anything other than convoluted and wrong-headed. Lukács's comments on aspects of Solzhenitsyn's texts are often acute and sound (certainly there are affinities with Hemingway, Conrad, Tolstoy and others), but in his excitement at the artistry in the novels, Lukács has overlooked the simple fact that they were both banned in the Soviet Union and that their author was about to be expelled from the Writers' Union. Moreover, of course, Lukács did not live long enough to see the object of his admiration expelled from the Soviet Union, or the collapse of the Soviet Union and of Marxism as preached (and practiced?) there. Neither was he to witness the increasingly religious and nationalist sentiments that Solzhenitsyn came to exhibit.

Curiously enough, there are arguments to support the view of Solzhenitsyn as a Socialist Realist—but only by ditching all the verbiage and taking the position that Socialist Realism is achieved when the "message" (socialist, capitalist, liberal, religious or whatever) in a given work outweighs its artistry, when it tries to direct the reader's imagination instead of stimulating it. Thus, *For the Good of the Cause* could, without too much difficulty, be billed as Socialist Realism; and indeed, lumpen readers of a left-wing bent and deprived of Lukács's erudition, did—after their initial honeymoon with Solzhenitsyn and what they perceived as the moral rejuvenation of Marxism—dismiss the author as a kind of anti-Socialist Realist, i.e., an instrument of Western anti-Soviet propaganda. In any event, it would not be difficult to find passages in some of Solzhenitsyn's books (not *Ivan Denisovich*, this author would argue) where the propaganda looms unpalatably large. The same can be said of Charles Dickens.

The eminent American literary scholar Irving Howe was one of several critics to challenge Lukács. Reminding his readers of Lukács's equivocation over the years, he suggests that the Marxist critic has actually identified in Solzhenitsyn qualities that are so lacking in himself, primarily "independence" and "courage," but buttressed by a clear-cut moral awareness. Howe notes, as does Lukács, Solzhenitsyn's (and Pasternak's) penchant for the anti-modernist, nineteenth-century realistic novel; but unlike Lukács, he does not attribute this to "a deliberate or ideological rejection of literary modernism." In Howe's view, such an approach rests instead on:

> moral-political grounds [. . .] a persuasion that genuinely to return to the Tolstoyan novel, which the Stalinist dogma of "Socialist Realism" had celebrated in words but caricatured in performance, would constitute a revolutionary act of the spirit. It would signify a struggle for human renewal, for the reaffirmation of the image of a free man as that image can excite our minds beyond all ideological decrees.

In discussing *The First Circle* and *Cancer Ward* Lukács detected a weakness in the author in that his good characters were "plebeian" rather than politically and socially aware—he cites Marx's phrase "ignorant perfection." Howe counters that they are indeed plebeian, but that this has little to do with being educationally deprived and a good deal more to do with religion. (Though the quarrel between the two critics here is based primarily on the novels, it does have some bearing on our interpretation of *Ivan Denisovich*):

> The plebeian stress in Tolstoy and Dostoevsky, which one hears again in Solzhenitsyn, draws upon a strand of Christian belief very powerful in Russian culture, a strand that favors egalitarianism and ascetic humility, as if to take the word of Jesus at face value. Platon Karataev may himself be an example of "ignorant perfection," but Tolstoy's act in creating him is anything but that. [. . .] And the same might hold in regard to Solzhenitsyn's "plebeian" sentiments.

In this difference of opinion there was at least some sound argumentation. As more of Solzhenitsyn's works were published in the West, all sorts of interest groups seized on him for their own ends. Standing midway between well-considered argument and political hijacking was, for example, Robin Blackburn's article for *New Left Review*. Concerned primarily with *The First Circle*, which the critic calls Solzhenitsyn's masterpiece (*Cancer Ward* being in his view "weaker"), the piece rates *Ivan Denisovich* "more modest but entirely successful," and informs us that "Above all Solzhenitsyn's work must be read politically." It concludes that "The sentimental moralism of Tolstoy's aristocrat is simply out of the question for those who have passed through the grinding ordeal of the labor camps. They do not affect to despise the material bases of life since they know how degrading [sic. no comma, R. P.] extreme and prolonged deprivation of them can be. At the same time they are quite beyond the empty consumerism of the West. In short they still want justice—above all else—but they never suppose that it is separable from food and drink."

At the really ludicrous end of politically inspired commentary, the following two instances are of particular entertainment value: i) *The Workers' Press*, which its own logo proclaims is "The daily paper that leads the fight against the Tory government" and was the organ of the "Socialist Labour League," a Trotskyist splinter group, ran a series of lengthy articles on Solzhenitsyn (February 25, 26, 27 and March 1 and 4, 1971) by Thomas Jackson, in which we read, for example, that Solzhenitsyn "stands four square in defense of the property values of October," and that Nerzhin, the hero of *The First Circle* was seeking the Trotskyist path) Some six-seven years later, with the author now exiled to the West and regularly lambasting the West for its weakness in the face of communism, we had the British Tory Party repeatedly invoking his name, usually in garbled form, in its electioneering.

Robin Blackburn may have a point that Solzhenitsyn must be read politically, but the same could be said of nearly all the great Russian writers. This notion came out in an engrossing exchange between two heavy-weight scholars of Russian literature, Max Hayward and Victor Erlich, when they addressed the early works of Solzhenitsyn. How comforting it is to see that their respective positions, based on a close reading of just a few works, have stood the test of time far better than the politically inspired exegeses of a far larger body of material. Erlich says of *Ivan Denisovich*:

> The unspeakable squalor and misery, the back-breaking labor, and the animal scrounging for scraps of food, is authenticated here by a wealth of detail and made more credible by the author's quiet, undramatic manner. *One Day* is not a horror story. Physical violence appears in the novel not as the central actuality but as an ever-present threat [. . .] One cannot but wonder about the cumulative impact of this meticulously honest reportage in which thousands of Soviet citizens as innocent as Ivan Denisovich, as admirable as the brave naval officer Buynovsky, and as appealing as the gentle, devout Baptist Aleshka, are doomed to years of subhuman existence.
>
> This is not to say, however, that *One Day* is an overt indictment of the system or that, as some over-enthusiastic Western exegetes have argued, it implies the notion of the forced labor camp as a microcosm of Soviet society. For one thing, no work of fiction which could be legitimately interpreted thus would ever secure Khrushchev's personal authorization. [. . .] Though technically *One Day* is a third person narrative, the point of view is provided here by a "simple" peasant, whose potential for survival is considerably greater than his ratiocinative powers.

Erlich then goes on to a discussion of the style of the work, which in his view is "a far cry from the colorless, puritan prose of socialist-realist fiction"; but he has reservations: "The sustained 'folksy' stylization which lends solidarity and color to the verbal texture of *One Day* limits the novel's scope and import," and he finds some of the praise that has been heaped on the book in the West to be exaggerated, citing in particular F. D. Reeve's assertion that *Ivan Denisovich* is "one of the greatest works of twentieth century European fiction."

Hayward responded in the same issue. He endorsed Erlich's plea that there should be a "viable balance between literary and political considerations" in assessing Soviet works of literature. He also makes the general point that it is impossible to separate politics and literature in the Soviet context. He disagrees with Erlich on the question of the literary worth of contemporary Soviet literature, saying that there are "no recognized standards for the measurement and comparison of aesthetic values"; for the time being we can only measure them, in Hayward's view, by "the impact they have on ourselves," and "this is all highly personal."

Specifically, Hayward disagrees with Erlich over *Ivan Denisovich* on two counts. Firstly, for Hayward the camp does indeed represent a microcosm of the Soviet Union, and he quotes the passage concerning the harsher construction site (Sotsgorodok), which Ivan is so keen to avoid. On this site the prisoners must first erect posts and surround themselves with barbed wire: "No Soviet reader would miss this ironic suggestion that in the enforced 'building of socialism' the people were in fact building their own prison. There are other equally explicit passages suggesting that there was no essential difference between life in the camp and life outside." At the end of his article Hayward takes his argument even further: "It seems to me that the concentration camp is to be seen not just as a microcosm of life in the Soviet Union but of life everywhere. The majority of the human race are condemned to a daily grind, a rat-race of which the concentration camp is the ultimate and most intense expression."

This universality is achieved, in Hayward's analysis, by the very device that Erlich found so constricting, namely the narrative style of the work. Solzhenitsyn was anxious that we should see the "whole experience" not through the eyes of an intellectual. The hero "belongs to a totally different world from that of the intellectuals who can still derive some solace from conversation, from the feeling of still belonging to a larger intellectual world outside." Hayward cites in support of this the passage where Ivan notes mentally that Muscovites can smell each other out and chatter away among themselves so that for him they might just as well be speaking in Latvian or Rumanian. Hayward concludes:

> Solzhenitsyn has achieved something which many Russian authors in the past have striven for but never quite managed. Tolstoy's attempts to depict "simple people" are not entirely successful. His *muzhiks* are too obviously intended to demonstrate some "truth," arrived at by Tolstoy in the course of his intellectual quest, to be convincing in their own right. To take another "classical" example, Sholokhov's Grigorii Melekhov is suspect as a genuinely "popular" type. He has all the external attributes of a Cossack, but one cannot help feeling that his attitudes, his responses to life are somehow "intellectualized." His inner doubts, his "Hamletism," the "romantic" flavor of his love for Aksinia—all this vaguely echoes literary models and leaves me at least with the suspicion that Sholokhov has introduced us to the workings of his own comparatively sophisticated mind rather than to a completely non-intellectual, even if highly intelligent, Cossack. Isaac Babel's Cossacks, by contrast, are far more convincing because they are observed only *externally*. Babel was aware of the dangers of the intellectual trying "to get under the skin" of the simple man and did not even attempt it. I am inclined to believe that Solzhenitsyn has come nearest to achieving this almost, by its very nature, impossible task. One feature of Stalin's concentration camps was that for the first time the intelligentsia really got to know the *narod*; and *One Day* is an attempt to transmute this knowledge, obtained in such tragic circumstances, into a work of literature.

Hayward does not accept Erlich's opinion that Khrushchev would hardly permit the publication of a thorough-going indictment of the Soviet system, arguing that the Soviet leader was more than capable of embarking on schemes which misfired. Hayward's purely literary perceptions, quoted at length above, are worthy of the most serious consideration. Of particular note is his notion that *Ivan Denisovich* is applicable in ways far broader than its immediate geographical-temporal setting suggests. Elsewhere, Hayward returns to the same theme:

> One day in the life of Ivan Denisovich seems uncannily symbolic of one day in *anybody's* life. Like Kafka's *The Trial*, Solzhenitsyn's novel shows the human condition as a captive state from which there is no escape and for which there is no rational explanation. The feeling of being trapped and doomed is considerably heightened by making the reader see the concentration camp through the eyes of an illiterate peasant who is unable to rationalize his predicament as an intellectual would.

Hayward refers to the adapted form of *skaz* that the author uses, and in another article again raises the issue of *Ivan Denisovich* having more universal appeal than a first reading might suggest: in a wide-ranging survey "Themes and Variations in Soviet Literature, 1917–1967" he identified an exact parallel between the image of the prisoners in *Ivan Denisovich* building their own compound with the same metaphor in The Epilogue to *Doctor Zhivago*, where one of the hero's friends who survived the purges describes how they, as prisoners, were brought to an open field in a forest: "We cut down the wood to build our own dungeons, we surrounded ourselves with a stockade, we equipped ourselves with prison-cells and watch-towers." In "The Decline of Socialist Realism" he states again, with specific reference to *Ivan Denisovich*, that the building of socialism in Russia is expressly likened to the setting up of a concentration camp.

The politics, the message, the style, the characters, the plot of *Ivan Denisovich* all figure in the views we have alluded to so far. However, does the book possess some definable "philosophy," a *mirovozzrenie* (world outlook)? Hayward certainly hints at one, but it was left to Geoffrey Hosking to expatiate on the matter, and it is significant that he does so by coupling his interpretation of the work with *Doctor Zhivago*. He points out that Pasternak and Solzhenitsyn stood out from so many other writers of the Thaw period because they "rediscovered philosophy and folk culture." The philosophy which many of the post-Stalin authors found so attractive was, according to Hosking, that of the *Landmarks* (*Vekhi*) group and before them, Dostoevsky. These intellectuals—Russian intellectuals—rejected Marxism and they attached importance to spirit and individual personality, rather than to social groups, classes. They were suspicious of causality in man's behavior, and they were attracted to the Russian Orthodox Church. Such profound considerations are not immediately apparent in *Ivan Denisovich*; and one must guard against reading into the text all the aspects of Solzhenitsyn's life and thought which he was later to develop at great length in his publicistic works as well as in his creative writing.

We can, however, isolate one aspect of his philosophy, implicit in Hosking's analysis, namely, the existentialist preoccupation with the here and now as opposed to some teleological contemplation of a bright future. This outlook is summed up in Yuri Zhivago's over-quoted words: "Man is born to live, not to prepare for life." Ivan Denisovich Shukhov is, in the view of the present critic, the living embodiment of this dictum. As such, he doubtlessly owes something to anti-Marxist Russian philosophy, but he also—perhaps inadvertently as far as his creator is concerned—owes something to Camus' *The Myth of Sisyphus*.

There are many commentaries in books and journals on *Ivan Denisovich* and most of them have a lot to recommend them. The ones that have been mentioned here more or less define the parameters of all the various discussions that the book has spawned. Our own close reading of the text is not likely to go much *beyond* what has already been said, but it will have its own special emphases and will, at times, take issue with the individual interpretations put forward by other critics.

Aleksandr Solzhenitsyn
FROM *THE GULAG ARCHIPELAGO*[1]

Chapter 10
Behind the Wire the Ground Is Burning

No, the surprising thing is not that mutinies and risings did not occur in the camps, but that in spite of everything they *did*.

Like all embarrassing events in our history—which means three-quarters of what really happened—these mutinies have been neatly cut out, and the gap hidden with an invisible join. Those who took part in them have been destroyed, and even remote witnesses frightened into silence; the reports of those who suppressed them have been burned or hidden in safes within safes within safes—so that the risings have already become a myth, although some of them happened only fifteen and others only ten years ago. (No wonder some say that there was no Christ, no Buddha, no Mohammed. There you're dealing in thousands of years . . .)

When it can no longer disturb any living person, historians will be given access to what is left of the documents, archaeologists will do a little digging, heat something in a laboratory, and the dates,

---

[1]   From: Aleksandr Solzhenitsyn, *The Gulag Archipelago: 1918–1956: An Experiment in Literary Investigation*, translated from the Russian by Thomas P. Whitney (Parts I–IV) and Harry Willetts (Parts V–VII), abridged by Edward E. Ericson, Jr. (Harper & Row; Perennial Classics, 1985), 386–93; 403–418. Copyright © 1985 by The Russian Social Fund. Reprinted by permission of Harper Collins Publishers.

locations, contours of these risings, with the names of their leaders, will come to light.

Perhaps we (no, not we ourselves) shall learn at the same time about the legendary rising in 1948 at public works site No. 501, where the Sivaya Maska-Salekhard railway was under construction. It was legendary because everybody in the camps talked about it in whispers, but no one really knew anything. Legendary also because it broke out not in the Special Camp system, where the mood and the grounds for it by now existed, but in a Corrective Labor Camp, where people were isolated from each other by fear of informers and trampled underfoot by thieves, where even their right to be "politicals" was spat upon, and where a prison mutiny therefore seemed inconceivable.

According to the rumors, it was all the work of ex-soldiers (recent ex-soldiers!). It could not have been otherwise. Without them the 58's[2] lacked stamina, spirit, and leadership. But these young men (hardly any of them over thirty) were officers and enlisted men from our fighting armies, or their fellows who had been prisoners of war. These young men still retained in 1948 their wartime élan and belief in themselves, and they could not accept the idea that men like themselves, whole battalions of them, should meekly die. Even escape seemed to them a contemptible half-measure, rather like deserting one by one instead of facing the enemy together.

It was all planned and begun in one particular team. An ex-colonel called Voronin or Voronov, a one-eyed man, is said to have been the leader. A first lieutenant of armored troops, Sakurenko, is also mentioned. The team killed their convoy guards. Then they went and freed a second team, and a third. They attacked the convoy guards' hamlet, then the camp from outside, removed the sentries from the towers, and opened up the camp area.

Arming themselves with weapons taken from the guards, the rebels went on to capture the neighboring Camp Division. With

[2]   Those prisoners who were charged with Article 58 of the Soviet Penal Code for anti-Soviet propaganda and agitation, the most widely used article in political cases.

their combined forces they decided to advance on Vorkuta! It was only sixty kilometers away. But this was not to be. Parachute troops were dropped to bar their way. Then low-flying fighter planes raked them with machine-gun fire and dispersed them.

They were tried, more of them were shot, and others given twenty-five or ten years. (At the same time, many of those who had not joined in the operation but remained in the camp had their sentences "refreshed.")

The hopelessness of this rising as a military operation is obvious. But would you say that dying quietly by inches was more "hopeful"?

Riddle: What is the quickest thing in the world? Answer: Thought.

It is and it isn't. It can be slow, too—oh, how slow! Only slowly and laboriously do men, people, society, realize what has happened to them. Realize the truth about their position.

In herding the 58's into Special Camps, Stalin was exerting his strength mainly for his own amusement. He already had them as securely confined as they could be, but he thought he would be craftier than ever and improve on his best. He thought he knew how to make it still more frightening. The results were quite the opposite.

The whole system of oppression elaborated in his reign was based on keeping malcontents apart, preventing them from reading each other's eyes and discovering how many of them there were; instilling it into all of them, even into the most dissatisfied, that no one was dissatisfied except for a few doomed individuals, blindly vicious and spiritually bankrupt.

In the Special Camps, however, there were malcontents by the thousands. They knew their numerical strength. And they realized that they were not spiritual paupers, that they had a nobler conception of what life should be than their jailers, than their betrayers, than the theorists who tried to explain why they must rot in camps.

The old camp mentality—you die first, I'll wait a bit; there is no justice, so forget it; that's the way it was, and that's the way it will be—also began to disappear.

A bold thought, a desperate thought, a thought to raise a man up: how could things be changed so that instead of us running from them, they would run from us?

Once the question was put, once a certain number of people had thought of it and put it into words, and a certain number had listened to them, the age of escapes was over. The age of rebellion had begun.

Suddenly—a suicide. In the Disciplinary Barracks, hut No. 2, a man was found hanging. (I am going through the stages of the process as they occurred in Ekibastuz. But note that the stages were just the same in other Special Camps!) The bosses were not greatly upset; they cut him down and wheeled him off to the scrap heap.

A rumor went around the work team. The man was an informer. He hadn't hanged himself. He had been hanged.

As a lesson to the rest.

"Kill the stoolie!" That was it, the vital link! A knife in the heart of the stoolie! Make knives and cut stoolies' throats—that was it!

Now, as I write this chapter, rows of humane books frown down at me from the walls, the tarnished gilt on their well-worn spines glinting reproachfully like stars through cloud. Nothing in the world should be sought through violence! By taking up the sword, the knife, the rifle, we quickly put ourselves on the level of our tormentors and persecutors. And there will be no end to it . . .

There will be no end . . . Here, at my desk, in a warm place, I agree completely.

If you ever get twenty-five years for nothing, if you find yourself wearing four number patches on your clothes, holding your hands permanently behind your back, submitting to searches morning and evening, working until you are utterly exhausted, dragged into the cooler whenever someone denounces you, trodden deeper and deeper into the ground—from the hole you're in, the fine words of the great humanists will sound like the chatter of the well-fed and free.

The oppressed at least concluded that evil cannot be cast out by good.

Murders now followed one another in quicker succession than escapes in the best period. They were carried out confidently and anonymously: no one went with a bloodstained knife to give himself up; they saved themselves and their knives for another deed. At their favorite time—when a single warder was unlocking huts one after another, and while nearly all the prisoners were still sleeping—the masked avengers entered a particular section, went up to a particular bunk, and unhesitatingly killed the traitor, who might be awake and howling in terror or might be still asleep. When they had made sure that he was dead, they walked swiftly away.

They wore masks, and their numbers could not be seen—they were either picked off or covered. But if the victim's neighbors should recognize them by their general appearance, so far from hurrying to volunteer information, they would not now give in even under interrogation, even under threat from the godfathers, but would repeat over and over again: "No, no, I don't know anything, I didn't see anything." And this was not simply in recognition of a hoary truth known to all the oppressed: "What you don't know can't hurt you"; it was self-preservation! Because anyone who gave names would have been killed next 5 a.m., and the security officer's good will would have been no help to him at all.

And so murder (although as yet there had been fewer than a dozen) became the rule, became a normal occurrence. "Anybody been killed today?" prisoners would ask each other when they went to wash or collect their morning rations. In this cruel sport the prisoner's ear heard the subterranean gong of justice.

Out of five thousand men about a dozen were killed, but with every stroke of the knife more and more of the clinging, twining tentacles fell away. A remarkable fresh breeze was blowing! On the surface, we were prisoners living in a camp just as before, but in reality we had become free—free because for the very first time in our lives, we had started saying openly and aloud all that we thought! No one who has not experienced this transition can imagine what it is like!

An invisible balance hung in the air. In one of its scales all the familiar phantoms were heaped: interrogation officers, punches, beatings, sleepless standing, "boxes" (cells too small to sit or lie down in), cold, damp punishment cells, rats, bedbugs, tribunals, second and third sentences. But this could not all happen at once, this was a slow-grinding bone mill, it could not devour all of us at once and process us in a single day. And even when they had been through it—as everyone of us had—men still went on existing.

While in the other scale lay nothing but a single knife—but that knife was meant for you, if you gave in! It was meant for you alone, in the breast, and not sometime or other, but at dawn tomorrow, and all the forces of the Cheka-MGB could not save you from it! It was not a long one, but just right for neat insertion between your ribs. It didn't even have a proper handle, just a piece of old insulation tape wound around the blunt end of the blade—but this gave a very good grip, so that the knife would not slip out of the hand!

And this bracing threat weighed heavier!

So that now the bosses were suddenly blind and deaf.

The information machine on which alone the fame of the omnipotent and omniscient *Organs* had been based in decades past had broken down.

Foremen started *escaping* into the Disciplinary Barracks— hiding behind stone walls! Not only they, but bloodsucking work assigners, stoolies on the brink of exposure or, something told them, next on the list, suddenly took fright and *ran for it!*

This was a new period, a heady and spine-tingling period in the life of the Special Camp. It wasn't we who had taken to our heels— they had, ridding us of their presence! A time such as we had never experienced or thought possible on this earth: when a man with an unclean conscience could not go quietly to bed! Retribution was at hand—not in the next world, not before the court of history, but retribution live and palpable, raising a knife over you in the light of dawn. It was like a fairy tale: the ground is soft and warm under the feet of honest men, but under the feet of traitors it prickles and burns.

The masters of our bodies and souls were particularly anxious not to admit that our movement was political in character. In their menacing orders (warders went around the huts reading them out) the new trend was declared to be nothing but *gangsterism*. This made it all simpler, more comprehensible, somehow cozier. It seemed only yesterday that they had sent us gangsters labeled "politicals." Well, politicals—real politicals for the first time—had now become "gangsters." It was announced, not very confidently, that these gangsters would soon be discovered (so far not one of them had been), and still less confidently, that they would be shot. The orders further appealed to the prisoner mass to *condemn* the gangsters and *struggle* against them!

The prisoners listened and went away chuckling. Seeing the disciplinary officers afraid to call "political" behavior by its name, we were aware of their weakness.

The orders were of no avail. The prisoner masses did not start *condemning* and *struggling* on behalf of their masters. The next measure was to put the whole camp on a punitive routine.

The object of the camp administration was to make things so hard for us that we would betray the murderers out of exasperation. But we braced ourselves to suffer, to hang on a bit: it was worth it! Their other object was to keep the huts closed so that murderers could not come from outside, and so would be easier to find. But another murder took place, and still no one was caught—just as before no one had ever seen anything or knew anything. Then somebody's head was smashed in at work—locked huts are no safeguard against that.

They revoked the punitive regime. Instead they had the bright idea of building the "Great Wall of China." This was a wall two bricks thick and four meters high, to cut across the width of the camp. They were preparing to divide the camp into two parts. We greatly resented that wall—we knew that the bosses had some dirty trick in store—but we had no choice but to build it. Only a little of us was as yet free—our heads and our mouths—but we were still stuck up to our shoulders in the quagmire of slavery.

Two warders came into a hut after work, and casually told a man, "Get ready and come with us."

The prisoner looked around at the other lads and said, "I'm not going."

In fact, this simple everyday situation—*a snatch, an arrest*—which we had never resisted, which we were used to accepting fatalistically, held another possibility: that of saying, "I'm not going!" Our liberated heads understood that now.

The warders pounced on him. "What do you mean, not going?"

"I'm just not going," the zek[3] answered, firmly. "I'm all right where I am."

There were shouts from all around:

"Where's he supposed to go? . . . What's he got to go for? . . . We won't let you take him! . . . We won't let you! . . . Go away!"

And the wolves understood that we were not the sheep we used to be. That if they wanted to grab one of us now they would have to use trickery, or do it at the guardhouse, or send a whole detail to take one prisoner. With a crowd around, they would never take him.

Purged of human filth, delivered from spies and eavesdroppers, we looked about and saw, wide-eyed, that . . . we were thousands! that we were . . . *politicals!* that we could *resist!*

We had chosen well; the chain would snap if we tugged at this link—the stoolies, the talebearers and traitors! Our own kind had made our lives impossible. As on some ancient sacrificial altar, their blood had been shed that we might be freed from the curse that hung over us.

The revolution was gathering strength. The wind that seemed to have subsided had sprung up again in a hurricane to fill our eager lungs.

Chapter 12

The Forty Days of Kengir

In that fateful year, 1953, the fall of Beria made it urgent for the security ministry to prove its devotion and its usefulness in some signal way. But how?

The mutinies which the security men had hitherto considered a menace now shone like a beacon of salvation. Let's have more

---

3   Zeks—prisoners. From the acronym *ZK* (*zakliuchennyi kanaloarmeets*), meaning "an imprisoned builder of the canal." Used in the Gulag since the construction of the White Sea-Baltic Sea Canal.

disturbances and disorders, so that *measures will have to be taken.* Then staffs, and salaries, will not be reduced.

In less than a year the guards at Kengir opened fire several times on innocent men; and it cannot have been unintentional. They shot Lida, the young girl from the mortar-mixing gang who hung her stockings out to dry near the boundary fence.

They winged the old Chinaman—nobody in Kengir remembered his name, and he spoke hardly any Russian, but everybody knew the waddling figure with a pipe between his teeth and the face of an elderly goblin. A guard called him to a watchtower, tossed a packet of makhorka[4] near the boundary fence, and when the Chinaman reached for it, shot and wounded him.

Then there was the famous case of the column returning to camp from the ore-dressing plant and being fired on with dumdum bullets, which wounded sixteen men.

This the zeks did not take quietly—it was the Ekibastuz story over again. Kengir Camp Division No. 3 did not turn out for work three days running (but did take food), demanding punishment of the culprits.

A commission arrived and persuaded them that the culprits would be prosecuted. They went back to work.

But in February, 1954, another prisoner was shot at the wood-working plant—"the Evangelist," as all Kengir remembered him (Aleksandr Sisoyev, I think his name was). This man had served nine years and nine months of his *tenner.* His job was fluxing arc-welding rods and he did this work in a little shed which stood near the boundary fence. He went out to relieve himself near the shed— and while he was at it was shot from a watchtower. Guards quickly ran over from the guardhouse and started dragging the dead man into the boundary zone, to make it look as though he had trespassed on it. This was too much for the zeks, who grabbed picks and shovels and drove the murderers away from the murdered man.

The woodworking plant was in an uproar. The prisoners said that they would carry the dead man into camp on their shoulders.

---

4   Potent, minimally processed tobacco.

The camp officers would not permit it. "Why did you kill him?" shouted the prisoners. The bosses had their explanation ready: the dead man himself was to blame—he had started it by throwing stones at the tower. (Can they have had time to read his identity card; did they know that he had three months more to go and was an Evangelical Christian? . . .)

In the evening after supper, what they did was this. The light would suddenly go out in a section, and someone invisible said from the doorway: "Brothers! How long shall we go on building and taking our wages in bullets? Nobody goes to work tomorrow!" The same thing happened in section after section, hut after hut.

A note was thrown over the wall to the Second Camp Division. In this division, which was multinational, the majority had *tenners* and many were coming to the end of their time—but they joined in just the same.

In the morning the men's Camp Divisions, 2 and 3, did not report for work.

This bad habit—striking without refusing the state's bread and slops—was becoming more and more popular with prisoners.

They held out like this for two days. But the strike was mastered . . .

For the second time in Kengir, a ripening abscess was lanced before it could burst.

But then the bosses went too far. They reached for the biggest stick they could use on the 58's—for the thieves!

The bosses now renounced the whole principle of the Special Camps, acknowledged that if they segregated political prisoners they had no means of making themselves *understood*, and brought into the mutinous No. 3 Camp Division 650 men, most of them thieves, some of them petty offenders (including many minors). "A *healthy batch* is joining us!" the bosses spitefully warned the 58's. "Now you won't dare breathe."

The bosses understood well enough how the restorers of order would begin: by stealing, by preying on others, and so setting every man against his fellows.

But here again we see how unpredictable is the course of human emotions and of social movements! Injecting in Kengir

No. 3 a mammoth dose of tested ptomaine, the bosses obtained not a pacified camp but the biggest mutiny in the history of the Gulag Archipelago.

* * *

Events followed their inevitable course. It was *impossible* for the politicals not to offer the thieves a choice between war and alliance. It was *impossible* for the thieves to refuse an alliance. And it was *impossible* for the alliance, once concluded, to remain inactive.

The obvious first objective was to capture the service yard, in which all the camp's food stores were also situated. They began the operation in the afternoon of a nonworking day (Sunday, May 16, 1954) . . .

All these quite undisguised operations took a certain time, during which the warders managed to get themselves organized and obtain instructions . . .

The service yard was now firmly held by the punitive forces, and machine-gunners were posted there. But the Second Camp Division erected a barricade facing the service yard gate. The Second and Third Camp Divisions had been joined together by a hole in the wall, and there were no longer any warders, any MVD authority, in them.

How can we say what feelings wrung the hearts of those eight thousand men, who for so long and until yesterday had been slaves with no sense of fellowship, and now had united and freed themselves, not fully perhaps, but at least within the rectangle of those walls, and under the gaze of those quadrupled guards? So long suppressed, the brotherhood of man had broken through at last!

Proclamations appeared in the mess hall: "Arm yourselves as best you can, and attack the soldiers first!" The most passionate among them hastily scrawled their slogans on scraps of newspaper: "Bash the Chekists, boys!" "Death to the stoolies, the Cheka's stooges!" Here, there, everywhere you turned there were meetings and orators. Everybody had suggestions of his own. What demands shall we put forward? What is it we want? Put the murderers on trial! — goes without saying. What else? . . . No locking huts; take the numbers off! But beyond that? . . . Beyond that came the most frightening thing—the real reason why they had started it all, what they really wanted. We want freedom, of course, just freedom—but who can give it to us? The judges who condemned us in Moscow. As long as our complaints are against Steplag or Karaganda, they will go on talking to us. But if we start complaining against Moscow . . . we'll all be buried in this steppe.

Well, then—what do we want? To break holes in the walls? To run off into the wilderness? . . .

Those hours of freedom! Immense chains had fallen from our arms and shoulders! No; whatever happened, there could be no regrets! That one day made it all worthwhile!

Late on Monday, a delegation from command HQ arrived in the seething camp. The delegation was quite well disposed. Our side learned that generals had flown in from Moscow. They found the prisoners' demands *fully justified!* (We simply gasped: justified? We aren't rebels, then? No, no, they're *quite* justified!) "Those responsible for the shooting will be made to answer for it!" "But why did they beat up women?" "Beat up women?" The delegation was shocked. "That can't be true." Anya Mikhalevich brought in a succession of battered women for them to see. The commission was deeply moved: "We'll look into it, never fear!" "Beasts!" Lyuba Bershadskaya shouts at the general. There were other shouts: "No locks on huts!" "We won't lock them anymore." "Take the numbers off!" "Certainly we'll take them off." "The holes in the wall between camp areas must remain!" They were getting bolder. "We must be allowed to mix with each other." "All right, mix as much as you like." "Let the holes remain." Right, brothers, what else do we want? We've won, we've won! We raised hell for just one day, enjoyed ourselves, let off steam—and we won! Although some among us shake their heads and say, "It's a trick, it's all a trick," we believe it! We believe because that's our easiest way out of the situation . . .

* * *

All that the downtrodden can do is go on hoping. After every disappointment they must find fresh reason for hope.

So on Tuesday, May 18, all the Kengir Camp Divisions went out to work, reconciling themselves to thoughts of their dead.

That morning the whole affair could still have ended quietly. But the exalted generals assembled in Kengir would have considered such an outcome a defeat for themselves. They could not seriously admit that prisoners were in the right!

When the columns of prisoners returned to camp in the evening after giving a day's work to the state, they were hurried in to supper before they knew what was happening, so that they could be locked up quickly. On orders from the general, the jailers had to play for time that first evening—that evening of blatant dishonesty after yesterday's promises.

But before nightfall the long-drawn whistles heard on Sunday shrilled through the camp again—the Second and Third Camp Divisions were calling to each other like hooligans on a spree. The warders took fright, and fled from the camp grounds without finishing their duties.

The camp was in the hands of the zeks, but they were divided. The towers opened fire with machine guns on anyone who approached the inside walls. They killed several and wounded several.

Once again zeks broke all the lamps with slingshots, but the towers lit up the camp with flares . . .

They battered at the barbed wire, and the new fence posts, with long tables, but it was impossible, under fire, either to break through the barrier or to climb over it—so they had to burrow under. As always, there were no shovels, except those for use in case of fire, inside the camp. Kitchen knives and mess tins were put into service.

That night—May 18–19—they burrowed under all the walls and again united all the divisions and the service yard. The towers had stopped shooting now, and there were plenty of tools in the service yard. Under cover of night they broke down the boundary fences, knocked holes in the walls, and widened the passages, so that they would not become traps.

That same night they broke through the wall around the Fourth Camp Division—the prison area—too. The warders guarding the jails fled. The prisoners wrecked the interrogation offices. Among those released from the jail were those who on the morrow would take command of the rising: former Red Army Colonel Kapiton Kuznetsov and former First Lieutenant Gleb Sluchenkov.

Mutinous zeks! These eight thousand men had not so much raised a rebellion as escaped to *freedom*, though not for long! Eight thousand men, from being slaves, had suddenly become free, and now was their chance to . . . live! Faces usually grim softened into kind smiles. Women looked at men, and men took them by the hand. Some who had corresponded by ingenious secret ways, without even seeing each other, met at last! Lithuanian girls whose weddings had been solemnized by priests on the other side of the wall now saw their lawful wedded husbands for the first time—the Lord had sent down to earth the marriages made in heaven! For the first time in their lives, no one tried to prevent the sectarians and believers from meeting for prayer. Foreigners, scattered about the Camp Divisions, now found each other and talked about this strange Asiatic revolution in their own languages. The camp's food supply was in the hands of the prisoners. No one drove them out to work line-up and an eleven-hour working day.

The morning of May 19 dawned over a feverishly sleepless camp which had torn off its number patches. Many took their street clothes from the storerooms and put them on. Some of the lads crammed fur hats on their heads; shortly there would be embroidered shirts, and on the Central Asians bright-colored robes and turbans. The gray-black camp would be a blaze of color.

Orderlies went around the huts summoning us to the big mess hall to elect a commission for negotiations with the authorities and for self-government. For all they knew, they were electing it just for a few hours, but it was destined to become the government of Kengir camp for forty days.

* * *

The days ran on. And the generals were regretfully forced to conclude that the camp was not disintegrating of its own accord, and that there was no excuse to send troops in to the rescue.

The camp *stood fast* and the negotiations changed their character. Golden-epauleted personages, in various combinations, continued coming into the camp to argue and persuade. They were all allowed in, but they had to pick up white flags, and they had to undergo a body search. In return, the rebel staff guaranteed their personal safety! . . .

They showed the generals around, wherever it was allowed (not, of course, around the secret sector of the service yard), let them talk to prisoners, and called big meetings in the Camp Divisions for their benefit. Their epaulets flashing, the bosses took their seats in the presidium as of old, as though nothing were amiss.

The discussions sometimes took the form of direct negotiations on the loftiest diplomatic model. Sometime in June a long mess table was placed in the women's camp, and the golden epaulets seated themselves on a bench to one side of it, while the Tommy-gunners allowed in with them as a bodyguard stood at their backs. Across the table sat the members of the Commission, and they, too, had a bodyguard—which stood there, looking very serious, armed with sabers, pikes, and slingshots. In the background crowds of prisoners gathered to listen to the powwow and shout comments. (Refreshments for the guests were not forgotten!)

The rebels had agreed on their demands (or requests) in the first two days, and now repeated them over and over again:

—Punish the Evangelist's murderer.
—Punish all those responsible for the murders on Sunday night in the service yard.
—Punish those who beat up the women.
—Bring back those comrades who had been illegally sent to closed prisons for striking.
—No more number patches, window bars, or locks on hut doors.
—Inner walls between Camp Divisions not to be rebuilt.
—An eight-hour day, as for free workers.
—An increase in payment for work (here there was no question of equality with free workers).
—Unrestricted correspondence with relatives, periodic visits.
—Review of cases.

Although there was nothing unconstitutional in any of these demands, nothing that threatened the foundations of the state (indeed, many of them were requests for a return to the old position), it was impossible for the bosses to accept even the least of them, because these bald skulls under service caps and supported by close-clipped fat necks had forgotten how to admit a mistake or a fault. Truth was unrecognizable and repulsive to them if it manifested itself not in secret instructions from higher authority but on the lips of common people.

Still, the obduracy of the eight thousand under siege was a blot on the reputation of the generals, it might ruin their careers, and so they made promises. They promised that nearly all the demands would be satisfied—only, they said, they could hardly leave the women's camp open, that was against the rules (forgetting that in the Corrective Labor Camps it had been that way for twenty years), but they could consider arranging, should they say, *meeting days*. To the demand that the Commission of Inquiry should start its work inside the camp, the generals unexpectedly agreed. (But Sluchenkov guessed their purpose, and refused to hear of it: while making their statements, the stoolies would expose everything that was happening in the camp.) Review of cases? Well, of course, cases would be re-examined, but prisoners would have to be patient. There was one thing that couldn't wait at all—the prisoners must get back to work! to work! to work!

But the zeks knew that trick by now: dividing them up into columns, forcing them to the ground at gunpoint, arresting the ringleaders.

No, they answered across the table, and from the platform. No! shouted voices from the crowd. The administration of Steplag have behaved like provocateurs! We do not trust the Steplag authorities! We don't trust the MVD!

"Don't trust even the MVD?" The vice-minister was thrown into a sweat by this treasonable talk. "And who can have inspired in you such hatred for the MVD?"

A riddle, if ever there was one.

There were weeks when the whole war became a war of propaganda. The outside radio was never silent: through several loudspeakers set up at intervals around the camp it interlarded appeals to the prisoners with information and misinformation, and with a couple of trite and boring records that frayed everybody's nerves.

Through the meadow goes a maiden,
She whose braided hair I love.

(Still, to be thought worthy even of that not very high honor—
having records played to them—they had to rebel. Even rubbish
like that wasn't played for men on their knees.) These records also
served, in the spirit of the times, as a *jamming device*—drowning the
broadcasts from the camps intended for the escort troops.

On the outside radio they sometimes tried to blacken the whole
movement, asserting that it had been started with the sole aim of
rape and plunder. At other times they tried telling filthy stories about
members of the Commission. Then the appeals would begin again.
Work! Work! Why should the Motherland keep you for nothing?
By not going to work you are doing enormous damage to the state!
(This was supposed to pierce the hearts of men doomed to eternal
katorga!) Whole trainloads of coal are standing in the siding, there's
nobody to unload it! (Let them stand there—the zeks laughed—
you'll give way all the sooner!)

The Technical Department, however, gave as good as it got.
Two portable film projectors were found in the service yard. Their
amplifiers were used for loudspeakers, less powerful, of course, than
those of the other side. (The fact that the camp had electricity and
radio greatly surprised and troubled the bosses. They were afraid
that the rebels might rig up a transmitter and start broadcasting
news about their rising to foreign countries.)

The camp soon had its own announcers. Programs included
the latest news, and news features (there was also a daily wall
newspaper, with cartoons). "Crocodile Tears" was the name of
a program ridiculing the anxiety of the MVD men about the fate of
women whom they themselves had previously beaten up.

But there was not enough power to put on programs for the only
potential sympathizers to be found in Kengir—the free inhabitants
of the settlement, many of them exiles. It was they whom the
settlement authorities were trying to fool, not by radio but with
rumors that bloodthirsty gangsters and insatiable prostitutes were
ruling the roost inside the camp; that over there innocent people
were being tortured and burned alive in furnaces.

How could the prisoners call out through the walls, to the workers one, or two, or three kilometers away: "Brothers! We want only justice! They were murdering us for no crime of ours, they were treating us worse than dogs! Here are our demands"?

The thoughts of the Technical Department, since they had no chance to outstrip modem science, moved backward instead to the science of past ages. Using cigarette paper, they pasted together an enormous air balloon. A bundle of leaflets was attached to the balloon, and slung underneath it was a brazier containing glowing coals, which sent a current of warm air into the dome of the balloon through an opening in its base. To the huge delight of the assembled crowd (if prisoners ever do feel happy they are like children), the marvelous aeronautical structure rose and was airborne. But alas! The speed of the wind was greater than the speed of its ascent, and as it was flying over the boundary fence the brazier caught on the barbed wire. The balloon, denied its current of warm air, fell and burned to ashes, together with the leaflets.

After this failure they started inflating balloons with smoke. With a following wind they flew quite well, exhibiting inscriptions in large letters to the settlement:

> "Save the women and old men from being beaten!"
> "We demand to see a member of the Presidium,"

The guards started shooting at these balloons.

Then some Chechen prisoners came to the Technical Department and offered to make kites. (They are experts.) They succeeded in sticking some kites together and paying out the string until they were over the settlement. There was a percussive device on the frame of each kite. When the kite was in a convenient position, the device scattered a bundle of leaflets, also attached to the kite. The kite fliers sat on the roof of a hut waiting to see what would happen next. If the leaflets fell close to the camp, warders ran to collect them; if they fell farther away, motorcyclists and horsemen dashed after them. Whatever happened, they tried to prevent the free citizens from reading an independent version of the truth. (The leaflets ended by requesting any citizen of Kengir who found one to deliver it to the Central Committee.)

The kites were also shot at, but holing was less damaging to them than to the balloons. The enemy soon discovered that sending up counter-kites to tangle strings with them was cheaper than keeping a crowd of warders on the run.

A war of kites in the second half of the twentieth century! And all to silence a word of truth.

In the meantime the Technical Department was getting its notorious "secret" weapon ready. Let me describe it. Aluminum corner brackets for cattle troughs, produced in the workshops and awaiting dispatch, were packed with a mixture of sulfur scraped from matches and a little calcium carbide. When the sulfur was lit and the brackets thrown, they hissed and burst into little pieces.

But neither these star-crossed geniuses nor the field staff in the bathhouse were to choose the hour, place, and form of the decisive battle. Some two weeks after the beginning of the revolt, on one of those dark nights without a glimmer of light anywhere, thuds were heard at several places around the camp wall. This time it was not escaping prisoners or rebels battering it down; the wall was being demolished by the convoy troops themselves!

In the morning it turned out that the enemy without had made about a dozen breaches in the wall in addition to those already there and the barricaded gateway. (Machine-gun posts had been set up on the other side of the gaps, to prevent the zeks from pouring through them.) This was of course the preliminary for an assault through the breaches, and the camp was a seething anthill as it prepared to defend itself. The rebel staff decided to pull down the inner walls and the mud-brick outhouses and to erect a second circular wall of their own, specially reinforced with stacks of brick where it faced the gaps, to give protection against machine-gun bullets.

How things had changed! The troops were demolishing the boundary wall, the prisoners were rebuilding it, and the thieves were helping with a clear conscience, not feeling that they were contravening their code.

Additional defense posts now had to be established opposite the gaps, and every platoon assigned to a gap, which it must run to defend should the alarm be raised at night.

The zeks quite seriously prepared to advance against machine guns with pikes.

There was one attack in the daytime. Tommy-gunners were moved up to one of the gaps, opposite the balcony of the Steplag Administration Building, which was packed with important personages holding cameras or even movie cameras. The soldiers were in no hurry. They merely advanced just far enough into the breach for the alarm to be given, whereupon the rebel platoons responsible for the defense of the breach rushed out to man the barricade—brandishing their pikes and holding stones and mud bricks—and then . . . from the balcony, movie cameras whirred and pocket cameras clicked (taking care to keep the Tommy-gunners out of the picture). Disciplinary officers, prosecutors, Party officials, and all the rest of them—Party members to a man, of course—laughed at the bizarre spectacle of the impassioned savages with pikes. Well-fed and shameless, these grand personages mocked their starved and cheated fellow citizens from the balcony, and found it *all very funny.*

Then warders, too, stole up to the gaps and tried to slip nooses with hooks over the prisoners, as though they were hunting wild animals or the abominable snowman, hoping to drag out a *talker.*

But what they mainly counted on now were deserters, rebels with cold feet. The radio blared away. Come to your senses! Those who come over will not be tried for mutiny!

The Commission's response, over the camp radio, was this: Anybody who wants to run away can go right ahead, through the main gate if he likes; we are holding no one back!

In all those weeks only about a dozen men fled from the camp.

Why? Surely the rest did not believe in victory. Were they not appalled by the thought of the punishment ahead? They were. Did they not want to save themselves for their families' sake? They did! They were torn, and thousands of them perhaps had secretly considered this possibility. But the social temperature on this plot of land had risen so high that if souls were not transmuted, they were purged of dross, and the sordid laws saying that "we only live once," that being determines consciousness, and that every man's a coward when his neck is at stake, ceased to apply for that short time in that circumscribed place. The laws of survival and of reason told people that they must all surrender together or flee individually, but they did not surrender and they did not flee! They rose to that spiritual plane from which executioners are told: "The devil take you for his own! Torture us! Savage us!"

And the operation, so beautifully planned, to make the prisoners scatter like rats through the gaps in the wall till only the most stubborn were left, who would then be crushed—this operation collapsed because its inventors had the mentality of rats themselves.

No one supported the island of Kengir. It was impossible by now to take off into the wilderness: the garrison was being steadily reinforced. The whole camp had been encircled with a double barbed-wire fence outside the walls. There was only one rosy spot on the horizon: the lord and master (they were expecting Malenkov) was coming to dispense justice. But it was too tiny a spot, and too rosy.

They could not hope for pardon. All they could do was live out their last few days of freedom, and submit to Steplag's vengeance.

There are always hearts which cannot stand the strain. Some were already morally crushed, and were in an agony of suspense for the crushing proper to begin. Some quietly calculated that they were not really involved, and need not be if they went on being careful. Some were newly married (what is more, with a proper religious ceremony—a Western Ukrainian girl, for instance, will not marry without one, and thanks to Gulag's thoughtfulness, there were priests of all religions there). For these newlyweds the bitter and the sweet succeeded each other with a rapidity which ordinary people never experience in their slow lives. They observed each day as their last, and retribution delayed was a gift from heaven each morning.

The believers . . . prayed, and leaving the outcome of the Kengir revolt in God's hands, were as always the calmest of people. Services for all religions were held in the mess hall according to a fixed timetable. The Jehovah's Witnesses felt free to observe their rules strictly and refused to build fortifications or stand guard. They sat for hours on end with their heads together, saying nothing. (They were made to wash the dishes.) A prophet, genuine or sham, went around the camp putting crosses on bunks and foretelling the end of the world.

Some knew that they were fatally compromised and that the few days before the troops arrived were all that was left of life. The theme of all their thoughts and actions must be how to hold out longer. These people were not the unhappiest. (The unhappiest were those who were not involved and who prayed for the end.)

But when all these people gathered at meetings to decide whether to surrender or to hold on, they found themselves again in that heated climate where their personal opinions dissolved, and ceased to exist even for themselves. Or else they feared ridicule even more than the death that awaited them.

And when they voted for or against holding out, the majority were *for.*

Why did it drag on so long? What can the bosses have been waiting for? For the food to run out? They knew it would last a long time. Were they considering opinion in the settlement? They had no need to. Were they carefully working out their plan of repression? They could have been quicker about it. Were they having to seek approval for the operation up top? How high up? There is no knowing on what date and at what level the decision was taken . . .

On several occasions the main gate of the service yard suddenly opened—perhaps to test the readiness of the defenders? The duty picket sounded the alarm, and the platoons poured out to meet the enemy. But no one entered the camp grounds.

In the middle of June several tractors appeared in the settlement. They were working, shifting something perhaps, around the boundary fence. They began working even at night. The unfriendly roar made the night seem blacker.

Then suddenly the skeptics were put to shame! And the defeatists! And all who had said that there would be no mercy, and that there was no point in begging. The orthodox alone could feel triumphant. On June 22 the outside radio announced that the prisoners' demands had been accepted! A member of the Presidium of the Central Committee was on his way!

The rosy spot turned into a rosy sun, a rosy sky! It is, then, possible to get through to them! There *is*, then, justice in our country! They will give a little, and we will give a little. If it comes to it, we can walk about with number patches, and the bars on the windows needn't bother us, we aren't thinking of climbing out. You say they're tricking us again? Well, they aren't asking us to report for work *beforehand!*

Just as the touch of a stick will draw off the charge from an electroscope so that the agitated gold leaf sinks gratefully to rest, so did the radio announcement reduce the brooding tension of that last week.

Even the loathsome tractors, after working for a while on the evening of June 24, stopped their noise.

Prisoners could sleep peacefully on the fortieth night of the revolt. He would probably arrive tomorrow; perhaps he had come already . . .

In the early dawn of Friday, June 25, parachutes carrying flares opened out in the sky, more flares soared from the watchtowers, and the observers on the rooftops were picked off by snipers' bullets before they could let out a squeak! Then cannon fire was heard! Airplanes skimmed the camp, spreading panic. Tanks, the famous T-34's, had taken up position under cover of the tractor noise and now moved on the gaps from all sides. (One of them, however, fell into a ditch.) Some of the tanks dragged concatenations of barbed wire on trestles so that they could divide up the camp grounds immediately. Behind others ran helmeted assault troops with Tommy guns. (Both Tommy-gunners and tank crews had been given vodka first. However *special* the troops may be, it is easier to destroy unarmed and sleeping people with drink inside you.) Operators with walkie-talkies came in with the advancing troops. The generals went up into the towers with the snipers, and from there, in the daylight shed by the flares (and the light from a tower set on fire by the zeks with their incendiary bombs), gave their orders: "Take hut. number so-and-so! . . ."

The camp woke up—frightened out of its wits. Some stayed where they were in their huts, lying on the floor as their one chance of survival, and because resistance seemed senseless. Others tried to make them get up and join in the resistance. Yet others ran right into the line of fire, either to fight or to seek a quicker death.

The Third Camp Division fought—the division which had started it all. They hurled stones at the Tommy-gunners and warders, and probably sulfur bombs at the tanks . . . Nobody thought of the powdered glass. One hut counterattacked twice, with shouts of "Hurrah."

The tanks crushed everyone in their way. (Alia Presman, from Kiev, was run over—the tracks passed over her abdomen.) Tanks rode up onto the porches of huts and crushed people there. The tanks grazed the sides of huts and crushed those who were clinging to them to escape the caterpillar tracks. Semyon Rak and his girl threw themselves under a tank clasped in each other's arms and ended it that way. Tanks nosed into the thin board walls of the huts and even fired blank shells into them. Faina Epstein remembers the corner of a hut collapsing, as if in a nightmare, and a tank passing obliquely over the wreckage and over living bodies; women tried to jump and fling themselves out of the way: behind the tank came a lorry, and the half-naked women were tossed onto it.

The cannon shots were blank, but the Tommy guns were shooting live rounds, and the bayonets were cold steel. Women tried to shield men with their own bodies—and they, too, were bayoneted! Security Officer Belyaev shot two dozen people with his own hand that morning; when the battle was over he was seen putting knives into the hands of corpses for the photographer to take pictures of dead gangsters. Suprun, a member of the Commission, and a grandmother, died from a wound in her lung. Some prisoners hid in the latrines, and were riddled with bullets there.

As groups of prisoners were taken, they were marched through the gaps onto the steppe and between files of Kengir convoy troops outside. They were searched and made to lie flat on their faces with their arms stretched straight out. As they lay there thus crucified, MVD fliers and warders walked among them to identify and pull out those whom they had spotted earlier from the air or from the watchtowers. (So busy were they with all this that no one had leisure to open *Pravda* that day. It had a special theme—a day in the life of our Motherland: the successes of steelworkers; more and more crops harvested by machine. The historian surveying our country as it was *that day* will have an easy task.)

The victorious generals descended from the towers and went off to breakfast. Without knowing any of them, I feel confident that their appetite that June morning left nothing to be desired and that they drank deeply. An alcoholic hum would not in the least disturb the ideological harmony in their heads. And what they had for hearts was something installed with a screwdriver.

The number of those killed or wounded was about six hundred, according to the stories, but according to figures given by the Kengir Division's Production Planning Section, which became known some months later, it was more than *seven hundred*.

All day on June 25, the prisoners lay face down on the steppe in the sun (for days on end the heat had been unmerciful), while in the camp there was endless searching and breaking open and shaking out.

The members of the Commission and other suspects were locked up in the camp jail. More than a thousand people were selected for dispatch either to closed prisons or to Kolyma (as always, these lists were drawn up partly by guesswork, so that many who had not been involved at all found their way into them).

May this picture of the pacification bring peace to the souls of those on whom the last chapters have grated.

On June 26, the prisoners were made to spend the whole day taking down the barricades and bricking in the gaps.

On June 27, they were marched out to work. Those trains in the sidings would wait no longer for working hands!

The tanks which had crushed Kengir traveled under their own power to Rudnik and crawled around for the zeks to see. And draw their conclusions . . .

Translated by Harry Willetts

Varlam Shalamov
(1907, Vologda — 1982, Moscow)

Born to the family of a priest. In 1924 moved to Moscow where he worked for two years at a factory. From 1926 to 1928 studied at the Law School of Moscow State University but was expelled for hiding his "social origins." Arrested in 1929 for participating in a Trotskyite group and distributing Lenin's testament containing criticism of Stalin. After three years in a labor camp, he returned to Moscow where he began working as a journalist and published several short stories. In 1937 he was arrested again for "counter-revolutionary Trotskyite activities." Sentenced to five years of camp in Kolyma. In 1943, while in Kolyma, he was sentenced to another ten years for calling Ivan Bunin (an émigré poet and the first Russian Nobel Prize laureate in literature) a great Russian writer. Began writing poetry in 1949 while in prison. In 1951 Shalamov was released from labor camp but had no right to return to Moscow as a political criminal. Until 1956, when he was formally acquitted, he worked as a medical attendant in the Far East and Kalinin region. Returned to Moscow in 1956. Met with Solzhenitsyn, Nadezhda Mandelstam, and Alexander Galich. Boris Pasternak highly praised Shalamov's poetry. After his release from the Gulag, Shalamov worked on his major book *Kolyma Tales*. Shalamov intended "On prose," included in this volume, as the introduction to *Kolyma Tales*. The stories were unanimously rejected by Soviet journals and presses; they were published separately in Western journals and in book format in London in 1978. In 1988–89, after Shalamov's death, *Kolyma Tales* appeared in the Soviet press. Some of his poems were published in the USSR even before *perestroika*. In 1973 Shalamov became a member of the Union of Soviet Writers. In the same year, he was forced into a retirement home, from which he was transported to a psychiatric asylum in 1982. Shalamov died after contracting pneumonia during the forced transport.

On Prose[1]

The best modern prose is Faulkner. The novel is broken, exploded, and only Faulkner's authorial rage helps him complete the job, to build a world up from the wreckage.

The novel is dead. And no force in the world will resurrect this literary form.

People who have gone through revolution, war and concentration camps have no time for the novel.

The author who aims at the depiction of an imaginary life, of artificial collisions and conflicts (the author's inadequate personal experience that cannot be hidden in art) irritates the reader, who puts aside the bloated novel.

The need for the author in art has been retained, but faith in literature has been undermined.

What literary form has the right to exist? What literary form retains the interest of the reader?

In recent years science fiction has become popular worldwide. The fantastic successes of science have given rise to the success of science fiction.

But science fiction is nothing but a pitiful surrogate for literature, an ersatz literature, and it is of no use to the reader or the writer.

[1]   Translated from: Varlam Shalamov, "O proze," in *Sobranie sochinenii. V 4–kh tt.* Tom 4 (Moscow: Khudozhestvennaia literatura, Vagrius, 1998), 357–70.

Science fiction does not confer knowledge; it passes ignorance off as knowledge. Capable authors of this type of work (Bradbury, Asimov) aim only at narrowing the gaping chasm between life and literature without attempting to bridge it.

The success of literary biographies, from those by André Maurois to Irving Stone's literary biography of Van Gogh,[2] is also witness to the reader's demand for something more serious than the novel.

The enormous interest worldwide in the genre of the memoir is a voice and a sign of the times. Today's man checks himself and his actions not against the actions of Julien Sorel or Rastignac or Andrey Bolkonsky, but against the events and people of real life, that life in which the reader himself is a witness and participant.

Again, the believable author, to use the expression of Niels Bohr, should be "not only a witness, but a participant in the great drama of life." Niels Bohr used this phrase to refer to scholars, but it can justifiably be used to refer to literary authors.

Faith in the genre of the memoir is limitless. This genre is characterized by that "effect of presence" which constitutes the essence of live television. I can't watch a recorded soccer match when I already know the result.

Today's reader engages only with documents and is persuaded only by documents. Today's reader has the strength, knowledge and personal experience to make this argument. And he trusts this literary form. The reader doesn't feel that he has been deceived, as he does when he reads a novel.

Before our eyes the entire range of demands on the literary work change, demands which a literary form such as the novel does not have the strength to fulfill.

Bloated and verbose descriptiveness becomes a vice that nullifies the work. The description of a character's appearance impedes understanding of the author's idea.

Scenery is not accepted at all. The reader has no time to think about the psychological meaning of digressions about scenery.

---

[2]   Irving Stone, *Lust for Life*. A novel of 1934 about Vincent Van Gogh.

If scenery is incorporated, then it should be used extremely economically. Any detail of the landscape becomes a symbol, a sign, and only then does it retain its meaning, vitality, necessity.

Doctor Zhivago is the last Russian novel. *Doctor Zhivago* is the collapse of the classic novel, the collapse of the authorial precepts of Tolstoy. *Doctor Zhivago* was written according to Tolstoy's formula, but what emerged was a novel-monologue, without "characters" and other attributes of the nineteenth-century novel. In *Doctor Zhivago* the moral philosophy of Tolstoy scores a victory and endures the defeat of Tolstoy's artistic method.

The symbolic cloaks in which Pasternak wrapped his heroes, which effect a return to the ideas of his literary youth, diminish rather than increase the force of *Doctor Zhivago*, which is, again, a novel-monologue.

To debate "character development" and so forth is not merely old-fashioned, it is unnecessary and, therefore, harmful. The modern reader understands what the work is about in two words and has no need for detailed descriptions of appearance, has no need for classical plot development and the like. When Anna Akhmatova was asked how her play ends, she answered: "Modern plays do not have an end." This isn't a fad or a nod to "modernism," it's just that the reader does not need authorial efforts directed toward "rounding out" the plot through those well-trodden methods known to the reader since high school.

If a writer attains literary success, genuine success, success in its own right and not merely positive reviews, then who cares whether there are "characters" in the work or not, whether there is "individualization of characters' discourse" or not.

In art the only type of individualization is the distinctiveness of the authorial personage, the distinctiveness of his artistic handwriting.

The reader searches, just as he searched before, for answers to the "eternal" questions, but he has lost hope of finding them in belles-lettres. The reader does not want to read nonsense. He demands a solution to genuinely important questions, searches for answers about the meaning of life, about the links between art and life.

But the reader does not pose these questions to literary writers, not to Korolenko or Tolstoy, as in the nineteenth century, but searches for the answers in memoirs.

The reader no longer believes in fictional details. Any detail that does not contain a symbol seems extraneous in the literary fabric of the new prose.

Diaries, travelogues, memoirs, and scientific descriptions have always been published and have always enjoyed success, but now the interest in them is unusually high. They constitute the main section of any journal.

The best example of this is *My Life* by Charlie Chaplin. A mediocre thing in the literary sense, it's the number-one bestseller, having surpassed each and every novel.

Such is the trust in the memoir. A question: should the new prose be of a documentary nature? Or can it be more than a document?

One's own blood, one's own fate—these are the demands of today's literature.

If the author writes with his blood, then there is no need to collect material while visiting the Butyrka prison or "transit" stations, no need for research trips to regions like Tambov. The very notion of preparing to write is outdated and invalid; not only are other aspects of depiction sought after, but other paths of knowledge and cognition as well.

All the "hell" and "heaven" in the writer's soul, and vast personal experience, confer not only moral superiority, not only the right to write, but also the right to judge.

I am deeply convinced that the memoirs of Nadezhda Mandelstam[3] will become a milestone in Russian literature, not only because they are a monument to an era, a passionate condemnation of the era of the wolf-hound. Not only because the reader will find in this manuscript the answers to a whole series of questions troubling Russian society. Not only because memoirs are the fate of the Russian intelligentsia. Not only because questions on

---

[3] The widow of Osip Mandelstam, who authored the memoirs *Hope Against Hope* (1970) and *Hope Abandoned* (1972).

the psychology of creativity are posed here in brilliant form. Not only because the testament of Osip Mandelstam is set forth here and his fate recounted. It is clear that any aspect of the memoir will arouse enormous interest worldwide and among Russia's readers. But the manuscript of Nadezhda Mandelstam has yet another very important quality. It is a new form of memoir, very capacious and very comfortable.

The chronology of Osip Mandelstam's life is interwoven with everyday scenes, portraits of people, philosophical digressions, and observations on the psychology of creativity. From this angle the memoirs of Nadezhda Mandelstam present enormous interest. A major new figure enters the history of the Russian intelligentsia and the history of Russian literature.

The great Russian writers have long felt the loss, the false stature of the novel as a literary form. Chekhov's attempts to write a novel were fruitless. "A Boring Story," "Story of an Unknown Man," "My Life," "Black Monk"—all these are persistent yet unsuccessful attempts to write a novel.

Chekhov still believed in the novel, but failed at it. Why? A longstanding habit of writing story after story had been implanted in Chekhov, who held only one theme, one topic in his head. After a story was written, Chekhov would begin a new one in turn, without even thinking it over to himself. Such a method is not suitable for the novel. They say that Chekhov didn't find the strength in himself to "ascend to the novel," that he was too "grounded."

The prose of *Kolyma Tales* has no relationship to the sketch. The pieces in sketch form are sprinkled in for the greater glory of the document, but only here and there, each time dated and with intent. Real life appears on the page by entirely different means. In *Kolyma Tales* description is absent, as are data, deductions, and journalistic material. The point of *Kolyma Tales* is the depiction of new psychological patterns, the artistic investigation of a terrible theme, not in an "informative" tone, not in the collection of facts. Although, to be sure, any fact in *Kolyma Tales* is irrefutable.

Fundamental to *Kolyma Tales* is that it shows new psychological patterns, what is new in the behavior of a man who has been brought down to the level of an animal. Incidentally, animals are made from better material; not one animal would endure the torments man has endured. There is something new in the behavior of man, new—despite the enormous literature on prisons and their prisoners.

These changes of the psyche are irreversible, like frostbite. The memory aches like a frostbitten hand at the first cold wind. No one who has returned from imprisonment lives a day without remembering the camp, the humiliating and terrible labor of the camp.

The author of *Kolyma Tales* considers the labor camp a negative experience for man—from the first to the last hour. Man should not know, should not even hear about it. Not one man becomes better or stronger after the labor camp. The labor camp is a negative experience, a negative school, and the defilement of all—of the staff and the prisoners, of the security guards and the onlookers, the passersby and the readers of belles-lettres.

Kolyma Tales examines people without a biography, without a past or a future. Does their present resemble a savage or humane present?

In *Kolyma Tales* there is nothing that could be considered the overcoming of evil or the triumph of good, in terms of the big plan, the artistic plan.

If I had had a different goal, I would have found an entirely different tone, different colors, using the very same artistic principle.

Kolyma Tales is about the fate of martyrs, who were not, could not be, and did not become heroes.

The need for documents of this type is extremely urgent. After all in every family, and in the village and the city, among the intelligentsia, the workers and the peasants alike, there were people, or relatives, or acquaintances, who perished while imprisoned. The Russian reader—and not only the Russian reader—is waiting for an answer from us.

It is necessary and possible to write a story that is indistinguishable from a document. But the author must research his material with his own hide, not only with his mind; not only with his heart, but with every pore of his skin, his every nerve.

A conclusion has been lying in my brain for a long time, a kind of judgment about this or that side of human life, of the human psyche. I came to this conclusion at the dear price of blood and protect it as the most important thing in life.

There comes a time when one is overcome by the need to put this conclusion forward, to give it real life. This persistent desire acquires the character of a resolution. And you no longer think about anything else. And when you sense that you once more feel with that same strength as you did then, when you encountered events, people and ideas in real life (maybe the strength is different, on a different scale, but that's not important now), when once again warm blood flows through your veins . . .

Then you begin to search for a plot. It's very simple. There are so many encounters in life, and so many of them are retained in your memory, that to find the essential one comes easily.

The writing begins—it is very important to retain its immediacy and not spoil it with corrections. The rule in effect for poetry, that the first version is the most sincere, is in effect and retained here as well.

The completeness of plot. Life is endlessly plotted, as are history, mythology; fairy tales and myth are all encountered in real life.

It is not important whether the *Kolyma Tales* have plot. There are tales with plot, and tales without, but no one will say that the latter are less of a story or are less important.

It is necessary and possible to write a story that is indistinguishable from a document, from a memoir.

But in the higher, more important sense, any story is always a document, a document about the author—and it is this characteristic, probably, that makes one see in *Kolyma Tales* the triumph of good, not evil.

The shift from the first to the third person, the entry into the document. The use of authentic names here and fictional names there, the transitory protagonist—all this is material serving one goal.

All the tales have a common musical pitch that the author knows. Noun-synonyms and verb-synonyms must strengthen the desired impression. The author has thought out the composition of the collection. The author has rejected the short phrase as literary pretentiousness, has rejected the physiological measure of

Flaubert: "the human breath dictates the phrase." He has rejected Tolstoy's "that" and "which," rejected Hemingway's discovery: jagged dialogue, combined with phrases drawn out into moral admonitions, into pedagogical examples.

The author wanted only to capture real life.

What qualities should a memoir possess besides verisimilitude? . . . And what is historical accuracy? . . .

I had a conversation in the editorial office of a Moscow journal with regard to one of the *Kolyma Tales*.

"Did you read 'Cherry Brandy' when you were at the university?"

"Yes, I did."

"Was Nadezhda Mandelstam there?"

"Yes, Nadezhda Mandelstam was there."

"That means your legend about the death of Mandelstam is being canonized?"

I say:

"In the story 'Cherry Brandy' there are fewer historical inaccuracies than in Pushkin's 'Boris Godunov.'"

Keep in mind:

1) "Cherry Brandy" describes that very same transit prison in Vladivostok where Osip Mandelstam died and where the author of the story had been a year earlier.

2) Here one finds an almost clinical description of death from nutritional edema, or simply speaking, from hunger, that same hunger of which Mandelstam died. Death from nutritional edema is particular. Life returns to a person, then departs from him, and you may not know whether or not the person has died for five days. And whether he can still be saved, returned to the world.

3) Here the death of a man is described. Is that really too little?

4) Here the death of a poet is described. Here the author attempted to imagine with the help of personal experience what Mandelstam may have thought or felt as he was dying—that great equality of bread rations and high poetry, that great indifference and serenity that death from hunger brings, in contrast to all "surgical" and "infectious" deaths.

Is that really too little for "canonization"?

Do I really not have the moral right to write about the death of Mandelstam? This is my duty. Who can refute a story like "Cherry Brandy," and how? Who will dare to call this story a legend?

"When was the story written?"

"The story was written right after I returned from Kolyma in 1954 in Reshetnikov in the Kalinin region, where I wrote day and night, trying to nail down something that was most important, to leave witness, to put a cross on a grave, to not allow a name dear to me my whole life to be hidden, to commemorate this death, which cannot be forgiven or forgotten."

And when I returned to Moscow I saw that Mandelstam's poetry was in every house. It had gotten along without me. And if I had known this, I perhaps would have written differently, not that way.

Contemporary new prose may be created only by people who know their material to perfection, for whom the mastery of material, its artistic transformation, is not purely a literary exercise, but a duty, a moral imperative.

Similar to the way that Saint-Exupéry opened the skies for man, people will come from every corner of life who will be able to tell about what they know and what they have lived through, not just what they have seen and heard.

There is this notion that a writer should not know his material too well, overly well and intimately. The notion that the writer should narrate to the reader in the language of those very readers in whose name the writer began to prepare his material. That the understanding of what is depicted should not depart too far from the moral code, from the worldview of the reader.

Orpheus descending into hell, not Pluto ascending from hell.

According to this idea, if the author knows his material too well, he will go over to the side of his material. Values will change, the scale will be shifted. The writer will measure life by new measures, which are unknown to the reader and which frighten and alarm him. Inevitably the connection between writer and reader will be lost.

According to this idea, the writer is always a bit of a tourist, a bit of a foreigner, a bit too much of a man of letters and a craftsman.

An exemplar of such a writer-tourist is Hemingway, no matter how much he fought in Madrid. It's possible to fight and live an active life and at the same time to be "outside." It makes no difference whether one is "above" or "on the side."

The new prose rejects this principle of tourism. The writer is not an observer, not an onlooker, but a participant in the drama of life, and not in the guise of a writer or in a writer's role.

Pluto ascending from hell, not Orpheus descending to hell.

What has been earned by suffering with one's own blood enters the page like a document of the soul, transformed and enlightened by the fire of talent.

The writer becomes the judge of his time, not someone's assistant; it is precisely the deepest knowledge, the triumph in the very depths of real life that bestows the right and strength to write. It even suggests the method.

Writers of the new prose, like memoirists, should not place themselves higher than everyone else, smarter than everyone else, should not lay claim to the role of judge.

On the contrary the writer, the author, the storyteller should be lower than everyone, less than everyone. Only here can one find success and trust. This is the moral and artistic demand of contemporary prose.

The writer should remember that there are a thousand truths in the world.

How are results achieved?

Above all, through a serious and vitally important theme. Such a theme may be death, destruction, murder, Golgotha . . . It should be told smoothly, without declamation.

With brevity, simplicity, and the elimination of everything that could be called "literature."

Prose should be simple and clear. Enormous conceptual weight, and chiefly, enormous emotional weight does not allow for patter, trifles and rattling. It is important to resurrect feeling. Feeling should return, conquering the control of time, the changing of values. Only under these conditions is it possible to resurrect life.

Prose should be a simple and clear statement of what is vitally important. Details—new and unusual particulars, new kinds of description—should be brought in, planted in the story. The novelty, accuracy and exactitude of these particulars in and of themselves will make one believe in the story and in everything else, not as information, but as an open wound to the heart. But their role is much greater in the new prose. It is always the detail-symbol, detail-sign that translates the entire story into a different plan, giving it a "subtext" that serves the author's will and is an important element of the artistic resolution, the artistic method.

An important aspect of the work in *Kolyma Tales* was prompted by artists. In *Noa Noa* Gauguin writes: if the tree seems green to you, take the very best green paint and draw. You will not err. You found it. You solved it. Here it is a matter of the purity of tone. With regard to prose this question is solved with the elimination of everything extraneous not only in descriptions (a blue axe, etc.), but in the elimination of all the chaff of "halftones" in the depiction of psychology. Not only in the elimination of the dryness and uniqueness of adjectives, but in the very composition of the story, where much is sacrificed for the sake of this purity of tone. Any other solution leads away from the vital truth.

Kolyma Tales is an attempt to pose and answer certain important moral questions of the time, questions that simply cannot be solved using other material.

The question of the encounter between man and world, the struggle of man with the governmental machine, the truth of this struggle, the struggle for oneself, inside oneself, and outside of oneself. The possibility of influence over one's fate, ground up by the cogs of the governmental machine, the cogs of evil. The illusoriness and gravity of hope. The possibility of relying on forces other than hope.

The author destroys the border between form and content; better yet, he does not understand the difference. For the author it seems that the importance of the theme itself dictates particular artistic principles. The theme of *Kolyma Tales* does not find an outlet in ordinary stories. Such stories are a debasement of the theme. But in place of the memoir *Kolyma Tales* offers a new prose, the prose of real life, which at the same time is reality transformed, a document transformed.

The so-called labor camp theme is a very big theme, one with room for a hundred writers like Solzhenitsyn and five writers like Tolstoy. And no one will feel crowded.

The author of *Kolyma Tales* strives to prove that the most important thing for the writer is to preserve the living soul.

Compositional unity is no small component of *Kolyma Tales*. In this collection it is possible to replace and move around only a few stories, but the main ones, the supporting ones, must stay in their places. Everyone who has read *Kolyma Tales* as one book, not as separate stories, has acknowledged the great and powerful impression it makes. All its readers say this. This is explained by the deliberateness of selection, the careful attention to composition. The author considers all the stories of *Kolyma Tales* to be in their place. "Typhoid Quarantine," which finishes the description of the circles of hell, and the machine that throws out people into new suffering, into a new stage (stage!), is a story that cannot begin a book.

"The Red Cross" is brought into service here, embedded, and journalistic in its fabric, for in the camp the criminal world is of great significance, and he who does not understand this has understood nothing about the camps and understands nothing about modern life.

Kolyma Tales is the depiction of new psychological patterns in the behavior of man, of people in new conditions. Will they remain human? Where is the border between man and animal? The tales of Vercors or Wells' *Island of Doctor Moreau,* with its ingenious "Sayer of the Law," are only eye-opening and amusing in comparison with the fearsome face of real life.

These patterns are new, new despite the copious literature on prisons and prisoners. This proves once again the force of the new prose, its necessity. Overcoming the document is a matter of talent, of course, but the theme of the labor camp places very high demands on talent, most of all from the moral angle.

These psychological patterns are irreversible, like frostbite of the third or fourth degree. The author considers the labor camp to be a negative experience for man—negative from the first to the last hour—and regrets that his own strength must be directed toward overcoming this material in particular.

The author has asked former prisoners a thousand times, a million times, whether there has been even one day in their lives when they did not recall the labor camp. The answer was always the same: no, there has been no such day in their lives.

Even the highly educated and cultured people who spent time in the camps—if they weren't crushed and if they fortuitously came out unscathed—tried to erect a barrier of jokes and anecdotes, a barrier protecting their own soul and mind. But the labor camp deceived them as well. It made these people proponents of principled unprincipledness, and their enormous cultural knowledge served them as an object of intellectual entertainment, of mental gymnastics.

The analysis of *Kolyma Tales* lies in the absence of analysis. Here people are taken without a biography, without a past and without a future, taken in the moment of their present—a savage or humane one? To whom is the material more suited—to beasts, to animals, or to people?

Kolyma Tales is the fate of martyrs, who were not and did not become heroes.

In *Kolyma Tales*—so it seems to the author—there is nothing that could be considered the overcoming of evil or the triumph of good.

If I had wanted something else, I would have found a completely different tone, different colors, employing the very same artistic principle.

My own blood—that is what cemented the phrases of *Kolyma Tales*. The questions that life poses—these questions are not only not solved, but not even posed correctly. My memory has retained thousands of plot variants on the answer, and it remains for me simply to choose and drag a suitable one onto the page. Not in order to describe something, but in order to answer. I have no time for description.

Not one line, not one phrase in *Kolyma Tales* exists that could be called "literary."

What's more: life of the present day retains the features of fairy tales, epics, legends, mythology, religions, works of art (which bothered Oscar Wilde quite a bit).

The author hopes that in the 33 tales of the collection no one will doubt that this is the truth of real life.

The change and transformation were achieved not only by embedding documents. "The Injector" is not picturesque padding in the vein of "Elfin Cedar." Actually it is not picturesque at all, for it has no picturesque lyrics whatsoever, only the author's conversation with his reader.

"Elfin Cedar" is necessary not as picturesque information, it is the soul's necessary condition for the struggle in "Shock Therapy," "The Lawyers' Plot," and "Typhoid Quarantine."

This is a kind of picturesque padding.

None of the repetition or the slips of the tongue that the readers upbraided me for were the product of accident, carelessness, or haste.

They say that if an announcement has a typographical error it is easier to remember. But this is not the only reward for carelessness.

Authenticity and immediacy themselves require this type of mistake.

Sterne's *Sentimental Journey* breaks off in mid-sentence yet it does not evoke disapproval in anyone.

Why do all readers of the story "How it Began" manually write out and correct my unfinished phrase "Are we still wor . . . ?"

And how does one fight for a style, how does one defend the author's rights?

The utilization of synonyms, verb-synonyms and noun-synonyms, serves that same dual purpose—the underscoring of the main point and the creation of musicality, aural support, intonation.

When an orator gives a speech a new phrase is formed in his brain while synonyms exit upon his tongue.

The preservation of the first variant is unusually important. Corrections are inadmissible. It is better to wait for further inspiration and write the story again from the start with all the truth of the first version.

Everyone who writes poetry knows that the first version is the most sincere, most unmediated, subjugated to the haste of expressing the heart of the matter. The subsequent finishing—correction (in its various meanings)—is the control and the violence of the idea over feeling, the interference of the idea. In 12–16 lines of poetry of any of the great Russian poets I can guess which line was written first.

I have correctly guessed what was most important for Pushkin and Lermontov.

Thus for this prose, conditionally called "new," the success of the first draft is unusually important. [. . .]

They will say that none of this is necessary for inspiration, for sudden insight.

The author answers: sudden insight appears only after an indispensable waiting, intense work, searching, summoning.

God is always on the side of the big battalions. A la Napoleon. These big battalions of poetry get in line and march, learn to shoot while hidden, while in the depths.

The artist always works, and reworking of material always, constantly, carries on. Sudden insight is the result of this constant work.

Of course there are secrets in art. They are the secrets of talent. No more and no less.

The correction, the "finishing" of any story of mine is unusually difficult, for it has particular tasks, stylistic ones.

You correct a little and it destroys the strength of authenticity, of immediacy. That's how it was with the story "The Lawyers' Plot." The deterioration of quality after correction was immediately noticeable (N. M.).[4]

Is it true that the new prose relies on new material, and this material makes it powerful?

Of course, there are no trifles in *Kolyma Tales*. The author thinks, maybe mistakenly, that it's a matter, after all, not only of the material, and even not so much of the material . . .

The author has a story called "The Cross." It is one of the best stories in terms of compositional completeness; in essence, the principles of the new prose are observed, and it seems to me the story succeeded.

Why the theme of the labor camps. The camp theme, broadly interpreted, in its fundamental sense, is the foundational and chief

[4]   On Sept. 2, 1965, Nadezhda Mandelstam wrote to Shalamov: "In 'The Lawyers' Plot' it seems as if I had read a more detailed variant, and it was stronger."

question of our day. Is the destruction of man with the help of the state not the main question for our time, for our ethics, that has entered into the psychology of every family? This question is much more important than the theme of war. War in some sense plays the role of psychological camouflage (history says that in times of war the tyrant draws closer to the people). They want to hide the "camp theme"[5] behind the statistics of war, statistics of any kind.

When I am asked what I am writing I answer: I am not writing memoirs. There are no memoirs of any kind in *Kolyma Tales*. I am not writing stories either. Better to say, I am trying to write, not stories, but something that is not literary.

Not the prose of a document, but prose, long-suffering like a document.

Translated by Brian R. Johnson

---

[5]   That is, to hide any discussion of the Gulag.

Eulogy[1]

They all died . . .

Nikolai Kazimirovich Barbe, one of the organizers of the Russian Komsomol, a comrade who had helped me drag a large rock out of a narrow pit, a work brigade boss, was shot because the camp section where Barbe's brigade worked didn't fulfill the plan—according to the report of the young camp section commandant, the young communist Arm. He received a medal for his work in 1938 and later was director of a gold mine, the head of the administration; Arm made a great career for himself. Nikolai Kazimirovich Barbe had one thing which he took special care of: a camel hair scarf, a long, warm, light-blue scarf, real camel wool. Thieves stole it in the bathhouse when Barbe turned away—they simply took it, and that was that. And the next day Barbe got frostbite on his cheeks, bad frostbite—the blisters never healed to the day he died.

Ioska Ryutin died. He was my work partner; the hard workers didn't want to work with me. But Ioska worked with me. He was much stronger and more agile than me. But he understood why they had brought us here. And he didn't resent me for working badly. In the end a senior overseer—the mining ranks used in 1937

[1]   This translation first published in *50 Writers: An Anthology of 20th Century Russian Short Stories*, selected, with an introduction by Mark Lipovetsky and Valentina Brougher, translated and annotated by Valentina Brougher and Frank Miller (Boston: Academic Studies Press, 2011), 365–77.

were the same as those used in tsarist times—ordered them to give me a "single measure"[2] . . .

And Ioska was paired with somebody else. But our places in the barracks were next to each other, and someone in leather, who smelled of sheep, was moving clumsily and woke me up suddenly. This someone, with his back turned to me in the narrow passageway between the bed boards, was trying to wake up my neighbor: "Ryutin? Get dressed." And Ioska started to hurry and get dressed, and the man who smelled of sheep began searching through his few things. A chess set was found among his few belongings, and the man in leather put it aside.

"That's mine," Ryutin said quickly. "My property. I paid money for it."

"So what?" the sheepskin said.

"Leave it."

The sheepskin burst out laughing. And when it got tired of laughing and wiped its face with a leather sleeve, it said, "You won't be needing it any more . . ."

Dmitry Nikolayevich Orlov, the former assistant to Kirov, died.[3] He and I sawed wood on the night shift in the mine and, as possessors of a saw, worked during the day in the bakery. I remember well what a critical look the toolsmith and stock keeper gave us when he was issuing the saw, an ordinary crosscut saw.

"Here's what, old man," the toolsmith said. We were all called old men even back then, and not only twenty years later. "Can you sharpen a saw?"

"Of course," Orlov said hurriedly. "Is there a setting block?"

"You can separate the teeth with an ax," said the stock keeper, who realized that we were people who knew what to do, not like those intellectuals.

---

2   As Shalamov's story "A Single Measure" illustrates, a prisoner whom the authorities feel is not able to do his share of the work in a brigade is assigned a quota he must fulfill by working by himself. If he cannot meet that quota, he is executed.

3   Sergei Kirov (1886–1934): a rising star in the Communist Party when he was assassinated in 1934. His death was used by Stalin as a reason to initiate the Great Terror.

Orlov walked down the path hunched over, his hands in his sleeves.

He held the saw under his arm.

"Listen, Dmitry Nikolayevich," I said, skipping along to catch up with him. "I don't know how. I've never sharpened a saw."

Orlov turned to me, stuck the saw in the snow, and put on his gloves. "I think," he said in an instructive tone, "that every man with a higher education is obliged to know how to set and sharpen a saw."

I agreed with him.

The economist Semyon Alekseyevich Sheinin, my work partner, a good man, died. For a long time he didn't understand what was being done to us, but finally he understood and waited calmly for death. He had more than enough courage. One day I got a package—the fact that the package reached me was a great rarity—and in it was a pair of felt aviator boots and nothing more. How little did our relatives know about the conditions in which we lived! I knew perfectly well that the boots would be stolen, taken away from me that first night. And I sold them without walking out of the commandant's office for one hundred rubles to Andrei Boyko, a foreman. The boots cost seven-hundred, but I sold them for a good price. I could buy a hundred kilograms of bread, and if not a hundred, then some butter and sugar. The last time I had butter and sugar was in prison. And I bought a whole kilo of butter. I remembered how good it was for you. The butter cost forty-one rubles. I bought it during the day (we worked at night) and ran to Sheinin—we lived in different barracks—to celebrate receiving the package. I bought some bread too . . .

Semyon Alekseyevich became emotional and happy.

"But why me? What right do I have?" he mumbled, utterly overcome by emotion. "No, no, I can't . . ."

But I persuaded him and he ran joyfully to get some boiling water.

And that very moment I fell to the ground from a terrible blow to my head.

When I jumped up, the bag with the butter and the bread was gone. The one-meter long log used to hit me was lying next to the cot. And all around everyone was laughing. Sheinin came running with the boiling water. For many years afterward I couldn't recall the theft without getting terribly, overwhelmingly emotional. And Semyon Alekseyevich—died.

Ivan Yakovlevich Fedyakhin died. He and I were on the same train, the same steamboat. We wound up in the same gold mine, in the same work brigade. He was a philosopher, a peasant from Volokolamsk,[4] the organizer of the first collective farm in Russia. Collective farms, as is well known, were organized by the SRs[5] in the twenties, and the Chayanov-Kondratiev group represented their interests "above" . . . Ivan Yakovlevich was also an SR, from a village, one of the million who voted for that party in 1917. And for organizing the first collective farm, he got to do time—five years in prison.

One day at the very beginning, during the first fall in Kolyma,[6] in 1937, he and I were working on unloading a cart—we stood in the infamous mine production line. There were only two carts, the kind that could be detached. While the man handling the horse was taking one to the washing apparatus, two workers would barely manage to fill the other. There wasn't enough time to smoke and, what's more, the overseers didn't allow it. Our horse handler, on the other hand, did smoke—he'd smoke a huge cigar, rolled out of almost half a pack of *makhorka*[7] (there was still *makhorka* back then), and leave it on an edge of the coal seam so that we could have a drag.

Mishka Vavilov, the former deputy chairman of the "Industrial Imports Trust," was the horse handler, and Fedyakhin and I were face workers.

---

[4]   A town, about 80 miles northwest of Moscow.

[5]   A party of Socialist Revolutionaries, one of the oldest socialist parties in Russia. Its representatives were heavily persecuted by Bolsheviks since 1918.

[6]   Remote region in the Russian Far East, where a large number of Gulag camps were located.

[7]   Cheap, inferior tobacco.

Without hurrying to throw the ore into the cart, we talked with one another. I told Fedyakhin about the lesson they gave to the Decembrists in Nerchinsk[8]—according to *The Memoirs of Maria Volkonskaya*—three poods[9] of ore per man.

"And how much does our quota weigh, Vasily Petrovich?" Fedyakhin asked.

I counted: about 800 poods.

"Just look, Vasily Petrovich, how the quotas have increased . . ."

Later, during the hungry winter, I'd get tobacco—I'd beg, save up, and buy some—and trade it for bread. Fedyakhin didn't approve of my "commerce."

"It doesn't become you, Vasily Petrovich, you shouldn't do that . . ."

I saw him for the last time in the winter in the mess hall. I gave him six dinner meal tickets that I had received that day for making copies by hand of some materials in the office. My good penmanship sometimes helped me. The meal tickets were good only for so long—they had dates stamped on them. Fedyakhin got the dinners. He sat at the table and poured the portions of the watery soup into one bowl—the soup was terribly thin and not one drop of grease floated in it . . . The barley kasha he received for all six meal tickets didn't even fill a half-liter bowl . . . Fedyakhin didn't have a spoon, and he licked up the kasha with his tongue. And wept.

Derfel died. He was a French communist who had even been in the stone quarries of Cayenne.[10] Besides being hungry and cold, his morale had plummeted—he didn't want to believe that he, a member of the Comintern,[11] could find himself here, doing Soviet hard

---

8   The Decembrist uprising took place in December 1825. A group of officers commanding about 3,000 men refused to swear allegiance to the new tsar, Nicholas I. For a variety of reasons, the revolt failed and within weeks five leaders were executed, other exiled for decades to Siberia. Nerchinsk is one of places of their hard labor.

9   16 kilos, approximately 30 pounds.

10   Capital of French Guiana, where the notorious French penal colony, Devil's Island, was located.

11   Comintern: Communist International, also known as the Third International;

labor. His horror would have lessened had he noticed that he wasn't the only one. Everyone he came with, lived with, and was dying with, was like that. He was a small, weak man and beatings were now becoming popular . . . One time the work brigade boss hit him, hit him simply with his fist, to maintain order, so to say, but Derfel fell and didn't get up. He was one of the first to die, one of the more fortunate. In Moscow he worked for TASS[12] as an editor. He had a good command of Russian. "In Cayenne it was bad too," he said to me once. "But here it's really bad."

Fritz David died. He was a Dutch communist, a Comintern worker, who was accused of espionage. He had beautiful wavy hair, deep blue eyes, and a child-like shape to his mouth. He knew very little Russian. I met him in a barracks packed with so many people that you could sleep standing up. We stood side by side; Fritz smiled at me and closed his eyes.

The space under the bed boards was packed with people to overflowing; you had to wait to sit down, to squat down, and then lean against some bed boards, a post, or someone's body—and fall asleep. I waited with my eyes closed. Suddenly something next to me fell down. My neighbor Fritz David had fallen. He got up embarrassed.

"I fell asleep," he said, startled.

Fritz David was the first man in our transport of prisoners who received a package. His wife sent him the package from Moscow. In the package there was a velvet suit, a nightshirt, and a large photograph of a beautiful woman. It was in this velvet suit that he squatted next to me.

"I want to eat," he said, smiling and turning red. "I really want to eat. Bring me something to eat."

Fritz David went insane and he was taken away somewhere.

---

founded in 1919 to coordinate the efforts of the communist parties around the world in order to bring about an international communist revolution.

[12] TASS: The Telegraph Agency of the Soviet Union (established in 1925), which was responsible for gathering and disseminating all news, domestic and international.

The nightshirt and the photograph were stolen from him the first night. When I was telling people about him later, I always felt perplexed and indignant: why did anyone need someone else's photograph?

"Even you don't know everything," some clever fellow said one day when I was talking to him. "It's easy to guess. This photograph was stolen by the professional criminals and, as these criminals say, for a 'séance.' For masturbation, my naive friend . . ."

Seryozha Klivansky died, my friend from my first year at the university, whom I met in Butyrka Prison[13] ten years later in a cell of prisoners bound for transport. He was expelled from the Komsomol in 1927 for a report on the Chinese revolution in a current politics club. He managed to finish the university, and he worked as an economist with Gosplan[14] until the atmosphere changed there and Seryozha was forced to leave. He won a competition for a position in the Stanislavsky Theater Orchestra and was its second violinist—until his arrest in 1937. He was a cheerful man, a wit, and always full of irony. He showed an interest in life, in its events too.

In the cell for prisoners bound for transport, everybody walked around almost naked, poured water on himself, and slept on the floor. Only a hero could endure sleeping on the bed boards. And Klivansky would joke, "This is torture by steaming. After this, we will be subjected to torture by freezing in the North."

This was an accurate prediction, but it was not the whining of a coward. At the mine Seryozha was cheerful and sociable. He tried to master thieves' vocabulary with enthusiasm and was as happy as a child when he could repeat thieves' expressions with the appropriate intonation.

"Right now, I think I'll kip down for a bit," Seryozha would say, as he crawled onto the upper bed boards.

---

[13]   Butyrka Prison: located in Moscow, built in 1879; during the Great Purge of the 1930s, thousands of prisoners were shot there and hundreds of thousands passed through it to various labor camps.

[14]   The state planning agency in the USSR.

He loved poetry and often recited it from memory in the prison. In the camp he didn't recite poetry.

He would share his last piece of bread, that is to say, he still shared . . . It means that he never lived to see the time when no one had a last piece, when no one had anything to share with anyone.

The work brigade boss Dyukov died. I don't know and didn't ever know his first name. He was one of the "non-political prisoners" and his sentence had nothing to do with Article 58.[15] In the camps on the mainland he was a so-called chairman of a collective; he wasn't exactly disposed toward revolutionary romanticism, but he was ready "to play a role." He arrived in the winter and gave a remarkable speech at the first meeting. The non-political prisoners had meetings because, you see, those who had committed "non-counter-revolutionary" or work-related crimes as well as the recidivist thieves were considered "friends of the people," subject to being reformed and not subject to punitive measures. Unlike the "enemies of the people"—sentenced under Article 58. Later, when the recidivists began to be sentenced under Point Fourteen of Article 58—for sabotage (refusing to work)—the whole fourteenth paragraph was eliminated from Article 58, which removed various punitive measures that could go on for many years. The recidivists were always considered "friends of the people"—up to and including Beria's famous amnesty of 1953. Hundreds of thousands of unfortunate people were sacrificed to theory and Krylenko's[16] "elasticity" and notorious "reeducation."

At that first meeting Dyukov proposed taking a brigade of men sentenced under Article 58 under his leadership; usually the work

[15]   Article 58: part of the Soviet Penal Code put in force in 1922, it authorized the arrest of people suspected of counter-revolutionary activities. It was revised, expanded and "updated" a number of times, and used with increasing frequency against millions of prisoners during the purges of the 1930s. Those sentenced under Article 58-1, were "traitors"; those under 58-14, "saboteurs."

[16]   Nikolai Krylenko (1885–1938): served in a variety of posts in the Soviet legal system; rose to the position of Commissar of Justice and Prosecutor General of the RSFSR. He believed that political considerations more than anything else should guide the application of punishment. Perished during the Great Purge himself.

brigade boss of the "political prisoners" was a political himself. Dyukov wasn't a bad fellow. He knew that peasants work very well in camps, best of all prisoners, and he remembered that there were a lot of Article 58 men among the peasants. Ezhov's and Beria's[17] special wisdom should be seen in this, for they realized that the labor value of the intelligentsia was not high and consequently the camps might not be able to fulfill the production goals, unlike the political goals. But Dyukov didn't go into such lofty considerations; it's doubtful anything came into his head except the men's capacity for work. He selected a brigade for himself—exclusively of peasants—and began working. This was in the spring of 1938. Dyukov's peasants had already stayed there the whole hungry winter of 1937–38. He didn't go to the bathhouse with his brigade, otherwise he would've realized long before what the problem was.

They didn't work badly and just needed to be given more food than they were getting. But the administration refused Dyukov's request in the harshest way. The hungry brigade kept reaching its quota by working with tremendous effort. Then Dyukov began to be shortchanged: by the men who measured the output, the bookkeepers, the overseers, and the work bosses. He began to complain, to protest more and more sharply, the brigade's production output kept falling and falling, and the food kept getting worse. Dyukov tried turning to the higher-ups, but the higher-ups advised the relevant workers to add Dyukov's brigade, including the work brigade boss himself, to the infamous lists. This was done and all were executed at the infamous Serpentine Mine.[18]

Pavel Mikhailovich Khvostov died. The most frightening thing in hungry people is their behavior. Everything's like in healthy people, and yet they're half-insane. The hungry always fiercely defend the cause of justice—if they're not terribly hungry, not

[17]   Lavrenty Beria (1899–1953): head of the NKVD from 1940 to 1953. One of the most cruel and amoral men of the Soviet regime. Executed in 1953. Nikolai Ezhov (1895–1940): People's Commissar and "Stalin's loyal executioner," NKVD (secret police) chief. Succeeded by Beria after his execution.

[18]   A notorious place of prisoners' executions at Kolyma. Shalamov compares it with Auschwitz.

terribly emaciated. They're eternal squabblers, desperate fighters. Usually only one out of a thousand people who have quarreled with someone, their voices strained to the limit, will go on to fight. Hungry people always fight. Arguments flare up for the wildest, the most unexpected of reasons: "What are you doing with my mining pick . . . why did you take my place?" The one who is shorter, not as tall, tries to trip his opponent and bring him down. The one who is taller—to fall upon his enemy and bring him down with his weight, and then scratch, hit, and bite him . . . All of this is done weakly— it's not painful and not fatal—and all too often, just to arouse the interest of those around. Fights are not broken up.

Khvostov was just like that. He fought with someone every day—in the barracks and in the deep drainage trench that our brigade was digging. He was my *winter* friend—I didn't see his hair. He had a hat with ear flaps, with torn white fur. And his eyes were dark—hungry, shining eyes. I sometimes recited poetry, and he looked at me like I was half-crazy.

Suddenly he began to hit the rock in the trench desperately with his pick. The pick was heavy; Khvostov kept making swinging blows and hitting the rock almost non-stop. I marveled at such strength. We'd been together for a long time, had been hungry for a long time. Then the pick fell and made a ringing sound. I glanced back. Khvostov was standing with his legs spread apart and swaying. His knees were buckling. He swayed and fell face down. He stretched his hands out in front of him in the same mittens that he mended every evening. His arms became exposed—there were tattoos on both forearms. Pavel Mikhailovich had been a sea captain.

Roman Romanovich Romanov died before my very eyes. At one time he had been something like our company commander. He distributed packages and kept an eye on cleanliness in the camp compound, in a word, he was in such a privileged position as not one of us could dream of—we of Article 58 and *lityorki*, as the professional criminals called us, or *liternki*, as the higher administrators of the camp said.[19] The best we could dream of was laundry work in the

---

[19]   *Lityorki*: the diminutive and pejorative form of *liternki*. Liternki, or literally "the

bathhouse or mending clothes on the night shift. Except for rocks, everything was forbidden to us by Moscow's "special instructions." Such a document was included in each of our files. And so, Roman Romanovich occupied such a position, beyond our reach. And he even quickly grasped all its secrets: how to open a box with a parcel in it so that the sugar would spill onto the floor; how to break a jar with preserves; and how to throw dried bread crusts and dried fruit under the trestle-bed. Roman Romanovich learned all this very quickly and didn't maintain any contact with us. He was rigidly official and conducted himself as a polite representative of those higher authorities with whom we couldn't have personal contact. He never gave us any advice. He only explained: one letter may be sent per month, packages are given out from 8 to 10 in the evening in the camp commandant's office, and so on. We didn't envy Roman Romanovich, we were just amazed by him. Evidently, some personal chance acquaintance of Roman's played a role here. However, he wasn't the company commander for long, just two months in all. Either there was the next scheduled staff review (such reviews took place from time to time and without fail by New Year's), or someone "ratted" on him, to use the colorful camp expression. And Roman Romanovich disappeared. He had served in the military and was a colonel, it seems.

And so four years later I found myself on a "temporary vitamin assignment"—gathering the needles from trailing shrubs, the only year-round green plants there. These needles were brought from many hundreds of miles to a vitamin plant. There they were cooked and the needles turned into a gooey, brown mixture with an unbearable smell and taste. It was poured into barrels and sent to various camps. In terms of the local medicine at that time, it was considered the main remedy—available to all and obligatory—against scurvy. Scurvy was rife and rampant and,

letter ones," were prisoners who had been sentenced according to one of the categories listed in Article 58. The categories were reduced to a letter or two; for example, anti-Soviet elements would be AS, S would be a member of a sect, etc. Shalamov himself had a letter T, which meant "Trotskyite" and implied the use for hard labor only.

what's more, appeared in combination with pellagra and other vitamin deficiency diseases. But everybody who had to swallow even a drop of the horrible potion agreed it was better to die than to be treated with such a hellish brew. But there were orders, and orders are orders, and you wouldn't get any food in camp until a dose of this medicine was swallowed. The man on duty stood right there with a special tiny scoop. You couldn't enter the mess hall and bypass the dispenser of the needle brew, and so the very thing that a prisoner values—dinner, food—was irreparably spoiled by this preliminary, obligatory exercise. And so it continued for more than ten years . . . Doctors who were a bit more competent were bewildered—how could vitamin C, which is unusually sensitive to all temperature changes, be preserved in such a sticky "ointment"? The treatment made no sense at all, but the extract continued to be handed out. Right there, next to all the settlements, were a lot of wild rose bushes. But no one even dared to gather the rose hips— nothing was said about them in the orders. And only much later after the war, in 1952 I think, a letter was received—again, however, from the local medicine folk—in which giving out the extract of needles from trailing shrubbery was categorically forbidden since it had a destructive effect on the kidneys. The vitamin plant was closed. But at the time I met Roman, the needles from the trailing shrubs were being collected with a vengeance. They were collected by the "goners"—the mine slag and refuse of gold mine work— semi-invalids, hungry and chronically sick. The gold mines made invalids out of healthy people in just three weeks: hunger, lack of sleep, heavy work for many hours on end, and beatings . . . New people would join the brigade and Molokh[20] would chew them up . . . By the end of the season there was no one in Ivanov's work brigade except the work brigade boss Ivanov. The rest went to the hospital, to "boot hill," and on "vitamin" assignments, where they were fed once a day and where it was impossible to receive more than 600 grams of bread daily. That fall Roman and I did not work

---

[20]   Molokh: in the Old Testament represented as an old man with ram's horns, holding a scythe, to whom small children were sacrificed.

collecting needles. We worked in "construction." We were building a dwelling for ourselves for the winter; in the summer we lived in torn tents.

An area was measured off in footsteps, stakes were driven in, and then we put in a widely-spaced fence consisting of two rows. The space between them was filled with pieces of frozen moss and peat. Inside was a sleeping platform made of poles, just one level. In the middle stood an iron stove. We were given a ration of wood, figured out empirically, for every night. However, we had neither a saw nor an ax—those sharp objects were kept by the guards who lived in a separate, heated tent covered with plywood. Saws and axes were handed out only in the morning when we were marched off to work. The problem was that in a neighboring brigade on temporary "vitamin" duty some criminals had attacked the work brigade boss. Professional criminals are unusually disposed to theatrics, and introduce it into their lives in a way that even Evreinov[21] would envy. A decision was made to kill the work brigade boss, and the proposal of one of the professional criminals—to saw off the boss's head—was met with excitement. His head was sawed off with an ordinary crosscut saw. That's why there was an order forbidding axes and saws to be left with prisoners for the night. Why only for the night? But no one ever tried to find logic in the orders.

How do you cut wood so that the logs fit in the stove? The thinner ones were broken with our feet, and all the thick ones were put in the opening of the burning stove, the thinner end first, and gradually burned away. Someone would push them deeper into the stove with his foot—there was always someone to look after this. The light from the open stove door was the only light in our dwelling. Until snowfall, the wind went through our small house, but then we piled up snow around the walls and poured water on

---

[21]   Nikolai Evreinov (1879–1953): theater director, dramatist, and author. He believed in the theatricalization of life and developed his theories in a number of books, including the three-volume *The Theater for Oneself* (1915–1917). In his early and most famous essay, "Apology for Theatricality" (1908), he wrote that "the stage must not borrow so much from life as life must borrow from the stage."

it—and our winter hut was ready. A piece of tarpaulin was hung over the door opening.

It's here, in this very shed, that I met Roman Romanovich again. He didn't recognize me. He was dressed like a "flame," as the hardened criminals say and, as always, appropriately—clumps of cotton stuck out of his padded jacket, pants, and hat. Quite a few times, it's true, Roman Romanovich had to run "behind a corner" to light the cigarette of some criminal . . . His eyes had a hungry shine, and his cheeks were red like before, only they didn't bring to mind balloons but were stretched rather tightly over his cheekbones. Roman Romanovich was lying in a corner and loudly breathing in and out. His chin rose and fell.

"He's dying," Denisov, his neighbor, said. "He has good footcloths . . ." And after nimbly pulling off the felt boots from the dying man's feet, he unwrapped his footcloths of green blanket material that was still holding together . . . "That's the way," he said, looking at me threateningly. But I didn't care.

Roman's corpse was carried out when we were lined up before being marched off to work. He didn't have a hat either. The flaps of his open jacket dragged along the ground.

Did Volodya Dobrovoltsev, the *pointist* die? *Pointist*—is that a job or a nationality? This was a job which evoked jealousy in the barracks of Article 58 prisoners. Separate barracks for the political prisoners in the general camp, where there were also barracks behind barbed wire for the "non-political prisoners" and the recidivist criminals, were a mockery of the legal system, of course. This didn't protect anyone from attacks and bloody settling of scores by the professional criminals.

A *point*—that's an iron pipe with hot steam. This hot steam warms the rock layer, the frozen pebble bed; from time to time a worker scoops out the warmed rock with a metal spoon, the size of a human hand, which has a three-meter handle.

This work is considered skilled labor, since the *pointist* must open and close the valves that control the hot steam moving through the pipes from a boiler in a shed—a primitive steam contraption. To be a boiler man is even better than to be a *pointist*. Not every Article 58 engineer mechanic could dream of work like that. And not because this was skilled labor. It was pure chance that out of thousands of people Volodya was sent to do this work. But this changed him. He didn't have to think how to get warm—the eternal thing on your mind . . . The freezing cold didn't go through his whole being, didn't stop his mind from working. The hot pipe was his salvation. That's why everybody envied Dobrovoltsev.

There was talk that it was no accident that he was a *pointiest*—it was reliable proof that he was an informer, a spy . . . Of course, the professional criminals always said that if you worked as a medical orderly in camp, it meant you drank working men's blood, and people knew the price of judgments like that; envy is a poor advisor. Volodya somehow grew immeasurably in our eyes, as if a remarkable violinist had been found among us. The fact that Dobrovoltsev would leave alone (he had to because of the conditions of his work) and, as he was walking out of camp past the guard shack, would open the guard window and shout out his number "twenty five" in such a cheerful, loud voice—that was something we had gotten unused to a long time ago.

Sometimes he worked near our coal seam. And since we knew him, we ran and took turns warming ourselves by his pipe. The pipe was about one and half inches in diameter; you could put your hand around it, hold it tightly in your fist, and feel the warmth passing from your hands to your body, and then you couldn't bear to break away and return to the coal seam, into the freezing air . . .

Volodya didn't chase us away like other *pointists*. He never said a word to us, although I know the *pointists* were forbidden to allow our kind to warm themselves by the pipes. He'd stand, surrounded by clouds of thick white steam. His clothing would be stiff from the cold. Every fiber on his jacket glistened like a crystal needle. He never talked with us—this work was evidently worth too much.

On Christmas Eve of that year we were sitting by the stove. Its iron sides were redder than usual on account of the holiday. A human being senses the difference in temperature instantly. Sitting by the stove, we were getting sleepy and longed for some lyric poetry.

"It would be nice to return home, brothers. There are miracles, you know . . . ," said Glebov the horse handler and former professor of philosophy, famous in our barracks because a month before he had forgotten his wife's name. "Only mind you, the truth."

"Home?"

"Yes."

"I'll tell the truth," I answered. "It would be better to return to prison. I'm not joking. I wouldn't want to return to my family now. They would never understand me, they wouldn't be able to understand me. What seems important to them I know is a mere nothing. What's important to me—the little that I have left—isn't given for them either to understand or feel. I'd bring them a new fear, one more fear added to the thousands of fears that their lives are more than full of. What I've seen—a human being shouldn't have to see or even know about. A prison—that's another matter. A prison—that's freedom. It's the only place I know where people weren't afraid and said everything that was on their mind. Where they rested spiritually. Where they rested physically, because they didn't work. There every hour of existence had meaning."

"Oh, come on! You're talking nonsense," said the former professor of philosophy. "It's because they didn't beat you during the investigation. But anyone who passed through method number three[22] has a different opinion . . ."

"Well, and you, Pyotr Ivanych, what will you tell us?"

Pyotr Ivanovich Timofeyev, the former director of the Ural Trust, smiled and winked at Glebov.

"I'd return home to my wife, to Agniya Mikhailovna. I'd buy rye bread—a whole loaf! Cook some millet kasha—a bucketful! Soup with little dumplings—also a bucketful! And I'd eat it all. For the first time in my life I would have my fill, eating this good stuff, and what would be left, I'd force Agniya Mikhailovna to eat."

"And you?" Glebov turned to Zvonkov, the coal miner in our brigade, and in his first life a peasant—from either the Yaroslavl or Kostroma area.

"Home," Zvonkov answered seriously, without smiling. "I think I'd go home now and not take a step away from my wife. Wherever

---

[22]   A code number for the use of tortures during investigation in 1937–39.

she goes, I go too—wherever she goes, I go too. Only they have broken me of the habit of working—I've lost my love for the land. Well, I'll find something somewhere . . ."

"And you?" Glebov's hand touched the knee of our barracks orderly.

"First thing I would go to the district committee of the party. There, I remember, they had cigarette butts on the floor—an endless amount . . ."

"Don't joke . . ."

"But I'm not joking."

Suddenly I saw that only one man was left who hadn't answered. And this man was Volodya Dobrovoltsev. He raised his head without waiting for the question. The light from the glowing coals in the open door of the stove fell on his eyes—his eyes were lively and sparkled.

"And I," and his voice was calm and deliberate, "would want to be a trunk. A human trunk, you understand, without hands or feet.

Then I would find the strength in myself to spit in their ugly mugs for everything that they're doing to us."

1960

Translated and annotated
by Valentina Brougher and Frank Miller

Vasily Grossman
(1905, Berdichev — 1964, Moscow)

Born into an educated and wealthy Jewish family. From 1912 to 1914 lived with his mother in Switzerland. Later lived in Kiev where he began his higher education in 1921. In 1923 was transferred to the Department of Chemistry in the School of Physics and Mathematics at Moscow State University, from which he graduated in 1929. Worked as a chemical engineer and taught chemistry in Ukraine. From 1933 lived in Moscow and continued working as a chemist. Began writing fiction in the late 1920s. In 1934 *The Literary Gazette* (*Literaturnaia gazeta*) published his short story "In the Town of Berdichev" (adapted for film in 1967 as *Commissar* by Aleksandr Askol'dov). The story was praised by Maxim Gorky and Isaac Babel. In the 1930s Grossman published several collections of short stories and two novels. When WWII began, he was mobilized as a frontline correspondent for the army newspaper *The Red Star*. His frontline articles and short stories earned him broad popularity. Eye-witnessed the Battle of Stalingrad and was one of the first to write about the Holocaust. His mother perished along with other Jews during the German invasion of Berdichev in 1941. His article "The Hell of Treblinka" (1944), one of the first published articles about a Nazi death camp, was used in the Nuremberg Trials. After the war, Grossman, with Ilya Ehrenburg, compiled *The Black Book* (1947), an account of the Holocaust on the territory of the USSR. Published in the United States and Israel, *The Black Book* was banned in the Soviet Union, as it contradicted the post-war nationalism and anti-Semitism promoted by Stalin's regime. In 1952 published the novel *For the Right Cause* (initially titled *Stalingrad*), which became the target of violent ideological critique. During the Thaw, Grossman completed the sequel to this novel, titled *Life and Fate*. This epic novel, modeled after *War and Peace*, unfolds as a large-scale comparison of the Soviet and Nazi regimes as two similar forms of the "super-violence of totalitarian systems." Its challenge to the Soviet ideological regime was so obvious that the editorial board of the journal to which Grossman submitted his manuscript reported it to the KGB. As a result, all copies of *Life and Fate* that were found in Grossman's home were confiscated. The head of the ideological department of the Central Committee explained to the desperate writer that his manuscript could not be returned and his book would be published in the Soviet Union only after 200 or 300 years had passed. One copy of *Life and Fate* was hidden outside of Grossman's home: in 1980 it was published in Switzerland, and in 1988, during *perestroika*, in the USSR. Along with this novel the KGB confiscated a manuscript of Grossman's novella *Forever Flowing* (begun in 1955), which developed on the themes of *Life and Fate*. In 1963, Grossman completed a new version of this novella, which was published for the first time in 1970 (abroad) and in 1989 in the USSR. Shocked by the persecution of his novels and deprived of the ability to publish his works, Grossman died of cancer in 1964.

From *Forever Flowing*[1]

The province authorities sent the plan down to the district authorities in the form of a total number of "kulaks." And the districts then assigned proportionate shares of the total number to the individual village soviets, and it was in the village soviets that the lists of specific names were drawn up. And it was on the basis of these lists that people were rounded up. And who made up the lists? A troika—three people. Dim-witted, unenlightened people determined on their own who was to live and who was to die. Well, that makes it all clear. Anything could happen on this level. There were bribes. Accounts were settled because of jealousy over some woman or because of ancient feuds and quarrels. And what kept on happening was that the poorest peasants kept getting listed as kulaks while those who were more prosperous managed to buy themselves off.

Now, however, I can see that the heart of the catastrophe did not lie in the fact that the lists happened to be drawn up by cheats and thieves. There were in any case more honest, sincere people among the Party activists than there were thieves. But the evil done by the honest people was no less than that done by the dishonest

[1] Published in: Vassily Grossman, *Forever Flowing*, trans. Thomas P. Whitney (London and New York: Harper & Row, 1970), 141–160. Copyright © 1970 by Possev-Verlag. English translation copyright © 1972 by Thomas P. Whitney. Reprinted by permission of Harper Collins Publishers.

ones. These lists were evil in themselves; they were unjust. It was all the same who got included in them. Ivan was innocent, and so was Peter. Who had established the plan's master figure for the whole of Russia? Who had ordered this plan for the entire peasantry? Who had signed it?

The fathers were already imprisoned, and then, at the beginning of 1930, they began to round up the families too. This was more than the GPU could accomplish by itself. All Party activists were mobilized for the job. They were all people who knew one another well and knew their victims, but in carrying out this task they became dazed, stupefied. They would threaten people with guns, as if they were under a spell, calling small children "kulak bastards," screaming "Bloodsuckers!" And those "bloodsuckers" were so terrified they had hardly any blood of their own left in their veins. They were as white as clean paper. The eyes of the Party activists were glassy, like the eyes of cats. They were in the majority after all, and they were dealing with people who were acquaintances and friends. True, they were under a spell—they had sold themselves on the idea that the so-called "kulaks" were pariahs, untouchables, vermin. They would not sit down at a "parasite's" table; the "kulak" child was loathsome; the young "kulak" girl was lower than a louse. They looked on the so-called "kulaks" as cattle, swine, loathsome, repulsive: they had no souls; they stank; they all had venereal diseases; they were enemies of the people and exploited the labor of others. And, on the other hand, the poor peasants, the members of the Young Communist League, and the militia—they were all Chapayevs, heroes of the Civil War. Yet these activists were in reality ordinary people like all the rest; many of them were just plain whiners and cowards; and there were plenty of ordinary scoundrels as well.

These slogans began to have their impact on me too. I was just a young girl. And they kept repeating them at meetings and in special instructions and on the radio; they kept showing them at the movies; writers kept writing them; Stalin himself, too: the kulaks are parasites; they are burning grain; they are killing children. And it was openly proclaimed "that the rage and, wrath of the masses must be inflamed against them, they must be destroyed as a class, because they are accursed." And I, too, began to fall under the spell of all this, and it began to seem as if everything evil had sprung from the kulaks and that if they were destroyed a happy time would instantly ensue for the peasantry.

And there was no pity for them. They were not to be regarded as people; they were not human beings; one had a hard time making out what they were—vermin, evidently. I became a member of the Party activist committee too. The activist committee included all kinds—those who believed the propaganda and who hated the parasites and were on the side of the poorest peasantry, and others who used the situation for their own advantage. But most of them were merely anxious to carry out orders from above. They would have killed their own fathers and mothers simply in order to carry out instructions. And the worst were not those who really believed the destruction of the kulaks would bring about a happy life. For that matter, the wild beasts were not the most poisonous among them either. The most poisonous and vicious were those who managed to square their own accounts. They shouted about political awareness and settled their grudges and stole. And they stole out of crass selfishness: some clothes, a pair of boots. It was so easy to do a man in: you wrote a denunciation; you did not even have to sign it. All you had to say was that he had paid people to work for him as hired hands, or that he had owned three cows. I was aroused and unhappy, but I did not suffer deeply. It was as if the cattle on a farm were being slaughtered in violation of the rules. I was unhappy, of course, very much so! But I did not lose sleep over it.

Do you remember how you answered me? I will not forget your words. One can tell they were daytime words. I asked you how the Germans could kill Jewish children in gas chambers, how they could go on living after that. Could it be that there would be no retribution, either from God or from other people? And you said: only one form of retribution is visited upon an executioner—the fact that he looks upon his victim as something other than a human being and thereby ceases to be a human being himself, and thereby executes himself as a human being. He is his own executioner. While the man who has been done in, has been executed, remains a human being for all eternity, no matter how he has been murdered. Do you remember that?

So now I understand why I came here to be a cook. Why I did not want to be a collective farm chairman. Yes, I have spoken of this before.

And nowadays I look back on the liquidation of the kulaks in a quite different light—I am no longer under a spell, and I can see the human beings there. But why had I been so benumbed? After all, I could see then how people were being tortured and how badly they were being treated! But what I said to myself at the time was "They are not human beings, they are kulaks." And so I remember, I remember and I think: Who thought up this word "kulak" anyway? Was it really Lenin? What torture was meted out to them! In order to massacre them, it was necessary to proclaim that kulaks are not human beings. Just as the Germans proclaimed that Jews are not human beings. Thus did Lenin and Stalin: kulaks are not human beings. But that is a lie. They are people! They are human beings! That's what I have finally come to understand. They are all human beings!

And so, at the beginning of 1930, they began to liquidate the kulak families. The height of the fever was in February and March. They expelled them from their home districts so that when it was time for sowing there would be no kulaks left, so that a new life could begin. That is what we all said it would be: "the first collective farm spring."

It is clear that the committees of Party activists were in charge of the expulsions. There were no instructions as to how the expulsions should be carried out. One collective farm chairman might assemble so many carts that there would not be enough household possessions to fill them up. They called them "kulaks," but they went off in half-empty carts.

From our village, on the other hand, the "kulaks" were driven out on foot. They took what they could carry on their backs: bedding, clothing. The mud was so deep it pulled the boots off their feet. It was terrible to watch them. They marched along in a column and looked back at their huts, and their bodies still held the warmth from their own stoves. What pain they must have suffered! After all, they had been born in those houses; they had given their daughters in marriage in those cabins. They had heated up their stoves, and the cabbage soup they had cooked was left there behind them. The milk had not been drunk, and smoke was still rising from their chimneys. The women were sobbing—but were afraid to scream. The Party activists didn't give a damn about them. We drove them off like geese. And behind came the cart, and on it were Pelageya the blind, and old Dmitri Ivanovich, who had not left his hut for ten whole years, and Marusya the Idiot, a paralytic, a kulak's daughter who had been kicked by a horse in childhood and had never been normal since.

In the district center there was no space left in the prisons. Yes, and when you get down to that, what kind of prison was there in the district center anyway? A hole in the wall. And there were many more coming than just this one column—a column from each village. The movie theater, the club, the schools were all inundated with prisoners. But they did not keep them there long. They drove them to the station, where trains of empty freight cars were waiting on the sidings. They were driven there under guard—by the militia and the GPU-like murderers: grandfathers and grandmothers, women and children, but no fathers, for the fathers had already been taken away in the winter. And people whispered: "They are driving off the kulaks." Just as if they were wolves. And people even shouted: "Curses on you!" But the prisoners had already stopped weeping. They had become like stone.

I myself did not see how they took them away in the trains. But I heard from others. Some of our people, for instance, went to visit them way beyond the Urals, so as to save their own lives during the famine that came later. I myself got a letter from a girlfriend. And some of the so-called "kulaks" escaped from their special resettlement areas. I spoke with two of them.

They were transported in sealed freight cars, and their belongings were transported separately. They took with them only the food they had in their hands. And at a particular transit station, my girlfriend wrote, they put the fathers of the families on the train. And that day there was a great gladness and weeping in those cars. They were en route more than a month. The railways were full of trainloads of similar peasants. Peasants were being transported from all over Russia. They were all tightly packed. There were no berths in the cattle cars. Those ill died en route. But they did get fed. At the main stations along the way they were given a pail of gruel and about seven ounces of bread per person.

The guard consisted of military units. The guards were not vicious. They merely treated them like cattle, and that was that. That is what my friend wrote.

And I was told by those who escaped what it was like when they got there. The provincial authorities scattered them in the Siberian taiga. Wherever a small village was nearby, the ailing and handicapped were put into huts as crowded as the prisoner-transport trains. And where there was no village nearby, they were simply set down right there on the snow. The weakest died. And those able to work began to cut down timber and didn't bother to take out the stumps. They hauled out the tree trunks and built shacks, lean-tos, makeshift sheds and dwellings. They worked almost without sleeping so that their families would not freeze to death. Only afterward did they begin to build real log cabins with two rooms, one room to a family. They "puttied" them together with moss to make them warm in the winter.

Those able to work bought timber tracts from the NKVD and got equipment from the lumber enterprises and rations for their dependents. Their settlements were called "labor settlements," and they had a commandant and foremen over them. They were paid, they told me, the same as local workers, but their entire pay was kept in special accounts. Our men are strong, and soon they began to earn more than the local people. But they did not have the right to leave their settlements or their logging area. Later on, during the war, I heard they were permitted to move about freely within their own administrative districts. And after the war, heroes of labor were given permission to move about freely even outside the immediate district. Some were even allowed to have passports, which meant they were able to travel.

My girlfriend wrote me that they began to found special colonies consisting of kulaks who couldn't do ordinary work — to make them self-supporting. They were given seed on loan and got a ration from the NKVD till their first harvest. And they had a commandant and guards, just as in the labor settlements. Later on they were organized into artels, and, in addition to the commandant, they had their own elected elders.

Meanwhile back at home our new life began without the so-called "kulaks." They started to force people to join the collective farms. Meetings were under way from morning on. There were shouts and curses. Some of them shouted: "We will not join!" Others shouted: "All right, we will join, but we are not going to give up our cows." Stalin's famous essay on "dizziness from success" appeared. There was a mess all over again: they roared that Stalin had promised he would not allow them to be herded forcibly into collective farms. They wrote their declarations on the margins of newspapers: "I am leaving the collective farm to become an independent farmer." And again the officials began to drive them into the collective farms. And all the things that the so-called "kulaks" had left behind were for the most part simply stolen.

And we thought, fools that we were, that there could be no fate worse than that of the kulaks. How wrong we were! The ax fell upon the peasants right where they stood, on large and small alike. The execution by famine had arrived. By this time I no longer washed floors but was a bookkeeper instead. And, as a Party activist, I was sent to the Ukraine in order to strengthen a collective farm. In the Ukraine, we were told, they had an instinct for private property that was stronger than in the Russian Republic. And truly, truly, the whole business was much worse in the Ukraine than it was with us. I was not sent very far—we were, after all, on the very edge of the Ukraine, not more than three hours' journey from the village to which I was sent. The place was beautiful. And so I arrived there, and the people there were like everyone else. And I became the bookkeeper in the administrative office.

It seems to me that I saw and learned about everything that went on. It was not for nothing that the old man had called me a "minister"—I tell this only to you, exactly as I myself remember it, because I never brag about myself to an outsider. I kept all the accounts in my head, memorized them. And when commands came, and our troika went into session, and the leaders got drunk on vodka, I heard everything that was said.

How was it? After the liquidation of the kulaks the amount of land under cultivation dropped very sharply and so did the crop yield. But meanwhile people continued to report that without the kulaks our whole life was flourishing. The village soviet lied to the district, and the district lied to the province, and the province lied to Moscow. Everything was apparently in order, so Moscow assigned grain production and delivery quotas to the provinces, and the provinces then assigned them to the districts. And our village was given a quota that it couldn't have fulfilled in ten years! In the village soviet even those who weren't drinkers took to drink out of terror. It was clear that Moscow was basing its hopes on the Ukraine. And the upshot of it was that most of the subsequent anger was directed against the Ukraine. What they said was simple: you have failed to fulfill the plan, and that means that you yourself are an unliquidated kulak.

Of course, the grain deliveries could not be fulfilled. Smaller areas had been sown, and the crop yield on those smaller areas had shrunk. So where could it come from, that promised ocean of grain from the collective farms? The conclusion reached up top was that the grain had all been concealed, hidden away. By kulaks who had not yet been liquidated, by loafers! The "kulaks" had been removed, but the "kulak" spirit remained. Private property was master over the mind of the Ukrainian peasant. Who was it who then signed the act which imposed mass murder? I often wonder whether it was really Stalin. I think there has never been such a decree in all the long history of Russia. Not the czars certainly, not the Tatars, nor even the German occupation forces had ever promulgated such a terrible decree. For the decree required that the peasants of the Ukraine, the Don, and the Kuban be put to death by starvation, put to death along with their tiny children. The instructions were to take away the entire seed fund. Grain was searched for as if it were not grain but bombs and machine guns. The whole earth was stabbed with bayonets and ramrods. Cellars were dug up, floors were broken through, and vegetable gardens were turned over. From some they confiscated even the grain in their houses—in pots or troughs. They even took baked bread away from one woman, loaded it onto the cart, and hauled it off to the district. Day and night the carts creaked along, laden with the confiscated grain, and dust hung over the earth. And there were no grain elevators to accommodate it, and they simply dumped it out on the earth and set guards around it. By winter the grain had been soaked by the rains and began to ferment—the Soviet government didn't even have enough canvas to cover it up!

And while they kept on hauling grain from the villages, the dust rose everywhere and one had the illusion that smoke was hovering in the air, over everything. One peasant went out of his mind and kept shouting and screaming: "Heaven is burning, the earth is burning!" He just kept on screaming and screaming. No, it was not heaven that was burning, but life itself.

So then I understood: the most important thing for the Soviet government was the plan! Fulfill the plan! Pay up your assessment, make your assigned deliveries! The state comes first, and people are a big zero.

Fathers and mothers wanted to save their children and hid a tiny bit of grain, and they were told: "You hate the country of socialism. You are trying to make the plan fail, you parasites, you pro-kulaks, you rats." They tried to answer, but it was to no avail: "We aren't trying to sabotage the plan. All we want is to feed our children and to save ourselves. After all, everyone has to eat."

I can tell you the story, but stories are words—and what this was about was life, torture, death from starvation. Incidentally, when the grain was taken away, the Party activists were told the peasants would be fed from the state grain fund. But it was not true. Not one single kernel of grain was given to the starving. Who confiscated the grain? For the most part, local people: the Workers and Peasants Inspection officials, the district Party committee, the Komsomol, local people, and, of course, the militia, the NKVD; and in certain localities army units were used as well. I saw only one man from Moscow who had been mobilized by the Party and sent out to assist collectivization, but he didn't try very hard; instead, he kept trying to get away and go home. And again, as in the campaign to liquidate the kulaks, people became dazed, stunned, beastlike.

Grisha Sayenko, a militiaman, was married to a local village girl, and he came to the village to celebrate a holiday. He was gay, and he danced the tango and waltz and sang Ukrainian village songs. And one of the old, gray-haired men went up to him and said: "Grisha, you are making us all paupers and that's worse than murder. Why is the Workers and Peasants Government going against the peasantry, doing things the czar wouldn't do?" Grisha pushed him in the face and then went to the well to wash his hands, and he said to those who were there: "How will I be able to pick up a spoon with the hand that touched that parasite's face?"

And the dust kept rising day and night while they were hauling away the grain. The moon hung halfway up the sky like a stone, and beneath that moon everything seemed fierce and wild, and it was as hot at night as though one lay under sheepskins and the field was trampled over in all directions like an execution ground.

And people became confused, and the cattle, too, became wild and kept lowing and mooing plaintively in their fright, and the dogs howled loudly at night. And the earth crackled.

And autumn came without any rain, and the winter was a snowy winter. And there was no grain to eat. No bread.

It could not be bought in the district center because rationing was in effect. And it could not be bought at the railway stations either, in booths or kiosks. A military guard refused to let anyone near. Nor was bread being sold in nonrationed, "commercial" stores.

With the autumn people began to use up their potatoes, and, since there was no bread, they disappeared very quickly. By Christmas they began to slaughter their cattle. The cattle were by then mostly skin and bones anyway, and the meat was stringy and tough. Then, of course, they killed the chickens. All the meat went swiftly. Not a drop of milk was to be had. Not an egg was left in the village either. But the worst thing was that there was no grain, no bread. They had taken every last kernel of grain from the village. There was no seed to be sown for spring wheat or other spring grains. The entire seed fund had been confiscated. The only hope was in the winter grains, but the winter grains were still under the snow. The spring was far away. And the villagers were already starving. They had eaten their meat, and whatever millet they had left; they were eating the last of their potatoes, and in the case of the larger families the potatoes were already gone.

Everyone was in terror. Mothers looked at their children and began to scream in fear. They screamed as if a snake had crept into their house. And this snake was famine, starvation, death. What was to be done? The peasants had one thing only on their minds— something to eat. They would suck, move their jaws, and the saliva would flow and they would keep swallowing it down, but it wasn't food. At night, one would wake up, and all around was silence. Not a conversation anywhere. Not an accordion either. Like the grave. Only famine was on the move. Only famine did not sleep. The children would cry from morning on, asking for bread. And what could their mothers give them—snow? And there was no help. The Party officials had one answer to all entreaties: "You should have worked harder; you shouldn't have loafed." And then they would also say: "Look about your village; you've got enough buried there to last you three years."

Yet in the winter there was still no real honest-to-God starvation. Of course, people became weak. Stomachs puffed up somewhat from potato peelings, but there was no real swelling as yet. They began to dig up acorns from beneath the snow and dried them out, and the miller set his stones wider apart and they ground the acorns up for flour. They baked bread from the acorns—more properly, pancakes. They were very dark, darker even then rye bread. Some people added bran to them or ground-up potato peelings. But the acorns were quickly used up because the oak forest was not a large one and three villages rushed to it all at once. Meanwhile a Party representative came from the city and said at the village soviet: "There you see, look at the parasites! They went digging for acorns in the snow with their bare hands—they'll do anything to get out of working."

At school the upper grades continued to attend classes until nearly spring. But the lower grades stopped during the winter. And in the spring the school shut down. The teacher went off to the city. And the medical assistant left too. He had nothing to eat. Anyway, you can't cure starvation with medicines. And all the various representatives stopped coming from the city too. Why come? There was nothing to be had from the starving. There was no use coming any more. No use providing them with medical help and no use teaching them anything either. Once things reached the point where the state could not squeeze anything more out of the human being, he became useless. Why teach him? Why cure him?

The starving people were left to themselves. The state had abandoned them. In the villages people went from house to house, begging from each other. The poor begged from the poor, the starving begged from the starving. Whoever had fewer children or none might have something left by spring. And those with many children kept begging from them. And occasionally they were given a handful of bran or a couple of potatoes. But the Party members gave nothing. Not out of greed, nor because of viciousness. They were just very afraid. And the state gave not one tiny kernel to the starving. Though it was on the grain of the peasants that the state was founded, that it stood. Could Stalin not know what was happening? Old people recalled what the famine had been like under Czar Nicholas. They had been helped then. They had been lent food. The peasants went to the cities to beg "in the name of Christ." Soup kitchens were opened to feed them, and students collected donations. And here, under the government of workers and peasants, not even one kernel of grain was given them. There were blockades along all the highways, where militia, NKVD men, troops were stationed; the starving people were not to be allowed into the cities. Guards surrounded all the railroad stations. There were guards at even the tiniest of whistle stops. No bread for you, breadwinners! And in the cities the workers were given eight hundred grams—a pound and a half—of bread each day. Good Lord, could that even be imagined—eight hundred grams! And the peasant children in the villages got not one gram. That is exactly how the Nazis put the Jewish children into the Nazi gas chambers: "You are not allowed to live, you are all Jews!" And it was impossible to understand, grasp, comprehend. For these children were Soviet children, and those who were putting them to death were Soviet people. These children were Russians, and those who were putting them to death were Russians. And the government was a government of workers and peasants. Why this massacre?

It was when the snow began to melt that the village was up to its neck in real starvation.

The children kept crying and crying. They did not sleep. And they began to ask for bread at night too. People's faces looked like clay. Their eyes were dull and drunken. They went about as though asleep. They inched forward, feeling their way one foot at a time, and they supported themselves by keeping one hand against the wall. They began to move around less. Starvation made them totter. They moved less and less, and they spent more time lying down. And they kept thinking they heard the creaking of a cart bringing flour, sent to them by Stalin from the district center so as to save the children.

The women turned out to be stronger and more enduring than the men. They had a tighter hold on life. And they had more to suffer from it too. For the children kept asking their mothers for something to eat. Some of the women would talk to their children and try to explain and kiss them: "Don't cry. Be patient. Where can I get anything?" Others became almost insane: "Stop whining, or I'll kill you!" And then they would beat the children with whatever was at hand just to put an end to their crying and begging. And some of them ran away from their homes and went to their neighbors' houses, so as not to hear their children cry.

No dogs and cats were left. They had been slaughtered. And it was hard to catch them too. The animals had become afraid of people and their eyes were wild. People boiled them. All there was were tough veins and muscles. And from their heads they made a meat jelly.

The snow melted and people began to swell up. The edema of starvation had begun. Faces were swollen, legs swollen like pillows; water bloated their stomachs; people kept urinating all the time. Often they couldn't even make it out of the house. And the peasant children! Have you ever seen the newspaper photographs of the children in the German camps? They were just like that: their heads like heavy balls on thin little necks, like storks, and one could see each bone of their arms and legs protruding from beneath the skin, how bones joined, and the entire skeleton was stretched over with skin that was like yellow gauze. And the children's faces were aged, tormented, just as if they were seventy years old. And by spring they no longer had faces at all. Instead, they had birdlike heads with beaks, or frog heads—thin, wide lips—and some of them resembled fish, mouths open. Not human faces. And the eyes. Oh, Lord! Comrade Stalin, good God, did you see those eyes? Perhaps, in fact, he did not know. After all, he was the one who wrote the essay on "dizziness from success."

And now they ate anything at all. They caught mice, rats, snakes, sparrows, ants, earthworms. They ground up bones into flour, and did the same with leather and shoe soles; they cut up old skins and furs to make noodles of a kind, and they cooked glue. And when the grass came up, they began to dig up the roots and eat the leaves and the buds; they used everything there was: dandelions, and burdocks, and bluebells, and willowroot, and sedums, and nettles and every other kind of edible grass and root and herb they could find. They dried out linden leaves and ground them into flour—but there were too few linden in our region. The pancakes made from the linden leaves were greenish in color and worse than those made of acorn flour.

And no help came! And they no longer asked for any. Even now when I start thinking about it all, I begin to go out of my mind. How could Stalin have turned his back on human beings? He went to such lengths as this horrible massacre! After all, Stalin had bread. He had food to eat. What it adds up to is that he intentionally, deliberately, killed people by starvation. He refused to help even the children. And that makes Stalin worse than Herod. How can it be, I keep thinking to myself, that he took their grain and bread away, and then killed people by starvation? Such things are simply unimaginable! But then I think and remember: it did take place, it did take place! Then again I think that it simply could not really have happened.

Before they had completely lost their strength, the peasants went on foot across country to the railroad. Not to the stations where the guards kept them away, but to the tracks. And when the Kiev-Odessa express came past, they would just kneel there and cry: "Bread, bread!" They would lift up their horrible starving children for people to see. And sometimes people would throw them pieces

of bread and other scraps. The train would thunder on past, and
the dust would settle down, and the whole village would be there
crawling along the tracks, looking for crusts. But an order was issued
that whenever trains were traveling through the famine provinces
the guards were to shut the windows and pull down the curtains.
Passengers were not allowed at the windows. Yes, and in the end
the peasants themselves stopped going to the railroads. They had
too little strength left to get to the tracks—in fact, they didn't have
enough strength to crawl out of their huts and into the yard.

I can still recall how one old man brought the farm chairman
a piece of newspaper he had found near the tracks. There was an
item in it about a Frenchman, a famous minister, who had been
taken to Dnepropetrovsk Province where the famine was at its
worst, even worse than ours. People had become cannibals there,
but his hosts had taken him to a local village, to a collective farm
nursery school, and he had asked them: "What did you have for
lunch today?" And the children answered, "Chicken soup with
pirozhki and rice cutlets." I read it myself and I can still see that
piece of newspaper right now. What did it mean? It meant that they
were killing millions and keeping the whole thing quiet, deceiving
the whole world! Chicken soup! Cutlets! And on our farm they had
eaten all the earthworms. And the old man said to the farm chairman:
"When Nicholas was Czar, the whole world wrote about the famine
and was urged to give: 'Help, help! The peasantry is dying.' And
you Herods, you child-killers, are showing off Potemkin villages,
making theater out of it!"

The village moaned as it foresaw its approaching death. The
whole village moaned—not out of logic, but from the soul, as leaves
moan in the wind or straw crackles. And I myself saw red; why
were they moaning so plaintively? One had to be made of stone to
hear all that moaning and at the same time eat one's own ration of
bread. I used to go outdoors with my bread ration and I could hear
them moaning. I would go farther, and then it would seem as if
they had fallen silent. And then I would go on a little farther, and it
would begin again. At that point, it was the next village down the
line. And it seemed as if the whole earth were groaning, together
with the people on it. There was no God. Who could hear them?

One of the NKVD men said to me: "Do you know what they call your villages in the provincial center? A hard-school cemetery." But when I first heard those words, I did not understand them.

And how wonderful the weather was! At the beginning of summer there were rains, quick-falling, light, and the hot sun mingled with the rain, and as a result the lush wheat stood there like a wall. You could cut it with an ax, it was so strong and good. And it was high, taller than a man. And I saw so many rainbows that summer, and thundershowers and warm rain. That whole winter they had wondered whether there would be a harvest. They had asked the old men what they thought, and they searched for good omens. Their whole hope was in the winter wheat. And their hopes were justified, but they were too weak to harvest it. I went into a hut. People lay there, barely breathing, or else not breathing at all, some of them on the bed and others on the stove, and the daughter of the owner, whom I knew, lay on the floor in some kind of insane fit, gnawing on the leg of the stool. It was horrible. When she heard me come in, she did not turn around but growled, just as a dog growls if you come near when he is gnawing on a bone.

Deaths from starvation mowed down the village. First the children, then the old people, then those of middle age. At first they dug graves and buried them, and then as things got worse they stopped. Dead people lay there in the yards, and in the end they remained right in their huts. Things fell silent. The whole village died. Who died last I do not know. Those of us who worked in the collective farm administration were taken off to the city.

First I went to Kiev. At that time they had begun to sell unrationed bread at high prices in the "commercial" stores, as they were called. You should have seen what went on! The lines were half a kilometer in length the night before the stores even opened. As you know yourself, there are all kinds of queues. In some of them people stand and smile and laugh and eat sunflower seeds. And in others people write down their number in the line on a piece of paper. And in a third kind, the kind in which people do not laugh or joke, they write their number in chalk either on the palm or the back of their hand. But these lines were of a special kind. I have never ever seen any like them. People held onto the belts of those ahead and clung for dear life. If one person stumbled, the whole line would shake and quaver as if a wave had passed along it. It was as if a dance had begun—from side to side. All of them staggered heavily. They were terrified of being unable to keep hold of the person in front, of their hands slipping, and losing their place. And the women began to scream out of fear. And the whole long queue howled, and it seemed as if some of them had gone out of their minds—they kept singing and dancing. Now and then, some young hoodlums would break into the line. They would look for the places where the links in the chain were weakest. And when the hoodlums came near, everyone would start to howl again with fear—it seemed as though they were singing. They were city people standing there in line for unrationed "commercial" bread—deprived people, non-Party people, craftsmen—or else people from the suburbs. Many of them were people who had been refused ration cards.

And the peasants kept crawling from the village into the city. All the stations were surrounded by guards. All the trains were searched. Everywhere along the roads were roadblocks—troops, NKVD. Yet despite all this the peasants made their way into Kiev. They would crawl through the fields, through empty lots, through the swamps, through the woods—anywhere to bypass the roadblocks set up for them. They were unable to walk; all they could do was crawl. People hurried about on their affairs, some going to work, some to the movies, and the streetcars were running—and there were the starving children, old men, girls, crawling about among them on all fours. They were like mangy dogs and cats of some kind. And they had the nerve to want to be treated like human beings! They were modest. A young girl would crawl along, swollen up, looking like an ape; she would whine, but she would pull down her skirt and hide her hair beneath her kerchief. She was a peasant girl, and this was the first time she had come to Kiev. But the ones who had managed to crawl their way there were the more fortunate, one out of ten thousand. And even when they got there, they found no salvation. They lay starving on the ground, and they spluttered and begged but were unable to eat. A crust might lie right next to them, but they couldn't see it, and they lay dying.

In the mornings horses pulled flattop carts through the city, and the corpses of those who had died in the night were collected. I saw one such flattop cart with children lying on it. They were just as I have described them, thin, elongated faces, like those of dead birds, with sharp beaks. These tiny birds had flown into Kiev and what good had it done them? Some of them were still muttering, and their heads were still turning. I asked the driver about them, and he just waved his hands and said: "By the time they get where they are being taken they will be silent too."

I saw one young girl crawl across the sidewalk; a janitor kicked her, and she slid into the street. She didn't even look back. She just kept crawling along swiftly, trying to find the strength to go on. She brushed off her dress, too, where it had gotten dusty. I bought a Moscow paper that very same day and read an article by Maxim Gorky in which he said that children needed cultural toys. Are we to suppose that Maxim Gorky did not know about those children being hauled off on a flattop cart drawn by dray horses? What kind of toys did they need? But perhaps he did know, too, for that matter. And perhaps he, too, kept silent, like all the rest. And perhaps he, too, wrote, as others had written, that those dead children were eating chicken soup. The very same drayman told me that the greatest number of corpses were near the unrationed "commercial" bread stores. A swollen, starving person would eat a crust and it would finish him off. I can still remember the Kiev of those days, even though I spent only three days there in all.

And this is what I came to understand. In the beginning, starvation drives a person out of his house. In its first stage, he is tormented and driven as though by fire and torn both in the guts and in the soul. And so he tries to escape his home. People dig up worms, collect grass, and even make the effort to break through and get to the city. Away from home, away from home! And then a day comes when the starving person crawls back into his house. And the meaning of this is that famine, starvation, has won. The human being cannot be saved. He lies down on his bed and stays there. Not just because he has no strength, but because he has no interest in life and no longer cares about living. He lies there quite quietly and does not want to be touched. And he does not even want to eat.

He keeps urinating constantly and he has continuous runs and he becomes sleepy. All he wants is to be left alone, and for things to be quiet. Starving men lie there dying. And I have heard the same from POWs too. If the POW lay down on his bunk and did not try to get up and get his ration, it meant he would soon die.

Some went insane. They never did become completely still. One could tell from their eyes—because their eyes shone. These were the people who cut up and cooked corpses, who killed their own children and ate them. In them the beast rose to the top as the human being died. I saw one. She had been brought to the district center under convoy. Her face was human, but her eyes were those of a wolf. These are cannibals, they said, and must all be shot. But they themselves, who drove the mother to the madness of eating her own children, are evidently not guilty at all! For that matter, can you really find anyone who is guilty? Just go and ask, and they will all tell you that they did it for the sake of virtue, for everybody's good. That's why they drove mothers to cannibalism!

It was then that I saw for myself that every starving person is like a cannibal. He is consuming his own flesh, leaving only his bones intact. He devours his fat to the last droplet. And then his mind grows dim, because he has consumed his own mind. In the end the starving man has devoured himself completely.

I thought, too, that every starving person dies in his own particular way. In one hut there would be something like a war. Everyone would keep close watch over everyone else. People would take crumbs from each other. The wife turned against her husband and the husband against his wife. The mother hated the children. And in some other hut love would be inviolable to the very last. I knew one woman with four children. She would tell them fairy stories and legends so that they would forget their hunger. Her own tongue could hardly move, but she would take them into her arms even though she had hardly the strength to lift her arms when they were empty. Love lived on within her. And people noticed that where there was hate people died off more swiftly. Yet love, for that matter, saved no one. The whole village perished, one and all. No life remained in it.

What I found out later was that everything fell silent in our village. The children were no more to be heard. They didn't need any cultural toys, nor any chicken soup either. They no longer moaned. There was no one left to moan. I found out that troops were sent in to harvest the winter wheat. The army men were not allowed to enter the village, however. They were quartered in their tents. They were told there had been an epidemic. But they kept complaining that a horrible stink was coming from the village. The troops stayed to plant the spring wheat too. And the next year new settlers were brought in from Orel Province. This was the rich Ukrainian land, the black earth, whereas the Orel peasants were accustomed to frequent harvest failures. The new settlers left their women and children in temporary shelters near the station and the men were brought into the village. They were given pitchforks and told to go through the huts and drag out the corpses. The dead men and women still lay there, some on the floor and some in their beds. The stink in the huts was still frightful. The new settlers covered their noses and mouths with kerchiefs and began to drag out the bodies, but the bodies fell apart in pieces. Then they buried the pieces outside the village. And it was then that I understood what was meant by the phrase "a hard-school cemetery." When they had removed the corpses from the huts, they brought in the womenfolk to clean the floors and to whitewash the walls. Everything was done as it was supposed to be done. But the stink remained. They were unable to either eat or sleep in those huts, and they returned to the Orel Province. But of course the land did not remain empty. It is a rich land.

And now it is as though they had never lived at all. Yet many, many things took place there. There was love. And wives left husbands. And daughters were married off. And there were drunken brawls, and people came to visit, and they baked bread. And how they worked! And they sang songs. And children went to school. And a movie projector was brought in, and the people went to see the films.

And nothing was left of it at all. Where has that life gone? And what has become of all that awful torment and torture? Can it really be that nothing at all is left of it? Can it really be that no one will ever answer for everything that's happened? That it will be forgotten without even any words to commemorate it? That the grass has grown over it?

So I ask you: how can all this be?

There, you see how our night has passed, that it is already dawn and growing light. It is time for both of us to pull ourselves together and go to work.

Vasily Timofeyevich had a soft voice and his gestures were somehow quiet, hesitating, gentle. And when he and Hanna talked together, her black eyes lowered their gaze, and she would answer him in a barely audible voice.

After their marriage they became even more shy and retiring than they had been before. He was a man of sixty, whom the neighborhood children called "grandfather." And he was really very shy, very embarrassed, that he had married a young girl even though he was gray-haired, somewhat balding, and wrinkled, and that he was happy in his love, and that when he looked upon her he would whisper: "My dear darling . . . my sweetheart." Once upon a time, as a slip of a girl, she had imagined what her future husband would be like. He would be a Civil War Hero like Shchors, and the best accordion-player in the village, and he would write heartfelt verses like Taras Shchevchenko. But her gentle heart nonetheless understood the strength of the love Vasily Timofeyevich bore her, that unlucky, poor, shy, elderly man who had always lived someone else's life and never his own. And he could understand and appreciate her youthful hope too. A peasant cavalier would suddenly appear and take her away from her father's crowded hut. But here was Vasily Timofeyevich, who had come for her in old boots, with the big dark hands of a peasant, coughing in a guilty sort of way, and gazing upon her with admiration, with happiness, with guilt, with grief. And she, too, felt guilty in his presence and was meek and silent. And their son, Grisha, was a quiet child. He never cried.

His mother, who was still like a thin slip of a girl after he was born, sometimes went up to the cradle at night and, seeing the boy lying there with open eyes, she would say: "You should at least cry a little, Grishenka. Why are you always silent, silent and still?"

In their hut the wife and the husband spoke in soft voices and their neighbors were astonished. "Why do you speak so quietly?"

It was strange that she, a young woman, and he, an elderly, homely peasant, were very much alike in meekness of heart, gentleness, shyness.

They both worked without letup, and they even hesitated to raise their voices when their brigadier drove them out to work in the fields unfairly and out of turn.

On one occasion Vasily Timofeyevich rode to the district center with the collective farm chairman on an errand for the collective farm stable. While the chairman went about his business at the district offices for agriculture, finance, and such, he, after tying the horses to a hitching post, went to the district store and bought his wife a present—poppyseed cakes, sugar candies, ring-shaped crackers, and nuts, a little of each, maybe five ounces. And when he entered their hut and untied his white kerchief, his wife held up her hands and clapped them joyously, and cried: "Oh, oh!" And Vasily Timofeyevich went off into the passageway, shyly, so that she would not see the tears in his happy eyes.

She embroidered a shirt for him. And she never ever did know that Vasily Timofeyevich Karpenko hardly slept all night long and kept going barefooted up to the chest of drawers on which the shirt still lay, and stroked it with his hand, his fingers feeling the cross-stitch of the simply embroidered design. When he brought his wife home from the maternity ward of the district hospital, and she held her child in her arms, it seemed to him that if he were to live a thousand years he would never forget that day.

Sometimes he was simply overcome with dismay: how could it possibly be that such happiness had come into his life? How could it possibly be that he could wake in the middle of the night and listen to the breathing of his wife and his son?

And this is how it went. He came home from work and he saw the diaper drying on the wattle fence and the smoke rising from his chimney. He looked upon his wife—she was bent down over the cradle. Then she was putting a plate of borsch on the table and smiling about something. He looked at her hands, at her hair escaping a little from beneath her kerchief. He listened to her gossip. Sometimes, briefly, she went out into the passageway, and he felt pangs of loneliness; his heart ached while he waited for her, and when she returned, he was overjoyed. And she, catching his glance, smiled at him meekly and sadly.

Vasily Timofeyevich was the first to die. He was two days ahead of tiny Grisha. He had given nearly all the crumbs he had to his wife and child, and that is why he died before they did. In all likelihood, there was no self-sacrifice in the whole world greater than his and no desperation greater than the desperation he suffered as he looked upon his wife, disfigured by the swelling dropsy of starvation, and upon his dying son.

He felt no reproach or wrath against the great and meaningless thing that the state and Stalin had committed—even in his final hour. He did not even ask the question "Why?" He did not ask why the torment of death by starvation had been meted out to him and his wife, meek, obedient, submissive people, and to his quiet year-old baby boy.

The skeletons spent the winter together in their rotting rags— the husband, the wife, and the small son—smiling pallidly. They had not been parted in death.

And then in the spring when the starlings came, the representative of the agricultural section entered their hut, with his kerchief covering his nose, and he looked at the kerosene lamp without any glass, at the icon in the corner, at the chest of drawers, at the cold frying pans there, at the bed, and he said: "In here, two adults and one small one."

The brigadier, standing there on the threshold made sacred by love and meekness, nodded his head and made a mark on a piece of paper.

When they went out into the fresh air, the representative of the agricultural department looked at the white huts, at the green orchards, and said: "Once you have removed the corpses, don't bother to try to restore all this mess."

Translated by Thomas P. Whitney

Vladimir Tendryakov
(1923, Makarovskaya — 1984, Moscow)

Vladimir Tendryakov was born into a peasant family. Right after graduating from school, he went to the front. In 1943 he was severely wounded and returned to his village. From 1946 to 1951 studied at the Literary Institute in Moscow. In the 1950s and 1960s was famous for his sociological novellas depicting the Soviet village, among which one of the strongest was *Konchina* (The Death, 1968), which depicted a local countryside boss as a "little Stalin." In the 1970s Tendryakov published a series of novellas about moral conflict, which triggered a heated debate about the dead-ends of morals founded upon Soviet ideology. "Bread for a Dog" belongs to a cycle of autobiographical stories told from the perspective of a child that describes collectivization and the famine (Holodomor) it caused. Tendryakov wrote these stories in 1969–71. However, due to their irreconcilability with the official discourse on collectivization, they were published only after his death during *perestroika*.

Bread for a Dog

Summer of 1933.

There is a small public garden with birch trees that one can walk through; it's behind a fence with its paint peeled off, next to a soot-covered train station building painted in government ochre. In it, right on its beaten paths, on the tree roots, on the surviving dusty grass lay those who were no longer considered people.

True, each one had to keep somewhere deep in his lice-covered rags a well-thumbed document—if it had not been lost—proving that its bearer had such-and-such family name, first name and patronymic, was born there and there, and based on such and such a decision exiled with the deprivation of his civil rights and the confiscation of his property. But no one cared any more that he, so-and-so, deprived of his civil rights, exiled by the administration,[1] hadn't reached his destination; no one was interested that he, so-and-so, deprived of his rights, wasn't living anywhere, wasn't working, and didn't have anything to eat. He was no longer a member of the human race.

For the most part, these were dispossessed[2] peasants from around Tula, Voronezh, Kursk, Oryol, and from all over Ukraine.

---

[1] That is to say, without a formal court hearing.

[2] Collectivization: Stalin's First Five-Year Plan (1928–32) called for combining individually owned farms into large state collective farms. Peasants were

The southern word *kurkul*[3] came with them to our northern parts as well.

Even in their outward appearance the *kurkuls* didn't resemble people.

Some of them were skeletons, with dark, wrinkled, seemingly rustling skin drawn tight around them—skeletons with huge, timidly burning eyes.

Others, on the contrary, were tautly bloated—any minute their skin, blue from being stretched, could split open; their bodies swayed, their feet looked like pillows, their dirty fingers seemed sewn on and were covered with cankerous white flesh.

And they also didn't behave like people.

Someone would be pensively gnawing the bark on the trunk of a birch tree and peering into space with inhumanely big, smoldering eyes.

Someone, lying in the dust and emitting a bad, sour smell with his half-rotten rags, would be wiping his fingers in disgust with such energy and persistence that it seemed he was ready to clean the skin off them.

Someone would be spread out on the ground like jellied meat, not moving and only screeching like a large bird, and his insides would make gurgling sounds like a huge, boiling tea urn.

And someone would be dolefully stuffing into his mouth a small piece of station garbage picked up from the ground . . .

Those who had already managed to die had the most resemblance to people. They were lying peacefully—sleeping.

---

forced to give up their land and cattle, and those who resisted were killed or exiled. This policy of forced collectivization devastated agriculture and led to the horrific famine of 1932–33, during which millions of people starved to death.

[3]   *kurkul*: Ukrainian word (equivalent to the Russian "kulak") for a comparatively well-to-do peasant who had cattle, or could hire laborers, etc., the kind who in the late 1920s and early 1930s were dispossessed of their property and forcibly collectivized or exiled, or even killed. Historical studies indicate that the term "kulak" was also applied indiscriminately when the city or regional authorities wanted to fulfill the quota of people being shipped to the Gulag.

But before dying, one of the meek who had been gnawing bark quietest of all, who had been eating garbage, would suddenly rebel. He'd stand up straight, clasp the smooth, strong birch trunk with his stick-like, fragile hands, press his bony cheek against it, and open his black, blindingly toothy mouth wide, undoubtedly getting ready to shout a curse to reduce things to ashes, but only a rattle would come out and foam would bubble up around the mouth. Tearing off the skin on his bony cheek, the "rebel" would slide down the trunk and . . . grow silent forever.

Ones like this, even in death, didn't resemble people; they squeezed the trees like monkeys.

The adults avoided the public garden. Only the stationmaster in his new uniform cap with a bright red top strolled out of duty along the platform and the low fencing. He had a swollen, leaden-colored face, looked down at his feet, and didn't say anything.

From time to time Vania Dushnoi the policeman would show up, a staid fellow with a frozen expression—"just you watch out!"

"No one's crawled out?" he'd ask the stationmaster.

But the latter wouldn't answer; he'd just walk past without raising his head.

Vania Dushnoi watched to make sure that the *kurkuls* didn't crawl away from the public garden—either onto the platform or onto the tracks.

We, the small boys, also didn't go into the public garden itself but watched from behind the small fence. No horrors could stifle our beastly curiosity. Petrified with fear, overcome with squeamishness, breaking down from hidden pity, we watched the bark-eaters and the outbursts of the "rebels" which ended in a rattle, foam and sliding down a tree trunk.

The stationmaster—"the red cap"—once turned his reddened, dark face in our direction, looked for a long time and finally said either to us or to himself or to the indifferent sky in general, "What will such children grow up to become? They enjoy looking at death. What kind of a world will there be after us? What kind of a world . . ?"

We couldn't stand the garden for long. We'd tear away from there, breathing deeply—as if we were airing all the nooks in our poisoned souls—and run to the settlement.

There, where there was a normal life, where you could often hear the song:

Don't sleep, arise, my curly-headed one!
Filling the workshops with clanging,
The country rises in glory
To greet the day . . .

When I was already an adult, I wondered in amazement for a long time why I, a generally impressionable, vulnerable small boy, didn't fall ill and didn't go mad right after I saw a *kurkul* for the first time, dying with foam and a rattle right before my eyes.

Probably because the horrors of the public garden didn't appear right away, and I had a chance to get used to them somewhat, to become callous.

I experienced my first shock, by far stronger than the death of a *kurkul*, during a quiet street incident.

A woman in a worn-out coat of a simple, nice design with a velvet collar, and her face just as nice and worn-out, slipped right in front of my eyes and broke a glass jar with milk in it which she had bought on the station platform. The milk spilled into a dirty, ice-encrusted horse's hoofprint. The woman dropped down before it like before a daughter's grave, let out a stifled sob, and suddenly took a simple, chewed-up wooden spoon out of her pocket. She cried and scooped up the milk with her spoon from the small hole left on the road by the horse's hoof; she cried and ate, cried and ate—carefully, not greedily, in a refined way.

But I stood to the side and—no, I didn't wail with her—I was afraid that passers-by would start laughing at me.

My mother would give me lunch to be eaten at school: two pieces of black bread heavily smeared with cranberry jam. And so there came a day when during a noisy break I took out my bread and with my whole being sensed the silence that had set in around me. I got flustered and didn't dare offer any of the bread to the kids at the time. However, the next day I took now not two but four pieces . . .

During the long recess, I took them out and, afraid of the unpleasant silence which is so hard to break, I cried out much too hastily and awkwardly, "Who wants some?!"

"Me a tiny piece," Pashka Bykov, a kid from our street, answered.

"Me too . . ! Me too . . ! Me too . . !"

Hands stretched out from all directions, eyes glistened.

"There won't be enough for all!" Pashka tried to push away the pressing kids, but no one backed off.

"Me! Me! A small piece of crust . . !"

I broke off a little piece for everybody.

Somebody pushed my hand, probably out of impatience without any evil intent, the bread fell, the kids in the back who wanted to see what had happened to the bread pressed against the ones in the front, and several feet stepped on the pieces and crushed them.

"You butterfingers!" Pashka scolded me.

And he walked away. All the others followed him and then crept off in different directions.

The bread lay in pieces on the floor colored with the jam. We felt as if we had accidentally killed an animal in the heat of the moment.

Olga Stanislavna, the teacher, walked into the classroom. Judging by the way she turned her eyes away, by the way she didn't ask any questions right away but only after some barely noticeable hesitation, I understood—she was hungry too.

"Who is so full here?"

And all those whom I had wanted to treat to some bread announced willingly, triumphantly, perhaps even with malicious joy, "Volodka Tenkov is full! He's the one . . !"

I lived in a proletarian country and knew full well how shameful it was to be full. But unfortunately I truly was full; my father, a high-ranking official, received a high-ranking man's rations. My mother even baked cabbage pies with chopped eggs, using white flour!

Olga Stanislavna began the lesson.

"Last time we covered spelling . . ." And she fell silent. "Last time we . . ." She tried not to look at the crushed bread. "Volodya Tenkov, get up and pick up after yourself!"

I got up obediently without arguing, picked up the bread, and wiped the cranberry jam off the floor with a sheet of paper torn from my notebook. The whole class was silent; the whole class was breathing over my head.

After that, I flatly refused to take any lunch food to school.

Soon after that I saw the emaciated people with the huge, meekly sad eyes of Eastern beauties . . .

And those sick with dropsy, with swollen, smooth, featureless faces, with light-blue elephant legs . . .

The emaciated ones—just skin and bones—people in our area started calling them "shkeletons" and those sick with dropsy, "elephants."

And so the public garden with the birches near the train station . . .

I managed to get used to some things and not go mad.

I also didn't go mad because I knew that those who were dying in our birch grove by the train station in broad daylight were our enemies. It was about them that the great writer Gorky[4] had recently said, "If the enemy doesn't surrender, he's annihilated." They wouldn't surrender. So . . . they found themselves in the birch grove.

With some other kids I was a witness to an unexpected conversation between Dybakov and one "shkeleton."

Dybakov was the party first secretary in our district, a tall man in a semi-military jacket who had straight-hewn shoulders and wore a pince-nez on his thin, hooked nose. He walked around with his hands behind his back, his back bent in, and his chest—decorated with patch pockets—thrust forward.

Some kind of district conference was taking place in the railway workers' club. The whole leadership of the district with Dybakov at the head was making its way to the club along a path strewn with crushed brick. We, the kids, with nothing else to look at, also followed Dybakov.

Suddenly he stopped. Across the path, right in front of his feet in box calf boots, lay a man in rags—all bones with worn-out skin

---

[4] Maxim Gorky (pseud. of Aleksei Peshkov; 1868–1936): short story writer, novelist and playwright, who came to prominence at the end of the nineteenth century with his stories about the downtrodden and works in support of major social change. Recognized as "the father of Socialist Realism" for his novel *Mother* (1905).

that was terribly loose. He was lying on the crushed brick, his brown skull resting on the pathetic, dirty bones of his hands, and he was looking up as all those dying of hunger look—with timid sorrow in his unnaturally big eyes.

Dybakov took step after step, making a crunching sound on the brick-gravel path, and was about to skirt the living skeleton he had chanced to encounter when suddenly this skeleton opened his leathery lips, flashed his large teeth, and said hoarsely but distinctly, "Let's talk, chief."

Silence descended; far beyond the vacant lot by the barracks you could hear someone singing in a tenor voice from nothing to do, to the accompaniment of a balalaika:

> He who has one leg
> Is well off.
> A lot of boots aren't needed,
> Just one foot cloth.

"Or are you afraid of me, chief?"

District committee worker Comrade Gubanov, with an unlocked briefcase under his arm as always, emerged from behind Dybakov. "Si-lence! Si-lence!"

The man lying there looked up at him timidly and grinned in a terrible way. Dybakov waved off Comrade Gubanov to the side with a motion of his hand.

"Let's talk. You ask—I'll answer."

"Tell me before I die . . . what . . . what did I do . . ? Can it seriously be because I had two horses?" the murmuring voice asked.

"Because of that," Dybakov answered quietly and coldly.

"And you admit it! Lord, you're a beast . . ."

"Si-lence!" Comrade Gubanov ran up to him again.

And again Dybakov waved him off to the side nonchalantly.

"Would you have given bread to the worker for his cast iron?"

"What do I need your cast iron for, to eat it with my gruel?"

"That's exactly it. The collective farm needs it, and the collective farm is ready to feed the workers for their iron. Did you want to join a collective farm? Only be honest!"

"I didn't want to."

"Why?"

"Everybody wants his bit of freedom."

"It's not your bit of freedom that's the reason, but horses. You didn't want to part with your horses. You fed them, tended to them—and suddenly you're told to give them up. You didn't want to part with your property! Isn't that so?"

The goner said nothing, blinked sorrowfully, and seemed even ready to agree.

"Take away the horses, chief, and stop. Why take my life as well?" he asked.

"And you'll forgive us if we take them away? You won't start taking up arms behind our backs? Be honest!"

"Who knows . . ."

"And we don't know either. What would you have done with us if you had felt that we were taking up arms against you . . ? You're silent . . ? Nothing to say . . ? Then good-bye."

Dybakov stepped over the thin, stick-like legs of the man he had been talking to and moved on, his hands behind his back, his chest with the patch pockets thrust forward. Others started moving too and followed him, skirting the goner with disgust.

He lay there in front of us small boys, a flattened skeleton in rags, his skull on the crumbled brick—a skull preserving a human expression of submissiveness, weariness, and perhaps pensiveness. He lay there and we kept scrutinizing him with condemning looks. He had two horses, the bloodsucker! For the sake of those horses he would've taken up arms against us. "If the enemy does not surrender . . ." Dybakov got rid of him splendidly.

And nonetheless I felt sorry for the evil enemy. Probably not only I. No kid started to dance in joy over him or to tease:

> Enemy—big enemy,
> *Kurluk* big kulak,
> He gorges on tree bark,
> He kills lice,
> Strolls with his *kurkulikha*,
> And sways in the wind nice.

I would sit down at the table at home, reach for some bread, and memories of those images would unfold in my mind: quietly crazy eyes directed into the distance, white teeth gnawing bark, a cold

hulk with gurgling insides, a gaping black mouth, a rattle, foam . . .
And I'd feel nausea rising in my throat.

Before all this, when talking about me, my mother used to say,
"I can't complain about that one. No matter what you put before
him, he puts it away, wolfs it down." Now she'd raise a ruckus and
shout, "You've become so choosy! You don't know when you're
well off . . !"

I was the only one who "didn't know how well off" I was, but if
my mother began scolding, she always scolded the two of us right
away—me and my brother. My brother was three years younger; in
his seven years he knew only how to worry about himself, and for
this reason ate "wolfing things down."

"You've become so choosy! We don't want soup, we don't want
potatoes. All around people are happy, so very happy to get a stale
crust of bread. But I might as well serve you hazel-grouse!"

I had read only small lines of verse about hazel-grouse:
"Eat pineapples, chew hazel-grouse, your last day is coming,
you bourgeois louse!" I couldn't announce a hunger strike, and
I couldn't refuse food altogether. First of all, my mother wouldn't
have permitted it. Secondly, nausea is nausea, images are images,
but I still wanted to eat, though hardly bourgeois hazel-grouse.
I was made to swallow the first spoon, and the rest followed without
being forced on me. I'd finish my dinner quickly and get up from
the table heavier.

And here is where it all began . . .

It seems to me that it is more natural for conscience to awaken
in the bodies of people who are full rather than hungry. A hungry
man is forced to think more about himself, about getting daily bread
for himself; the very burden of hunger forces him to be selfish. A full
man has more of a chance to look around, to think about others.
For the most part ideological fighters emerged from the ranks
of the full with the satiety of a certain caste—the Gracchi[5] in all
times.

---

[5]   Gracchi: one of the very rich and politically important families of Rome in the
second century BC.

I'd get up from the table. Isn't that the reason why people in the station public park are gnawing bark? Isn't it because I ate too much?

But those are *kurkuls* gnawing bark! Why are you pitying them...? "If the enemy doesn't surrender, he's annihilated!" And they are "annihilated" probably like this, that's probably how it's supposed to look—skulls with eyes, elephant legs, and foam around a black mouth. You're simply afraid to face up to the truth.

My father happened to relate at one point that there were villages in other places where the inhabitants had all died to the last soul—the adults, old people, and children. Even nursing infants . . . There's no way you can say about them, "If the enemy doesn't surrender . . ."

I'm full, very full—totally satiated. I just ate so much that there probably would've been enough for five people to save themselves from a hungry death. I didn't save five, I ate their lives. But whose? The lives of enemies or non-enemies . . ?

And who's an enemy . . ? Is the one gnawing bark an enemy? He was—yes!—but now animosity is far from his mind, there's no flesh on his bones, and there's no strength left even in his voice . . .

I ate my whole dinner and didn't share it with anyone.

I have to eat three times a day.

Once toward morning I suddenly woke up. I hadn't dreamt of anything; I simply went and opened my eyes and saw my room in the twilight that was mysteriously ashy—there was a nice, cozy, grey dawn outside my window.

Far off on the station tracks a "goat"[6] whistled. Early, blue titmice were chirping on an old linden tree. A father starling was clearing his throat, trying to sing like a nightingale and botching it! A cuckoo began cuckooing softly, with conviction, in the back part of the swamp. "Cuckoo bird! Cuckoo bird! How many years will I live?"[7] And it lets out its "cu-ckoos" like silver eggs.

---

[6]   goat: railroad term for locomotives used in yard switching operations.

[7]   Russians believe that the number of times you hear the cuckoo bird go "cuckoo" is the number of years you are fated to live.

And all this takes place during twilight, surprisingly peaceful and grey, an intimate, cozy world. In the minute unexpectedly stolen from sleep, I suddenly quietly rejoice at an obvious fact: a certain Volodka Tenkov, a human being about ten years old, exists in the wide world. He exists—how wonderful! "Cuckoo! Cuckoo!" How many years will I . . ? "Cu-ckoo! Cu-ckoo. Cu-ckoo . . !" It's unceasingly generous.

At that point there was a thundering sound far off, at the very end of our street. Ripping open the silence of the sleepy settlement, a rickety cart was drawing near, replacing the silver voice of the cuckoo, the chirping of the blue titmice, and the vain attempts of the untalented starling. Who is this, and where is he so angrily rushing so early in the morning . . ?

And suddenly it strikes me: who? It's clear who! The whole settlement is talking about these early trips. The *komkhoz*[8] stableman, Abram, is going "to collect carrion." Every morning he drives his cart straight into the birch grove and shakes the people lying there—alive or not? He doesn't bother with the living, and he piles the dead into the cart like blocks of wood.

The rickety cart thunders, waking up the sleeping settlement. It thunders and grows quiet.

After its appearance, you can't hear the birds. For about a minute you can't hear anyone or anything. Anything . . . But what's strange—there's no silence either. "Cu-ckoo! Cu-ckoo . . !" Oh, don't! Does it really matter how many years I will live in this world? And do I really want to live that long . . ?

But just like heavy rain pouring off a roof, sparrows that have awakened come swooping down. Buckets start ringing, women's voices resound, and the well crank begins squeaking.

"Roofs fixed! Wood cut! Garbage cans cleaned! Any work at all!" a strong baritone shouts, calling out to people.

"Roofs fixed! Wood cut! Garbage cans cleaned!" a boyish alto repeats.

---

[8]   *komkhoz*: acronym for *kommunal'noe khozyaistvo*, communal services.

These are exiled *kurkuls* as well—father and son. The father is a tall man with bony broad shoulders, bearded, sternly important; the son is sinewy thin, freckled, very serious, and two or three years older than me.

Every day begins with their two voices offering loudly, almost haughtily, to clean the settlement's garbage cans.

I mustn't eat my dinner alone.

I'm obligated to share it with someone.

With whom . . ?

Probably with the most, most hungry person there is, even if he's an enemy.

Who's the most hungry . . ? How to find out?

It's not difficult. I should go to the park with all the birches and extend my hand with a piece of bread to the first person who comes along. It's impossible to make a mistake; everyone there is the most, most hungry, there are no others. Extend my hand to one and not notice the others . . ? Make one happy and hurt ten others by denying them food? That would be truly a mortal wrong. The ones to whom my hand won't be extended will be taken away by the stableman Abram.

Can the ones who are passed over agree with you . . ? Isn't it dangerous to extend a helping hand openly?

Of course, I didn't think like that then and use the words with which I now write, thirty-six years later. Most likely I didn't think at all at the time but had a keen feeling like an animal that senses intuitively the complications to come. At that time I realized not with my rational mind but intuitively that the noble intention—break your daily bread in half and share it with your neighbor—could be carried out only secretly from others, only thievishly!

Furtively, thievishly, I saved a part of what my mother had placed before me on the table. I thievishly packed my pockets with three pieces of bread saved honestly, a lump of millet porridge wrapped in paper and the size of a fist, and a clean, crystal-perfect lump of sugar. In broad daylight I walked out to do my thievish deed—to hunt secretly for the most, most hungry person.

I met Pashka Bykov, who was in my class and lived on the same street as me, with whom I wasn't really friendly, but with whom I was careful not to quarrel either. I knew that Pashka was always hungry—day and night, before and after dinner. The Bykov family—seven people in all—lived on the ration cards of the father who worked as a coupler on the railroad. But I didn't share my bread with Pashka—he was not the most . . .

I met the deformed old woman Obnoskova who lived on what she gathered—grasses and roots on the sides of the road, in fields, at the edges of the forest—and dried, cooked, and steamed what she found . . . Other old women like that who lived alone had all died. I didn't share with the old woman—still not the most . . .

Boris Isaakovich Zilberbruner, in galoshes tied with string to dirty anklebones, trotted past me. If I had met this Zilberbruner earlier, then who knows, I might have decided he was the one. Not long ago he had been one of the "shkeletons" who hung around a cafeteria, but he adapted and made fish hooks out of wire, and was paid for them even in chicken eggs.

Finally I ran into one of the "elephants" staggering through the settlement. He was very broad like a wardrobe, and wore a roomy, unbelted peasant caftan the color of plowed land; he had a rook's nest in his Zaporozhye Cossack hat. His swollen, pale-blue legs that shook with each step like oatmeal *kisel*, would have fitted in a bathhouse wash-tub only one at a time.

Perhaps even he wasn't the most . . . Had I continued my hunt, I probably would've run into a more unfortunate person, but the remains of my dinner in my pockets were burning me, demanding that I share immediately . . !

"Uncle . . ."

He stopped, breathing heavily, and directed his chink-like eyes at me from his towering height.

Standing near him, I was struck by his pale, swollen face with its unnatural gigantic size—cheeks that moved and floated like flabby buttocks, a chin crashing down to his chest, eyes which had totally disappeared under his eyelids, and a broad nose bridge stretched to a corpse's blueness. You can't read anything in a face like this—neither fear nor hope, neither emotionalism nor suspicion—it was a pillow.

Rummaging in my pocket, I began to free the first piece of bread awkwardly.

The flattened face twitched, the thickly swollen hand with the short, dirty, unbending fingers reached out and took the piece gently, insistently, and impatiently. A calf with a warm nose and soft mouth takes bread from a hand that way.

"Thank you, boy," the elephant said in a falsetto, using the Ukrainian word for "boy."

I laid out everything for him that I had.

"Tomorrow . . . In the vacant lot . . . Near the piles . . . Something more," I promised and ran away from there with lighter pockets and a lighter conscience.

I was happy the whole day. It was cool and quiet inside, under my ribs, where my soul lived.

In the vacant lot, near the piles . . . This time I was carrying eight pieces of bread, two pieces of fatback, and an old jar filled with fried potatoes. I was supposed to eat all this myself and didn't. I saved it all when my mother wasn't looking.

I ran, skipping along to the vacant lot, with both hands holding my shirt which bulged out in the front. Someone's shadow appeared under my feet.

"Young man! Young man! I beg you! Spare me a moment . . !"

Are people addressing me so respectfully . . . ?

Me.

A woman in a dusty hat, known to all by her nickname, Otryzhka,[9] stood blocking my way. She was neither an "elephant" nor a "shkeleton" but simply an invalid disfigured by some kind of strange illness. Her whole dried-up body was unnaturally crumpled, crooked, and twisted—her small shoulders were distorted, her back thrown back, and on her small bird-like head there was a greasy cloth hat with a dingy feather somewhere far in back of her body. From time to time this head shook despairingly as if its mistress were preparing to exclaim quickly, "And now I'll do a dance for

[9]   *Otryzhka*: literally, "Belch."

you!" But Otryzhka didn't dance and would usually start winking really, really hard, scrunching up her whole cheek.

Now she was winking at me and saying in a passionate, teary voice: "Young man, take a look at me! Don't be shy, don't be shy, take a careful look . . ! Have you ever seen a being wronged by God . . . ?" She kept winking and coming towards me, and I kept backing away from her. "I'm sick, I'm feeble, but I have a son at home . . . I'm a mother, I love him with all my heart, I'm ready to do anything to feed him . . . We've both forgotten how bread tastes, young man! A little piece, I beg you . . !"

The dreadful, cheerful winking with her whole cheek, the dark hand holding a dirty bit of rag for dabbing her eyes . . . How did she find out that I had bread under my shirt? The "elephant" that was waiting for me in the vacant lot wouldn't have told her. It was to the "elephant's" advantage to keep quiet.

"I'm prepared to get on my knees before you. You have such a good . . . You have an angel's face . . !"

How did she find out about the bread? From the smell? Sorcery . . ? I didn't understand then that I wasn't the only one trying to give some food to the exiled *kurkuls*, and that all simple-hearted rescuers had an eloquently thievish, guilty facial expression.

I was unable to resist Otryzhka's fervor, her gleeful winking, and her crumpled, dirty bit of rag. I gave her all the bread with the pieces of fatback, keeping only one piece and the jar of fried potatoes.

"I promised that . . ."

But Otryzhka was devouring the jar with her crow's eyes, shaking her dusty hat with the feather and moaning, "We're dying! We're dying! Me and my son—we're dying . . !"

I let her have the potatoes as well. She shoved the jar under her knitted jacket, flashed her greedy eyes at the last piece of bread left in my hand, jerked her head—"I'll do a dance!"—winked once more with her cheek and walked away, listing to the side like a sinking boat.

I stood and scrutinized the bread in my hand. The piece was small, dirty and squashed from being in my pocket, but I had called him myself—come to the vacant lot—I had forced the hungry man to wait a whole day, and now I was going to treat him to such a small piece. No, better not shame myself . . !

And from vexation—and hunger as well—without leaving the spot, I ate the bread. It was unexpectedly very tasty and . . . toxic. The whole day after eating it I felt poisoned: how could I have done that—I had torn it out of the mouth of a hungry man! How could I . . !

And in the morning when I looked out the window, I grew cold. The familiar "elephant" was hanging around our gate, under a window. He stood wrapped in his immense caftan the color of a newly plowed field, his toad's hands folded on his huge stomach, and a breeze ruffling the dirty fur on his Cossack hat—he was immovable and tower-like.

I immediately felt like a miserable fox cub, driven into a burrow by a dog. The "elephant" can stand until tomorrow, he can stand like that tomorrow and after tomorrow; he has nowhere to rush to, and standing promises bread.

I waited till my mother left the house, got into the kitchen, broke off a thick end piece of a loaf of bread, which was of considerable weight, got ten large, raw potatoes from the sack and ran out . . .

The caftan the color of plowed earth had bottomless pockets into which all our family supplies of bread could have probably disappeared.

"Son. Don't believe that vile old woman. She doesn't have anyone. No son, no daughter," he said in Ukrainian.

I had guessed even without his saying so. Otryzhka was deceiving me, but try and refuse her when she's standing before you all broken, winking with her cheek and holding a dirty bit of rag in her hand to dab her eyes with.

"Oh, what misery, my son, what misery. Death, and she's robbing people . . . Oh, what misery, what misery," he continued in Ukrainian. Sighing huskily, he pushed off slowly, dragging his swollen feet with difficulty on the settlement sidewalk along boards full of splinters. He was wide like a haystack and majestic like a dilapidated windmill. "Oh, woe is me, woe . . !"

I turned to go into the house and winced: my father was standing before me, a patch of sunlight playing on his smoothly shaven head. He was somewhat stout and solidly built, dressed in a canvas soldier's blouse tied with a thin belt from the Caucasus with metal decorations on it. His face wasn't sullen and his eyes weren't covered over by his eyebrows—it was a peaceful, tired face.

He stepped up to me, put his heavy hand on my shoulder, stared for a long time somewhere to the side, and finally asked, "You gave him some bread?"

"Yes."

And he again peered into the distance.

I love my father and I'm proud of him.

People now sing songs and write tales about the great revolution, about the civil war. It's my father they're singing about, it's him they write tales about!

He's one of those soldiers who were the first to refuse to fight for the tsar, who arrested their officers.

He heard Lenin at Finland Station. He saw him standing on an armored car in person, not as a statue.

He was a commissar of the Four-Hundred Sixteenth Revolutionary Regiment during the civil war.

He has a scar on his neck from a Kolchak[10] shell splinter.

He was awarded a silver watch with his name engraved on it. It was stolen later, but I held it in my hands myself and saw the engraving on the cover: "For demonstrated courage in battles with the counter-revolution . . ."

I love my father and I'm proud of him. And I'm always afraid of his silence. Right now he'll stay silent for a while and then say, "I fight our enemies my whole life, and you're feeding them. Are you a traitor, Volodka?"

But he asked quietly, "Why this one? Why not another one?"

"That one turned up . . ."

"Another turns up—you'll give?"

"I d-don't know. I probably will."

"And will we have enough bread to feed all of them?"

---

[10]   Admiral Aleksandr V. Kolchak (1874–1920): in 1917 supported Kerensky's Provisional Government. Appointed Minister of War and Navy in the anti-Bolshevik government established in Omsk, Siberia; led the White forces against the Reds in Siberia during the civil war. Executed by the Bolsheviks in 1920.

I kept silent and looked at the ground.

"The country doesn't have enough for all. You can't scoop out the sea with a teaspoon, my son." My father poked me lightly in the shoulder. "Go play."

The familiar "elephant" began to wage a silent duel with me. He'd come under our window and stand and stand—motionless, slovenly, and faceless. I tried not to look at him, I'd put up with him, and . . . the "elephant" would win. I'd run out to him with a piece of bread or a cold potato pancake. He'd receive the tribute and slowly go away.

Once running out to him with bread and the tail of cod fished out of yesterday's soup, I suddenly discovered that one more "elephant" was lying around near our fence on the dusty grass, covered with a wet, dirty railway worker's overcoat that had once been black. As I was walking toward him, he only raised his head of uncombed, matted hair covered in scabs, and said hoarsely, "Boy-y, I'm dy-i-ing . . !"

And I saw that it was true and gave him a piece of cooked cod. The next morning three more "shkeletons" were lying near our fence. I was now under total siege, now I couldn't take anything out to buy them off. You can't feed five with your dinners and breakfasts, and my mother wouldn't have had enough supplies for all.

My brother would run out to look at the guests and return excited and happy. "One more 'shkeleton' has come crawling to Volodka!"

My mother would swear. "Made a place for themselves to lie around in, as if we're richer than the rest. Found parasites to feed, those tyrants of mine!"

As always, she was scolding the two of us right away, although my brother had nothing to do with it whatsoever. My mother would swear, but she couldn't bring herself to walk out and chase away the hungry *kurkuls*. My father, too, walked past the ground where they lay. He didn't say a word to me in reproach.

My mother issued an order. "Here's a pitcher—run to the cafeteria and get some *kvas*.[11] And be quick!"

---

[11]   *kvas*: a fermented drink made from water and rye bread.

There was nothing to be done; I took the glass pitcher from her.

I darted through the gate to freedom without difficulty; it wasn't for the sluggish "elephants" and barely crawling "shkeletons" to stop me.

I spent a long time jostling people in the small cafeteria-café as I tried to buy the *kvas*. The *kvas* was the real thing, made of bread—it was by no means fruit water with vitamins added to it— because it was not sold to anyone who wanted it, but only to those on a list. But you can hang around all you want; you still have to return home.

They were waiting for me. All those who had been lying down were now standing solemnly. Cascades of patches, the copper color of skin showing through holes in their rags, ingratiating smiles with sinister bared teeth, burning eyes, faces without eyes, hands stretching towards me that were thin like bird claws and round like balls, and cracked, raspy voices saying, "Little boy, some bread . . ."[12]

"A crumb each . . ."

"I'm dying, b-boy-y. A bite before death . . ."

"Want me to, I'll eat my hand? Want me to? Want me to . . ?"

I stood before them and pressed the cold pitcher with the cloudy *kvas* to my chest.

"A bit of brea-ea-d-d . . ."

"A crust . . ."

"Want me to . . . my hand . . ?"

And suddenly Otryzhka swooped down from the side, the feather on her hat shaking energetically.

"Young man! I beg you! On my knees I beg you!"

She actually fell to her knees in front of me, wringing not only her hands but twisting her neck and back as well and winking at some point above, at the blue sky, at God . . .

And this was now too much. Everything went dark before my eyes. Someone else's wild cry escaped from me at a wailing gallop. "Go a-way! Go a-way! Bastards! Sons of bitches! Bloodsuckers! Go away!"

---

[12] This line and the dialogue that follows contains a mixture of Russian and Ukrainian.

Otryzhka got up matter-of-factly and shook the dirt off her skirt. The rest all grew feeble at the same time, dropped their hands, turned their backs to me and moved off slowly—unhurriedly, sluggishly.

But I couldn't stop and I kept screaming in a wailing tone, "Go a-way!"

The hard workers—the staid, bearded father with the freckled, very serious son who was only two years older than me—approached with tools on their shoulders. The son casually motioned with his chin in the direction of the *kurkuls* wandering off and said, "Jackals."

The father nodded in agreement with an air of importance, and they both looked with open contempt at me—disheveled, red-eyed, gently pressing the pitcher with the *kvas* to my chest. I wasn't a victim for them with whom one had to sympathize but one of the participants in the jackals' game.

They walked by. The father carried a saw on his straight shoulder, and it was bending in the sun like a wide cut of cloth, sending out soundless flashes of lightning; one step—a flash, another step—a flash.

My hysterics were probably perceived by the goners as my being completely cured of my boyish pity. No one stood near our gate any more.

Was I cured . . ? Perhaps. Now I wouldn't have taken out a piece of bread to the "elephant," had he stood in front of my window right up until winter.

My mother kept moaning and groaning that I wasn't eating anything and getting thin, that there were big, dark shadows under my eyes . . . Three times a day she'd torture me. "Again you're staring at your plate? Again I haven't pleased you? Eat! Eat! It's cooked in milk and I've added butter. Just you dare turn away!"

She baked pies for me with cabbage and chopped egg, using the flour set aside for the holidays. I liked those pies very much. I ate them. I ate them and suffered.

Now I always awoke before dawn and never missed the sound of the cart going by which the stableman Abram was driving to the station public park.

The morning cart was thundering . . .

> Don't sleep, arise, my curly-headed one,
> Filling the workshops with clanging . . .

The cart thundered—a sign of the times! The cart rushing to collect the corpses of the enemies of the revolutionary fatherland.

I listened for it and realized I was a stupid, incorrigible boy. I couldn't do anything with myself—I felt sorry for my enemies!

Somehow one evening I was sitting with my father on the porch at home.

Recently my father's face had turned somehow dark, his eyelids red; in some way he reminded me of the station master who would stroll along the station public park in his red cap.

Suddenly below, near the porch, a dog appeared as if from out of the ground. It had lifelessly dull, somewhat dirty-yellow eyes, and its abnormally rumpled fur lay in clumps on its sides and back. It stared at us for a minute or two with its lifeless eyes and disappeared just as instantly as it had appeared.

"Why is its fur growing like that?" I asked.

My father kept quiet, then explained reluctantly: "It's falling out . . . From hunger. Its owner is probably growing bald himself from starvation."

And suddenly it hit me. It seemed I had found the most, most unfortunate being in our small town. Someone will take pity on the "elephants" and "shkeletons" once in a while, be it even in secret and feeling ashamed of himself; once in a while a fool like me will be found who will slip them some bread . . . But a dog . . . Even my father felt pity not for the dog but for its unknown master— "growing bald from starvation." The dog will die and even an Abram won't be found who'll take it away.

The next day, from morning on, I sat on the porch with pockets full of pieces of bread. I sat and patiently waited—would that same dog appear . . . ?

It appeared just like yesterday—suddenly, noiselessly—and stared at me with its lifeless, unwashed eyes. I made a motion to get out my bread and it dashed aside . . . Out of the corner of its eye it had time to see the bread I'd taken out, stood frozen to the spot, and stared at my hands from afar—lifelessly, without any expression.

"Come . . . Come on! Don't be afraid."

It looked and didn't move, ready to disappear at any moment. It didn't believe either my affectionate voice or my ingratiating smiles, or the bread in my hand. No matter how much I entreated it—it didn't approach, but it didn't disappear either.

After a half-hour struggle I finally threw it the bread. Without taking its lifeless, impenetrable eyes off the bread, it drew close to it, moving sideways, always sideways. One jump—and . . . no piece of bread and no dog.

The next morning—a new encounter, with the same exchange of lifeless glances, the same unyielding distrust of any affection in my voice and the bread I was offering out of kindness. The piece was grabbed only when it was thrown to the ground. There was no chance to give it a second piece.

The same thing the third morning, and the fourth . . . We didn't let a single day go by without meeting, but we didn't get any closer to one another. I never could teach it to take the piece of bread from my hand. Not once did I see any kind of expression in its yellow, dull, and lifeless eyes—not even a dog's fear, not to mention a dog's sweetness and friendly disposition.

It seems that even here I had encountered a victim of the times. I knew that some of those people who had been exiled fed on dogs—enticing them, killing and cutting them up. My acquaintance had probably fallen into their hands too. They couldn't kill it, but on the other hand they killed its trust in people forever. And it seems it didn't trust me in particular. Raised on a hungry street, it couldn't imagine a fool who was ready to give it food simply like that, without demanding anything in return . . . even gratitude.

Yes, even gratitude. That's a kind of payment as well, but it was quite enough for me that I was feeding it and supporting a life. It meant that I too had the right to eat and live myself.

With those pieces of bread I was feeding not the dog that had lost his fur from starvation but my own conscience.

I can't say that my conscience really liked this suspicious food. I continued to have pangs of conscience from time to time, but not such strong ones and not so dangerous to life.

Written in 1969–1970; published posthumously in 1988.
This version was prepared by N. Asmolova-Tendryakov
and published in 1995.

Translated and with annotations
by Valentina Brougher and Frank Miller

Yulii Daniel (Nikolai Arzhak)
(1925, Moscow — 1988, Moscow)

Born to the family of the Jewish writer Mark Daniel, Yulii Daniel fought and was wounded in WWII. Graduated from the School of Philology at the Moscow Regional Pedagogical Institute, then worked as a schoolteacher. Began publishing his literary translations of poetry in 1957. From 1958, along with Andrey Sinyavsky, published his original works abroad under the pseudonym "Nikolai Arzhak." Among these works, his novellas *This is Moscow Speaking* and *Atonement* are the best examples in Russian literature of working through the historical trauma of Stalinism. Daniel was arrested in 1965 and sentenced to five years of hard labor. After his release in 1970, he lived in Kaluga and could only publish as a translator and under a pseudonym. Died in Moscow in 1988. In 1991, Daniel was acquitted (along with Sinyavsky) of charges for the "lack of criminal content" in his actions.

THIS IS MOSCOW SPEAKING[1]

1

"Mew!" the little kitten whimpers
"Mew!" it can't meow properly yet.
Oppressed by boundless solitude,
It wanders dejectedly among the park benches.

Lolling on the benches there
Are people—crude, all-powerful, big,
Cars growl around like dogs.
It is afraid. What lies ahead?

Independence has suddenly befallen
Its pitiful, feline intellect.
"Mew!" whimpers the emancipated cat.
"Explain to me! Show mercy!"

No matter, it will be seasoned by wearisome wanderings.
It will be equipped with claws and fangs,
Its yellow teeth will flash
Like the glass of broken vodka bottles.
It will master "Meow." It will proclaim in a strong voice
That it will take on anything;

But for the moment, its heart is in pieces,
For the moment, it's "Mew! Mew! Mew!"

—Ilya Chur, *Moscow Boulevards*[2]

---

[1]   Published in: Yulii Daniel, *This is Moscow Speaking*, trans. Stuart Hood, Harold Shukman, John Richardson (London: Collins and Harvill, 1968), 20–66.

[2]   All poems in epigraphs are ascribed to fictional authors. Their actual author was Daniel.

When I try now to recall what happened last summer, I find it very difficult to remember things in their proper order and to give a coherent and consistent account of all I saw, heard and felt; but the day when it began, I remember perfectly, down to the most trifling detail.

We were sitting in the garden of the dacha. We had all arrived the day before, for Igor's birthday. We had drunk and made a lot of noise until the small hours, and gone to bed at last, expecting to sleep until noon; but the quiet of the countryside woke us at seven. We got up and all set out on various absurd activities, such as running about the garden in our shorts or exercising on the bar (no one managed more than five press-ups), and Volodya Margulis even doused himself with water from the well, although it was common knowledge that he never washed in the morning, claiming that it would make him late for work.

We sat and argued cheerfully about how to spend our Sunday. Naturally, we considered bathing, volleyball and boating, and one enthusiast even suggested a cross-country walk to the church in the next village.

"It's a very nice church," he said. "A very old one, I don't remember which century . . ."

But we laughed at him—no one felt like walking five and a half miles in the heat.

We must have been a strange sight—men and women between thirty and thirty-five, stripped as though for the beach. We tactfully tried to ignore the unexpected, comic and sad things about our appearance: the narrow shoulders and incipient bald pates of the men, the hairy legs and thick waists of the women. We had known each other for a long time, we remembered one another's dresses, suits and ties, but had never so far visualized ourselves in a state of nature, almost without clothes. Who would have thought, for instance, that Igor, always so elegant and neat, and successful with his women colleagues at the college where he taught, would turn out to have bandy legs? Looking at each other in the raw was as interesting, amusing and shame-making as looking at dirty postcards.

We sat, backsides firmly wedged into our chairs which looked so out of place on the grass, and spoke of our forthcoming athletic feats. Suddenly Lilya appeared on the verandah.

"I don't understand a word of it," she said.

"What is it you are supposed to understand? Come and join us."

"I don't understand a word of it," she repeated, smiling plaintively. "A broadcast . . . I heard only the very end . . . They're repeating it in ten minutes."

"The latest, twenty-first reduction in the price of horse collars and harnesses," said Volodya in an announcer's voice.

"Come inside," said Lilya. "Please do . . ."

So we all trooped into the room where the small, square plastic box of the loud-speaker hung modestly on a nail. In answer to our puzzled questions, Lilya did nothing but sigh.

"Just like a steam engine!" Volodya joked. "Steam-engine sighs—that's a good expression, don't you think! Straight out of Ilf and Petrov."[3]

"Stop pulling our legs, Lilya," Igor began. "I know how boring it is to wash the dishes by yourself . . ."

At this moment, a voice came from the radio.

"Moscow speaking," it said. "Moscow speaking. We will now broadcast a Decree of the Supreme Soviet of the Union of Soviet Socialist Republics, dated 16th July, 1960. In view of the growing prosperity . . ."

I looked around. Everyone stood casually listening to the rich baritone of the announcer—all except Lilya, who buzzed around like a photographer in front of children, gesturing at the loud speaker.

". . . To meet the wishes of the wide masses of the workers . . ."

"Give me a match, Volodya," said Zoya. We all went "sh!" at her. She shrugged her shoulders and, dropping the unlit cigarette into her cupped hand, turned away to the window.

". . . Sunday, August 10th, 1960 is declared . . ."

"Here it comes!" cried Lilya.

---

[3]   Famous Soviet satirical writers.

". . . Public Murder Day. On that day all citizens of the Soviet Union, who have reached the age of sixteen, are given the right to exterminate any other citizen with the exception of those listed in the first paragraph of the annex to this decree. The decree will be in force from 6 a.m. Moscow time until midnight. Annex . . . Paragraph 1. It is forbidden to kill (a) children under sixteen, (b) persons wearing the uniform of the armed forces or the militia and (c) transport workers who are on duty. Paragraph 2. Murders committed before or after the above mentioned period, and murders committed in the course of robbery or rape, will be regarded as crimes and punished in accordance with the existing laws. Moscow. The Kremlin. Chairman of the Presidium of the Supreme . . ."

The radio went on:

"We will now broadcast a concert of light music . . ."

We stood and looked at each other, dazed.

"Strange," I said. "Very strange. I can't see what can be the point."

"They'll explain," said Zoya. "The papers are bound to give an explanation."

"Comrades, it's a provocation!" Igor bustled about the room, looking for his shirt. "It's a trick. It's the Voice of America transmitting on our wave-length!"

He hopped on one foot, pulling on his trousers.

"Oh, sorry!" He ran out onto the verandah to do up his fly. No one smiled.

"The Voice of America?" said Volodya thoughtfully. "No, that's impossible. It's technically impossible." He looked at his watch. "It's half past nine. Our broadcasts are on the air. If they were transmitting on our wavelength, we'd be hearing theirs and ours . . ."

We went out again. Half-dressed people had come out onto the verandahs of the neighboring dachas. They huddled together in groups, shrugging their shoulders and gesticulating absurdly.

Zoya lit her cigarette at last. She sat on the steps, her elbows on her knees. I looked at her hips in the tight bathing suit, and her breasts half revealed by the low cut top. She was plump, but very pretty. Prettier than any of the other women. Her face was as always calm and a little sleepy. Behind her back they called her "Lady Phlegmatic."

Igor stood among us fully dressed, like a missionary among Polynesians. He had looked thoughtful ever since Volodya had asserted that the broadcast could not have been a trick played by trans-Atlantic gangsters. Evidently, he regretted having dismissed the whole thing as a provocation. But in my opinion he had nothing to worry about: there were not supposed to be any informers among us.

"What are we getting excited about, anyway?" he said cheerfully, "Zoya is right: there will be an explanation. What do you think, Tolya?"

"Damned if I know," I mumbled, "There's still almost a month to go before that—what d'you call it—Public . . ."

I broke off. Again we stared at one another puzzled.

"I know!" Igor shook his head. "It's all connected with international politics."

"With the Presidential elections in America? Is that what you mean?"

"Lilya dear, I wish you'd shut up! You don't know what you're talking about!"

"Let's go swimming," said Zoya, getting up. "Tolya dear, get me my bathing cap."

Even Zoya must have been shaken; or she would never have called me "Tolya dear" in front of everyone. But no one seemed to notice.

As we were walking to the river, Volodya caught up with me, took my arm and said, looking at me sadly with his Old Testament eyes:

"You know, Tolya, I think they're planning something against the Jews."

2

> Who would be able, who could stand it,
> If they hadn't arranged
> For the sale of masks to wear at home
> For every day, for every hour
> Disguise yourself as a lift-man or poet,
> Enthusiast or dandy,
> Knock at the window for a ticket.
> Shout!—but don't forget
> "No admittance without masks."
>
> —Ilya Chur, *Tickets Are Being Sold*

So here I am, writing it all down, and wondering just why I'm doing it. I can never have these notes published in our country. There's no one I can even show them to. Should I send them abroad? But firstly, that's impossible in practice, and secondly, what I intend to write about has already been written up in hundreds of foreign newspapers, and the radio has rattled on about it day and night; no, it's already been done to death abroad. Besides, to tell the truth, it isn't very pretty to appear in print in anti-Soviet publications.

I'm pretending, of course. I know why I'm writing. I need to work out for myself what really did happen. Above all, what happened to me. Here I sit at my desk. I'm thirty-five. I still work for that idiotic technical publishing house. My appearance hasn't changed. Nor have my tastes. I still like poetry as I did before, I still like a drink, I still like women. And they, by and large, like me. I fought in the war. I killed. I was nearly killed myself. Every time a woman touches the scar on my hip, she snatches back her hand and asks in a shocked whisper: "Good heavens, what's that?" "It's a wound," I say, "a scar from a bullet." "You poor thing," she says. "Did it hurt very much?" In general, everything is as before. Anyone of my acquaintances, friends, colleagues might easily say: "Well, Tolya, you haven't changed a bit!" Only I know: that day pulled me up with a start and made me face myself. I know that I had to get to know myself all over again.

And there's another thing. I'm not a writer. I used to write poetry as a boy, and still do on special occasions; I've reviewed a few plays—I thought I might gain a foothold in literature in this way, but nothing came of it. Yet I continue to write. I'm not a graphomaniac. I meet a lot of them in my profession: every graphomaniac believes he is a genius, whereas I know that I have little or no talent. But I very much want to write. The great advantage of my position—the really pleasant thing about it—is that I know in advance that no one will read me, so I write fearlessly whatever comes into my head! If I want to write,

> And like black Africa the piano
> Bares its negroid teeth,

I write it. And no one will accuse me of pretentiousness or of holding colonialist views. If I want to write about the government and say that they're all rabble-rousers, hypocrites and, in general, no good—I write that as well . . . I can afford the luxury of being a communist when I'm all by myself.

To be completely honest, I still hope that I'll have readers—not now, of course, but after many many years, when I'm dead. As Pushkin said: "One day, some industrious monk will read my diligent, anonymous work . . ." And it's nice to think about it.

Well, now that I have revealed myself to my imaginary reader, I can continue.

We never managed to have any fun at all that day. Our jokes fell flat, our games bored us, we didn't drink and broke up early.

When I went to work next morning in Moscow I foresaw the inevitable commotion about the Decree and thought that some people would say what they thought and others would keep quiet. To my surprise, almost everyone kept quiet. Two or three people asked me: "Well, what d'you think of it?" I mumbled: "I don't know . . . We'll have to wait and see," and there the conversation ended.

A day later, a long editorial entitled "In Preparation for Public Murder Day" appeared in *Izvestia*. It said very little about the Decree itself, but talked as usual of "growing prosperity . . . tremendous advances . . . true democracy . . . only in our country . . . for the first time in history . . . visible signs . . . the bourgeois press" and so on. It added that no damage was to be done to public property—arson and dynamiting were therefore forbidden—and that the Decree did not apply to prisoners serving their sentence in jail. And that was that. The article was read and re-read from the first word to the last, no one was any the wiser, but, for some reason, everyone felt more confident. I suppose the actual style of the article—its routine solemnity and prosy pomposity—was somehow reassuring. There was nothing so extraordinary after all—we had "Artillery Day" and "Soviet Press Day", so why not "Public Murder Day"? . . . Buses and trains would be running as usual, and the police were not to be harmed, so public order would be assured. Everything reverted to normal.

About ten days passed. Then something started which is difficult to define: a kind of restlessness, a general feeling of unease. I don't know how to put it into words. People were on edge and rushed about. In the underground, at the cinema, in the street, people would go up to one another, smile obsequiously and begin a conversation—about their ailments, about fishing, about nylon stockings—about anything at all. And, provided they were not immediately interrupted but given a hearing, they shook hands for a long time with their listeners, looking gratefully and confidently into their eyes. Others—chiefly young people—became rowdy and insolent, each in his own way; more than usual, they sang and recited poetry (for the most part Esenin) at the top of their voices in the street. Incidentally, on the subject of poetry, *Literature and Life* published a selection of poems devoted to the forthcoming event by Bezymensky, Mikhalkov, Sofronov and others.[4] Unfortunately, I can't get a copy of the issue now, although I've tried, but I remember part of Sofronov's poem:

> The lathes of Rostov's Agricultural
> Machinery Plant were humming,
> The factory whistles were singing,
> And our great Party
> Seized the Trotskyists by the collar.
>
> I was seventeen at the time,
> I was far from maturity,

---

[4]   Loyalist Soviet poets well known for their capacity to turn out verses on the Party's rulings and slogans.

I couldn't tell people apart,
So my aim when hitting them was poor.

Perhaps I sang more tunefully then,
But I was not calm and brave;
Feeling pity, I left some alive,
Others I could not finish off . . .

Jokes circulated in great numbers. Volodya Margulis, hurrying from one friend to another, repeated them, roaring with laughter. Having fired off his entire supply at me, he told me that Igor, addressing a meeting at his college, had said that the Decree showed the wisdom of the Party's policy, that it was added evidence of the growth of creative initiative among the masses—and so on in the usual vein.

"Can you believe it, Tolya!" he said, "I always knew Igor was a careerist and all that, but I didn't expect this of him."

"Why not?" I asked. "What's so special about it? He was told to make a speech, and he did. If you were a party member like Igor, you'd have reeled one off, too."

"Me! Never! First, I wouldn't join the Party for anything, and second . . ."

"First, second! Stop shouting! Are you any better than Igor? Didn't you jabber about nationalism[5] at school at the time of 'the Doctors' Plot?'"

The moment I said this, I was sorry. It was a sore point with him. He could not forgive himself for having for a while believed what the newspapers had said about the "Plot."

"Better tell me how you're getting on with Nina," I said amicably. "How long is it since you've seen her?"

Volodya brightened up.

"You know, Tolya, it's not easy to love as I do," he said. "It's not easy. I called her up yesterday, and said I wanted to see her, but she said . . ."

---

[5] The "critique of Zionist nationalism" was used to orchestrate the anti-Semitic campaign in 1950–52. The campaign reached its highest point with the so-called "Doctor's Plot," in which Jewish doctors were charged for the attempted murder of several Soviet leaders. The accusation was dismissed as false after Stalin's death.

And he told me, in great detail, there and then, what she had said to him and he to her, and what they had both said to one another.

"Tolya, you know me, I'm not a sentimental type, but at that point I very nearly burst into tears . . ."

I listened to him and wondered how people manage to create problems for themselves out of nothing. Volodya was married, he had two children, he taught literature, he was the best schoolmaster in the district and was altogether no fool. But his love affairs! True, his wife was a bitch, you'd run to any woman from a wife like that. All right, let him run! But why the agonies, the red-hot passions, the small-town Hamlet act? And why the talk of "moral obligations" and "divided loyalties" and "she believes in me"? Incidentally, "she believes in me" was said of both his wife and his latest heart-throb. I look at this kind of thing more simply. Right from the start—no play acting, no diplomacy, no obligations: let's be honest. If I marry, I won't worry about problems of Volodya's kind, I'll simply say in advance: "I'm married, you know, I don't intend to divorce, but I like you very much. Does that suit you? Wonderful, where and when shall we meet? It doesn't suit you? That's too bad, goodbye, perhaps you'll think it over . . ." Just like that, though not quite so crudely, of course. And I think that's much better than talking a lot of blah about incompatibility with your wife and saying: "I admire her, of course, but . . ." I've never really hurt a woman up to now, and that's only because I've never let them have illusions about me.

Volodya talked for another half hour about his complicated love life and went away. I showed him out but he immediately rang the bell again, put his head through the half-open door and whispered so that the neighbors shouldn't hear:

"Tolya, if there's a Jewish pogrom on the 10th of August, I'll fight. It's not going to be a Babii Yar.[6] I'll shoot the bastards. Look."

He opened his jacket and showed me the butt of an officer's pistol sticking out of his inside pocket; he had kept it since his army days.

---

[6]   Nazis massacred Jews at Babii Yar, near Kiev, in 1941.

"They won't get me as easily as that . . ."

When at last he left, I stood for a long time in the middle of the room.

Who were "they"?

3

> No, Alcinous, you are wrong: there
> is indeed infinity in nature,
> The stupidity and baseness of people
> are an illustration of it.
>
>   —Cyril Zamoysky, *Experiments and Sermons*

"Tolya, why can't you be serious! Try to understand one simple thing . . ."

My neighbor was washing dishes with a mop. His stomach, covered with grey hair and bulging out of his tight undershirt and his trousers, rested on the edge of the sink. He was getting very worked up, although I had not said a word.

". . . no, no, don't misunderstand me. You know me, I'm the last man in the world to be impressed by newspaper clichés. But facts are facts, and you've got to face them . . . It's true that the political consciousness of the masses has increased! Therefore the State has the right to carry out a wide-scale experiment, it has the right to hand over some of its functions to the people! Look at our squads of volunteers co-operating with the militia, our Komsomol patrols, our People's Home Guard for the maintenance of public order— these are facts! And facts which are highly significant. Of course the volunteers make their mistakes too, they have lapses so to speak— some tight trousers have been slashed and some girls have had their heads shaved[7] but that's inevitable! That's production wastage! You can't make an omelet without breaking eggs! The present Decree is nothing but the logical continuation of a process which has already

---

[7] The formation of vigilante groups who assist the police to fight "hooliganism" is a notable feature of the post-Stalin era. There have been frequent cases of these groups persecuting young people who dress in Western style (*stiliagi*).

begun the process of democratization. Democratization of what, you'll ask? Democratization of the organs of executive authority. The ideal, of course—don't misunderstand me—is the gradual assumption of executive authority by the masses, at the lowest level, so to speak. No, I've put that badly—we don't have any low levels— but you know what I mean . . . And believe me—an experienced old lawyer, hundreds, thousands, tens of thousands have been through my hands—believe me, what the people will do in the first place is settle accounts with spongers, the dregs of society . . . You remember Tolstoy! "They want to fall on them, to make an end of them once and for all!" That's what they want to do Tolya—as a community, collectively, in the good old Russian way . . ."

I was hoping against hope that he would drop the soapy dish and he finally cracked it against the sink. The noise brought his wife hurrying from their room: she gave a disapproving look at the pieces and at me, and said in an even voice:

"Peter, go to your room."

They didn't keep that fool long enough in the concentration camp, I said to myself as I went to answer the doorbell. Zoya came in. We went through to my room and Zoya, sighing with relief, threw off her shoes. I like seeing a woman taking off her shoes— the shape of the leg changes, the line immediately becomes cozy, friendly, unsophisticated.

"You look as if you were wearing white slippers," I said, pointing to her untanned feet. "Show me where else you're white."

"I wanted to have a talk with you," she said. "Oh well, all right, later on . . ."

I kissed her.

"Lock the door," she said.

. . . We lay a little away from one another; Zoya's skin was cool in spite of the heat; her light-brown body had three white bands round it—on the breasts, the hips and the feet. She lay beside me, sprawling free and unashamed, beautiful and resplendent, like a clown at the circus, and I felt that I loved her very much. Equally freely and unashamedly, I felt like winking at some imaginary observer and saying to him: "look what a woman has fallen to my lot!" I lay and thought that probably what went on between us was what is called "life": struggle, conquest, mutual capitulation, assertion and violent denial, a deep awareness of oneself and complete loss of self-alienation—all at one and the same time. At that moment I didn't care that she was married, or that I was not the only one to possess her intelligent, submissive, ever-waiting flesh, that she had a husband who made love to her in accordance with his legal rights, or that in a month my sister would return from the seaside and Zoya would no longer be able to come to my flat—we would once more climb into attics and loiter in doorways, like stray cats, and I would again be surprised and even a little shocked by her ability to surrender in the most unsuitable circumstances, and be very grateful to her for doing so—at the moment I cared nothing for any of this. I lay and wailed for her to speak.

And she spoke.

"Tolya," she said. "It will soon be Public Murder Day."

She said it in a very simple, business-like way, just as she might have said: "It will soon be New Year's Day" or "May Day."

"What about it?" I asked. "What has that got to do with us?"

"Haven't you had enough of hiding?" she asked. "Now we can change everything."

"I don't understand," I muttered. But it was a lie—I understood at once.

"Let's kill Paulie."

That's exactly what she said: "Paulie." Not "my husband" or "Paul," but "Paulie." I felt my lips turning to wood. "Zoya, are you in your right mind? What are you saying!" Zoya slowly turned her head and rubbed her cheek against my shoulder.

"Tolya darling, please don't get excited, just think calmly. We'll never get another chance like this. I've thought it all out. You'll come to us the night before. You'll say you want to spend the Day with us. Paulie and I have already decided not to go out, and you and I will do it together. Afterwards you'll move in with me. And we'll get married. I wouldn't involve you in it, I'd do it all myself, it's just that I'm afraid I won't be able to manage it alone."

I lay and listened, and every word caught me by the throat and choked me, like a spasm.

"Tolya, why don't you say something?" I cleared my throat and said:

"Go away."

She didn't understand.

"Where?"

"To hell," I said.

Zoya looked me in the eyes for a few moments, then got up and began to dress. She put on her bra, her pants, her petticoat. I watched her disappear inside her clothes. She threw on her dress, thrust her feet into her shoes and began to do her hair.

Having finished, she picked up her bag and unlocked the door. On the threshold she turned and said softly:

"You sissy."

She went. I heard the front door click.

I got up and dressed. I made the bed. I swept the floor. I went through a great many movements, concentrating on each. I didn't want to think.

4

> I hate them so much that I have spasms,
> I scream and I tremble; oh, if only all these whores
> Could be gathered together and wiped out!
>
> —George Bolotin, *Trumpets of Time*

I had to think all the same. It may sound stupid, but what staggered me most of all was that word "sissy" which Zoya had flung at me: the fact is, I am not a coward, I proved it to myself during the war and several times since. Yet Zoya had decided that I was. No, it wasn't cowardice, it was just that it was crazy—suddenly to kill Paulie, poor, meek, uncomplaining, unsuspecting Paulie. All right, we had been deceiving him—if he'd known he would of course have suffered; we'd spent his money on drink, we made fun of him behind his back and to his face; but all the same—to kill him? Why? What for? If it came to that, if she just wanted to marry me, couldn't she get a divorce? It meant . . . Did it mean that for her murder was not merely the means of getting rid of an unloved, silly, elderly husband? It meant that there was some purpose in it which I couldn't understand. Did she hate him, and want to get even with him? Yes, of course, she wanted to get even with him because she had fallen in love with him at nineteen, and because all he could now talk about was "the fantastic achievements of science," remind her to take care of the key of their flat where they kept their money, and tell Jewish and Armenian anecdotes. Obviously she must hate him. And if she hated him, she was capable of killing. That I could understand. Hatred gives the right to kill. Out of hatred I could myself . . . could I? Yes, of course, I could. Undoubtedly. Whom do I hate? Whom have I hated in the course of my life? School years don't count, but since I've been grown up? At college, I hated one of the teachers who deliberately failed me four times running in my exams. Well, to hell with him, that was a long time ago. The bosses in various departments where I worked. Yes, they were crooks. They made my blood boil. I'd like to punch them on the nose, the bastards. Who else? The writer K who writes novels in the spirit of the Black Hundreds.[8] Yes, yes, I remember saying I would kill him if I were sure that nothing would happen to me. The swine deserves to be taught a lesson! Such a lesson that he'll never pick up his pen in his life again . . . And what about the fat-faced masters of our destiny, who sit at meetings and preside—our leaders and teachers, true sons of the people, who get congratulatory messages from collective farmers near Ryazan and metal workers in Krivoy Rog, from the Emperor of Ethiopia, and from teachers' congresses, and from the President of the United States, and the staffs of public lavatories? Those best friends of Soviet athletes, writers, textile workers, and the color-blind and the insane? What should be done with them? Should they be forgiven? Even for 1937?[9] And the post-war madness, when the country, hysterical, possessed, bedeviled, was devouring itself? They think that once they've desecrated the

---

[8]   It is interesting that a current term among Soviet intellectuals for the "reactionaries" is *chernosotentsy*, intended to indicate their spiritual kinship with the extreme right-wing, anti-intellectual, and anti-Semitic groups ("Black Hundreds") under Nicholas II. Their main appeal, as it was then, is to "working-class" chauvinism. Concomitantly, more progressive trends in art and literature are often colloquially described as "left-wing" (*Translator's Note*).

[9]   1937: Peak year of Stalin's pre-war purges (*Translator's Note*).

grave of the Great Moustache, they've done all that was required.[10]
No, they should be treated differently. Do you still remember how
it's done! The fuse. Pull out the pin. Throw. Fall flat on the ground.
Head down! The explosion—and now a leap forward. As you run,
fire your machine gun, fanning out at belly level. A burst. Another.
Another . . . And there they lie, cut to shreds and riddled with
bullets. It's slippery: your feet slip. Who's that? Crawling, dragging
his guts along the parquet floor strewn with plaster. And that one,
hung with medals, who accompanies the Chief on his trips? Why
is he so thin? Why does he wear a padded coat? I've seen him once
before, crawling up the slope, spilling his blue and red stomach
in the dust. And these! I've seen them too. Only then they were
wearing belt-buckles with the inscription "Gott mit Uns," caps with
red stars, knee boots, low boots, foot rags, forage caps—Russians,
Germans, Georgians, Rumanians, Jews, Hungarians, in tunics, with
placards, in medical squads, with spades. An army truck rolls over
the corpse, then two more, then eight, then forty, and you too will lie
there flattened like a frog—we've seen all that before!

I got up, went over to the window and wiped my sweaty face
on the curtain. Then I went into the kitchen, washed in the sink and
put on my jacket. I couldn't stay at home another moment.

I walked along the street sweltering in the August sun; coming
towards me were housewives with shopping bags; little boys
were flying toy airplanes; perspiring old men wandered along the
pavement, stopping at each mineral-water stall. I reached the corner
of Arbat and Smolensk Square and stopped. It would be nice to call
on someone. But who was there? It was summer, everyone was in
the country. Or if not in the country, then probably at the Silver
Copse[11] or somewhere else where they could bathe. It would be nice
to have a drink. It occurred to me that an artist friend of mine, Sasha

---

[10] Stalin: The desecration of his grave is to be understood figuratively: the story was
written before Stalin's body was removed from the Lenin Mausoleum (*Translator's
Note*).

[11] A riverside beach near Moscow.

Chuprov, lived near here, on the way to Kiev station. Even if he were out, I could sit in his room: he never locked his door.

I went into the food shop at the corner and wandered through, looking for the wine department. I walked up to the counters and watched the attendants. They were all alike in their uniforms, but their manner varied—businesslike and correct at the sausage counter, apathetic and supercilious in the fruit department, coy and obliging in the pastry section, muddled and inefficient in the grocery. In the wine department which I found at last, they were condescending and a little too familiar. I stood and watched the bottles on the revolving stand, a cone rising beside a pillar. Here emotions were stored. Poured into bottles and sealed with wax, they were given different labels: brandy, vodka, Georgian wine; but in actual fact the bottles were filled with sadness, gaiety, unbridled anger, touching trustfulness, irritability and recklessness. The emotions were biding their time. In due course they would come out of their glass prisons, and hear stupid farewell toasts, and run riot in hands clutching at tablecloths, on lips kissing at random, in lungs taking in extra air in order to sing "Moscow Nights" lustily. "Time is on our side," they told themselves, as their many colors gleamed in the electric light "Our cause is just, our day will come . . ."

I bought a bottle of brandy (Georgian, as I hadn't enough money for a better brand) and a lemon, and left the shop.

Chuprov was at home.

"Oh, it's you," he said gloomily. "Come in . . ."

The large, light room was incredibly untidy. There was an open sketch book on the floor, and rolls of paper on and underneath the desk and on the window-sill. The owner, fully dressed, tossed and turned on the bed, hitching his feet on and off the headboard.

"What's the matter?" I asked.

"Those bastards," he replied. "I worked and worked, and it was all a goddamned waste of time."

"What were you working at?"

"Posters, naturally." Chuprov painted left-wing pictures and was known in liberal circles as avant-garde. But he couldn't sell these pictures, tainted as they were by the corrupting influence of the West, he was afraid of getting involved with foreigners, and he had to eat. So he painted posters of girls with shining faces against a background of the Kremlin walls, of miners in full underground regalia, marching confidently towards the happy future, of young engineers in overalls, with calipers in their breast-pockets and the *History of the Communist Party* under their arms. He was paid well but at irregular intervals.

"Have they turned them down?" I asked. "Didn't you have a contract?"

"That's just the joke—I didn't. I thought there would be no competition, so in view of the occasion I decided to take a risk. I painted a non-conformist one, in my own, free manner, can you imagine? I took it to them, and they . . ."

"Wait a minute. In view of what occasion?"

"Where have you been all this time? Public Murder Day, of course. You don't suppose they'll manage without posters! Anyway, listen and don't interrupt. I took it to them, and the Chief—an academic stick-in-the-mud, all he needs is a skull-cap. 'You've brought it to the wrong place,' he says. 'This may be all right for *Life* but not for us.' And so on and so on: 'Great events in the life of the country . . . the Party has given us a lead . . . great ideas need clear expression . . . to inspire . . . to call to action . . . look at this! . . .' And he shows me a poster by Artemyev and Krants. Well, you won't believe me, but there was nothing to look at! I'm not saying it because they turned mine down and accepted theirs, you know how I regard this kind of work; it's just pot-boiling, nothing else. But you have to have a conscience all the same. If you do it, do it properly. Don't skimp it. Go through with it. All they'd painted, the bastards, was a lot of dummies, you couldn't tell the living from the dead, and a tower crane in the background—and there you are, a lovely, colorful poster! I don't give a damn for their money, I made plenty over May Day—but it's the work, the ideas! It's the waste I regret. When will they at last understand that we're living in the mid-twentieth century and that art must . . . I don't know . . . get into top gear, move at a new tempo . . ."

He fired it all off and swore; the ash fell off his cigarette and dropped onto the pillow.

"Listen, Sasha," I said cautiously. "That rejected poster of yours—could I have a look at it?"

"Why not? There it is, beside the wall."

I cleared a space on the floor and unrolled the poster. Against the background of an enormous, rising or possibly setting, sun stood the stylized figures of a boy and girl; the sun shone on their backs and their red shadows stretched right across the poster, merging in the bottom left hand corner with a dark red puddle at the foot of a stylized house; while in the bottom right hand corner lay a corpse, knees drawn up and arms outstretched.

"Well, how do you like it?" asked Sasha.

I thought for a moment and said:

"Lots of expression."

I risked nothing: I knew for certain that Sasha had never read Huxley.

"D'you mean it?" Sasha was radiant.

"Yes," I continued, "but I think the corpse is too garish."

Sasha jumped off the bed and, sticking out his lips, examined his work.

"You may be right," he said. "And you know why that is? I should have stylized it more, not made it so realistic, so true to life . . ."

We drank brandy. Sasha talked about his work; I listened, thinking it was all Zoya's fault. If it hadn't been for her I wouldn't have given that damned Murder Day a second thought. Why should it concern me? To hell with it . . . But Zoya was a bitch. Paulie should be told. No, there was no point in doing so now. Since I had refused, she would be too scared to do anything. Bitch, murderess! Everything had been so nice, we'd been so happy, but now I could never touch her again. She wouldn't let me, anyway. It was because of her I had to sit and listen to the drunken outpourings of Chuprov. Nonconformist! Avant-garde! If tomorrow they announced a "Homosexual Day" he'd jump up and reach for his brush. He'd draw a graph of the growth in the incidence of homosexuality since 1913. I don't want to kill any more. *I don't want to.*

"What don't you want?" asked Chuprov.

"I don't want any more to drink."

"There's none left anyway. But why don't you want to? Wait a minute, I'll go and buy some . . . Or I'll tell you what—would you like to meet a friend of mine, an old man. A wonderful old man! He writes poetry. Come on, come on, you'll be grateful to me afterwards, you've never seen anyone like it."

"All right."

I got up, feeling sick.

"Let's go, Sasha! Let's go, Alexander Chuprov! Let's go, you genius of a painter! Is he a genius too? Will he explain everything?"

"Everything! He can explain everything—he's a waiter."

5

> They lie in wait in any doorway,
> Reeking of carbolic acid.
> They're in the grass springing up from the earth,
> In old books, moldering on the shelf.
> Everywhere you can hear the muffled whisper,
> And every phrase conceals an evil purpose.
> They're in the water flowing in the shower,
> And in the hoarse gurgle of the toilet bowl.
>
> —George Bolotin, *Devils of Death*

While we were buying vodka, looking for a taxi and driving to somewhere near the Danilov market, I had time to sober up a little. "Why and where am I going?" I wondered. "What the hell have I to do with this old man? Though why not after all . . ." I had to get through Sunday somehow, so why not with the old boy? I'd quarreled with my girl, so what? I might as well go and see the old boy.

Sasha stopped the taxi and paid.

"You sit here a moment, I'll go up and find out if we can see him. I won't be long."

I sat on a bench on the boulevard. Trams were clanking behind my back. Young fathers wheeled baby carriages along the footpaths. Freshly scoured soldiers were out with their girls; talking decorously and keeping their hands to themselves: it was still daylight.

I looked up at the new, seven-and-eight-story buildings here and there on either side of the boulevard. Their light brick faces and clear-washed eyes gazed with benevolent encouragement at the young leaves in the front gardens. But in the gaps between these showy, optimistic frontages, the old buildings of the thirties stared, gloomily aware of their own superiority. Wedged at the back of the yards, their corners facing the boulevard, they stood motionless yet seeming to advance, and such was their evident self-righteousness and unshakeable loyalty to their ideals that were the Architect to rise from the grave and point with his finger, these grey flatirons would move forward, sweeping aside the cardboard facades, grinding to dust the automatic lifts, the volumes of Hemingway, and all the new and fashionable people who had been secretly thumbing their noses at them.

Chuprov appeared beside me suddenly, as though he had sprung out of the ground.

"Come on," he said. "The Maestro is at home."

I followed him, bumping against the bottles stuffed into his pockets.

A little old man with twitching eyebrows welcomed us into the spick-and-span one-room flat. He wore slacks and an old-fashioned pajama-top tied with a cord and looking like a hussar's tunic; from under it hung a black Russian shirt with white buttons like the stops on an accordion.

"Come in," he said. "Delighted to meet you. My name is Gennady Vasilyevich Arbatov. And yours? Do come in and sit down, and forgive the untidiness. I'm living a bachelor life, as my wife is away in the country."

We went into the large, long room. The furniture was new, the well-washed cloth on the solid round table was carefully protected by a transparent sheet of plastic; a range of cushions lay like peas in a pod on the divan bed. One wall was completely masked by grey curtains.

"My friend is very interested in your poems, Gennady Vasilyevich," said Chuprov. "Would you read us some?"

"You're so quick off the mark, Sasha. Always in a hurry, always rushing somewhere. And may I ask where? Everything in its turn. Time flies fast enough, you needn't hurry it. Now we'll have a drink with your friend, we'll talk about this and that, we'll put out feelers like ants: The poems won't run away. Poetry is good for the digestion, as an old friend of mine used to say. Don't you agree, Anatoli Nikolayevich?"

"You needn't stand on ceremony with him. Call him Tolya."

"Sorry, my dear Sasha, I can't. Your friend and I have only just met. I accept everything about modern life, I welcome it, I wish it well, but I can't accept this new-fangled habit. I've been called Gennady Vasilyevich ever since the age of fifteen. And rightly so, for when you address a man respectfully, it exalts him, it raises him, so to speak, above the sinful earth. What do you think, Anatoli Nikolayevich?"

"Whichever you prefer," I said. "Call me a pot if you like . . ."

"So long as you don't put me in the oven," the old man finished the saying. He was laying the table quickly and neatly; vodka glasses, forks, small plates, radishes, pickled cucumbers, sliced bread and salami appeared with lightning speed. During all this time he never stopped talking, his words rounded, cozy and old-fashioned, like forks with bone handles. He filled the glasses and we drank.

"Yes, you are right about the pot and the oven, Anatoli Nikolayevich. Though sometimes people call you a pot and put you into the oven as well . . ."

"People are like wild animals," Chuprov said gloomily. He was evidently thinking of his rejected poster.

"You shouldn't say that, Sasha. You shouldn't speak disparagingly of wild beasts. May I draw your attention to the fact that when people are in a kindly mood their favorite subject of conversation is the animal world. And why? Because everyone likes wild animals. They'll argue about anything else—pictures, say, or books, or sculpture. Not to mention politics. But never about animals. I read an illustrated article last spring about zoos in various countries. It was by the director of the Moscow Zoo. I enjoyed it enormously. You might wonder what I could possibly care about a tapir being born in Italy? Yet I read about it and felt happy. And a lot of other things like that. Soon wild beasts will be the only link, the only point of contact between human beings. Wild beasts are not just animals, my friends—they are the bearers and the guardians of the spirit."

His last words were so out of keeping with his cozy manner that I looked up in surprise. He noticed it and paused. Sasha broke in:

"Let's drink to the baby tapir! Cheers!"

We had several more drinks. The old man was getting drunk and the more drunk he got the more polished was his speech. Crossing his legs and darting his eyes to left and right at Sasha and me, he lowered his voice and spoke clearly and fast:

"No one knows what is hidden in another's heart. Our conversation now for instance is an insane, suicidal self-exposure. If you literally stripped your clothes off in the street, you'd be taken to the police station and fined, and people would disapprove—that's all! But it's much more serious to be frank, to bare your soul. Who knows if some word of mine, some idea I express will not sting you, wound you, burrow into you so deep that this poisoned dart can be extracted only at the cost of my life. And you will rush at me to kill me in self-defense! And who or what could stand in your way? How can you tell what hatred you may have inspired in someone else, or indeed many others? And why? By an ill-chosen word, or by your way of eating, or by the shape of your nose? Incidentally," he turned to me, "are you a Jew?"

"No," I replied, feeling my nose. "Why, do I look like one?"

"Yes, there's something about you. Now, those Jews are a wise people. They live in fear. Not in fear of God but in fear of man. They regard everyone as a potential enemy. And they are right. What can be more terrifying than a human being? A wild animal kills for food. It has no vanity, no lust for power, no ambition—it doesn't care a damn for all that. It isn't envious. But we—how can we know who is thirsting for our blood, or whom we have offended without knowing it, by the fact of our very existence. We don't know anything . . ."

"Wild animals fight to the death over their females," said Sasha.

Gennady Vasilyevich frowned.

"That's a different matter. That's the instinct of procreation. Animals have wisdom and simplicity: they don't fall in love. But a man has only to fall in love and he is ready to play the dirtiest of tricks, to commit any crime. No wonder the Romans used to say: 'Femina mors animae' — 'Woman is death to the soul.' But that's not what I'm talking about. I ask you, Sasha, and you, Anatoli: are you sure that among your friends and the people you know there is no one who could kill you? I know I can't be sure for myself. And thinking about death—you're young, you don't think about it, but I'm old. I lie at night on that divan over there—you see it has a wooden back—tossing and turning and knocking against the wood and I say to myself: 'That's what my coffin will be like—wood beside me, wood on top, wood all round . . .'"

He drew breath; his head was shaking.

"And there's nothing you can do about it. Being cautious, keeping to yourself—it's all a waste of time And so is all their talking and arguing and fussing . . ."

"Who are 'they,' Gennady Vasilyevich?" I asked.

"All those . . . those scribblers," he replied wearily.

He got up unsteadily and drew back the grey curtains; the wall behind it was lined with bookshelves. Gaudy in their bright cloth bindings, the authors burst into the room like a Tartar horde, tearing to shreds the semblance of security and the deceptive quiet of the middle class flat, bringing with them the lumbering, creaking carts of philosophical systems, the crooked mirrors and the swords of self-analysis, the blunt battering-rams of all-embracing pessimism, and the stallions of civilization, bared teeth covered with the yellow foam of hatred of mankind, hooves trampling into pulp the grey-haired evangelists who hold up to the oblivious skies the scrolls of their commandments decomposing into atomic dust . . .

"Everyone is ready to drown his neighbor in a spoonful of water." Chuprov sighed and poured out the last of the vodka.

Chuprov and I walked home through the deserted streets. Policemen stood at the crossroads, neon-signs glared on grocery stores, heels echoed sharply on the pavement, but not even this sound, which I usually liked, could please me now. There was only one week left till Public Murder Day.

6

> Revolt—you wouldn't dare:
> Run away—you couldn't if you tried,
> And anyway it's all the same;
> What can be the soldier's lot!
> Inglorious death
> Or deathless glory . . .
>
> —George Bolotin, *The Halt*

I stopped going to work. I rang up the office and said I was ill. I stayed in bed or wandered about my room, and spent hours drawing faces on the wrapping paper of the salami delivered from the shop.

The only visitor I had in all that time was Volodya Margulis who, the moment he came in, asked me idiotically: "All the same, why should they issue a Decree like that?" "They" were the government. I made no reply and Volodya, delighted at my having no opinion of my own, proceeded to explain that the whole business was inevitable, and lay at the very root of the doctrine of socialism.

"Why?" I asked.

"Well, of course it does. It's all in keeping: they were bound to legalize murder, to make it a commonplace happening, that's why they don't explain anything. Before, they used to explain, to try to persuade people."

"What rubbish. When?"

"During the Revolution."

"No, you're wrong. The Revolution wasn't made like this or for this purpose."

"And what about 1937?"

"What about it?"

"It was the same thing. Complete freedom to kill. Then, at least, they made more of a show of it. Now they just say: 'Go ahead and kill'—and that's that! And another thing, in those days the killers had a whole apparatus at their disposal, an enormous staff, whereas now you have to do it yourself—self-service!"

"Oh, shut up, Volodya. Your anti-Soviet monologues are no longer funny."

"Are you taking offence on behalf of the Soviet regime? Do you think one should stand up for it?"

"For the real Soviet regime—certainly one should."

"Would that be the one without any communists? Like in Sholokhov's *And Quiet Flows the Don*?"

"Go to hell!"

"A most convincing reply!" snapped Volodya. "And would you . . ."

"That's enough," I said.

We sat without talking, and after a while he left, offended. I lay down on the bed again, and thought things over. I didn't care why the Decree had been put out. And there was no point in producing scientific explanations and in jabbering about the Revolution. I don't like that sort of thing. My father was a commissar during the Civil War and it's my opinion that he knew what he was fighting for. I don't remember him well—he was one of the first to be arrested in 1936—but I found his letters after my mother's death. I read them, and in my opinion people of my generation have no right to talk loosely about those times. Each one of us can and must decide for himself. That's all we have left, it's all we can do, but even that's a lot. Too much, in fact.

That Arbatov, the old man on Danilov Boulevard, had upset me. I will not and I cannot kill, but others might be willing and able. And their target might be myself, Tolya Kartsev! Once again, as on the day of my last meeting with Zoya, I went over the list of my enemies. There was that one, but he could never bring himself to kill. This one might, but he would be scared. That other, now, he could and would—with a brick from behind a corner. Who else was there? Could so-and-so? No, he was not my enemy. Wasn't he? How could I be sure? Perhaps he was. Besides, must it be an enemy who killed me? Any passer-by, a drunk, a crazy fool might shoot me in the face just for the fun of watching me jerk my legs as I lay spilling out my life on the pavement, and as my nose sharpened, and my cheeks fell in and my jaw dropped. As my eyes, my hands, my words, my silence, my sea, my women, my clumsy poems all escaped through the hole in my head.

Damn it! To hell with it! I couldn't let them kill me! I must live. I'll go into hiding, I'll barricade myself, I'll sit it out in my room.

I don't want to die. *I do not want to.* There's no disgrace in wanting to live. Better live like a dog than . . .

Stop! I must get a grip on myself. I must calm down. Better a live dog. I'll buy food the night before, and I won't go out that Sunday. I'll lie in bed and read Anatole France. I'm very fond of Anatole France. *Penguin Island. The Revolt of the Angels.* And there's also *Anatole France in Carpet Slippers.* Whenever I happened to spend the night at Zoya's she'd make me wear Paulie's dressing gown and slippers, and she'd laugh and laugh. At the time I couldn't understand why it amused her so much, but now I know. She was imagining Paulie dead and herself married to me. I wonder how she meant to kill him. I'll sit it out at home on Sunday. So will my neighbors. People might break in, of course. I must put a bolt on the front door. Steal a crowbar from a building site and bar the door. Hit them on the head with the crowbar. If anyone breaks in, hit him on the head like a dog. Better a live dog. I went to a dog show recently. I liked the borzois, they have long, narrow heads like dueling pistols. Would I be capable of fighting a duel? Pushkin's bullet hit a button on d'Anthés's jacket. If I do go out on Sunday I'll put my cigarette case in the inside pocket of my jacket—the one on the left, where the heart is. *On the Left where the Heart is*—that's a very boring novel by Leonhardt Frank. Bruno Frank—that's somebody quite different, he wrote about Cervantes. Now, what would Don Quixote do on the 10th of August? He'd ride about Moscow on his Rosinante and defend anyone who was attacked. Riding his own personal Rosinante. An eccentric with a copper basin on his head, he would ride into Red Square, ready to break a lance in the name of his Beautiful Lady, in the name of Russia. Poor knight wandering about the Moscow streets in 1960, he would search for his friend and fellow thinker, the Ukrainian boy who once sang a song about Granada.[12] But the cobbles lie over the warring shadows, and the pits made by the staves of regimental banners are filled in with asphalt. The visionary from La Mancha

---

[12]   "Granada": a song by the Soviet poet Mikhail Svetlov, written in the 1920s and sung all over Russia. Written in the international spirit of the time, it describes the Civil War and a young Spaniard who fights in it for the sake of the peasants of his native Granada.

would find no one—not a soul. That much I know for certain. Where are they—those who would have followed Don Quixote? Would Chuprov follow him? Or Margulis? Or Igor? No, if they fight at all, each will fight for himself alone. Each will fight for himself, each decide for himself. Wait, wait, who was it who said "Each of us must decide for himself"? It was I who said it, I who thought of it for myself. So what business have I to judge other people? Are they any worse than I am? Am I any better than they?

I got up and looked in disgust at the hollow my head had left on the pillow. Was it I who had been lying there? Planning to stock up with food and to bolt the door? Trembling like the meanest cur for my precious skin, nearly wetting my pants in terror? Then what good was I, with all my splendid passion for unmasking others, despising them while I stood aside, disgustingly neutral? What good was I—a Pontius Pilate, daily betraying my own soul?

Yes, each one answers for himself. But only for his real self—not for the one others want to turn him into. I am responsible for myself, but not for the potential self-seeker, informer, chauvinist and coward. I cannot save my life by letting them kill me.

But what then shall I do? I'll go out into the street and shout: "Citizens, don't kill each other! Love your neighbors!" But what will I achieve? Whom will I help? Whom will I save? I don't know, I don't know anything . . . Perhaps I'll save myself. If it's not too late.

7

Stay here! Where are you going?
In senseless gloom, in blind fury—
Aren't angels skimming over the heads
Of the howling crowd?
Haven't thousands of reptiles crept from the bogs,
Forgetting the power of terrestrial laws
They hiss with huge gaping mouths,
And mothers have miscarriages.
Stay here! Life itself has summoned you
In the name of those who are herded here, on earth.
Drink it in, take your fill of inspiration
From the absurdity of Doomsday!

—George Bolotin, *To You, Poets!*

On the 10th of August, I got up at eight. I shaved, had breakfast, read a little. But whatever I started, I kept thinking that I must go out. I was continually being reminded of this by the loud-speakers blaring stirring marching-songs outside, by the cats walking in zigzags, delighted at the sudden dearth of people on the pavements, and also by the fact that my neighbors didn't go into the kitchen or the washroom but kept to their room.

At about eleven, I dressed, put my cigarette case into my left inside pocket as planned, and went down. I was walking down the stairs so slowly and so quietly that when I bumped into a tenant on the first-floor landing, it was a surprise for both of us. She gave a scream, stepped back, hit her shopping bag against the railing; there was a sound of breaking glass, and yogurt poured on the staircase. She slipped on the greasy pool, groaned, and sat down heavily. I rushed to help her. At this she screamed again and, shutting her eyes, pushed me weakly away from her with trembling hands.

Slowly she raised her head—her face was dead white—and looked up at me.

"Tolya, Tolya," she mumbled. "I used to hold you in my arms . . . when you were little . . . I knew your mother . . . Tolya!"

"Anna Filipovna, what's wrong? Mind the broken glass, you'll hurt yourself!"

"Tolya," she said. "I thought . . . I bought the yogurt for my granddaughter . . . Oh, Tolya!"

She burst into tears. Her stout, heavy, sixty-year-old body shook with sobs. I helped her to her feet and picked up the bag.

"Zina is sick, and Boris is away on a business trip, that's why I went out to buy the yogurt . . ."

Her daughter Zina, who had been at school with me, came hurrying down from the second floor, her dressing-gown unfastened.

"Mama! What's happened? Who was it? What have they done to you?"

"It's nothing, Zina darling, nothing at all. I fell down . . ."

"Didn't I tell you," Zina began.

"Take your mother home, Zina. I'll go and get the yogurt."

I took out of the bag the loaf of bread soaked in yogurt and gave it to Zina.

"Wait, Tolya. The money . . ."

By the time I had finished with the yogurt and gone out for the second time, it was very hot—as sultry as before a storm. I took my coat off and carried it on my arm, forgetting all about the cigarette case. I was feeling wretched; I kept seeing Anna Filipovna's corpse-like face and hearing her desperate, incoherent mumbling: "Tolya, Tolya . . ."

I walked along Nikitsky Boulevard. It was as usual cheerful, tidy, dappled like a horse with the shadows of leaves. Except that today there were no children. Teenage boys, in shirts with rolled up sleeves lounged on benches spitting on the grass, and an elderly man walked haughtily along the middle of the pavement, chin stuck up, a huge unmuzzled dog following him on a lead.

When I came to Arbat Square, I saw people running. They were hurrying towards some place behind the old Underground station, I couldn't see exactly where: the cinema was in the way. I ran across the road and pushed my way through the crowd.

A man lay on the ground, his head to the wall. He lay in the same position as the corpse in Sasha Chuprov's poster—arms flung out, legs bent at the knee. A red stain had spread over his shirt, a white one, from Vietnam—I have one like it, my sister bought it for me last spring. He lay motionless, and the sun flashed on the pointed toes of his fashionable shoes. Somehow I didn't realize at once that he was dead; when I did, a chill ran down my spine. What shook me was not the murder, not the death, but the amazing fact that Chuprov's nightmare had come true: why was the man lying in exactly that position? His head was almost touching the frame of a poster on which a dashing ballet dancer in black and white announced a ten-day exhibition of Caucasian books, and art. Next to it hung a tattered notice of a lecture at the Polytechnic Museum: "G. S. Hornfeld, Economist, on Planning and Organization of Labor and Industry . . ." The rest was torn off.

People in the crowd were talking in quiet voices.

"He's quite young."

"Perhaps he's still alive."

"Oh no! He's dead. I held a mirror to his mouth—this one, from my bag."

"Who did it?"

"The flower-woman said a tall sun-burnt man ran up and shot him. He called out to him and, when he turned, he fired."

"When who turned?"

"The dead man, of course!"

"And not a policeman in sight; just when he's needed!"

"When you don't need them, they're always there."

"Wait a minute, what have the police to do with it?"

"What do you mean? A man has been killed!"

"So what?"

"You're crazy! I'm telling you, a man has been killed."

"Don't you read the papers? Today it's allowed."

"Don't you shout in the presence of the dead, young man. Papers are papers, but there is such a thing as conscience."

"And is it your opinion that conscience and a Government Decree are not the same? I'd be careful what I said if I were you."

"You get out of here, young fellow, before I bash your head in!"

"For an old man you've got a lot of fight in you!"

"Somebody ought to chase the flies away. It looks so bad."

"Do you mean to say that any hooligan can come along and do a thing like that, and nothing will happen to him?"

"You should read the papers, dearie. It says 'Free extermination.' But don't worry your head. They'll kill those who deserve it, that's all."

"But who does deserve it?"

"They know who deserves it. They don't issue decrees for nothing."

"They'll strip the corpse if we don't look out. Look at his smart shoes."

"Looting is forbidden. This is a government matter."

I elbowed my way out and went off.

I don't remember where I wandered to, how many streets and squares I paced, or how I finally reached Red Square. Convex, rectangular, box-like, it was filled up to the roots and domes with the dense, the almost tangible, reverence of centuries. The bare, cement parallel lines of the grandstands, the three-tiered cubes of the Mausoleum, the right angles of the low parapet, the unsophisticated crenellated walls—all this had been familiar and dear to me since my childhood, it was a sight as unarguable and uncompromising as the illustration of a geometrical theorem—and it suddenly struck me afresh, hit me in the brain, the heart, the soul. The proposition is given; the proof is to be worked out. So the geometricians work away, transfixed in their zeal, fingers clamped to pencil, paper resting on the bowed back serving as a desk; they go on tracing their diagrams, failing to see, refusing to see that the paper is torn, the lead broken, that the pencil, turned into a scourge, furrows the skin, the flesh! Stop! You must not, you cannot do it at this price! These are human beings! This is not what he wanted, the one who was the first to lie within these marble walls![13]

I was thrown to the ground. Before I could get up a man flung himself on me and seized me by the throat, but I jerked away and freed my neck. We rolled over and over, bumping our heads on the cobbles, clutching each other, our feet slipping on the freshly watered stones. I caught glimpses of blue sky, of the many colors of St Basil's, the red marble cube of the tomb, and two statues with rifles, guarding the dead. We slithered to the feet of the sentries. Here I managed at last to drive my knee hard into the pit of his stomach and he let go. I jumped up, staggering, and stepped on the sentry's foot. My opponent got up too, but I hit him twice on the jaw, knocking him down again. He crawled away and tried to rise, propping himself up on his arms, but they folded up and he sat weakly down, leaning against the wall of the Mausoleum. Spitting blood, he rasped:

"Go on, then, kill me!"

I picked up the jacket I had dropped at the foot of the parapet and said, choking:

"You damned fool . . ."

He replied: "It was for the sake of the Motherland . . ."

I glanced at the sentries. They stood as still as three minutes earlier, except that one of them was squinting down at the dusty mark my heel had left on his polished boot . . .

I went home.

---

[13]   Lenin.

8

The Lord offended a shell:
He took a prickly grain of sand
and hurled it
Into its defenseless mouth.

And if Something comes into your house,
Where is the refuge from evil?
And a pearl grew there
Like a white globule, like a
transparent grain.

—Richard O'Hara, *The Lagoon*

We all gathered again in November, for the anniversary of the Revolution. After much discussion we agreed to hold the party at Paul and Zoya's: they had their own two-roomed flat, a tape recorder, recordings of songs by Vertinsky and Leshchenko,[14] and a lot of spare china and glass, so the women decided it was the best place.

When I was told where the party was to be held, I at first decided to stay away, but then I said to myself: "Why not, after all! We are all friends, the food will be good, and as to what I know about Zoya . . . well, we'll just pretend I don't." Actually, I wasn't sure that Zoya cared whether I came or not, so I told Lilya I was in a bad mood and hadn't yet made up my mind whether to go out at all—let Zoya ring me up the day before. I told myself I would decide in the course of the conversation.

And Zoya rang me up.

She said hullo as though nothing had happened, asked about my health, my mood, and whether I would come to the party. She spoke, and I replied, and listened to her breathing down the mouthpiece.

[14] Émigré Russian singers. Alexander Vertinsky (1889–1957) voluntarily returned to the Soviet Union after World War II and was highly praised in the USSR. Pyotr Leshchenko (1898–1954) was arrested in 1952 in Soviet Romania and died in a prison hospital. Foreign recordings of Leshchenko, smuggled in by returning Red Army soldiers, circulated widely in the post-war years.

"Do come," she said. I wish you would. I'll expect you. You'll spoil the party for me if you don't."

"Look here, Zoya," I said. "If I do, I won't come alone."

"Oh? Who with then?"

"You don't know her."

There was a fraction of a pause, then: "Well, of course. Bring anyone you like. You know we're always happy to meet your friends."

On that we said goodbye.

I had said "you don't know her" and this was the honest truth: I did not yet know myself, whom I meant to bring.

I thought of all the women I knew, the unattached ones, naturally. There were quite a few of them, but the trouble was that they would attach too much significance to an invitation of this sort, and I had not the slightest wish to start a new affair. Should I go by myself, after all? But I had a sudden access of schoolboy spite: I wanted at any price to prove to Zoya that I didn't care a damn for her. I decided to ring up Svetlana. She was twenty, an illustrator who worked for our publishing house, very attractive, clearly fond of me, and sufficiently unassuming not to get the wrong idea. Delighted at my invitation, she mumbled shyly that she wouldn't know anyone there, she wasn't sure and so on . . .

"Nonsense, Svetlana dear," I said. "They're all very nice people—so long as it doesn't bother you if they get a bit drunk and start singing prison songs and maybe using bad language . . . That's settled then, I'll meet you tomorrow at half past nine at the corner of Stoleshnikov Street in front of the bookshop."

We arrived long after the others had sat down to supper. The bottles were a third empty, the men in shirtsleeves, and someone was already dying to sing. But the festive atmosphere was still fairly decorous—cigarettes were not yet being stubbed out on the plates and people drank from their own glasses.

We were greeted by a cheerful burst of noise. Everyone stared at Svetlana.

"This is Svetlana," I said. "I hope you'll take her to your hearts. And hold on to the bottles—I warn you we're thirsty and ravenous."

"Svetlana, darling, come here," Lilya crooned. "These awful men have got completely out of hand, they're so busy with their food and drink, we might as well not be there. Still, we can't do without them, can we!"

"You certainly can't," Paulie roared with laughter. "We . . ."

"Here's your glass, Svetlana," Igor poured her some dry wine. "Or would you prefer brandy? I daren't offer you vodka."

"No, no of course not. Thank you." Svetlana's smile was a little forced.

"Tolya, where have you been all this time, why don't you come to see us? Misha keeps asking, 'Where's Uncle Tolya? When is he coming?'" Volodya's wife, Emma, leaned her chest on the table and made a round mouth and round eyes, imitating her son. She was dressed, as always, gaudily and without taste.

"Well?" Zoya handed me a glass of vodka.

"Well?" I replied.

"Happy holiday!" Paul leaned across the table to clink glasses with me. "I was beginning to be afraid you weren't coming. Zoya and I . . ."

"Paulie, you're spilling your drink."

"Sorry, dear . . . Zoya and I . . ."

"Paulie, pass the salad, will you . . ."

"Zoya and I . . . Why don't you let me get a word in?"

"I was only asking you to fill my glass."

It was getting noisier and noisier. All general conversation had come to an end. Yura was flirting with Svetlana for all he was worth, Lilya had left the table and was clinging to a lanky young fellow known to everyone as Yura the Geologist; Vladimir was reciting— bawling verses, with loose rhymes like dangling shoelaces, by a fashionable young poet. A sharp-nosed girl advanced upon him, shouting that the poet had no talent and was nothing but a hack.

"A hack, but what about his civic courage," yelled Volodya. "No talent, but at least he is attacked by *Komsomolskaya Pravda*!"

Everyone was having fun—Yura changing tapes on the recorder, Emma gobbling salad, Yura the Geologist saying again and again: "We've got quite unused to mayonnaise out there." I drank three glasses of vodka and for no reason became annoyed.

"Listen everybody!" I shouted above the din. "You know, I really love you all!"

"Tolya, darling!"

"Tolya, sweetypie!"

"You are a pet!"

"Isn't it idiotic that we meet so seldom," I went on. "When was the last time we all gathered together?"

"The last time?"

"Yes, when was it?"

"*I* know!" Lilya shouted. "It was at our dacha! The day they announced Public Murder Day!"

Suddenly there was dead silence. Even the tape recorder ground to a halt. Only Emma was saying:

". . . they get hot lunch at school now . . ." but looking round at the silent faces, she too stopped. The heavy silence dragged on and on, it was becoming indecent.

"Yes, indeed," said Igor. "So much time has passed, so much has happened. The tenth of August . . ."

"Zoya and I," Paul shouted, "we sat it out quietly at home . . . we watched the television, and we listened to the tape recorder . . . next day at work they asked me . . ."

It was as though a dam had burst, they all suddenly came to life:

". . . and I said to him: 'You'll be the first I'll do in! You're a swine,' I said, and I gave him a piece of my mind . . ."

"In Odessa, some crooks got hold of the Chief of Police. Well, he was in uniform, of course, so you know what they did? They dressed him in some old rags and they let him go. They let him go, imagine! Then they caught up with him and they finished him off! They were tried later on."

"And what happened?"

"They were convicted of robbery!"

"Listen, listen to what happened in Peredelkino![15] Kochetov hired thugs from the Moscow suburbs, to act as a bodyguard. He

---

[15]   Peredelkino: a village near Moscow where many writers, including the famous pro-Stalinist writer Vsevolod Kochetov, have summer homes.

had to keep them in food and drink, of course. But some other writers hired their own lot—guess why! To do in Kochetov!"

"Go on, what happened?"

"What d'you think? There was a fight. The thugs fought among themselves."

"Does anyone know how many victims there were in all?"

"Not many in the Russian Republic. Eight or nine hundred, I think, less than a thousand. A man from the Central Statistical Bureau told me."

"So few? Are you sure?"

"Yes, that's right. Those were the figures given over the wireless. The foreign wireless, of course."

"There was slaughter in the south. The Georgians went for the Armenians, the Armenians for the Azerbaijanians . . ."

"The Armenians for the Azerbaijanians?"

"Well, yes, in the High Karabakh—that's in Armenia."

"And what about Central Asia? I bet there was a lot of fighting there."

"Not among themselves. They all went for the Russians."

"Have you read the letter from the Central Committee?"

"Yes."

"No! What did it say?"

"First, about the Ukraine. There they took the Decree for a directive. And what a mess they made of it! Squads of young activists were formed and blacklists were drawn up. But of course the names on the blacklists became known at once—how can you keep a thing like that secret? So the special squads had nothing to do—all the people on the lists decamped. The whole thing was a fiasco. And on top of that, the Central Committee reprimanded them for cheapening the idea and going to extremes. Fourteen regional-committee and two area-committee secretaries were thrown out on their ear."

"Really?"

"It's absolutely true. And in the Baltic States no one was killed at all!"

"No one? How's that possible?"

"Just like that! They didn't kill anyone."

"But that amounts to a demonstration!"

"And how! They simply ignored the Decree and that was that. The letter from the Central Committee mentions the inadequacy of political education in the Baltic States. They've fired someone there as well."

". . . running along the sidestreet and shouting and firing and firing! Round after round at the windows! Where'd he get the automatic? He teaches at the Aviation Institute . . ."

"We locked the door, drew the blinds, and played chess . . ."

"I said to him: 'Don't you dare go out, think of the children.' But he kept saying: 'I'm going out.' He was even gritting his teeth. Misha was crying . . . I only just managed to talk him out of it."

". . . there's an article in *Izvestia* by what's her name . . . Elena Kolomeiko . . . about the educational value of the Decree for the young. And she somehow tied it up with polytechnic schools and with the virgin lands . . ."

"Did you see the cartoon in *Crocodile*? He's lying . . ."

"We only wished, Zoya and I, some of our friends had been with us in the flat. It would have been more cheerful . . ."

"It's over, it's over, it's over!" The unspoken words burst through the anecdotes, the nervous giggles, the digs at the government. For the first time since Public Murder Day, I heard people talking about what had actually happened. Until then, whenever I had tried to speak of it, people looked at me with an odd expression, and changed the subject. Sometimes I found myself wondering absurdly: "Could I have dreamed the whole thing?" But now it was over! Now we were celebrating the forty-third anniversary of the Great October Socialist Revolution!

Only four of us—Svetlana, Zoya, Volodya and I—were silent, while the whirlpool of impressions, rumors, anecdotes and facts eddied round us, hanging like the colors of the rainbow in mid-air, spraying the beige wallpaper:

"We were out on an expedition, so all was peace and quiet. You can't do anything out there, with the virgin forest all around you. If it's you today, it will be me tomorrow."

"Our neighbor committed suicide at dawn . . . He was a quiet old man, a waiter at the 'Prague' Restaurant."

"I couldn't sleep all night, I kept thinking someone was scratching at the door . . ."

I thought of how on the night of the 10th of August I went out and saw street-washing machines driving along Sadovaya Street; they drove side by side, covering the width of the street, their water-jets and brushes out, sweeping the road and the pavements . . .

Catching Svetlana's eye, I winked at the door. She went out and, a moment later, I followed. The kitchen was quiet and cozy.

"Well, Svetlana? Are you enjoying yourself?"

"I can't understand it, Tolya. They were all so nice at first, but then they started talking about that . . . What are they so pleased about?"

"They are pleased that they are still alive, Svetlana darling."

"But they all went into hiding! They've been . . ." she paused, looking for the right word. "They've been terrorized, frightened out of their wits!"

"Terrorized!" I took her by the shoulders. "Do you realize what you are saying . . ."

No, she didn't; she had no idea that by this one word she had given the answer to the question that millions of bewildered people were asking themselves and each other. That slip of a girl had no idea that she had shown herself the match of statesmen, the watchful guardians of the nation wisely rustling their papers in their dim-lit studies, officials muttering in hushed deferential tones: in a word, those who embody what is solemnly called the State. She thought she had spoken this word to me alone, but she had inadvertently flung it at the huge government buildings, the black-and-white acres of newsprint that daily blanket the country, at the unanimous roaring of general meetings, at the diabolical clanking of tanks and the gaping mouths of the guns mounted on them at ceremonial parades.

I hugged her and said:

"Forget it, Svetlana. I want to kiss you, I've been waiting to for a long time. Haven't you noticed? . . ."

And now, having seen Svetlana to her flat, I am on my way home. I walk through the familiar streets and alleys—I could find my way along them blindfold. Frilly crinolines of lampshades shine pink through net curtains. Couples say goodbye in doorways and can't bring themselves to part. Timiryazev in stone[16] looks as thoughtful as a finger pointed at a brow.

A wireless is blaring, there is a squeal of brakes somewhere; people walk in noisy groups, going home, like me, from parties. Other people sit in their rooms, muttering curses, or poems or confessions of love.

This is Moscow speaking.

I walk along the street, along the quiet, cozy avenue, feeling for the notebook in my pocket, and thinking of what I have written. I believe that it might equally well have been written by anyone else of my generation and my destiny, who loves this damned, this beautiful country as much as I do. I have judged it and its people and myself both more and less severely than I should. But who will blame me?

I walk along and tell myself: "This is your world, your life, you are a cell, a particle of the whole. You must not allow yourself to be intimidated. You must answer for yourself, and you are thereby answerable for others." And the endless streets and squares, embankments and trees, and the sleepy houses sailing like a convoy of ships to an unknown destination, hum softly in unconscious agreement and astonished approval.

This is Moscow speaking.

Translated by Stuart Hood,
Harold Shukman,
John Richardson

---

[16]   A Russian botanist (1843–1920), much honored in the Soviet Union.

Andrey Sinyavsky (Abram Tertz)
(1925, Moscow — 1997, Paris)

Born to the family of a former Socialist Revolutionary. During the war Sinyavsky served as a radio technician at the military aerodrome. He graduated from the School of Philology at Moscow State University in 1949. Worked as a researcher at the Institute of World Literature, taught at the School of Journalism at Moscow State University, and the School-Studio of the Moscow Art Theater. In the 1960s published scholarly articles in the journal *New World* (*Novyi mir*). Authored scholarly works on Gorky, Mayakovsky, Pasternak, and Babel. From the late 1950s began writing literary works under the pseudonym "Abram Tertz" (the name of a thief in an urban folk song) in the West. Among these works, most prominent are the grotesque short stories "Pkhentz," "Graphomaniacs," "In the Circus," the novellas *The Trial Begins* and *Liubimov* (*The Make-Peace Experiment*), and the essay "What is Socialist Realism?" For these publications, Sinyavsky, along with Yulii Daniel, was arrested in 1965 and put on trial for "anti-Soviet propaganda." The trial generated a wave of support for Sinyavsky and Daniel among the Soviet intelligentsia and is considered to be a catalyst for the dissident movement. Sinyavsky was sentenced to seven years of hard labor. While imprisoned, in letters to his wife, he wrote the book *Strolls with Pushkin* (first published in 1975), which caused a heated discussion in émigré circles and initiated a new wave of debates in the *perestroika*-era Soviet press.

Sinyavsky was released in 1971; in 1973 he immigrated to France. From 1973 he worked as a professor of Russian literature at the Sorbonne. From 1978, together with his wife, Maria Rozanova, he published the literary journal *Syntax* (*Sintaksis*). In his Paris period he wrote the novels *Good Night* (1983) and *Cat's House* (published in 1998), a number of critical articles (many in debate with Aleksandr Solzhenitsyn), and scholarly books, such as *Vasily Rozanov's* Fallen Leaves (1982), *The Russian Intelligentsia* (1997, released in Russian as *Sovetskaia tsivilizatsiia* [1989]), and *Ivan the Fool* (1991).

Dissent as a Personal Experience[1]

My experience of dissent is extremely individual, even though, like any personal experience, it reflects in some way broader, more general, and more ramified developments, and not only the events of my own life. I have never belonged to any dissident movement or dissident community, and my heterodoxy has manifested itself not in public activity, but exclusively in my writing; moreover in a kind of writing which was initially esoteric, and stylistically obscure for the general public, and not meant to evoke any openly political resonance.

The first period of my dissent as a writer takes up approximately ten years, from 1955 to my arrest. In those days I sent manuscripts abroad through secret channels and, hiding my real name, I published in the West under the pseudonym Abram Tertz. I was wanted as a criminal: this I knew, and I understood that I would be caught sooner or later, for as the saying goes, "Crime does not pay." As a result the process of writing itself assumed the nature of a rather thrilling detective story, although I do not write detective fiction and dislike it, and personally I do not care for the adventuresome. I just did not see any other way for my literary work to be published than this slippery path which was condemned by the state, and was

---

[1]   Published in *Yearbook of Comparative and General Literature*, 31 (1982): 21–29.

similar to a dangerous game of chance in which it was necessary to stake everything, one's existence, one's human interests, and one's personal attachments, on a single card. There was simply no other way. It was necessary to choose, in one's own mind, between one's existence as a human being and one's existence as a writer. The more so since the destiny of writers in the Soviet Union shows that literature is a risky and at times fatal path, and under Soviet conditions the writer who combines literature with his well-being often stops being a real writer.

From the very beginning of my literary career there was, whether I liked it or not, a kind of a split personality, which still has not been obliterated. This is a split between the authorial persona Abram Tertz and my human self (as well as my scholarly likeness), Andrey Sinyavsky. As a man I prefer a quiet, peaceful, and secluded life, and I am quite an ordinary person. Accordingly, people are usually nice and well-meaning to me as a human individual. The same may be said about my research and teaching activities, which even today run parallel to my work as a writer. To be sure there have also been various inconveniences in this regard—in connection, for example, with my study of the poetry of Pasternak—but, after all, those are trifles. On the whole my career as a scholar and a literary critic has developed successfully enough. And very likely I would still be a perfectly happy member of the Soviet Academy of Science and a prosperous literary critic of the liberal direction, if it were not for my dark literary double by the name of Abram Tertz. This person is, in contrast to Andrey Sinyavsky, inclined to go on forbidden paths and to take risky steps of different kinds, which has brought a great amount of trouble upon him and, accordingly, upon me. I think, however, that this "split personality" is not a question of my moral psychology, but rather a problem of the artistic style employed by Abram Tertz—an ironic, *outré* style, with elements of the fantastic and the grotesque. To write as is customary or as is ordered is simply of no interest to me. If I were supposedly asked to describe ordinary life in an ordinary realistic manner, I would refrain from writing at all. Inasmuch as politics and the social structure are not my discipline, it can be that my disagreements with the Soviet government were basically aesthetic. As a result Abram Tertz is a dissident primarily by virtue of his stylistic qualities. But he is an impudent, incorrigible dissident, who provokes indignation and aversion in a conservative and conformist society.

Here it is fitting to deviate a bit and point out that any real literature in modern times is most often a transgression of the rules *"du bon ton."* By its nature literature is heterodoxy (in the broader sense of the word) with regard to the prevailing view of things. Any writer is a heterodox element within a society of people who think in an orthodox manner or, in any event, think alike. Any writer is an outcast, a degenerate, a not fully legitimate being in the world, because he thinks and writes in opposition to the opinion of the majority — at least if he writes in defiance of the existing style and the already-determined, accepted course in literature.

In principle the writer should probably be killed — if for no other reason than because, when all people live like real people, he writes. Writing itself is heterodoxy in relation to life. In Russia one of the jailers admitted to me in a moment of intimacy, "I would put all writers without exception and independent of their greatness — Shakespeare, Tolstoy, Dostoevsky — into one big madhouse, because writers only disturb the normal development of life." I think that this man is somehow right in his own way. He is right in that the writer, by the mere fact of his existence, introduces a kind of anxiety into the social system. This is particularly the case in a standardized society, which lives and thinks according to state orders. In such a society the writer is a criminal, a more dangerous criminal than a thief or a murderer. In prison I was told with regard to my work, "It would have been better had you killed somebody!" Yet I had not written anything terrible in these works, and had not called for the overthrow of the Soviet government. It was sufficient that you think differently in some way, that you compose words in your own way and hereby enter into contradiction with the general official style, and with the official jargon, which determines everything. For such authors, as for dissidents in general, there exists a special juridical term in the Soviet Union: "especially dangerous state criminals." I personally fell into this category, and I hope to remain to the end of my days, in the eyes of Soviet society an "especially dangerous state criminal."

However, I was not always such a bad fellow. My childhood and adolescence, in the 1930s, were spent in a wholesome Soviet atmosphere, in a normal Soviet family. My father was admittedly no Bolshevik. He had been a left Socialist and after renouncing the aristocratic milieu by 1909 he had already joined the Revolution. He took an extremely loyal position towards the Bolshevik government, no matter how they persecuted him for his former revolutionary activities. Accordingly, I was raised in the best traditions of the Russian Revolution, or more precisely, in the traditions of revolutionary idealism, which, by the way, I do not any means regret. I do not regret it because in my childhood I adopted from my father the notion that one should not live in accordance with narrow, egotistic, "bourgeois" interests, and that it is necessary to see some higher meaning in life. Subsequently, art became this "higher meaning" for me. When I was fifteen, on the eve of the war, I was an enthusiastic Communist-Marxist, for whom there was nothing finer than the world revolution and the future universal brotherhood.

I would like to remark in passing that to the extent that we are talking about dissent as a concrete historical phenomenon, this is a very typical biography for Soviet dissidents in general. Most of the time, dissidents were formerly very high-minded Soviet individuals, people with strong convictions, with principles, and with revolutionary ideals. On the whole, dissidents are the product of the Soviet society of the post-Stalin era, and not some alien elements in this society nor remnants of some old, shattered opposition. In all periods of Soviet history there have been enemies of the Soviet government—people who have not been satisfied with it or who have suffered from it; people who have criticized it, but who nevertheless cannot be called dissidents. Nor can we call, for instance, Pasternak, Mandelstam, or Akhmatova, dissidents although they were heretics in Soviet literature. Through their heterodoxy they anticipated dissent; they supported and still support this later development. But one cannot call them dissidents for the simple reason that their roots go back to bygone, pre-revolutionary traditions of Russian culture. Dissidents, on the other hand, are a totally new phenomenon, which grew directly from the soil of Soviet reality. They are the people who were raised in Soviet society, who are children of the Soviet system, and who came into conflict with the ideology and the psychology of their fathers. And this, it seems to me, partly explains the interest of the contemporary West in the problems of Soviet dissent, because the dissidents represent a view of Soviet society from within. One cannot accuse them of being an alien class, nor of not accepting the Revolution, like those people who lost out in it. This is not a political opposition struggling for power. It is characteristic that the political accent of the dissident movement is generally low-key, while intellectual and moral questions come to the fore. This distinguishes the dissidents from the Russian revolutionaries of the past, and if they bring about some "revolution" —let us provisionally call it by that term—then it will be in the form of a reevaluation of values, which is the starting point for dissent. Within each dissident this process of re-evaluation takes its individual course under the influence of one or another of the contradictions in daily life. Each dissident encounters his own stumbling block, which serves as the catalyst of critical thought. For many of dissidents this stumbling block, as we know, was the Twentieth Party Congress in 1956, not only because their eyes were opened to the enormous crimes of the past, but also because, after having revealed to them some of these crimes, the Twentieth Party Congress and all of the subsequent Soviet ideology did not and could not give any sort of serious, historical explanation for the events. And although the regime has become more moderate since Stalin, this has not led to a more liberal and more democratic state system which would provide some guarantee of human rights and human liberty. In the aftermath of the Twentieth Party Congress, the Soviet people were simply told, as before, to trust the Party and the state in everything. In the recent past, however, this faith has cost too much and has led us too far astray. As a consequence each dissident's ideological or childish faith in the justice of Communism was replaced by individual reason and the voice of one's conscience. Thus the dissident movement is, in my opinion, primarily an intellectual movement; it is a process of independent and unintimidated thinking. At the same time these intellectual or spiritual aspirations are correlated to a feeling of moral responsibility, which is bestowed upon a man and forces him to think, speak, and write independently without regard for the norms and prescriptions of the state.

I personally experienced this normative process of dissent a little bit differently. My period of re-evaluating values and forming individual opinions was during the late forties and early fifties. That period of late, mature, and rampant Stalinism after the war coincided with the years of my studies when I began to study the humanities at Moscow University, and the main stumbling block, which led to the collapse of revolutionary ideals, were problems of literature and art, which arose with particular poignancy in those days. After all this was exactly the time when the frightful purges were carried out in the Soviet cultural world. To my misfortune, I loved modernism in art and everything that, as a result of the purges, was subject to destruction. I saw the purges as the death of culture and the end of any original thought in Russia. In the internal conflict between politics and art I opted for art and rejected politics. At the same time I started to look closely at the nature of the Soviet state in general, in the light of the devastation that was visited on life and culture. Consequently I was exhilarated at Stalin's death. Having attempted to write "something original and artistic," I understood in advance that there would not be and could not be any place for it in Soviet literature. I never tried, nor even so much as dreamed of publishing it in my own country, so I simply sent the manuscripts abroad. This was nothing less than dropping out from the prevailing literary system and the literary environment. Sending works to the West was, however, the best means of "preserving the text" and did not represent a political action or a form of protest.

I did not therefore consider myself guilty of a political crime, when they arrested me and when the second period of my career as a writer began. Now, this was a natural form of behavior, and not a result of cunning on my part. Generally, a man who is thrown into prison should behave naturally—this is the only thing that helps. It is natural for the writer to affirm that literature neither is nor can serve the purpose of political agitation and propaganda, as is maintained by the Soviet government—which, by the way, conducts political agitation freely and incompetently in the West. In this manner my friend Yulii Daniel and I managed to take the position of "pleading not guilty" despite the pressure of the court and the KGB. This rather strong pressure is exerted on your person and your family, and our denial of guilt played a specific role in the development of the dissident or, as it is called, the democratic movement, although we were not directly associated with this movement, but rather acted on our own. The problem was that earlier on in all public political trials in the Soviet Union, the "criminals" (in quotation marks and without quotation marks) confessed their guilt, repented, and publicly abased themselves before the Soviet court. Political justice in the Soviet Union was based on that. Of course, there had previously also been some people who repented and considered themselves not guilty, but no one ever heard about it. Outwardly everything went well: "the enemies of the people" confessed to being "enemies of the people" and asked to be good, honest Soviet citizens, or, even worse, not to be shot, so that they could improve, and by atoning for their crimes against the fatherland become good, honest Soviet citizens. For the state this meant reducing the people to a common denominator, to a "moral-political unity of the Soviet people and the Party." We, the dissidents, succeeded in breaking with this tradition. We succeeded in remaining ourselves and outside the Soviet "unity." What happened in mine and Yulii Daniel's court case was that it was made public and that it received support inside the country and in the West through "public opinion." All that happened without our willing it. Being in prison and being on trial we did not presume that another process was beginning around our prosecution. We were isolated and could not imagine that it would lead to a chain reaction. We were simply writers and persisted in our own course.

At this point it is appropriate to remember that a dissident (I am using the expression now in its most general and broadest meaning) is not only a man who disagrees with the system and has the courage to express himself: he is also a man who does not consider himself guilty. This is, of course, a matter of personal choice and nobody may impose upon anyone any "rules of behavior" before

Soviet justice. This is a problem to be resolved by each individual. But the concept of the "dissident" presupposes a specific kind of moral resistance or force of conscience, which does not allow him to repent and turn into an ordinary Soviet citizen who speaks at the bidding of the state all his life. There are those who do not repent their words and their deeds, and are consequently sent to labor camps, and remain dissidents. There are others who retract their dissent, repudiate themselves, get free and become again "honest Soviet citizens." The warrant of dissidence is prison.

I now turn to the third and last period of my experience as a dissident, namely the period from my emigration up to the present. I would like to dwell for a while on this point, since it is particularly complicated and, in my opinion, dramatic. I will hardly touch upon the West itself, because I am interested in the dissident émigré environment and its press, in which I had occasion to get involved deeply enough to gain an exceedingly unsettling experience.

What has recently been going on with the dissidents who have come to the West should, in my opinion, be designated by the expression "dissident NEP." I am using this expression not as a scientific term but rather as an image, an analogy to that colorful period of Soviet history which began in the twenties after the Civil War and continued for about five to seven years. In those days the government granted the country the so-called economic "breather" with the purpose of adjusting an economy devastated by war and revolution. As we know this was a comparatively peaceful and happy period, which allowed the people to breathe relatively freely and grow fat a bit. Simultaneously this was the time of crushing defeat of all opposition and the beginning of the powerful Stalinist consolidation. It was the time when the Revolution degenerated into its opposite, a conservative, petty bourgeois-bureaucratic system. It is amazing that during the years of NEP many heroes of the Revolution and the Civil War turned out to be cowards, opportunists, submissive executors of the new political system, veritable philistines and conformists. Does that mean that they had not been real heroes in the recent past? No, they were heroes without any doubt; had faced death and feared nothing. But the political climate changed and they entered a different environment, which demanded different human qualities. And yet it was also as if they had come into their own, they were the very medium of the triumphant Revolution. And so if they had not fallen in battle, the heroes of yesterday turned into mediocre bureaucrats.

Now let us transfer some characteristics of NEP to our dissident experience. Having come to the West we find ourselves not only in a different society but also in a different historical climate, at a different stage of its development. This is a peaceful and comparatively happy period in our personal histories. We have only to endure the test of prosperity, as well as the test of democracy and freedom, of which we had dreamed. As dissidents we are threatened by nothing except personal decadence. After all it is very easy to be a dissident in the West (that is, a dissident with regard to the Soviet system). What threatened us with prison in the Soviet Union promises us here, with a certain effort, prestige and material prosperity. Only the idea "dissident" itself fades somehow over here and loses its heroic, romantic, and moral aura. We essentially do not resist anything and risk nothing, but only shake our fists in the air in the belief that we are carrying on a battle for human rights. It is clear that we sincerely wish to help, and at times we actually do help those who are persecuted in the Soviet Union. But this has to be done: one has to think of those who are in prison over there. Only on our part (and this is worth remembering) all this is no longer a struggle, not a sacrifice nor an achievement; it is charity and philanthropy. It can even be an income, a living, and at times, unfortunately, a profitable enterprise. It is this last circumstance which sometimes adds a not altogether noble touch to the dissident cause in the West.

Everybody, of course, needs money, and if a dissident has no other specialty, he is forced to earn his living on this well-trodden path. Money is also necessary to publish books and journals, to organize conferences, etc. And all those are useful and absolutely necessary things in Russia as well as in the West. As everyone already knows, however, money not only makes it possible to do good and permits one to live independently, but, as it happens, it also corrupts and enslaves. And dissidents cannot escape this universal human law.

I do not mention any names, because it is not a question of names but of trends. And the trend unfortunately shows that there are cases when the dissident who comes to the West loses his distinguishing feature, his independence and his courage of mind, and enters the service of some dissident-émigré corporation, or the service of some dissident boss. And he no longer speaks his mind but rather what is demanded of him. His adaptation is justified with the words, "You cannot survive here otherwise!" Moreover, this may be said by someone who only yesterday risked his life for his own convictions. And what are we to make of this? Was it the case that in the Soviet Union, in prison, he was spiritually free and could live in his own way, different from the majority, and without yielding to any sort of pressure or bribery? And is it the case that here in an environment of freedom he adapts himself to the situation, because here, as it suddenly turns out, "you cannot survive otherwise"? Is freedom psychologically more dangerous for him, the dissident, than prison? Can it be that, given freedom, we become slaves? Or, was Dostoevsky's Grand Inquisitor right, when he said that people do not love freedom but fear it, and seek some support in life, in the form of bread, authority, and miracle? People seek someone to worship, and "in order to do it surely together," they look for a "community of worship" of some authority, to which they surrender their freedom? We are, however, not concerned here with the problems of human history and psychology in general, but with a concrete phenomenon: namely, the dissident movement. So with reference to dissidents in the West the greatest danger of opportunism and conformism arises, as it seems to me, from the need for a general, communal worship of something or somebody.

Here it is necessary to take the specific character of émigré life into account. When coming to the West, we become very lonely, and we suffer from our loneliness. This affects the Russian people in particular, for we are used to closer, more amicable contacts than we can notice in the West. Naturally, we look for *our* own people, for *our* environment, and we find it in the form of the dissident-émigré association. We easily make concessions to this environment and its authorities, in so far as we fear losing it; and the range of choices within the groups is extraordinarily limited. The community of thought which arises in this environment, the narrowness of the environment and its seclusion, and at times its conservatism and subordination to authority, sometimes even the émigré's material dependence on this authority and this environment—all these create the fertile soil to foster conformity. We ourselves do not always realize how we turn from dissidents into conformists. After all, we do not commit treason, we do not leave one camp for the other. We only adjust ourselves subtly. But in exactly that way, the heroes of the Revolution did not realize their degeneration during the NEP period. After all they did not betray the ideals of Communism. The revolutionaries only turned into obedient party officials. This is why I am afraid that in our emigration, under the warm wings of the democratic West, we reproduce the archetype of the Soviet system without wishing it or being aware of it—only with a different, anti-Soviet valence. There is another essential difference: we do not have our police and we do not have prisons. But there is already a censorship in its own right, and there are also informers. It is only that the Western police somehow do not accept our reports. Oh, yes, we forgot: after all, this is a democracy!

An outside observer interested in our problems does not always understand why and about what Soviet dissidents emigrating to the West argue so fervently among themselves. They do not understand why there is no agreement of opinions: after all, all of us are dissidents. I personally think that there is more agreement among us than is necessary. There is even an excess of agreement to the detriment of our dissent. After all, the dissidents are by nature not a political party and not even an ideology. The repudiation of Soviet ideology presumes not only different thinking with regard to this ideology, but also diversity of thought within heterodoxy. If we are heretics, then there should be many heresies. This is, in my view, the value of dissent, which in its ideal form is not the nucleus of a new Church, or of a new, unified, anti-Soviet state, but rather a pluralistic community, even if only on paper. I said before that the Soviet dissidents are by their nature an intellectual, spiritual, and moral opposition. The question is: opposition against what? Not simply against the Soviet system in general, but also opposition against the unification of ideas and their paralysis in Soviet society. And if we want a free Russian idea, a free Russian word and culture to develop, we need diversity of thought. This is the most important precondition for the development of Russian culture. Why should diversity of thought be possible in the West, yet not with us dissidents? We are, after all, like anyone else, equipped with the rudiments of reason and a sense of justice.

Apart from this there has recently been a clear split within the dissident movement, particularly on émigré soil. It is a split into two wings or directions, the first of which can provisionally be called the "authoritarian-nationalist" wing, and the second the "liberal-democratic" wing. By its nature dissent is liberal and democratic, and that is the way it started. Therefore the terms "Soviet dissidents" or "democratic movement" were and remain synonymous. The "national-authoritarian" wing appeared later and entered, as it seems to me, into a conflict with the main premises of the dissident movement. It is understandable that with the split now in process and later, when it is completed, serious and fundamental disagreements flare up. They form the basis of our quarrels.

I myself belong to the liberal-democratic wing—not because I believe in the imminent victory of freedom and democracy in Russia. On the contrary, I categorically do not believe in such a victory. At any rate I do not see such prospects in the near, foreseeable future. But under the circumstances of Soviet despotism it is correct for a Russian intellectual—in my opinion—to be a liberal and a democrat, and not to propose some other new kind of despotism. Let us assume that democracy as a social and government system has no future in Russia. All the same it is our vocation to remain proponents of freedom, because freedom, like some other "useless" concept, such as, for instance, art, goodness, or human thought, is an end in itself and does not depend on the historical or political trend.

This is why I cannot agree with those dissidents who propose to exchange Communism with another variety of despotism under the flag of nationalism and religion, even though such changes are probably historically feasible. Although I personally belong to the Russian Orthodox Church and like the Old Russian culture fully as much as many writers and thinkers of the Slavophile circle, with regard to contemporary Russian nationalism I am extremely suspicious of the idealization of the state order and the social customs of past Russia. I am against the mixture of spiritual and material values, or of religious and political ones. Let us say that many contemporary Russophiles tend to criticize the West for the formalized way of life, for the fact that here judicial and rationalistic categories of "law" and "justice" dominate, when the ideas of Christian "love" and "goodness" were indigenous to Russia from the very beginning. And "'Goodness' is higher than 'law.'" Yes, I agree. Divine goodness and love are higher and greater than all human laws made on earth. But this theory appears to me dangerous and insulting in reference to a government system— dangerous for man, and insulting for religion. After all it is not God, not Christ, who in reality rules a despotic state, but the tsar or the leader who, unfortunately, even if it is an orthodox tsar, frequently does not resemble God but rather the Devil. Of course, this tsar has the opportunity to show "goodness" in circumvention of "law." But this "goodness" itself, in order to be shown, requires unbelievable, uncontrollable, and autocratic power. And in practice such power does not turn into love or goodness, but into executions. More precisely: many, many executions, and a little bit of goodness. So, in my view, the formalized and rationalistic "law" is better than tsarist "goodness."

Russian dissidents who have come to the West are sometimes afraid of democracy here. They think that the West will gradually disintegrate under the pressure of the monolithic, totalitarian system of the Soviet Union. They advise the West to turn to more authoritarian principles. And correspondingly they want the Russia of the future not to be a democracy but a more solid authoritarian-theocratic state. In the end, the people who were, so it seems, saved from death by Western democracy, now would like to restrict it. Hence the moralistic and didactic pronouncements to the West on the part of some Soviet dissidents, who see this West for the first time and know it badly.

We should probably be more modest and, by transmitting our distressing experience to the West, be careful to teach the West how to live and build its fundamental, Western society. We have already built our society in the form of a Communist state, from which we do not know where to turn. The new Russian nationalists object to this argument by claiming that all our Russian misfortunes have come from the West. Marxism came from the West. From the West came liberalism, undermining the autocratical-patriarchal foundation of Russia. All foreigners (Poles, Jews, Latvians, Hungarians) who brought about the October Revolution were Western intruders. Yet all this is but a search for a "scapegoat" somewhere from without. It is not we who are guilty but someone alien (the West, a world conspiracy, the Jews, etc.). In essence, this means casting off one's own sins and omissions. We are actually the good ones, we are clean, we are most fortunate, because we are Russians. And it is the "Devil" who interfered in our history.

What I am saying here is a sacrilege from the point of view of the nationalists. For similar reasons Russian nationalists call Russian liberals (and me, specifically) *Russophobes*. Like the decadent, liberal atheist West, we—in league with the Communists—hate the Russian people and Russia. It is difficult to defend oneself against such an accusation. After all, should one shout loudly that one loves Russia? That would be ridiculous. As far as I have observed, there are not that many Russophobes in the West. The converse, "Russophile" position would betray a lack of respect for the Russian people. If Russia could be conquered by a bunch of foreigners, how could this great nation be so worthy? And if Russia is incompatible with democracy, would that not mean that, by this interpretation, the people itself is inclined to slavery? By the way, this fear of democracy applied to the Russian people has had bitter antecedents in our history. For the longest time the "Russian patriots" were afraid to abolish serfdom in Russia. Their concern: How could one grant freedom to a Russian peasant? After all, without the landowner's supervision he would immediately stop working and get drunk!

Such are our quarrels in the broadest and crassest outlines. These arguments are useful for the discovery of different views on the matter, but in practice they are rather utopian. The Soviet system is extremely solid and does not promise any freedom (including freedom for the founding of an orthodox theocracy or autocracy). But we are always arguing: Do we need freedom? And the needle of the compass turns, as has long been our custom, to the side of despotism. A very sad portent.

How odd it is that in our Western environment the authoritarian-nationalist wing enjoys greater success and influence than the democratic one. This is due to the fact that by its own psychological make-up the authoritarian direction is more party-oriented, more disciplined, more single-minded, and more obedient to the authority of the "leader" than the democrats, who possess by nature tolerance, pluralism, and diversity of thought. Moreover, nationalism and the proponents of the authoritarian system are supported by the largest part of the old émigrés, who make up the majority of the Russian public, and who are, so to speak, the Western Russian soil. They support the authoritarian-nationalist wing by virtue of their inveterate, monarchist conservatism. For the old émigrés pre-revolutionary Russia is an indisputable ideal, to which, according to their views, contemporary Russia occupied by the Bolsheviks dreams of returning. In Paris a nice, elderly lady asked me, after she found out that I had recently come from Moscow, whether I had met *ours* there. "Which ours?" I asked timidly. She replied, "The Whites!" At this level of understanding the democratic dissidents who come to the West are something like "Soviet devils," who are specially sent here by the Bolsheviks, in order to disarm the last bulwark of the Fatherland.

It is interesting, however, that even Western circles sometimes tend to support the Russian nationalists and authoritarian representatives, even though the democratic dissidents are psychologically much closer to them. The logic here is as follows: freedom and democracy are good for the West, but for Russia something simpler and more reactionary is required—as for savages. Let me pose a purely rhetorical question: Has democratic America not at times supported extremely reactionary, authoritarian and totalitarian regimes in developing countries, hoping thereby to save these countries from the Communist infection? And has it not lost with this policy? Yet I am not concerned with American politics, which I understand poorly, but with Russian culture. It is this difference of interests that keeps us sometimes from coming to a mutual understanding.

As an illustration I want to cite a private conversation, which I recently had with a very clever and perceptive western Sovietologist. According to his personal convictions and tastes he is a liberal and a democrat, but politically he counts on Russian authoritarianism and nationalism. As a sophisticated man he is shocked by the rudeness of this direction, and, if he were Russian, he would never become associated with it. But to him it seems a movement with more future and greater advantage to the West than that of the Russian democrats. I asked him, "Aren't you afraid that in the end, in succession to the Soviet system, or more likely, in the form of some kind of alliance with it, outright fascism will triumph in Russia?" It turns out that this does not upset him in any way. He regards Russian Fascism as a realistic alternative to Soviet Communism and hopes that Russian Fascism may save the West from Communism through its concern with nationalism. I myself am not so optimistic, and at any rate, in my opinion, the West should save itself from Communism by its own efforts, and not with the help of someone's fascism. But the greatest contradiction consists again in the fact that freedom is necessary for Russian culture, whereas for my Western interlocutor, Russian culture is of minor importance and not essential at all. To him it is important to save the world from a catastrophe. I personally do not undertake such great tasks as saving the world. My profession is narrower: I am a writer.

In conclusion I only want to confirm my "dissent." Under an avalanche of abuse, this is easy. In my emigration I began to understand that I am not an enemy of the Soviet government only, but generally: I am an enemy—an enemy as such—metaphysically, in principle. Not that I was someone's friend first and then became his enemy. I am not anyone's friend, but only an enemy.

The West, of course, only smiles gleefully at these "Russian specimens": exotics. After all, the West does not read Russian newspapers on this or that side of the ocean. But I do read them, and I can see. And this is my conclusion: there, in the Soviet Union, I was an "agent of Imperialism"; here, in emigration, I am an "agent of Moscow." Meanwhile I have not changed my position, but have said the same thing: art is greater than reality. A threatening retribution is following me from various corners—for one and the same books, for one and the same statements, for one and the same style, for one and the same crime.

Psychologically this somewhat resembles the sort of nightmare in one's sleep, that does not come to an end. You know what happens in a dream: you seem to wake up, but only to find yourself in an even more intense continuation of your dream. Wherever you turn, you are an enemy of the people. No, even worse, even more horrible: you are d'Anthés, who killed Pushkin; and you also killed Gogol. You hate culture. You hate "everything Russian" (earlier on, in the first dream, it could be heard: "you hate everything Soviet," and incidentally, that too meant that you hate everything Russian). You hate your own mother, even your deceased mother. You are anti-Semitic. You are a misanthrope. You are a Judas, who betrayed Christ in the form of the new, Communist, national-religious resurrection of Russia. I reason to myself that despite all deficiencies I am still not the Antichrist. But what I think does not matter. That is all subjective. Objectively, that is, socially and publicly, I am the enemy of everything that is fine in the world. What is more—of everything that is good, everything that is human. What a horror! I ask myself: how could I ever have sunk so low? After all I was a nice boy at some point, like all people. But apparently society knows better than I what sort of man I am. After Soviet justice, if you will, there is émigré justice—and the same evidence. Of course, they do not throw you into a concentration camp. But a camp is not the most frightful thing in the world. There it is even pleasant compared to emigration, where they say that you have not been in any camp at all, but that you are sent "on an assignment" to destroy Russian culture.

I am now interested in one question: Why did Soviet and anti-Soviet, émigré justice agree (agree literally) in their accusations of me, a Russian dissident? Most likely, because both of these organs of justice are just and therefore so similar to each other. Who needs freedom? Freedom is a danger. Freedom is irresponsibility before the authoritarian collective. Watch out for it—freedom!

But finally you awake in the morning after all these dreams and you smile ironically at yourself: didn't you wish that? Yes, all that is true. Freedom! Writing—this is freedom.

Translated by Maria-Regina Kecht

Poetry of the 1960s

Yevgeny Yevtushenko

Andrei Voznesensky

Alexander Galich

Yevgeny Yevtushenko
(b. 1932, Zima Junction, Siberia)

Born into an intelligentsia family. Began publishing in 1949 at the age of sixteen. From 1952–58 studied at the Moscow Literary Institute, from which he was expelled for "lack of discipline." While a student at the Institute in 1952, he published his first book and was accepted to the Union of Soviet Writers as its youngest member. During the Thaw, Yevtushenko became the poetic voice of his generation, the Sixties. His public readings attracted thousands of listeners. In his poetry, one finds an ardent anti-Stalinist position fused with an unusual openness and intimate intonation. Among his most famous works are the poems "Babii Yar" (1961), "The Heirs of Stalin" (1962), and the narrative poem *Bratsk Hydroelectric Station* (1965). Dmitrii Shostakovich set Yevtushenko's poems in his Symphony No. 13 ("Babii Yar") and the cantata "The Execution of Stenka Razin" (a fragment from *Bratsk*). Exceptionally prolific as a poet, Yevtushenko has also authored several novels and screenplays and has directed two feature films. Lives in Moscow and the United States.

BABII YAR

No monument stands over Babii Yar.
A drop sheer as a crude gravestone.
I am afraid.
        Today I am as old in years
as all the Jewish people.
Now I seem to be
        a Jew.
Here I plod through ancient Egypt.
Here I perish crucified, on the cross,
and to this day I bear the scars of nails.
I seem to be
        Dreyfus.
The Philistine
        is both informer and judge.
I am behind bars.
        Beset on every side.
Hounded,
        spat on,
           slandered.
Squealing, dainty ladies in flounced Brussels lace
stick their parasols into my face.
I seem to be then
        a young boy in Byelostok.
Blood runs, spilling over the floors.
The bar-room rabble-rousers
give off a stench of vodka and onion.
A boot kicks me aside, helpless.
In vain I plead with these pogrom bullies.
While they jeer and shout,
        "Beat the Yids. Save Russia!"

Some grain-marketeer beats up my mother.
O my Russian people!
              I know
                   you
are international to the core.
But those with unclean hands
have often made a jingle of your purest name.
I know the goodness of my land.
How vile these anti-Semites—
                   without a qualm
they pompously called themselves
"The Union of the Russian People"!
I seem to be
          Anne Frank
transparent
          as a branch in April.
And I love.
          And I have no need of phrases.
My need
          is that we gaze into each other.
How little we can see
          or smell!
We are denied the leaves,
          we are denied the sky.
Yet we can do so much—
          tenderly
embrace each other in a dark room.
They're coming here?
          Be not afraid.
Those are the booming
sounds of spring:
          spring is coming here.
Come then to me.
          Quick, give me your lips.
Are they smashing down the door?
          No, it's the ice breaking . . .
The wild grasses rustle over Babii Yar.

The trees look ominous,
      like judges.
Here all things scream silently,
       and, baring my head,
slowly I feel myself
      turning gray.
And I myself
    am one massive, soundless scream
above the thousand thousand buried here.
I am
  each old man
      here shot dead.
I am
  every child
      here shot dead.
Nothing in me
    shall ever forget!
The "Internationale," let it
      thunder
when the last anti-Semite on earth
is buried forever.
In my blood there is no Jewish blood.
In their callous rage, all anti-Semites
must hate me now as a Jew.
For that reason
I am a true Russian!

September 19, 1961

Translated by George Reavey

THE HEIRS OF STALIN

Mute was the marble.
                 Mutely glimmered the glass.
Mute stood the sentries,
                 bronzed by the breeze.
Thin wisps of smoke curled over the coffin.
                 And breath seeped through the chinks
as they bore him out the mausoleum doors.
Slowly the coffin floated,
                 grazing the fixed bayonets.
He also was mute—
              he also!—
                    mute and dread.
Grimly clenching
              his embalmed fists,
just pretending to be dead,
                 he watched from inside.
He wished to fix each pallbearer
                 in his memory:
young recruits
           from Ryazan and Kursk,
so that later he might
               collect enough strength for a sortie,
rise from the grave,
               and reach these unreflecting youths.
He was scheming.
              Had merely dozed off.
And I, appealing to our government,
                 petition them
to double,
         and treble,
               the sentries guarding this slab,

and stop Stalin from ever rising again
　　　　　　　　　　　　　and, with Stalin,
　　　　　　　　　　　　　　　　　　the past.
I refer not to the past,
　　　　　　　　　so holy and glorious,
of Turksib,
　　　　　and Magnitka,
　　　　　　　　　　and the flag raised over Berlin.
By the past, in this case,
　　　　　　　　　I mean the neglect
of the people's good,
　　　　　　　false charges,
　　　　　　　　　　the jailing of innocent men.
We sowed our crops honestly.
Honestly we smelted metal,
and honestly we marched,
　　　　　　　　joining the ranks.
But he feared us.
　　　　　　　Believing in the great goal,
he judged
　　　　all means justified
　　　　　　　　to that great end.
He was far-sighted.
　　　　　　　Adept in the art of political warfare,
he left many heirs
　　　　　　behind on this globe.
I fancy
there's a telephone in that coffin:
Stalin instructs
　　　　　Enver Hoxha.[1]
From that coffin where else does the cable go!
No, Stalin has not given up.
　　　　　　　　He thinks he can
　　　　　　　　　　　cheat death.

---

[1]　Communist dictator of Albania from 1944–1985.

We carried
      him
         from the mausoleum.
But how remove Stalin's heirs
              from Stalin!
Some of his heirs tend roses in retirement,
thinking in secret
         their enforced leisure will not last.
Others,
    from platforms, even heap abuse on Stalin
but,
  at night,
      yearn for the good old days.
No wonder Stalin's heirs seem to suffer
these days from heart trouble.
         They, the former henchmen,
hate this era
    of emptied prison camps
and auditoriums full of people listening
        to poets.
The Party
   discourages me
      from being smug.
"Why care?"
    some say, but I can't remain
        inactive.
While Stalin's heirs walk this earth,
Stalin,
  I fancy, still lives in the mausoleum.

1962

                  Translated by George Reavey

THE EXECUTION OF STENKA RAZIN[2]
(From *Bratsk Hydroelectric Station*)

In Moscow the white-walled capital
a thief runs with a poppy-seed loaf down the street.
He is not afraid of being lynched today.
There isn't time for loaves . . .
                     They are bringing Stenka Razin!

The Tsar is milking a little bottle of malmsey,
       before the Swedish mirror,
                     he squeezes a pimple,
and tries on an emerald seal ring—
and into the square . . .
                     They are bringing Stenka Razin!

            One after another they're following,
and following his mother as fat as a barrel,
a little boyar is rolling along,
gaily gnawing a bar of toffee with his baby teeth.
Today is a holiday!
                     They are bringing Stenka Razin!

The merchant shoves his way in,
                     flatulent with peas.
Two buffoons come rushing at a gallop.
Mincing rogues—cheats . . .
                     They are bringing Stenka Razin!

---

[2]   Stepan Timofeevich Razin, a seventeenth-century Cossack leader celebrated for the rebellion he led against the nobility and landlords. In the name of taking power from government officials and allowing peasants to govern themselves, Razin and his supporters led and inspired multiple uprisings. He was captured and quartered to death in 1671.

Old men, scabs all over them,
                        hardly alive,
thick cords round their necks,
mumbling something,
                while doddering along . . .
                        They are bringing Stenka Razin!
And shameless girls also,
jumping up tipsy from their sleeping mats,
with cucumber smeared over their faces,
come trotting up—
                with an itch in their thighs . . .
                        They are bringing Stenka Razin!

And with screams from the soldiers' wives
amid spitting from all sides
on a ramshackle cart
he
    comes sailing
                in a white shirt.
He is silent,
            all covered with the spit of the mob
                        he does not wipe it away,
only grins wryly,
smiles at himself:
"Stenka, Stenka,
                you are like a branch
that has lost its leaves.
How you wanted to enter Moscow!
And here you are entering Moscow now . . .
Right then
            spit!
                Spit!
                        Spit!
You're happy—this is a free show.
Good people
            you always spit
at those

who wish you well.
I so much wished you well
on the shores of Persia,
and then again
          when flying
down the Volga on a boat!
What had I known?
             Somebody's eyes,
a saber,
      a sail,
         and the saddle . . .
I wasn't much of a scholar . . .
Perhaps this was what let me down?
The official beat me deliberately across the teeth
repeating,
        fervently:
'Decided to go against the people, did you?
I'll show you!'
I held my own, without lowering my eyes.
I spat my answer with my blood:
'Against the boyars—true.
Against the people—
            no!'

I do not renounce myself,
I have chosen my own fate myself.
Before you,
      the people, I repent,
but not for what the official wanted.
My head is to blame.
I can see,
      sentencing myself:
I was halfway
        against things,
when I ought to have gone
            to the very end.
No,

it is not in this I have sinned, my people,
                    for hanging boyars from the towers.
I have sinned in my own eyes in this,
that I hanged too few of them.
I have sinned in this,
that in a world of evil
I was a good idiot.
I sinned in this,
                    that being an enemy of serfdom
I was something of a serf myself.
I sinned in this,
                    that I thought of doing battle for a good Tsar.
There are no good Tsars,
                    fool.
Stenka,
      you are perishing for nothing!"

Bells boomed over Moscow.
They are leading Stenka
                    to the place of execution.
In front of Stenka
                    in the rising wind
the leather apron of the headsman is flapping,
and in his hands above the crowd
                    is a blue ax,
                          blue as the Volga.
And streaming, silvery,
                    along the blade
boats fly,
      boats
            like seagulls in the morning.
Stenka,
      over the snouts,
            and washtubs
                    and ugly mugs
of the liquor sellers
            and the money changers,

like light through the fog,
Stenka
      saw
         faces,
distance and depth in their eyes,
and in those eyes,
              morosely independent,
as if in smaller, secret Volgas
the boats of Stenka's ax were flying.
It's worth bearing it all without a tear,
to be on the rack and wheel of execution,
if sooner or later
            something grows in those *faces*,
                     menacingly,
on the faces forming on the faceless ones . . .
And calmly
         (obviously he hadn't lived for nothing),
Stenka laid his head down on the block,
settling his chin in the chopped-out hollow,
and with that head gave the order:
                "Strike! The ax!" . . .
The head started rolling,
           burning in its blood,
and hoarsely the head spoke:
           "Not for nothing!" . . .
And along the ax there were not chips any more
but little streams,
        streams . . .
Why, good folk, are you standing,
           not celebrating?
Caps into sky—dance!
But the Red Square is frozen stiff,
the halberds are scarcely swaying.
Even the buffoons have fallen silent.
Amid the deadly silence
fleas jumped over from peasants' jackets
              onto women's coats.

The Square had understood something.
The Square took off their caps,
and three times, thrumming,
                              the bells
                                         struck.

But heavy from its bloody forelock
the head was still rocking,
                              still alive.
From the blood-wet place of execution,
there,
        where the poor were,
the head threw looks around
                              like anonymous letters . . .
Bustling,
        the poor trembling priest ran up,
wanting to close Stenka's eyelids.
But straining,
                frightful as a beast,
the pupils pushed away his hand.
On the Tsar's head,
                    chilled by those devilish eyes,
the crown[3] began to shiver,
and, savagely, not hiding anything of his triumph,
Stenka's head
                burst out laughing
                          at the Tsar!

1964

> *Translated by Tina Tupikina-Glaessner,*
> *Geoffrey Dutton, and Igor Mezhakoff-Koriakin[4]*

---

[3] A reference to the *Monomakh*, a bejeweled fur cap worn only by the Tsar.

[4] All poems in this selection are published in: Yevgeny Yevtushenko, *The Collected Poems, 1952–1990*, edited by Albert C. Todd with the author and James Ragan (New York: Henry Holt, 1991), 102–104, 113–14, 165–170.

Interview with Yevgeny Yevtushenko[5]

INTERVIEWER: Yevgeni, can I first ask you about the 1957 youth festival, the Moscow Youth Festival? How do you think that signaled something new that was happening? How do you recollect that as being something about a change at the time, something . . . ?

YEVGENI YEVTUSHENKO: How I could forget Moscow Youth Festival? For the first time in my life, my socialist lips touched so-called "capitalist lip[s]" because I kissed one American girl, breaking any Cold War rules. Not only me, many of my friends, too, they're doing the same too on the streets of Moscow, in all the parks. But if we'll speak seriously about it, it was a very important moment, because since 1935, since the beginning of Stalin's purges, [the] only visitors in our country were just some diplomats and spies from the West; and [the] only Russian tourists abroad were our diplomat[s] and our spies. And for the first time, we've seen such a lot of foreigners, from Africa, from South America, and . . . people was so happy to see, to feel as a part of humanity, as a part of humanity which was stolen from us; so it was a great signal, great beginning of liberalization in Russia.

INT: [A]t the same time, you were also engaged in poetry readings which were getting huge audiences . . . Can you describe to me what was it that appealed to the audiences so much about that poetry, what were you touching in people with this poetry?

---

[5]   The interview preserves Yevtushenko's oral speech including irregularities of his English.

YY: I could just quote you in English, in my own translation, a couple of stanzas from one of my poem[s] which I wrote in 1972, when Cold War was in full swing and many dissidents' trials. So I wrote that time poem: "I would like to be born in every country, have a passport for them all, to throw all bloody boring foreign officers into panic, to be every fish in every ocean and every dog in the streets of the world. I don't want to bow down before any idols or play at being a Russian Orthodox Church hippie. But I would like to plunge deep into Lake Baikal and surface somewhere. Why not in the Mississippi?" That was declaration, not only my own, it was declaration of our generation. That's why they, all people around me, my friends, they were dreaming when Russia again will be part of the common civilization. I mean, we didn't feel lost or completely culturally isolated, because we were continuing to read some great Western books, French, American, English books. We were brought up as European culture . . . in Russian culture as a part of European culture, but we wanted, I could say, physical connection with the rest of the world. That's why, when American exhibition in 1959 was opened in Moscow, so many Muscovites were lining up for exhibition of Edward Steichen, "Family of Man."

INT: Can you be a bit more specific about the poetry? I mean, what was different about the poetry that you were writing at that time from the previous official poetry in particular? What sort of barriers did you break through with it?

YY: [. . .] During Stalin's times, many poets died behind bars in concentration camps. Poetry became official poetry; we had some little islands of little poet . . . of great poet[s], like Pasternak, Akhmatova, but they were . . . inner emigrants. But poetry got back popularity during Second World War, because it was easier in that time to be sincere and to be published writing poetry. So, and after the Cold War began, again even good, best poets, they were keeping silence or they were silenced forcedly [sic], like Akhmatova and Pasternak. When Akhmatova appeared in Polytechnic Museum after the Second World War, all people stood up, applauding her during half an hour; and Stalin, when he knew it, he became very jealous and he gave order to close all her public appearance[s], because he was [the] only one man who could be applauded such a long time. And, you know, when Stalin died, the political stage . . . I mean social stage, was completely empty; we didn't have any kind of dissidents' movement because all potential dissidents, they were in concentrations camps or already killed. So, Sakharov was official nuclear physicist under the top secrets, and he was different man— he was even a little bit Stalinist in that time, he honestly confessed in his memoirs. So we young poets, new generation, we were [the] only free voices in that moment when political . . . so we jumped on this empty political stage and read our poems against chauvinism, against dictatorship of only one party, against censorship, against anti-Semitism. And that's why we . . . and we were longing for the opening of the world; we wanted to join to all the world. And that's why people sink their own unrealized hopes in our poetry. That's why, in Gorbachev['s] parliament we had so many writers, because our poetry was a cradle of *glasnost,* and *glasnost* was a cradle of our democracy. Our democracy is still very childish, undemocratic; it's probably inevitable because we don't know what to do with freedom. I don't think that in the rest of humanity people knows what to do with the freedom too. [. . .]

> INT: But . . . to take your poem "Stalin's Heirs," the presence of Stalin within the people at the time or within the bureaucrats in particular—I mean, it wasn't a real freedom, was it, in the Thaw: you still had controls, you still had constraints, you still had censorship, you still had bureaucracies who were trying to hold back, presumably because they feared the possibility of what would happen if things became too free . . . Where were Stalin's heirs in society? How would you describe their presence?

YY: It's very . . . What happened with my poem "Stalin's Heirs"— it's a very typical story, because when I wrote it, I couldn't publish it, and even most progressive editor of our magazine *Novyi Mir,* Tvardovsky, he, with the gloomy irony typical for him, he said to me: "I am not fool. If I'll publish this poem, they'll close my magazine immediately, so I give you good advice, boy: hide this poem as deep as you could; otherwise you'll [be] immediately accused of anti-Soviet activities." But I began to recite my poetry publicly, with some big . . . sometimes there's big scandals, because part of the audience were leaving the auditorium. And I sent it to Khrushchev or his assistant, and I was waiting about seven months, probably, and afterwards I just discovered, being in Cuba as a poetical journalist for *Pravda*, that poem was published just one day before Caribbean crisis [sic]. And they . . . without my knowledge, they changed my word, because I was using "my Motherland doesn't permit me to keep silence," and they changed "Motherland" for "Party," and they explained me that I was very far and they couldn't ask my permission. So what happened is the bureaucracy, they already felt necessity of the changes, but at the same time they were badly scared of these changes, because the changes, they began to overtake them, their minds, and sometimes even their fears, and so they were trying to use us during the liberalisa . . . we were trying to use them, because as one of my . . . er, a very clever man, he said . . . he said, "It's impossible to make progress without help of reactionary people," and this is true generally in history, it was true in Russia, because it is . . . whereas they were trying to use us, we were trying to use them, because in their hands were all newspapers, all mass media, and through official newspapers, through official magazine[s], Russian writers said so many things. For instance, *One Day in [the Life] of Ivan Denisovich* was published, my "Babii Yar" was finally published—they were attacked, but they were published and people had possibility to read it, and we had giant circulation of our magazines and our newspapers in that time. And so that's why influence of literature was absolutely great at that time.

INT: Can you describe the atmosphere at those poetry readings? Just give me a description of what it was like.

YY: You know, I remember very well, of course, these readings, because I created them, I was the first poet who after Stalin's death began to recite poetry open[ly] in the schools, in the factori[es], in the colleges, everywhere, in offices, in little café[s]. Sometimes

I recited more . . . I had more readings than days in the year. And we organized a giant poetry reading in the Mayakovsky Square once; it was about 35– or 40,000 people. And what I feel, you know, I've seen . . . I feel that [the] audience, it's my co-author who is writing poetry together with me, and I just voice of this voiceless people, that what I recite is their thought, their hopes, in . . . But I remember also so many sparks, beautiful sparks of hopes in young eyes. And if . . . I mean, Gorbachev, for instance, he told me one story: when he went to Moscow . . . he was with his wife—he was flirting, he was not yet married to Raisa, and he was sitting as a student, and he was a little bit Party apparatchik, young Party apparatchik, and he said . . . when he heard poetry of our generation, my poetry, it changed him; it was first time that he became . . . feel as a different man. So are many people who were born, reborn because of Russian poetry. That's why our generation, it's so powerful, the generation of Sixties. That's . . . Gagarin is our generation. Sakharov a little bit older, but he belongs to our generation. Best poets, best writers, many great scientists. So . . . and that's why even older people who didn't take us enough seriously during our first step, because some of our poetry readings were connected with very glamorous scandals, as Shostakovich, they began to respect us, support us. Shostakovich created two of his great opuses with my words, and we didn't have monument for Babii Yar [at] that time, but Shostakovich['s] symphony, 13th Symphony, was a really great monument for all Jewish victims. When . . . and this, mm, (unclear) or premiere of this symphony was not only event of art: it was a political event. It was a great day for all Russia. [. . .]

> INT: Can we talk a bit about Khrushchev? Because you met him frequently through your career. Do you think that he was genuinely a reformer, he genuinely wanted that liberalization? And do you think that he was restrained by other forces which limited the degree of liberalization that he would have liked?

YY: If I talk about Khrushchev, I could not to [but] talk about his successors—I mean, about Gorbachev, about Yeltsin—because all of them, they have something in common. All of them, they were children of very poor families, and they hated bureaucracy, they hated oppression, and at the same time, three of them, all of them, they were Party apparatchik[s], Party bureaucrats. And I admired Khrushchev when he, as a child of poor family who suffered not only under the landlord, but under the Stalin's bureaucracy too, he was accusing Stalin to being killer. Khrushchev was the first man who officially said it, and I admired this [in] Khrushchev. But Khrushchev was a Stalinist in the same time; it was inevitable dualism. Yeltsin is the same. Yeltsin was a Party apparatchik, but he was a child of very poor family; he was sleeping in the very cold barrack and trying to work up himself, he was embracing God during his childhood, according [to] his memoirs; and in the same time, Yeltsin many times behaved . . . before *perestroika* he behaved very rudely, attacking intellectuals in Urals. When he got instruction to explode the house where Tsar was killed, he did it as an obedient Party apparatchik. And I think that inside Khrushchev there were torments of conscience, because he was involved in Stalin's crimes, he was one of Stalin's closest aides, especially in the last years. I hope some torments of conscience were inside Yeltsin too, and inside Gorbachev—because Gorbachev['s] father was arrested, his uncle was arrested, and this was inevitable dualism. And how one Stalinist could be anti-Stalinist at the same time? But that is Khrushchev's character: very paradoxical. That's why I admire this . . . his . . . on his grave [a] little monument by sculptor Neizvestny, when he express this dualism in Khrushchev's character. But generally I could say I am very grateful to him. He was sometimes rude; he apologized, being retired. Of course, it's easier to apologize when you are retired, but he did it. I could forgive him many things—his rudeness, his lack of culture—for his great achievement when he opened the gates of the prisons and concentrations camp [sic] and so many people began to come back. [. . .]

INT: So when you were a young man and you began to discover this, you heard it first hand from people who'd been through the concentration camps. What effect did that have on people of your generation, this revelation of the truth from them?

YY: First of all, it must not to be repeated in the future, first of all. And only way it's to completely strip mask from the Stalin. But it was one mistake of our generation, very typical for my generation, because we began to discover the truth about Stalin, but we didn't know all truth about Lenin: we idealized Lenin because we didn't know many documents that were hidden in archives. And so we were fighting against the shadow of Stalin with the name of Lenin, and we didn't understand at that time that . . . Stalin was, unfortunately for Lenin, his very faithful disciple. Because, for instance, we didn't know at that time that Lenin was a man who signed first degree [sic] about the first concentration camp for political prisoners in 1918. We didn't know that Lenin, not anybody else, he was accusing Stalin [of] being too soft, too liberal. And when we began to discover this truth, when we . . . We didn't know that Lenin was behind the decision to kill Tsar's family, we didn't know that Lenin was signing many notes, secret notes to Cheka, which was first name of KGB, to Dzerzhinsky, to be pitiless, to hang some peasants, to hang some so-called *burzhui*, bourgeois, and even to put these so-called *burzhui* on the battlefield as human shield covering Red Guards, which is . . . was crime itself. So . . . and now I understand. I couldn't, of course, say that Stalin and Lenin were equal [sic] figures, but Lenin was really . . . Stalin called him his "father," and our generation [of] writer[s], we called Stalin a traitor who betrayed Lenin's ideals. It was not true: Stalin was realizing Lenin's ideals, Lenin's . . . he was fulfilling Lenin's instructions. But it's late discovery of our generation. [. . .]

> INT: Now can we move on to Daniel and Sinyavsky, the trial of Daniel and Sinyavsky? Can I ask you first of all, what was your reaction to it? And secondly, you've described it as a provocation. Can you tell me how it was a provocation? [. . .]

YY: During many years, two Soviet writers, under the pseudonyms Abram Terts and Daniel Arzhak, were published their pretty anti-Soviet, anti-Communist works in the West. So KGB was getting mad trying to find their real names. And so, when they caught two people—they were Sinyavsky and Yulii Daniel—they immediately organized trial. And I understood that this trial will be snowball and will have many dissidents processed. Because during Khrushchev's time we didn't have any kind of trials, dissidents' trials. [. . .]

In 1967, I was invited by Robert Kennedy to his New York flat. We . . . had a very long talk, and during this talk he unexpectedly invited me into his shower . . . toilet room, and he put on the shower, and only after, he said to me that he has some information, that names of Sinyavsky and Daniel were given to our KGB by one CIA agent. I was incredibly surprised, and I asked very naïvely why. I remember his grin full of irony—he said, "No, it was even . . . I could . . . it was very cynical, but it was very clever," because at that time America was bogeyman [sic] in the eyes of many European liberals, even in the eyes of American left-wing intellectuals, because it was a full-swing war in Vietnam. And so, when they arrested Sinyavsky and Daniel, on the first pages of all newspapers, Soviet Union become bogeyman instead of the United States. So it was a very skillful operation. So KGB didn't understand that they are swallowing hook. But probably they understood it, but that was absolutely not important for them, because they want to turn screws again, they want to come back to Stalinism; they were involved in conspiracy even against Brezhnev, because they thought that Brezhnev was an incorrigible liberal. And so they were using this conspiracy. And I think it's old [whole?] story. [. . .]

> INT: Now . . . can I then go back to ask you a question about Pasternak? How influential was Pasternak for you? You met him—what influence did he have on you, particularly in relation to . . . the fact that he was politically not really acceptable to Soviet society at that time? Was he a hero, an idol, somebody who you could . . . ?

YY: First of all, Pasternak was a great poet even in the early twenties. But it was typical for Cold War that they noticed his greatness only after political scandal around his name. I met him, and I fell in love with him completely. It was . . . you know, he was like Mother Nature itself, the most beautiful man, charming. And he was absolutely not political man—I could say in a way apolitical, but he was not indifferent to politics, which is . . . because indifference to politics is a snobbism, and he was never a snob. And his novel *Dr. Zhivago* . . . he put story of love about the history, about the political history, and he was speaking about human values, like about most priceless values in the world, which are always higher than politics, because Yura and Lara, they were divided by civil war, divided by practically, politics killed their love, killed them both. [. . .]

> INT: . . . Let's pick up where we just were, which is: where do you think was the end of the Cold War, in your opinion, which is to repeat what you said . . . what was the last moment for you?

YY: [. . .] I think it was 1989 . . . it was an international forum of intellectuals, when Gorbachev openly said in his speech, in the presence of the Graham Greene, of Arthur Miller, of many others Western writers, best Russian writers and scientists . . . he said that human values are above politics and above class struggle. Because Soviet doctrine was that class struggle is the dominant basis of socialism, and he said human values. And he probably didn't read Pasternak's novel *Dr. Zhivago*, but this is . . . was basis of Pasternak's novel: love story which is above the history of the politics, above the civil war. But something which was heresy in 1957, became official Soviet doctrine in 1989. So that was, I think, the end of Cold War.

> INT: And how do you think the Cold War affected Soviet culture and society? I realize it's a very broad question, but if you could sort of summarize how you think . . . the most important and the most prominent way that the Cold War affected Soviet culture and society.

YY: First of all, we were, for a long time, separated from many contacts with our colleagues in the West. For instance, Anna Akhmatova, great poet, when she was young, she was the mistress of Amadeo Modigliani, and she didn't know until 1940 . . . '42, that Modigliani became famous painter after his death. Many people thought that Chagall is dead; they didn't know that he'd become very famous painter. And we missed many Western great books. But despite of censorship, we were trying to keep this connection, because we were publishing some novels, some poetry . . . we published two . . . beautiful book of English poetry in 1937; in most terrible year of Stalin's purges, we published three anthologies of American poetry. And when Iron Curtain was finally broken, when Robert Frost came, Carl Sandburg, Edward Steichen, other great people of American, English or French art, it was just a great holiday for all of us. And so we were . . . I could say we were . . . in a way we were not in spiritual relation, but we didn't have enough information about what is going on abroad. For instance, even in the last years of Brezhnev, Xeroxes were forbidden; you couldn't have a personal Xerox or personal fax, so it was lack of information. It was impossible to buy foreign newspapers in Moscow; only in special sections of library, with a special permission. At the same time, I think that we, our intellectuals . . . this very hard period passed not losing faith, because many people created beautiful works. They probably didn't exhibit their paintings, they didn't publish some of their poems or novels, but they were writing; they were ready for the moment of openness. And when *perestroika* came, we published so many new, beautiful books, we exhibited so many beautiful paintings, and we began to discover ourselves.

> INT: And who in Soviet society do you think benefited from the Cold War?

YY: I think just bureaucracy, just bureaucracy. But also, unfortunately, I think that . . . unfortunately, there is nothing more profitable in the world than arms race, but . . . it's very profitable as a trade, it gives work for many people. And when, after Cold War was over and we began to close military factori[es], we began to cut budget of many scientists, so many people now without work—it's a big tragedy. So that's like vicious circle. At the same time, arms race, it's very expensive thing, but it makes some people rich, gives them money. That's why I think the wars, they exist and each moment someone kills someone. [. . .]

INT: Right. And what was the worst moment for you in the Cold War?

YY: I told you: when our tanks crossed Czechoslovakian border. That was the most terrible moment, because I didn't want to believe it till the last moment. I remember we were sitting with my writers colleagues in Crimea, and we were talking about it, and I remember . . . I was always idealist, and I am incorrigible idealist—I couldn't be different man; I don't lose hope even in the most difficult moments . . . and so I remember I very romantically exclaimed, "This couldn't happen!" And one more experienced writer, who was veteran of Second World War, he said to me, "Zhenya, Zhenya, I envy to you, I envy to your idealism. Probably now, in this moment when we are sitting and talking about it, Brezhnev's tanks are crossing Czechoslovakian borders." Next morning, I listened radio and I learned that it was true. I tell you, it was the first time in my life when I was absolutely thinking about suicide committing. And when some people congratulate me with my courage when I sent telegram of protest, and I wrote up a poem, it was not courage: it was my fear, because I saved myself from suicide committing, send in this telegram; otherwise I couldn't live with such a burden on my conscience, if I could keep silent.

INT: Now what do you think the Cold War achieved? (*Pause*) For good or ill. (*Pause*)

YY: There is only . . . you know, (*Pause*) If we'll . . . So, Cold War destroyed so many things in the world, in the both systems, I think. It made capitalism more cynical, it made us more cynical; it destroyed so many lives, so many hopes, so many talents. But probably when you think what was good in Cold War, probably one thing, but it was a competition of two systems, but it was dangerous competition; and I don't like if in the world will be only the same political system, because we need this competition, but without cold war, because such a competition could be very easily to transform into war from the Cold War. Because now, I mean, in the moment of this standardization of many systems—I call it the moment of "spiritual McDonaldization of the world"—we have other dangers, we have . . . and I don't think what world ha . . . Now America is . . . obvious it's a leader, and it's a pity. It doesn't mean what . . . it doesn't mean my lack of respect to America, but I think it's very dangerous when only one country takes on its shoulders responsibility for the rest of the world. And, you know, I think megalomania always is kind of weakness, and lack of knowledge. When you are leader of the world, lack of knowledge about other countries could be very dangerous, it could be very destructive for this country which has courage to be responsible for the rest of the world. I think responsibility for the world has to be common. United Nations is not perfect organization, of course. I don't know . . . I think in the future we'll have something else, government of the world—I don't know how to call it—council of the world, something, but responsibility could be only collective. And I think that if now NATO will expand and Russia will be outside of NATO, that could be again some *retsidivs* [he means recurrence] of the Cold War, and probably very dangerous. Because if you isolate someone, he feel lonely, he scares, and he feel humiliated—he or it. I think we have to . . . NATO has to be alliance for everybody, with open gates for everybody; and probably because we have so many common enemies for all humanity, we need new organization which will invite everybody, because we don't know in which country, tomorrow or after tomorrow, will be new dictatorship which could be dangerous for everybody else; and the rest of this union has to be united immediately, in each moment, and we don't know where this new kind of fascism or . . . we don't know names of new dictatorships which will come. Above all, it's very easy to produce now any kind of very dangerous bombs, very easy; probably privately some produce them privately even. So any kind of military blocs inevitably will lead to a new kind of Cold War.

INT: And can I just ask you one last question, which is about the publication of *One Day in the Life of Ivan Denisovich*: from your knowledge of Khrushchev, why do you think that he authorized the publication of this book?

YY: Yes. You know, this book, together with my poem "Heirs of Stalin," was waiting long time. And when Khrushchev was in Caucasus, and one chairman of Abkhazian collective farm, with tears in eyes, began to tell him how many people were killed in Caucasus during Stalin's purges, Khrushchev began to cry too, and in this moment his assistant [Vladimir Lebedev] gave him my poem "Heirs of Stalin"—he was keeping it . . . almost . . . more than half a year—and Khrushchev immediately has sent this poem by military plane to Moscow. It was published in *Pravda*; it was a big scandal, and some Party big cheeses, without any kind of knowledge that Khrushchev was behind this poem, they wrote letter accusing editor in chief of *Pravda* in anti-Soviet activities, publish Yevtushenko's . . . such a scandalous poem. And that time he gave order in a special meeting, when he has read also *One Day [in the Life]* of *Ivan Denisovich* after my poems, and he gave order to publish it, because censorship stopped this book, stopped my poem, and he said, "If I like this poem, if I like this novella, and censorship accuse them to being, then also it means I could be accused in anti-Soviet activities too." And he said, "Our people who lost so many lives during Stalin's purges before the war, behaved so patriotically during the war—they were trying to forget their own pain, their losses of their family. They deserve trust. And if you continue to have censorship, we insult our people, because it means that we mistrust to our own people." And he gave his order to ideological secretary Ilyichov to prepare this special decree of Central Committee of Communist Party of USSR about abolishment of censorship. And they were terribly scared because they couldn't imagine their lives, their survival, without censorship, and that's why they very urgently organized big provocation. They invited . . . knowing that Khrushchev will visit official exhibition of the painting Manège in Moscow, they called to some contemporary painter[s] [and] sculptors, and over one night or two, they brought some sculptures, some abstract paintings . . . they invited Khrushchev after his tour around other halls, and he never seen abstract painting. He asked, "There are some unfinished canvases?" They said, "No." "But why they have no human faces or landscapes of our Motherland?" he asked. And they answered him, "Because they hate the faces of our

Soviet workers, miners." And so, in only one painting, it was dirty spots, and title, unfortunately, was "October Revolution," and that's why they . . . Khrushchev became very furious. He was swearing at this sculpture of Ernst Neizvestny, but he [Neizvestny] behaved very courageously and he was swearing back, he was fighting back. A special, special story. So, the dictionary permits, and international TV doesn't permit to repeat their very juicy expressions during this talk. And now our bureaucrats, these coyotes of ideological jungle, they said, "Now you see, our dear Nikita Sergeyevich, it's too early to abolish censorship we have to wait a little bit. People is not enough mature." That's a history of great provocation.[6]

---

[6] This typescript transcript of a February 2, 1997 interview with Yevgeny Yevtushenko is reprinted here with the permission of the Trustees of the Liddell Hart Centre for Military Archives and the assistance of Lianne Smith, Archives Services Manager at King's College London Archives. Interview excerpted from *The Cold War: Television Documentary Archive, 1995-1998*, held in the Liddell Hart Military Archives of King's College London Archives.

Andrei Voznesensky
(1933, Moscow — 2010, Moscow)

Voznesensky's father was a professor of engineering, his mother an ardent reader of poetry. At the age of fourteen he sent his poems to Boris Pasternak, with whom he was acquainted. Graduated in 1957 from the Moscow Institute of Architecture. Started publishing in 1958. His poetry revived the avant-garde tradition that had been interrupted by the monopoly of Socialist Realism. Along with Yevtushenko and other poets from the generation of the Sixties, enjoyed wide popularity during the Thaw. Along with Yevtushenko and Aksyonov, Voznesensky was targeted by Khrushchev during the meeting with creative intelligentsia at the Kremlin in March 1963 (see the description of this meeting in Aksyonov's *A Mysterious Passion*, in this volume). His poetry provided the literary foundation for the theatrical production *Antiworlds*, performed at the Moscow Theater on the Taganka (dir. Yurii Liubimov), and his narrative poem *Yunona and Avos'* was adapted into a popular musical (composed by Aleksei Rybnikov, dir. Mark Zakharov). In 1979 he contributed to the almanac of uncensored literature *Metropol'*. During *perestroika* and through the 1990s, Voznesensky actively contributed to the cultural return of Russian poetry and art banned during the Soviet period.

ANTIWORLDS

The clerk Bukashkin is our neighbor.
His face is gray as blotting paper.

But like balloons of blue or red,
Bright Antiworlds
            float over his head!
On them reposes, prestidigitous,
Ruling the cosmos, a demon-magician,
Anti-Bukashkin the Academician,
Lapped in the arms of Lollobrigida's.

But Anti-Bukashkin's dreams are the color
of blotting paper, and couldn't be duller.

Long live Antiworlds! They rebut
With dreams the rat race and the rut.
For some to be clever, some must be boring.
No deserts? No oases, then.

There are no women—
            just anti-men.
In the forests, anti-machines are roaring.
There's the dirt of the earth, as well as the salt.
If the earth broke down, the sun would halt.

Ah, my critics; how I love them.
Upon the neck of the keenest of them,
Fragrant and bald as fresh-baked bread,
There shines a perfect anti-head . . .

. . . I sleep with windows open wide;
Somewhere a falling star invites,
And skyscrapers
             like stalactites
Hang from the planet's underside.
There, upside down,
               below me far,
Stuck like a fork into the earth,
Or perching like a carefree moth,
My little Antiworld,
             there you are!

In the middle of the night, why is it
That Antiworlds are moved to visit?

Why do they sit together, gawking
At the television, and never talking?

Between them, not one word has passed.
Their first strange meeting is their last.

Neither can manage the least *bon ton*.
Oh, how they'll blush for it, later on!

Their ears are burning like a pair
Of crimson butterflies, hovering there . . .

. . . A distinguished lecturer lately told me,
"Antiworlds are a total loss."

Still, my apartment-cell won't hold me.
I thrash in my sleep, I turn and toss.

And, radio-like, my cat lies curled
With his green eye tuned in to the world.

Translated by Richard Wilbur

Parabolic Ballad

Along a parabola life like a rocket flies,
Mainly in darkness, now and then on a rainbow.
Red-headed bohemian Gauguin the painter
Started out life as a prosperous stockbroker.
In order to get to the Louvre from Montmartre
He made a detour all through Java, Sumatra,
Tahiti, the Isles of Marquesas.

                            With levity
He took off in flight from the madness of money,
The cackle of women, the frowst of academies,
Overpowered the force of terrestrial gravity.

The high priests drank their porter and kept up their jabbering:
"Straight lines are shorter, less steep than parabolas.
It's more proper to copy the heavenly mansions."

He rose like a howling rocket, insulting them
With a gale that tore off the tails of their frock coats.

So he didn't steal into the Louvre by the front door
But on a parabola smashed through the ceiling.

In finding their truth lives vary in daring:
Worms come through holes and bold men on parabolas.

There once was a girl who lived in my neighborhood.
We went to one school, took exams simultaneously.
But I took off with a bang,

                           I went whizzing
Through the prosperous double-faced stars of Tiflis.

Forgive me for this idiotic parabola.
Cold shoulders in a pitch-dark vestibule . . .
Rigid, erect as a radio antenna rod
Sending its call sign out through the freezing
Dark of the universe, how you rang out to me,
An undoubtable signal, an earthly stand-by
From whom I might get my flight bearings to land by.
The parabola doesn't come to us easily.

Laughing at love with its warnings and paragraphs
Art, love, and history race along recklessly
Over a parabolic trajectory

He is leaving tonight for Siberia.
　　　　　　　　　　　　　Perhaps
A straight line after all is the shorter one actually.

Translated by W. H. Auden.

Ballad of 1941

The piano has crawled underground. Hauled
In for firewood, sprawled
With frozen barrels, crates, and sticks,
The piano is waiting for the axe.

Legless, a black box,
It lies on its belly like a lizard,
Droning, heaving, backed
In an empty mine shaft.

Blood-red, his frozen fingers swollen,
Three lost on one hand, he goes down
On his hand. and knees
To reach the keys.

Seven fingers of an ex-pianist play,
Their frost-bitten skin, steaming, peels away
As from a boiled potato. Their beauty,
Their godliness flame and reply,

Like the great northern lights.
Everything played before is a great lie.
All the reflections of flaming chandeliers,
The white columns, the grand tiers

In warm concert halls—a great lie.
But the steel of the piano howls in me.
I lie in that catacomb,
And I am huge as that piano.

I mirror the soot of the mine. I ape
Hunger, the light of fires, the human shape.
And for my crowning crescendo
I wait for the lick of the axe.

Translated by Stanley Moss

The Triangular Pear

Prelude I

Be discovered, America!
Eureka!

I measure, explore,
                 discover, all out of breath,
In America, *America*,
In myself, *myself*.

I peel the skin from the planet,
                     sweep away mold and dust;
Cut through the crust
              and go down
                    into the depths of things
As into the subway.

Down there grow triangular pears;
                   I seek the naked souls they contain.

I take the trapezoidal fruit, not to eat
Of it; but to let its glassy core
Glow with an altar's red heat.

Pry into it incessantly,
                do not relent;
Do not be misled
If they say your watermelon's green when in fact it's red.

I worry it like a retriever,
                 hack at it like a cleaver!
And if the poet's a hooligan,
Then so was Columbus—carry on!

Follow your mad bent—
                    head straight for shore . . .

You're looking for India—
                    look a hit more—

You'll find
          America!

Prelude II

I adore
The blaze of your buildings, shooting up to the stars,
                                   to heaven's outskirts!

I am a greyhound
                  unleashed, a greyhound
Ready to hunt you down and learn your breed!

Below, past the storefronts
                    you race, a barefoot, beatnik girl!

And under the firehoses of thundering highway
                    my ears like millwheels whirl

Round over godless
                    baseball-crazy
                              gasoline-hazy
                                        America!
Coca-Cola. Clangarola . . . Where
The hell am I?

Like hell—through penthouses, down alleyways
                         and gutters—you led me on,
My eyes shooting back at women
                         like the bolts of guns!

From shopwindows your whoring goods hurled themselves
                                                    at my neck.
But searching for your soul,
                        I thrust them back,
And dived under Broadway, as with an aqualung.
A blue flame in a basement,
                                one of your Negro women swayed!
I'd almost caught up with you
                            but, quivering, you got away.
Read this and forgive:
                    if I grasped nothing but the heat of the chase . . .

A gnome on a roof I perch; below, New York, unfurled.
And your sun, on my little finger,
                                    sits like a ladybird.

Translated by William Jay Smith[1]

[1] Published in: Andrei Voznesensky, *AntiWorlds* (London: Oxford University Press, 1967), 40–41, 49–50, 51, 66–68.

Alexander Galich
(1918, Ekaterinoslav — 1977, Paris)

Born into a Jewish intelligentsia family that moved to Moscow in 1923, Galich studied at the Literary Institute and at the Opera and Drama Studio of Konstantin Stanislavsky. Coauthored the play *The Dawn City*, produced by the studio of Alexei Arbuzov and Valentin Pluchek in 1940. In the 1940s–60s he wrote several plays and film scripts, among which was the script for the popular film *Faithful Friends* (1954). His play *Matrosskaia Tishina*, (1958), which treated the subject of the Holocaust, was banned from production at the newly opened Sovremennik Theater. From the late 1950s, Galich began to compose and perform songs on political themes. In the 1960s Galich could perform his songs only at home, as their content was deemed too critical of the Soviet regime for officially permitted public performances. In 1969 a book of his songs was published abroad, which led to Galich's expulsion from the Union of Soviet Writers in 1971. In the 1970s he actively participated in the dissident movement and in 1974 was forced to emigrate from the USSR. He worked at Radio Liberty in Munich then settled in Paris. It is believed that he died of electrocution while installing a recording antenna. According to some, Galich was assassinated. In 2003 *Matrosskaia Tishina* was released as the film *Papa*, directed by Vladimir Mashkov.

BEHIND SEVEN FENCES

We rode out into the country,
Far away from dirt and grime,
There we saw the fenced-in houses,
Where our leaders spend their time!

There the grass is greener
And the air is clear!
There they've got mint candies,
Truffles and éclairs!

Behind seven fences,
Under seven seals,
There they crunch mint candies,
After fancy meals!

They've got flora, they've got fauna,
They've got caviar and drinks,
But if you as much as peek in,
You'll be picked up by their finks.

Guards patrol the fences
In civilian duds,
While Stalin's loyal comrades
Chew their shish kebabs.

Behind seven fences,
Locked by seven locks,
Stalin's favorite comrades
Chew their shish kebabs!

And when it's fun they're after,
As Stalin's high command,
They get to screen the movies
That they themselves have banned.

And they all breathe heavily,
As they stare up at the screen:
Cause they like the raunchy blonde
That looks just like Marilyn.

Behind seven fences,
Under seven seals
They sure like the raunchy blonde
That looks just like Marilyn!

We walked about awhile
Round the fences in the rain,
Then we sighed at one another
And took the homebound train.

And as we rode the train back
We heard a radio talk
On democratic freedoms
Enjoyed by Soviet folk.

But behind seven fences,
Locked by seven locks,
They were too busy feasting
To hear that radio talk!

LENOCHKA

One April night our Lenochka
Was standing at her post,
That chestnut-haired young beauty
Was standing at her post
So stunning and sublime she was
One look and you were toast!
At city's exit Lenochka
Was standing at her post!

> And that's the story for you,
> She was standing at her post.

If you become a cop, you see,
You have to swear all day,
Don't matter if you're shy or not,
You have to swear all day.
Her girlfriends sniffed the lilacs,
Went into town to play.
But she patrolled the highways
So she had to swear all day!

> And that's the story for you,
> She had to swear all day!

So Lenochka was standing there,
A sergeant on patrol,
A girl out of Ostankino
A sergeant on patrol.
To each her very own, you see,
While others had a ball,
Our Lenochka was standing there.
A sergeant on patrol.

And that's the story for you,
A sergeant on patrol!

When suddenly she noticed
A cavalcade of lights!
From Moscow's central airport
A cavalcade of lights!
The sirens were all blaring,
Security's airtight!
Some foreigners were coming:
A cavalcade of lights!

And that's the story for you,
A cavalcade of lights!

So Lenochka just waved them through,
Her hand, it didn't shake!
Her knees went kind of wobbly,
But her hand, it didn't shake!
These weren't local taxis, see,
But cars of foreign make!
And Lenochka just waved them through,
Her hand, it didn't shake!

Ompa-ompa-ompa,
Her hand, it didn't shake.

But suddenly the lead car
Slowed down along its route,
Though everything was fine, you see,
It slowed down on its route.
The KGB surrounded it
Like something was afoot,
But right beside our Lenochka
It slowed down on its route.

And that's the story for you,
It slowed down on its route!

In that car sat a gorgeous
Young Ethiopian stud
He stared at our Lenochka
That Ethiopian stud,
And rising from his leather seat
(He would not miss, by God!)
He tossed her a chrysanthemum
That Ethiopian stud!

Ompa-ompa-ompa,
That Ethiopian stud!

A messenger arrived at dawn from
CC CPSU,
He zoomed in on a fancy bike from
CC CPSU.
He hurried right to Lenochka,
He was giving her the cue:
"They're calling L. Potapova
to CC CPSU!"

Right there on the Old Plaza
Was that Ethiopian guy,
He was getting all the honors,
That Ethiopian guy,
He thanked them very regally
And that is not a lie,
Cause it turned out he's a royal,
That Ethiopian guy!

His retinue drank vodka,
But he stared at the door,
He held on to his souvenirs

And he stared at the door,
They hailed the regal ally,
But he grunted like a boar,
Just then the music sounded
And they opened up the door . . .

All sheathed in tulle and velvet
She walked into the hall.
Left everybody speechless,
When she walked into the hall.
So that the royal stud himself
Ahmed Ali and all,
Cried out, "I must be dreaming!"
When she walked into the hall.

      Ompa-ompa-ompa,
      When she walked into the hall!

And afterwards our Lenochka
Around the world was known,
A girl out of Ostankino
Around the world was known.
When Prince Ali did his daddy in,
And got the royal throne,
The Sheik's wife L. Potapova
Around the world was known!

To the Memory of Boris Leonidovich Pasternak

> "The management of the USSR Literary Fund announces the death of the writer Boris Leonidovich Pasternak, a member of the Litfund, who died on March 30th of this year, in his seventy-first year, after a difficult and prolonged illness, and expresses its condolences to the family of the deceased."
>
> *The only announcement*
> *of Boris Pasternak's death that appeared*
> *in Soviet newspapers.*[1]

The funereal wreaths will be made into brooms,
But for a whole half-an-hour we looked sad.
We are proud to say, as his contemporaries,
That he died at home, in his bed!

The hired orchestra was torturing Chopin,
And the farewell was properly solemn:
He did not soap a noose in Elabuga[2]
And he did not go mad in Suchan!

Poetasters all the way from Kiev
Came to offer respects to the dead! . . .
We are proud to say, as his contemporaries,
That he died at home, in his bed!

He didn't just make it past forty,
He was seventy — an age ripe and mortal!

---

[1]   Literary Fund is an organization to which all members of the Union of Soviet Writers belonged. After Pasternak's expulsion from the Union in 1958 (as a part of the campaign against his novel *Doctor Zhivago*), he was allowed to remain a member of the Litfund.

[2]   The place of Marina Tsvetaeva's suicide.

And he wasn't some penniless castoff,
The deceased was on Litfund's payroll!

... O the fir branches are all stripped bare now,
His snowstorms have knelled out and fled,
See how proud we are, lousy bastards,
That he died at home in his bed!

"The snow was swept across the land,
It swirled and swirled.
A candle on a table glowed
A candle glowed."[3]

It wasn't candlelight back then:
The main chandelier was lit up,
And on the executioner's face
The glasses nimbly glinted.

The groggy audience was bored:
The same old thing again!
He wasn't getting jail, Suchan,[4]
And not a bullet through the brain!

They weren't flaying him alive
To let him earn a martyr's grace
His martyrdom would be by vote,
Cast like a whip across his face.

And someone really plastered asked,
"What is it now? Who are they after?"
And someone chewed amidst the jokes
And someone shook with laughter.

---

[3]   An excerpt from Boris Pasternak's poem "Winter Night."

[4]   The location of a Gulag labor camp.

But we will not forget their laughter,
And their jaded boredom,
We will recall the names of all
Who dared to vote against him!

"The noise died down. I came out on the stage.
As I lean against the doorframe there,
I attempt to hear in distant echoes . . ."[5]

. . . So the slurs and the insults are over,
Eternity lowers the curtain on their part
And now marauders rise over his coffin,
For they will be his ceremonial guard!

[5]   An excerpt from Pasternak's poem "Hamlet."

* * *

Comrades, I'll tell you like it is:
We live in Russia, not just anywhere!
You prefer your ethnic cap over a hat?
You are free to decide what to wear!

But our work it is really quite subtle.
We can't stop being watchful and rest,
Instead, we must strive day and night
To act as guards of our State's interest.

We're not playing cards here or ball games,
This isn't some train station, open to all,
What matters most to us? Cadres!
You recall who set that for our goal!?

So you are not just sitting here fishing,
And there is one key thing you should know:
All is clear when it comes to Rabinowitz,
But it's who Ivanov is that you must show.

Ivanov writes in our form that he's Russian—
The real thing, but don't make any bets.
See, he's born in that Jew-town of Bobruisk,
And his grandmother's last name was Katz.

So you'll have to take note of that grandma
(Keep Ivanov himself in the dark),
But put his form into a separate file,
And mark it off with a separate mark.

Translated by Maria Bloshteyn[6]

[6] Published in: Alexander Galich, *Dress Rehearsal* (Bloomington: Slavica, 2008), 169–92.

Vassily Aksyonov
(1932, Kazan — 2009, Moscow)

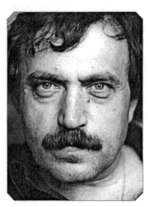

Born to a family of Party activists. His mother was Evgenia Ginzburg, known as the author of the Gulag memoir *Journey into the Whirlwind* (*Krutoi marshrut*, 1967). In 1937 Aksyonov's parents were arrested and sentenced to the imprisonment in the Gulag. Only in 1947 could Aksyonov join his mother in Magadan, where she lived in exile. Graduated from a Moscow medical college in 1956. His first stories and novels (*Colleagues* [1959], *A Starry Ticket* [1961], *Oranges from Morocco* [1963], *Surplussed Barrelware* [1968]) were published in the journal *Youth* (*Iunost'*) in the early sixties and made him one of the literary leaders of his generation. Although his works were harshly condemned by critics, his use of irony and the grotesque contributed to his popularity among Soviet readers. In the sixties and seventies, the "realist" approach of his early works gave way to an idiosyncratic mixture of modernism and Socialist Realist parody, resulting in something quite close to the aesthetics of postmodernism. Examples of Aksyonov's works of this period are his experimental novels *In Search of a Genre* (1978), *The Burn* (1980), and *The Island of Crimea* (1981). The latter two were rejected by Soviet censors. He coedited the uncensored literary almanac *Metropol'*, and in 1980, after the scandal that ensued following its attempted publication, he immigrated to Washington, DC.

Free from the strictures of Soviet literary control, Aksyonov's late fiction was, strangely enough, a return to traditional realism, as the novels *Generations of Winter* and *The Winter's Hero* attest (published in three volumes in Russian as *Moskovskaia saga* [1993–1996]). His works enjoyed wide distribution and popularity in post-Soviet Russia. His 2004 novel *Voltairians and Voltairiennes* was awarded the Russian Booker Prize for the Best Novel. From the late nineties Aksyonov divided his time between Moscow and Biarritz, France. His autobiographical novel *A Mysterious Passion* (*Tainstvennaia strast'*, 2007) offers a broad panorama of cultural life in 1960s Moscow. After Aksyonov's death in 2009, a new edition of the novel appeared with all fragments omitted in the previous edition restored.

From *A Mysterious Passion*[1]

On March 7, 1963,[2] Moscow entered the eye of a western hurricane. Thick, wet snow had been falling since morning. Galoshes were almost completely out of fashion by then, so at least half of the guests invited to the Kremlin—the young writers, filmmakers, stage actors and artists—arrived with wet feet. The other half, namely, the party elite, flaunted the dry soles of their shoes. They didn't wear galoshes. The sedans from the Central Committee's garages chauffeured them right to the doors of the Sverdlovsky Theater.

Vakson[3] crossed Red Square on the adjacent side, opposite the angle formed by Kuibysheva Street, passed GUM department store, then went toward the Spassky Tower. Through the falling snow he espied his friend, the film director Ryurik Turetsky,[4] quickly walking toward the tower along the hypotenuse from 25 October Street. He

---

[1]   Translated from: Vasilii Aksenov, *Tainstvennaia strast'* (Moscow: Sem' Dnei, 2009), 82–86, 88–95, 96–100, 105–107, 119–133. © 2009 Sem' Dnei Publishing House.

[2]   The exact date of Nikita Khrushchev's infamous "meeting with the creative intelligentsia." The following chapter is based on actual events.

[3]   Pseudonym for Aksyonov. As a roman à clef, *A Mysterious Passion* presents real persons under invented names.

[4]   The film director Andrei Tarkovsky. The screenplay described here is Tarkovsky's *Andrei Rublev*, initially titled *The Passions According to Andrei*.

picked up his pace and their paths intersected at a defined point, as in a geometry problem.

"Hi, Ryur!"

"Hi, Vaks!"

Each slowed his pace so they could have some time to catch up. Vakson wanted to know how things were going with "The Passions of Feodosii." Ryurik had sent his screenplay about the medieval Russian artist to the State Committee for Cinema for consideration. Ryur gave a dismissive wave.

"Those bastards are gonna sit on it for at least a year. We're flat broke. Irka makes a bit with her sewing and we live off that." Then, with genuine interest, he asked, "Have you ever been there?"

"Where?" Vakson didn't understand.

"You know, the fortress?" Ryurik pointed to the Kremlin. "I should really be going up there for the view and not to sit at their moronic ideological committee meetings."

They came to the end of Red Square. The snow that had been accumulating along a tangent by the walls and towers came to its senses and calmed down a little. Even so, their boots had grown heavy, and their socks, in the gap between their boots and trousers, were soaking.

"Hey, Ryur, have you ever seen the mummy?"[5]

Ryurik, walking quickly and dressed like a Hollywood industry type despite having no money, chuckled sarcastically.

"You know, I've never gotten around to it."

Vakson recalled how as a sixteen-year-old kid he'd stood in line to see the mummy. He didn't feel any kind of spiritual devotion to it. He was just doing what all the tourists from the provinces did then. As soon as you got to Moscow, you went straight to see the main attraction in Red Square, free of charge. As for Ryurik, being a native Muscovite meant that he'd never gone there because in principle he could go whenever he wanted.

The large crowd was at the coat check in the Sverdlovsky Theater. It smelled of wet clothes. After dropping off their overcoats,

---

[5]   A reference to Lenin's embalmed body in the mausoleum in Moscow's Red Square.

they formed little groups to draw attention to their ostentatious aloofness, or to their authority. Elderly men with all kinds of lapel pins dominated the crowd. There was one with the colors of the Supreme Soviet, one with service ribbons, even one with a laureate's badge. Catastrophically few, and unattractive, women were in attendance. Even fewer young people without badges were there. They almost all knew each other.

All the liberals dutifully kissed each other on the cheek, as if they were attending a premiere at the Contemporary.[6] They exchanged brief phrases. What's going on? Nothing. What's happening here tonight? We'll soon find out. For a moment Vakson considered the expression "nothing." In Russia nothing meant that things were good. At least for the moment. If something is happening, it's invariably bad. Antoshka Andreotis rushed past, produced multiple copies of his book "Pear-shaped Triangle"[7] from his pockets, quickly signed them with a felt-tip pen and presented them to the people in the left wing. And not only to those in the left wing. He even autographed a copy for that notorious behemoth Sufronyev.[8] Sufronyev glowed and boastfully glanced around: these progressive young people, these cocky punks, respect me! It occurred to Vakson that he should have brought at least one copy of the journal with his "Citruses"[9] in it. He could have given it to someone, to Ehrenburg,[10] for example. Ehrenburg was standing solemn and alone, an empty pipe in his mouth. I hope that old Parisian beatnik remembers how a group of young, free spirits—

[6]   The Sovremennik Theater, a popular, liberal-oriented Moscow theater founded during the Thaw.

[7]   A reference to the poet Andrei Voznesensky. His collection *The Triangular Pear* had just been published in 1962.

[8]   Anatolii Sofronov (1911–1990), a Stalinist poet, playwright, and editor-in-chief of the magazine *Ogonyok*.

[9]   A reference to Aksyonov's famous novella *Oranges from Morocco* (1962).

[10]   Ilya Ehrenburg (1891–1967), Soviet novelist and journalist. Author of the novel *The Thaw*, from which the period takes its name. One of the intellectual leaders of the liberals in the 1960s.

Atamanov[11], Mish, Podgursky and Vakson—all looking to the New Jerusalem, came to his place for the night and shook the foundations until his watchful collie could no longer sleep under the table. Vakson moved forward to give him the journal, then remembered that he hadn't brought it, and maneuvered himself over to the opposite side.

The crowd began to advance into the round hall with the heavenly blue cupola. If the Bolsheviks hadn't seized the fortress,[12] it might have been possible to paint the cupola with something like a Michelangelo. It's entirely possible that something sacred had been there before the Cheka wiped it away.

To the right of the entrance towered an enormous state-owned table of polished oak, and almost right up against it stood a heavy state-owned podium with a microphone. Several microphones were also set up on the table. Past the podium, rows of state-owned armchairs were spread out in semi-circles. Today they were reserved for state-owned asses, and for the asses of the Soviet creative intelligentsia. There were also some reserved for the asses of the not-quite Soviet creative intelligentsia, that is to say, for those asses that were going to get a whipping. Maybe my ass will get whipped too, thought Vakson, as he thought about the asses to be whipped. Hopefully not as badly as others. After all, my bold and spirited story just came out in print with the consent of the Central Committee. Well, maybe they'll whip me once or twice for "Heads and Tails," but not more than that. They didn't put me down to speak today. I need to sit somewhere closer to my people, we need to stick together, as the Kyoto prophet once said.

Kukush[13] and Henrik Izvestnov,[14] both in jackets and ties, drew closer to the crowd as they walked together. Shoot, I should have

---

[11]   Yurii Kazakov (1927–1982), a prose writer, master of the short story.

[12]   An allusion to a well-known quote by Stalin: "There are no fortresses in the world that the Bolsheviks could not seize."

[13]   A reference to the singer and poet Bulat Okudzhava (1924–1997), identified later as "Oktava."

[14]   Ernst Neizvestnyi (b. 1925), an artist and sculptor, among those attacked by

worn a tie too. I was even planning to wear one, and for some reason I didn't. Idiot. I look kind of out of it with this unbuttoned collar. Suddenly Kukush and Henry were gone. Where did they go? They must have taken their seats, but I'll never get to them now, trying to walk against this crowd. He scanned the hall. This wasn't the British Parliament, with Tories and Whigs exchanging their unyielding positions. This assembly was characterized by its absence of characteristics. It was more like consensus, the consolidation of governance. One of his buddies called out to him over the sea of heads, "Over here, Vaks!" but at that moment the hall burst into applause: His Majesty the Politburo appeared behind the presidium's table. The applause grew louder and soon became a rhythmic thunder, punctuated by occasional cries of "Glory to our Communist Party!" "Long live the members of the presidium of the Central Committee of the Communist Party of the Soviet Union!" "Long live the leader of the people of the USSR, Comrade Khrushchev, our Nikita Sergeyevich!"

Vakson clapped a little, then turned his attention to physiognomy. All of the members of the Politburo were here. The Party emphasized the tremendous importance it accorded to its dialogue with the Soviet creative intelligentsia. Like a crocodile who had basked in the sun, the chief ideologue Suslov made his way to his designated seat. Frol Romanovich Kozlov, who had the most heavy-set physique, got settled. Comrade Kirilenko majestically turned his well-baked snout. A rotten smell emanated from Kosygin's misanthropic mien. The Belorussian Comrade Mazurov, who looked like a soccer coach, stood behind his chair with a barely perceptible, but nonetheless perceptible, sardonic smile. Comrade Shelest brought to mind a superb illustration to accompany Lombroso's theory of criminal atavism.[15] Only Comrade Podgorny, who was also in attendance,

Khrushchev at the 1962 exhibit "The New Reality" at the Manezh gallery in Moscow. Later he was commissioned to design the monument at Khrushchev's grave. Since 1977 he has lived in the United States.

[15]   Cesare Lombroso (1835–1909) proposed that criminals could be distinguished by ape-like facial features and particular measurements and proportions of the skull and face.

could challenge him there. The seats at the end of each row were occupied by Kil'kichev,[16] Andropov, and Demichev, both candidates to become members and secretaries of the Politburo. They did not capture Vakson's physiognomical interest. It was time to focus on Him.

Nikita[17] was for the most part pale, but ruddy in places. The applause had clearly aroused him. Round as always. A magnificent white shirt of pure nylon. They say a Central Committee courier goes to Vienna for those shirts. The neck measurements are given in code, K to S, Khrushchev to Suslov. The emerald cufflinks on his sleeves were a gift from Fidel Castro (expropriated from the house of Batista). The crowd parted and he made his way to his chair, sustaining the applause by applauding his applauders. Then he held up his palms to extinguish the applause, because if you didn't do that in the Kremlin they would go on clapping for a year. Greetings, boys. Please, have a seat.

He looked into the hall disapprovingly. He smirked as if to say, eh, what kind of shit do I have to deal with today. "At this time I ask all spies and collaborators with the bourgeois press to please leave the room. I'm joking, I'm joking. Please sit, comrades."

* * *

Shchipkov[18] spoke in a kind, grandfatherly voice about the successes of the Moscow Writer's Union, the conferences and seminars, the propaganda brigades, the sponsored trips to support the building of communism, and so on. Then he easily transitioned into his favorite theme: bringing young members into the creative ranks of the Union. Established writers are being called in to work with

---

[16]   Leonid Ilichev (1906–1990), secretary of the Central Committee of the Communist Party of the Soviet Union, the head of the Ideological Commission of the Central Committee. Except for "Kil'kichev," all names in this paragraph are real.

[17]   Nikita Sergeyevich Khrushchev, referred to variously as "Nikita,""Nikita Sergeyevich," "the leader" and the "General Secretary."

[18]   Stepan Shchipachev (1899–1980), Soviet poet, head of the Moscow Writer's Union.

young writers. The relevant department has already begun its work. In due course we will discover new talents and recommend them to publishers and journals that print poetry and prose. These publications will provide us with the opportunity to induct young people into the ranks of the Writer's Union. A large group of young people became members of our organization this spring, and in turn rejuvenated our admittedly mature ranks with their promising diversity of opinions.

It was at this moment, at what was certainly the most opportune moment, that the delightful speech of this connoisseur of love and familial harmony was interrupted by some discordant sounds, momentarily bringing to mind Prokofiev's "Peter and the Wolf." Nikita Sergeyevich coughed into the microphone, reminding the hall of the trombone's existence: "We don't particularly appreciate your activities, Comrade Shchipkov."

The speaker stammered and from that moment on could not utter a single phrase without faltering. Any question of clarification would be taken as a challenge. What unimaginable insolence, what an egregious violation of Party etiquette!

"So who did you induct into the Writer's Union?"

"..."

"Are you confident that you have selected those who are worthy, proud, patriotic, and sworn to our cause?"

"..."

"As a communist do you swear upon your Party card that you have not inducted any beatniks or another Petofi Circle?"[19]

Three question marks, and he could not answer to any of them with a single exclamatory, proud or patriotic remark. Why couldn't he respond with the authority of his post, his Party card, or his Russian pride?

Because the use of the question mark on this stage is terrifying, that's why. And to respond with an exclamation would be

---

[19]   The Petofi Circle was formed in April 1956 and named after Sándor Petőfi, the poet who fought for Hungarian freedom in 1848 against the Austrian Empire. The Circle is credited with initiating the popular uprising against communist dictatorship in Hungary.

a disgrace! Pyotr Stepanovich Shchipkov hung his head and stepped down from the podium into the hall. A single, but weighty, thought occupied his mind: "When all is said and done, only ten years have passed since the death of the Firebreather."[20]

Vakson and Gol'tsev[21] exchanged meaningful looks during the reference to the Petofi Circle. Vakson couldn't think about anything other than the fact that the leader still remembered the anti-Soviet writers' club formed in Budapest in 1956. In the meantime, his neighbor to the right was clapping enthusiastically along with all the other blowhards. "Who's that on the right, Elizar?" Vakson asked in a whisper.

"Nalbandian, state artist," Gol'tsev whispered back. "Replicated Stalin."[22]

Vakson recalled the enormous painting above the staircase at the House of Scientists in Kazan. In it, Stalin and his closest associates were descending the staircase of the Great Kremlin Palace toward the people. A staircase above a staircase, clever. The magnificent procession of heroes of the communist empire stretched to infinity. In the spring of 1953 Vakson and a group of young friends were moving in the opposite direction on those stairs. They were going up to the second floor of the House of Scientists, where a student jazz group was playing on the sly. Taking a fleeting glance at the painting, he stopped: something strange had happened to Nalbandian's ever-present opus. Looking closer, he realized what was up: Lavrenty Pavlovich Beria had disappeared! He'd vanished from that close-knit party of eminences! All the others were there, but he, the exposed and obliterated agent of imperialism, had disappeared from the canvas! This was some kind of magic, a devil's trick! Then it all became clear: Beria was made over! His bald head was now adorned with parted, dark chestnut locks, his pince-nez

---

[20] A reference to Stalin.

[21] Elizar Mal'tsev (1916/17–2004), author of popular novels about peasant life.

[22] Dmitrii Nalbandian (1906–1993), Soviet artist, known for his numerous portraits of Soviet leaders from Lenin to Brezhnev. The painting described in the following paragraph is *At the Kremlin* from 1945.

was transformed into a large pair of glasses, mustaches embellished his upper lip. Among those painfully recognizable leaders and behind Stalin's left shoulder strode an Ordinary Soviet Man!

Vakson felt an urge to ask the artist if he had repainted Beria himself or if he'd sent someone else to do it, but at that moment Comrade Kil'kichev invited the poet Robert R[23] to the podium in a thoroughly imposing tone.

Robert coincidentally had taken the seat to the right of Pyotr Shchipkov, and as the latter returned from the podium dripping with sweat and shaking from the horror he'd endured, Robert wanted to dash out of the hall, snatch his coat from the cloakroom and run to freedom . . . "there, where the poplars are dazed, where the distance is afraid, where a house is terrified of falling, where the air is blue, like the bundle of linen a discharged patient takes from the hospital," . . . from bedlam! And now they were calling him forward.

Pyotr Shchipkov all but tore the pages of the poem "Yes, lads!" from his hands. Don't read it, Robert! Surely you know never to read it! The one called to the rostrum yanked his pages back from the fingers of the One Who Had Already Been There. He went forward. His head was spinning. In it hovered a thought completely unbefitting the circumstances: "Why doesn't anyone consider the fact that I have a terrible case of the flu?" Tall and muscular, he moved toward the aisle, brushing against the knees of those sitting in his row. Mumbling "excuse me" several times, he made his way to the carpeted path in the aisle. I need to make it to the podium without staggering. Without falling. Should I smile or not?

> Don't cry, don't purse your swollen lips,
> Don't gather them into creases.
> You'll peel open the dried scabs
> Left by a vernal fever.[24]

---

[23] Robert Rozhdestvensky (1932–1994), a poet who rose to prominence in the 1960s. Friend of Voznesensky, Yevtushenko, and Akhmadulina. Became an official Soviet writer in the 1970s.

[24] A poem by Boris Pasternak.

If you smile, you will annoy them as well. So don't cry, but don't smile either. A more businesslike attitude and I'll get my composure together. Remember, at Luzhniki Stadium I stood before a crowd of 15,000 and I didn't shit my pants!

Having made his way to the podium, he laid a hand along its side and glanced at the faces of those who were attentively watching him from the table. Attentively, yet indifferently. Only one of them, Mazurov, had eyes that hinted at some warmth. He, with the well-defined jaw, seemed to be a decent guy. All the rest were no good. Khrushchev was also no good. With Mazurov you might be able to go have a drink. The three of us: Yustas, me, and Mazurov. You couldn't have a drink with Khrushchev the way you could with Mazurov. He's the leader, he demands deference. Awe and deference. No friendly drink with him.

These are the sorts of thoughts that were flashing through his head, and perhaps through his bronchi and lungs, before he climbed up to the podium. Now some words about the podium itself. It was a tour de force of podium-making. Made from oak of exceptional quality. No one has fallen from it, not even once. On its front panel hung a remarkable exemplar of wood carving. True, it was not quite realistic and somewhat abstract. Something that looked like a crab with two claws, and in the center, some swallowed objects that were hard to make out. It was the emblem of the USSR. The podium was positioned a bit lower than the table on the stage, almost flush with its center. Nikita Sergeyevich Khrushchev hung right over it with his microphone, and when he heaved forward with both of his fists raised, it appeared from some corners of the hall that he was tackling the speaker.

Robert R had the floor: "Dddear comrades . . . dddear Nikkiita Sssergeyevich . . ."

Silence. While the silence drags on, let's say a few more words about another one of the advantages of this podium. The speaker cannot see a single member of the presidium from it. To see anyone on the committee from it you have to turn your back to the hall, and then the microphone ends up behind you. This would seem to be a trivial detail, but this layout plays a rather critical role in the scene before us. Robert went on torturing speech therapists: "Iiit ssseems . . . ttthat wwwe . . . aaare eeentttering a nnnnew eeera iiin ourrr hhhistory." Vakson and Gol'tsev wiped the sweat from their foreheads. You know, Elizar, this isn't for the fainthearted. Nalbandian sniffed disdainfully. All of R's friends knew that he occasionally experienced bouts of tortuous stuttering. Sometimes even at social gatherings, though that was rare. It happened often in public, although at poetry readings his admirers were always captivated by his manner of speaking. They saw his stuttering as a charming affectation, similar to Simonov's. He would even flaunt it at parties, pretending that he had difficulty speaking at moments of inspiration or deep thought. Despite all this, he hated being a stutterer and would have preferred to compete at oratory with Tushinsky.[25] One drunken evening he confessed to Vakson that he hadn't always stuttered. It started after a terrible scare when he was five years old. He didn't elaborate further and never uttered, allow us this pun, a word on the topic again. One significant detail is worth noting: Rob never stuttered when he read poetry, no matter how large the audience that crushed him with its admiration. The passion that took over him while in the flow of declaiming verses eclipsed that childhood fear.

Standing behind the podium in front of the attentive hall, two-thirds of which consisted of the Party's ideological apparatchiks and its "armed detachment," feeling on the back of his head the squinting gaze of the dictator and the indifferent presence of two dozen indifferent and powerful men, Robert could not control his stuttering. He tried to convey his main idea to the supreme council: that Soviet youth were in no way trying to break away from the older generation, they were imbued with patriotism and enthusiasm, possessed by a romantic drive toward the future, to outer space, to science, ready to rebuff NATO imperialists, to defend heroic Cuba, resist slanderers and demagogues, challenge the petty bourgeoisie, renounce the backwardness of those who did not keep up with the policies of the Twentieth Congress of our Party, maintain their dignity before those who cast unfounded accusations at them and

---

[25]   Yan Tushinsky is the poet Yevgeny Yevtushenko.

threatened them with the slogan "No, lads!" He was ready to say all this and in fact he did say it, but the terrible and humiliating anxiety turned everything into unintelligible slogans amid painful stuttering. Covered in sweat, his ears on fire, he stood with his back to the leader and forced his speech into the microphone, one prepared phrase after another garbled by stuttering. Of course he did not notice that Khrushchev had passed a note down to Kil'kichev, and how Kil'kichev, walking behind the armchairs, bent his head to the leader's ear. Finally, the celebrated and stellar youth poet Robert R reached his concluding pages, the poem "Yes, lads!" And his stuttering stopped instantaneously.

He was transformed. His head was proudly held high. He gripped the podium with both hands; it was he who took the podium in his hands, and not the other way around. The shaking stopped. Dry land rose up before him. His voice gathered sonorousness and held onto it with resounding strength. He read:

> We are to blame!
> Very much to blame!
> We were not with the paratroopers
> Who fell through the mist,
> And in this
> Autumn trampled by war
> We were not at the front,
> But on the homefront.
> We did not start with fear at a knock in the night,
> We saw
> Neither captivity
> Nor jail . . .
> We are to blame,
> For being born too late.
> We beg forgiveness,
> We are to blame . . .

Now he was in the flow, where he always felt himself the master of the situation. Reading, he saw, in place of an indistinguishable mass, a multitude of faces—perplexed, knit-browed, beaming, fixed in embarrassment—but he did not see the leader's cloddish face gushing beet juice. At these moments he completely forgot about the leader. Unlike his friends Yan Tushinsky and Antosha Andreotis, he did not like to gesticulate while reading. But here, coming to the conclusion, he raised his right arm powerfully, as if blocking a spike in volleyball:

> Yes, lads!
> Cheerful seekers,
> Who've escaped
> The cold hand of fate!
> Let them wail
> About unruly children
> In the swirling
> Artificial smoke
> Bold dealers in ideas,
> Who have learned
> Nothing!
> Yes, lads!
> We're stepping onto
> An uneven path.
> Fight against lies,
> Hold your own!
> You are true
> To what is most valued
> In the flag
> Under which
> We
> Live!

* * *

The hall erupted. Many were applauding and smiling. Many were outraged: aggressively, churlishly, drearily. Robert hadn't waited for a response from the presidium and had stepped away from the podium when the hall resounded with, "Would you look at that!" He stopped, one foot still on the podium, and turned toward the leader. The leader looked at him with a strange, almost vulgar, nearly thuggish smirk. "How is it that you are so arrogant with your poems, Comrade R?" Robert could not come up with anything better than a questioning face: "Are you talking to me, Comrade?" Khrushchev stood and dug his fists into the table. "I would advise you to be more modest. Your poems sound as if you are summoning the youth to stand under your own personal flag. Nothing will come of this, Comrade R!"

He moved back slightly from his microphone, as if to summon applause. He did not have to wait long. In the hall rose "boisterous applause, becoming an ovation," and the accompanying din of welcoming cries. Vakson looked around and saw that many people were standing and waving their arms. Shouts sliced through the uniform rumble: "That's right, Nikita Sergeyevich!" "Drive out these youth!" Sitting beside him, Nalbandian jumped in, "It's time to end this, Nikita Sergeyevich!"

Heat poured from Khrushchev. Beet-red spots appeared on his head and cheeks. His nose swelled. He had only just calmed the expressions of ecstasy when he launched into an extended paragraph: "Look, comrades, at these leaders and what surrounds them, these 'lads with upturned collars'! What are they worth in this world, where a historic battle is being waged? They are worth nothing! R is polemicizing with the verses of Apollon Gribochuyev[26] and his poem, 'No, lads!' He wants to suggest that communists are out of touch with life. As if only they, these new poets, could convey the feelings of our youth. You're wrong, R, you're off the mark! Who are you to deny the poet-soldier, whose keen eye and precise aim hits ideological enemies without missing? Comrades, let's salute the poet-communist Comrade Gribochuyev!"

The hall broke into complete hysteria. Paroxysms of delight. Many brushed away tears, pounded their chests, raised clenched fists, and in heroic ecstasy shouted to "those lads," "No pasaran!" Gribochuyev's freshly-wiped bald pate appeared above the rows of heads. He thanked the comrades for their solidarity.

Khrushchev continued: "Of course, it is not at all the case that we wish to make a negative example of everything. Now and then poets present an advantage to history and circumstances. Our ambassadors in France and West Germany speak favorably of Tushinsky's performances. Although I would advise Comrade

[26]   Nikolai Gribachev (1910–1992), an orthodox Socialist Realist poet.

Tushinsky to be a bit more humble at home. Our youth will NEVER wear t-shirts with his portrait on them! (A shout went up in the hall—Never! Never! Never!) I would strongly recommend Comrade Tushinsky to stay within the law, stop making yourself the subject of sensationalist stories, avoid pandering to consumerist tastes. One must rise above, and not wriggle along! And you, R, I advise you to stand under our proud banner, and not hunker down under your own, out of step with the times! That is all! Go to your seat! Sit down!"

He lowered his own bottom into his seat, then suddenly noticed that Robert R was still standing and looking askance at him, as if he wanted to choke out something awkward, inappropriate, aggravating. He waved off this feeble attempt with an aggressive sweep of his hand. Go, Comrade R, sit down. Put a lid on it! Robert shrugged. A protest rose up inside him, as if to shout, "How can you laugh, you bastard, and be so coarse, so dismissive? Just watch, your bullying will come back and bite you in the ass!" And just like that, the protest withered. He lowered his head and went to his place. Put a lid on it.

From that point on everything moved along fairly decently. The General Secretary champed at the bit and bolted along his favorite bumps in the road. He peddled an example for the poets to imitate, one frozen in his skull since his early days as a miner: "Pavel Makhinya was a true proletarian poet, not some kind of philistine or bourgeois. The entire Donbass region was inspired by his verse:

> The working class is a great power!
> When the motherland requests,
> Their work so venturous,
> They mine the coal for us.

At this time I'd like to make an interesting observation. I'm looking into the hall and I notice that not everyone is applauding. Comrades, not everyone enjoys these patriotic pronouncements. I see Ilya Ehrenburg—he isn't applauding. How is that, Comrade Ehrenburg? Hitler once condemned you to a death sentence, and here you're holding back? By the way, thank you for giving me a copy of your book *People, Years, Life*[27] with the kind inscription inside. But I must confess I can't make heads or tails of it. Somehow you put everything together in an unfamiliar way. There's hardly any Socialist Realism in it. You recall that the characters are not always straightforward with regard to their Marxism. It seems that somehow it isn't a Soviet writer who is telling the story, but a grand dame of the old regime. Well? Would you like to challenge this Bolshevik from the rostrum? Please do, dear sir!"

Ehrenburg understood, of course, that this was a game of cat and mouse in which he was not the cat. But he refused to see himself as a grumpy old rodent, so in response to every one of the General Secretary's outrageous statements, he moved his palms in a contrary gesture and kept his mouth shut. He shot sharp glances at the General Secretary from under his bushy eyebrows; he could not understand what was going on. Why was he suddenly so concerned for art and carrying on about it so ineffectively? Why is this outdated campaign being waged in our post-Stalin society? Only last year Khrushchev came up to him at a reception held at the Kremlin and for a half-hour they talked about enjoying their golden years. And now look, we are refusing to engage in dialogue. Stay quiet, don't say anything, put a lid on it!

Khrushchev held his gesture of invitation—please, please do come to the rostrum—but without waiting for a response to his invitation, he continued in a not at all comic, severe, leaderly tone: "Ehrenburg depicts our revolution as a catastrophe, but to me, and I am certain, to the majority of people in this hall, to the great Soviet people, the revolution is not a catastrophe, but a magnificent celebration of freedom, comrades!"

The roar that followed this outcry could have been compared with the revolution itself, or at least with the staged storming of the Winter Palace in that Soviet movie about the revolution. Khrushchev the Triumphator beamed. If he considered Pavel Makhinya the best proletarian poet, then he saw himself, of course, as the best orator.

---

[27] Ilya Ehrenburg's memoirs, written in the 1960s, in which he created an alternate cultural history of the Soviet Union and mentioned a number of significant avant-garde and modernist writers who had been banned under the Soviet regime.

Done with beaming, he turned and left the stage. Intermission. Refreshments.

* * *

Yan Tushinsky had sat with his friends for not quite three minutes when it was time to stand. It was announced that the intermission was over and everyone was asked to return to the conference hall. Everyone started moving. This time Yan put his arm around Vakson. "Listen, Vaks, I have to tell you something. Let's step into the bathroom." Passing the resplendent Kremlin toilets, which, according to rumor, never smell of stale piss, he dragged his friend further around the corner:

"There's a separate one over here, it's more private."

Vakson was genuinely surprised.

"Amazing! How do you know the Kremlin toilets so well?"

Tushinsky winked slyly.

"This isn't the first time I've been here. This is where I was awarded the Order of the Red Banner of Labor."

The separate bathroom had two stalls, two urinals, and two sinks. The door also had a lock on the inside, which Yan promptly secured. Then he ran the water from both faucets and in the urinals. Even then he couldn't feel completely at ease. He went into the stalls to periodically flush the toilets. He asked Vakson to do the same. Of course he followed suit. The water swirled, snarled and fizzled all the way to the Dnieper Hydroelectric Station.

"This is how everyone in New York talks when they have a heart to heart," Tushinsky said by way of explanation.

"You need to stage this for the theater," proposed Vakson.

"For which theater?" asked Tushinsky, stunned.

"The Moscow Art Theater."

Tushinsky waved all of this aside and got down to business:

"All your wisecracking keeps you from seeing that you're just farting in the wind. Bleak times are ahead. The Thaw is over. They're hammering into Khrushchev's skull that a conspiracy is brewing among Russia's youth. You think I was just kidding around when I pretended not to see you during the intermission? It's so they wouldn't think that we were scheming, discussing some sinister plot. By the way, a guy on the Central Committee told me, in this same bathroom to the roar of Niagara Falls, that some kind of shift is on the horizon, maybe even a return to Stalinism. You've got to be careful not to stir anything up. Tomorrow's another day, and who the hell knows in what direction Khrushchev will turn? You understand me, Vaks? Get it?"

"Got it, got it," mumbled Vakson. "Let's shut off the faucets or we'll burst the pipes in here."

* * *

The Polish poet Bandera Brigadska,[28] a representative of the international women's vanguard, replaced Shchavelenkov at the rostrum. As a Pole, she could be at once a dyed in the wool Stalinist who lived in Moscow with her husband, and a poet laureate who received her honors from Khrushchev during the Thaw. Unlike the chattering Shchavelenkov, this woman was a founding member of the Peace Council and the Information Bureau of the Communist and Workers' Parties. In a sober tone, almost without an accent and devoid of any humor, she observed that we live in difficult times, indeed, such complicated times that the subversive forces of imperialism are just waiting for the opportunity to use any of our mistakes, any slip of the tongue, against us. Bandera noted that she had just returned from the People's Republic of Poland, and our communist-internationalist comrades there were complaining that Soviet youth were obstructing the Polish Workers' Union's efforts to build socialism.

All at once either the ceiling of the hall caved in or the floor gave way. No, thought Antosha, the sleeping giant has been awakened. The entire hall was aroar: "Shame! Shame! Shame!"

Bandera Brigadska calmly waited for her male comrades to stop shouting. She waited for more than five minutes. Only toward the end of the howling did Antosha realize that this was about him.

---

[28]   Vanda Vasilevskaya (1905–1964), a Soviet writer of Polish origin.

Finally, Khrushchev muttered into the microphone: "Comrade Brigadska, explain to us in more detail what these complaints were about."

The roar quieted down.

"In Warsaw there is a disreputable journal called *Politics*. You might say that it has strongly revisionist tendencies. Two interviews were published in it, one after the other; one with a famous young Soviet poet, the other with a well-known prose writer. Their class consciousness leaves much to be desired. In short, it simply doesn't exist. The views and ideas of these young people undermine our foundations. This is especially dangerous in the Polish context, where the reactionary camp is gathering strength among those who want revenge after the suppression of the Hungarian counter-revolution . . ."

From the middle of the hall, where the ideological core of the gathering was concentrated, a deep, booming, and demonic voice rose up:

"Name names!"

The crowd joined in on the frenzied and impassioned chant: "Names! Names! Names!"

At these moments Bandera Brigadska (we can now reveal that this pseudonym means "Banner of the Brigade"), who seemed to be entirely at one with the body of the Party, allowed herself a demonstration of femininity that was strange coming from such an internationalist: she pressed a manicured hand to her bosom.

"I am not convinced, comrades, that it is necessary to name these two young individuals."

The crowd barked indignantly, like a caged lion whose meat had been stolen by a pair of magpies. And once again the frenzied and impassioned chant took flight: "Names! Names! Names!" Khrushchev coughed into the microphone over the clamor:

"Name their names, Comrade Brigadska. We won't pull any punches, why pull any punches, but in order not to pull any punches, we need to know who we're dealing with. We need names."

"Fine, Nikita Sergeyevich, I'll name them," Brigadska intoned, overcoming her fleeting demonstration of femininity. "The poet Andreotis and the prose writer Vakson."

The crowd howled joyfully, "Andreotis! Vakson! For shame! For shame! Teach them a lesson! They're not Russian! Where did they come from? Exile them! Cut them off!"

"What exactly is the issue here?" Khrushchev coughed again.

If before, everyone, including the Central Committee, pampered Antosha as if he were a mischievous, but happy child, he was now so thoroughly shaken by this unexpected and spontaneous turn, personally directed at him and of such a thoroughly negative and thoroughly adversarial character, that he sat gripping the armrests of his chair with his hands.

As for Vakson, who strategically had sat far away from Antosha, his feelings were almost completely the opposite. He was not pitched aloft. On the contrary, he was dragged down uncontrollably, as if an avalanche on a steep slope had pulled the ground from under his feet. A thought flashed through his mind: I believed these bastards in 1956 after the Twentieth Congress, I proposed the idea of escape, now it's time to pay.

The revolutionary poetess pulled a thick notebook out of her jacket pocket and flipped it right open to the relevant page:

"In conversation with Adam Glotissky, Moscow correspondent for the journal *Politics*, Andreotis presented himself as an apolitical versifier who dismisses Marxist principles of class struggle. Specifically, he claimed, and I quote, 'Beauty rules the world,' and he insisted upon this several times."

Antosha was seized by the fact that he could not at all remember when he said this, where, to whom, why, where to, where from, from without, from within, who this Adam was, and so forth.

The poetess continued:

"In a conversation with the same correspondent, Vakson stated that in the Soviet Union a battle is being waged between Stalinists and liberals, and he counted himself among the latter. 'Stalinists, and their name is legion,' he said, 'still hope for revenge, but we will conquer them.'"

Vakson remembered Adam. A quiet intellectual type to whom he hadn't even considered offering vodka. What exactly they talked about, he certainly couldn't remember; it was entirely possible that they talked precisely about what this brigade bitch was attributing to him. In any case, the avalanche was rumbling.

"Andreotis to the rostrum!" the crowd roared, like a seething cesspool. "Vakson to the rostrum! Make them answer! There's no reason to listen to them! Exile them! Cut them off from society!"

The subdued, civil, and somewhat absentminded, given that he is an academic, Secretary of the Central Committee Comrade Kil'kichev intoned into the microphone: "Comrade Andreotis has the floor."

Antosha stepped forward, implanting in his mind the one thought that would save him: I know what to say, I know how to say it, I know what to say, I know how to say it, I know . . . The march was complete, and he found himself at the well-crafted podium of the terrifying Bolsheviks, a pale boy with protruding nose and ears, in a name-brand sweater and fashionable scarf. He placed both hands on the edge of the podium to try to control his shaking. The microphone in front of him was buzzing strangely with feedback. The hostile turbulence of the crowd may have been flying around in circles inside him. Finally things more or less calmed down.

"Comrades!" Antosha exclaimed, and in the pause he noticed the face of a loyal Party worker distorted by a smirk: you're no comrade of mine. I know what to say, I know how to say it . . . Anton began, "Like my great teacher Vladimir Mayakovsky, I am not a communist . . ."

And he stopped there, without even adding the critical preposition "but" at the end. From behind and over the vulnerable nape of his neck a powerful proud voice roared:

"And you are proud of this, Andreotis? I am proud to be a communist!"

In response to the fatal blow of this bold and emotional cry everything but the smallest particles in the room roared. "For shame! Away with him! Forward, communists!"

Antosha's internal incantation was trampled by his body's panicked scream: I'm done for! I'm done for! I'm done for! They won't allow me to say anything else, they'll put me in chains right here, they'll throw me in the crawl space under an old fort and beat me with whips.

The proud voice behind his back continued to boom:

"I am proud to be a member of our great and victorious Communist Party of the Soviet Union, which has demonstrated its historical rectitude! You've miscalculated, Mister Andreotis! You wanted to lead our youth down the wrong path? Well it won't happen, we will wipe you off the face of the earth! These young people come to the Kremlin in their sweaters as if they're going to nursery school to ski or something, so we'll take you for a little ride until your asses start belching smoke, isn't that right, comrade communists?"

He withdrew slightly from the microphone so that the audience, cracking grins at the words "asses," could release their intense emotions: "That's right, Nikita Sergeyevich! Their asses! Their asses! Exile them! Cut them off!"

Antosha jerked oddly while standing at the podium, as if he were on the brink of fainting. From his seat Vakson wondered if his friend would suddenly topple from the podium and then have to clamber back up to hear his death sentence. For the moment he continued his inevitable downward slide. There was not a single kindred soul around him, only the unrecognizable backs of heads. No, Anton managed to hold on, and he was jolted by the thought of a last chance at redemption—poetry!

"Allow me, comrades, to read one of my recent poems."

His appeal, or his last request, was nearly drowned out by the excited roar of the crowd. Nikita pounded on the table with his fist:

"Do you see, he, this Mister Andreotis, thinks he knows how to save the world. Beauty, it turns out, is in his hands. He's taken it upon himself to save the world with the beauty of his rhymes! What a load of nonsense, Mister Andreotis!"

At this point Ilya Ehrenburg thought, with his characteristically ironic scorn, why is Khrushchev so stuck on the word "mister"? Was he deliberately firing up the crowd to get them ready for a public execution? Perhaps that complex of class resentment has surged up within him after all? Antosha, after all, is the son of a professor. He didn't grow up a farm boy.

Nikita Sergeyevich again pounded the table with his fist. It's too bad he could never pound this table with his shoe: this isn't the rabble from the United Nations here, but the cream of our Communist Party.

"In our world, beauty is found in the great teachings of Lenin, comrades!" (A powerful, enthusiastic outburst on the verge of an explosion.) The proud advance of our Party, that's where beauty is! You, Mister Antonov, with your tricks and stunts so alien to us, you'll never comprehend this! (The terrible roar of the crowd, which hadn't even noticed Khrushchev's slip of the tongue, continued to penetrate into every crack: For shame! For shame! For shame! One person exclaimed in a soprano through the roar: Shame to the ass-kissers! A bewildered pause. A correction: Kissers of bourgeois asses!) I understand that you are suffocating amid the beauty of labor's great achievements? Then away with you! Get a foreign passport and get (he barely refrained from adding the fuck) out! (Out! Out with them! That's right, Nikita Sergeyevich! The air will be cleaner!)

"Allow me to read one of my recent poems," mumbled Antosha, ostensibly into the microphone, ostensibly to the crowd, but at the moment he said it he turned his right eye to the table where the presidium sat, that is, to the one ridiculing him. The latter sat, apparently knocked out by his bellowing, his hands covering the loveliness of his face, but his eyes zeroing in on someone deep in the crowd.

"Read, then," he grumbled to the diminished and abused Andreotis.

Antosha began to read "The Lenin Sequoia," a poem that, according to his strategic reasoning, would steamroll right through the American editorial boards. He'd been to Sequoia National Park in California. The giant trees there are named after notable Americans: the Washington Tree, the Lincoln, Roosevelt, Edison, General Macarthur, Sherman, and many others. Unexpectedly, the guides, friends of our country and "progressive Americans," led him to a magnificent tree and said it was the Lenin Sequoia. This sequoia was majestic and filled with a noble communist spirit. It began to speak with the poet, just as the Eiffel Tower once spoke with Mayakovsky. He felt a profound sense of connectedness with its mighty trunk and stately crown. He imagined that one day this tree could fly away to an unknown world like a spaceship, with a message that contained all of the collected knowledge of mankind.

As always happened when he read his poems, he stopped thinking about everyone and everything. He even forgot the meaning of the poem and gave himself over to the resonance of the words. Even now this magic of words took precedence over strategy and the need to save himself from the beast. He forgot about the crowd and about the one who would judge his verse. He moved his hands, got into the rhythm, raised and lowered his voice, and highlighted the phonetic contiguity of the rhymes. Somehow the hall grew quiet, as if it had fallen under the spell of this snake charmer. But alas, everything comes to an end, and this poem, having served its protective function, concluded. Anton, debilitated, bowed his head. Nikita Sergeyevich sat for some time, his hands still covering his face. He didn't like the poem. It wasn't at all like the work of Pavel Makhinya. It wasn't driven by ideas. It was a cream puff. It smelled of formaldehyde, in the sense that it reeked of formalism.

"Mmmhmm," Khrushchev said, and immediately lapsed into a pause that made the liberals exhale and the Stalinists inhale. "Mmmhmm," he repeated, then began to elaborate. "That poem isn't particularly good. It tries too hard. You need to write more simply, Comrade Andreotis, more transparently."

The crowd gasped: the wretched, untrustworthy "mister" had unexpectedly been replaced with our own, indigenous "comrade." What did it mean? Khrushchev recognized that he'd ill-advisedly gone soft, and he needed to do away with this "comrade." A sow is no match for a goose, as they say in the country.

"Work patiently, Andreotis," he said, "and most importantly, identify who you are writing for: are you writing for us, or against us? If you write against us, then we'll wipe you off the face of the earth! If you are with us, then the fruits of your labor will flourish. Here is my hand, Andreotis, I advise you to come with us!"

The crowd gasped: the terrifying accuser of the "mister" has extended his hand to the "almost-comrade"! The latter, trusting like a child, took the hand that was lowered to him. "You may go," the hand said to him, "Take your seat." A great roar rose up in the hall, but it was no longer the unified shout of like minds and hinted at discord. The suddenly visible liberals began to applaud the leader enthusiastically; they understood the handshake extended to Antosha to mean that he had permission to live. The loyalists also applauded, although they clapped asynchronously and without rhythm. As Nikita Sergeyevich once said, "Oh, how changed I seem, I can hardly recognize myself!" The fragmentation was evidence of dissatisfaction. The Michelangelo of the Soviet era, State Artist of Labor and Happiness Nalbandian called out, shaking the heavy badges on his chest: "Nikita Sergeyevich, we're sick of democracy! Time for justice!"

Amid this discontent someone crowed like a showy rooster: "Now Vakson should answer for his phrase-mongering!" The crowd jumped in, emboldened by the enthusiasm: "Vakson! Vakson to the rostrum!" Vakson stood. The avalanche beneath his feet flowed ever faster. In a second it would all come crashing down. When they officially summon me, then I'll go. Then the avalanche will crash for sure. I don't know if I'll make it up to the podium or if I'll have to crawl there. For now I'll just stand. "I see him!" declared Nikita Sergeyevich, in the manner of Gogol's ghost, and he pointed to the section of the hall across from where Vakson sat. "I recognized him right away! Yes, yes, I see you in your red sweater. Everyone was applauding, and he, you see, wasn't. Come here! Climb out! C'mon, comrades, help him dig himself out of his lair!"

It wasn't Vakson to whom the finger of the leader of the working class pointed, but the artist Philarion Phophanoff,[29] a well-built fellow in a splendid red sweater and velvet trousers. He'd clearly come straight from his studio. He had a short haircut à la Brecht and wore eyeglasses of foreign manufacture.

His round Slavic features expressed absolute astonishment. Putting his hand to his chest, he tried to explain himself. He's not Vakson, after all, there had been a little mistake.

"To the rostrum!" snapped Nikita Sergeyevich. Anger stirred in him like the ova in a fish ready to spawn. "Come forward!"

---

[29]   A reference to the painter Ilarion Golitsyn (1927–2007).

It was notable that here he stopped trying to sugar-coat things by addressing the accused politely.

Meanwhile, Vakson raised his hand to show that he was the one being called to the rostrum, but no one paid attention to him. Everyone was fixed on the pseudo-Vakson, the distinguished artist of the RSFSR, and his progression toward the podium. He did not march like a guard, no way; you could tell that he was pigeon-toed, his socks circling around his feet as he shuffled.

Lots of people in the art world knew Phil as a first-rate easel painter and book illustrator. In the thirties, having grown into a beautiful child, he arrived from France, where he'd been born the spoiled brat of White officers, together with his parents, who had become ardent enthusiasts of the Great Utopia. Here in the USSR everything got sorted out and their identities were unmasked. The boy was lucky that his grand-uncle, a metallurgist, took him in. He grew up without a father, true, but nonetheless among people with manners.

Now he was getting closer to the tribunal. Nikita Sergeyevich, not waiting until he had reached his judges, expressed his irritation into the microphone for the entire hall:

"I know you're retaliating against us for the death of your father!"

Pseudo-Vakson was at the podium. He laid his hand on his chest:

"Yes, Nikita Sergeyevich, my father was shot, but this was during the Great Purges and the cult of personality around Stalin . . ."

It was difficult for him to speak. A deep, asthmatic pause followed every word. At this point Comrade Kil'kichev crept behind the chairs of the members of the Politburo and whispered something to Nikita Sergeyevich into the ear cherished by mankind. It cleared things up, obviously, to find out that there had been some confusion and it was not Vakson standing at the podium, but a wholly respectable, if young, artist who shared something of a coincidental situation with Vakson in that his father had been shot.

"Fine, go," N. Sergeyevich glumly said, "take your seat."

And Phil, who hadn't understood anything, with his head spinning and chasms opening to his left and his right, set off toward the depths of the hall and his comfort zone. Along the way two or three sympathetic hands were offered to him in support.

"Comrade Vakson has the floor," the scholar of proletarian studies Kil'kichev intoned in a soft voice into the government-owned microphone. Vakson, carried along and nearly buried by his avalanche, didn't notice how he'd arrived at the rostrum from the infinite depths below. Let's slow down, he said to himself, slow down, slow down, slow down . . . Drag a plow, your feet, your ass, anything, just slow down!

"And are you, Vakson, retaliating against us for the death of your father?" For a second time that same phrase thundered through the hall, having just ricocheted off of Philarion.

This phrase was especially written for me, thought Vakson, who then understood that there was nowhere to crawl to, that for the moment he was standing at a sturdily nailed together oak object and for the moment he had to stand there and somehow, even just a little, avoid getting smeared.

Later, when analyzing everything that remained in his memory, he figured out from the phrase that Khrushchev repeated that they had been part of an elaborate scenario for a public execution that had been planned in advance. Bandera Brigadska didn't appear at the rostrum by chance, nor was the Polish journal named without reason—in the last year he'd given quite a few interviews that were more daring than that one—and the General Secretary was supplied with incriminating information about them, and even that phrase was calculated to destroy me by mentioning my father and retaliation.

"My father is alive, Nikita Sergeyevich," he said, turning his back to the hall and his face to the leader.

The General Secretary was so taken aback that he began to squawk: "Alive? . . . How do you mean, alive? . . . He isn't alive . . ." Then he flew into a rage:

"Speak into the microphone!"

Vakson turned to the electrified crowd and spoke. The task put before him was difficult in that it was so stupid. He had to look at several hundred people in front of him, but answer to one person sitting behind him. Oh well, he had to speak.

"In 1937 my parents were sentenced to extended terms in the prison camps and exile . . ." Later he came to yet another curious conjecture. His father had been sentenced to death without the right to appeal, but after three months of awaiting execution the sentence was reduced to 15 years in the camps and three years of exile. Obviously, when the Central Committee was preparing the materials about Vakson for the General Secretary, they had only read up to the initial sentence. "After 18 years they were rehabilitated and returned. (Here he had to butter up the bastard.) We attribute the rehabilitation of our family to you, Nikita Sergeyevich."

That Vakson manages to turn everything around. He'll say something, then turn it right around, thought the General Secretary. He won't let himself get it from behind. I might have met his father. It isn't impossible that we met in 1919 in the courses for young commanding officers that Lenin visited. He was from Ryazan, it seems, that Vakson, and evidently by mistake he wasn't executed. And this Vakson, unlike the others, has shown up in a nice suit and tie, and kind of . . . damn, I'm all screwed up again . . .

He stood up, and shaking his fists in their nylon cuffs, roared:

"So you are spitting into the fountain that you drink from, Vakson?!" (damn it to hell, it's all screwed up, I confused a well with a fountain, goddamn it.)

Why a fountain anyway, what fountain, I don't drink out of a fountain, I drink from a faucet, well, sometimes I drink from the faucet when I'm out of beer, but where would I get a fountain from, Vakson's train of thought darted about like a laboratory mouse as he watched the leader turning crimson, clearly warming up for a big impromptu performance.

Finally the flood came, more or less as follows:

"You, Vakson, take note, that we will not allow you beatniks to build a Budapest here! Homegrown beatniks have sprung up and banded together, but we will not allow you to build a Petofi Circle in our untainted homeland! We will grind all of you, and you personally, Vakson, into dust if you try to band together! A repetition of the Hungarian counterrevolution will never happen here! The workers' fist, led by the Party, will smash everything! We'll scrub Soviet literature clean of all beatniks so you'll get the message! They write all sorts of crap, all sorts of fancy stories, they disgrace their fathers who made it through the war! We will not allow you to spit on Stalin! Stalin made mistakes, but he also achieved great things— and you have done nothing! We'll show you, the same way the Party dragged abstractionists by their noses into the fountain! Well, speak into the microphone about your so-called writing!"

Here we go with the fountain again, shot Vakson out of the corner of his mouth. One is the more or less clean one that you drink out of, and the other, the one they're dragging people into, stinks. He turned to the microphone and made an uncharacteristically concise statement:

"If my stories do not suit the Party and our leadership I can leave literature. I have a profession. I am a doctor, and I hope that in this capacity I will be useful to our motherland."

Khrushchev was taken aback: there you go, another revelation floats to the surface. Vakson, it turns out, is a doctor. His father is still alive, and he's not some scribbler, but a doctor useful to the homeland. Well, decide Nikita, what is he—a doctor or an enemy? He got confused again. He wanted to grab the water pitcher by its neck and smash it on the historic parquet floor. He refrained, but howled terrifyingly:

"What motherland are you talking about, Vakson?! Pasternak also swore by the motherland! Ehrenburg also writes about the motherland! And you, Vakson, what motherland are you talking about?"

"About our Soviet motherland, Nikita Sergeyevich. There is no other."

"Speak like this from now on," Khrushchev said, unexpectedly bringing the decibel level down to normal. "And remember, Vakson, if you deviate from that path, we will grind you to dust. But if you walk with us, you'll refine your talent. I offer you my hand."

And again the liberal representatives of literature and art blazed with delight. There won't be a blacklist! We'll work with our youth, with strict discipline of course, but also with a fatherly eye to their development!

Khrushchev's handshake hadn't left even the slightest impression on Vakson. He couldn't remember exactly what Khrushchev's hand was like: strong or weak, dry or sweaty, calloused or smooth? "They shook hands, but without any impressions." Or, as Oktava sang, "Take your coat, let's go home."

After his so-called presentation, an intermission was announced and the whole gang trickled toward the snack bar as if they hadn't just bellowed like crowing peacocks but only beamed with liberal smiles. Along the way, Stalin's favorite film actor, a giant man by the name of, say, Cherkashin,[30] hitched onto Vakson. "Whaaat a niiice surpriiiise!" he warbled, assuming the voice of an actor of the pre-revolutionary Aleksandriisky Theater. "And it turns out you're a doctor, Vaks! I dare say I would never have guessed. I presume you know about my family, yes? That my father's cousin also was a doctor of some kind?" After making this pretentious display of support, he waited for Vakson to respond. No response followed. Vakson didn't even turn his head. He imagined that the entire crowd was traipsing out, not to get something to eat, but to soak in a bath. This would mean they weren't wearing their regalia. You can't pin regalia onto a naked body.

Translated by Lisa Ryoko Wakamiya

[30] The actor Nikolai Cherkasov (1903–1966) played Alexander Nevsky and Ivan the Terrible in Eisenstein's eponymous films.

Part II

LITERATURE OF THE STAGNATION

INTRODUCTION

The period called the Stagnation (1968–1987) was one of the longest in Soviet cultural history. It began with the suppression of the Prague Spring, which itself was a logical continuation of the Soviet Thaw and a precursor to the period of *perestroika* (1987–1991) under Gorbachev. The Soviet authorities perceived the Czech attempt to democratize the communist regime and initiate a public discussion about its failures and crimes as a dangerous "diversion" that had to be stopped by military means. Milan Kundera's novel *The Unbearable Lightness of Being* captured the effect of this event on Czech (and more broadly, European) intellectuals. For the Soviet intelligentsia, the tragedy of the Prague Spring and the collapse of the project's efforts to introduce "socialism with a human face" led to their ultimate disappointment in communist ideology and utopia. This disappointment shifted late Soviet culture into a post-utopian dimension.

Although in political terms the Stagnation represented societal decline, especially in comparison with the highly dynamic Thaw years, in terms of cultural development the Stagnation was one of the most productive periods in Soviet history. The literary process in these years became divided into two parallel realms that hardly communicated with each other. One was so-called "official" literature, that is, works published in the Soviet Union. The other was represented by underground and émigré works that circulated in *samizdat* and *tamizdat*. Official literature, despite the constant pressure of censorship, was far from homogeneous. Along with orthodox Socialist Realism, mainly written by functionaries of the Union of Soviet Writers (and sarcastically called "secretaries' literature"), this sphere also included works by writers who used various methods, from Aesopian language to phantasmagoria, to continue the cultural work launched by the Thaw—that is, analyzing the Soviet past and trying to understand the legacy of Stalinism in the present. Writers such as Fazil Iskander, Yury Trifonov, Bulat Okudzhava, Chingiz Aitmatov, the Strugatsky brothers, and the "war prose" writers (Vasil Bykov, Grigory Baklanov, Konstantin Vorobiev, Viacheslav Kondratiev, and others) are especially significant in this respect. Another influential trend was represented by "village" prose and poetry. Authors of this group, such as Vasily Shukshin, Vasily Belov, Valentin Rasputin, Boris Mozhaev, and Nikolai Rubtsov, critiqued Soviet rule by imagining a peasant paradise ruined by Stalin's collectivization policies of the 1930s. This traumatic event in their version of history gradually developed into a full-fledged nationalist ideology expressed in their writing.

Underground and émigré literature was equally, if not more, diverse than official literature. On the one hand, it included texts that were aesthetically traditional, but ideologically radical. Along with Solzhenitsyn's works (published exclusively abroad since the 1970s), this type of writing was represented by the satirical novels of Vladimir Voinovich, the historical allegories of Yurii Dombrovsky and Georgii Vladimov, and the phantasmagoric novels of Vassily Aksyonov. On the other hand, most underground and émigré literature was represented by poetry and prose that seemed to be politically indifferent but explored new ways of seeing the world that overcame the ideological binary of Soviet vs. anti-Soviet. Among these tendencies, the neo-avant-garde (Gennady Aigi, Vladimir Kazakov) co-existed with surrealism (Sasha Sokolov), postmodern poetry (Venedikt Erofeev, Vsevolod Nekrasov, Moscow Conceptualism, Genrikh Sapgir), and various versions of modernism and the neo-baroque (Olga Sedakova, Elena Shvarts, Viktor Krivulin, and Aleksandr Kushner). Interestingly, the latter tendency was present in both underground and officially published literature.

If one attempted to identify the common denominator of all these tendencies, it would be an "incredulity towards grand narratives," to use Jean-François Lyotard's definition of the postmodern. Even orthodox Socialist Realism was no longer characterized by sincere faith in communist quasi-religious dogma. Instead it became overrun with stereotyped scenes and characters, and the reader's primary interest in these novels was driven by the features it shared with popular culture, namely, a clear-cut representation of good vs. evil and the occasional steamy sex scene. In other types of writing, whether official or non-official, the defining feature was the attitude toward the concept of truth: writers either presented their own version of "truth" as an alternative to Soviet ideological myths, or they exposed the ideological nature of any claim to truth and the constructedness of any reality.

One may be tempted to see parallels between the Stagnation and the postmodern period that followed the student revolutions of 1968 in Western Europe and the United States. However, the late Soviet cultural condition was quite different from that of the West. In Western liberal democracies, the postmodern critique of binary oppositions as a source of social, political, and cultural oppression led to the growing role of feminism, multiculturalism, and post-colonialism, as well as to the development of postmodern literature. In the Soviet Union, the cultural situation was dominated by the purely formal character of official ideology and politics, the shortage of consumer goods, widespread corruption and cynicism, rigid censorship, the quiet restoration of Stalinism, growing Russian nationalism (often inseparable from anti-Semitism), and the persecution of political dissent. The unifying strategy of the intelligentsia in response to these and similar features of late Soviet society may be described as various forms of escape that also proved to be effective strategies of cultural critique.

By escape we mean not only the literature of emigration and the literary underground, which in the seventies and early eighties turned toward aesthetic, rather than political, critique. As Alexei Yurchak demonstrated in his book *Everything Was Forever Until It*

Was No More, splitting one's life between official activities (necessary for one's career but intellectually and culturally meaningless) and informal circles (full of intellectual and emotional vigor) became typical for a large part of the Soviet intelligentsia and normalized escape as a form of cultural resistance. Among those who explored this strategy are Andrei Bitov, Evgeny Kharitonov, Genrikh Sapgir, Lev Rubinshtein, Dmitry Prigov, and the Mit'ki (see Vladimir Shinkarev's narrative, included in this section). Yuz Aleshkovsky's and Vladimir Vysotsky's songs were among the first works to explore the effects of the new cultural situation outside of intelligentsia circles.

In all these texts, despite their differences, one may notice shared features, such as an ironic attitude toward official discourses and a profound sense of individual loss—a loss of belief in the goals and values of existence. Outside the intelligentsia milieu, the exposure of the fictitious and absurd nature of Soviet ideology produced an existential crisis that could lead to alcoholism as a form of escape, or an individual quest for real values that extreme, often life-threatening, situations (abundant when life is experienced under the influence) could reveal. This literature finds common ground with European existentialism in its quest for ultimate freedom amid extraordinary situations. But unlike the French existentialists (Sartre and Camus, in particular), late Soviet writers were lighthearted and uproariously funny. After all, for them even loss and crisis are liberation from deadly Soviet dogma. Even self-destruction in this context assumes new meaning. It may give birth to a new identity, one that daringly transgresses the limits of propriety in the name of genuine, non-simulated, values.

Escape as a strategy for cultural critique took on broad and diverse forms in Stagnation literature. In his autobiographical essay "Less Than One," Joseph Brodsky, the Nobel Prize laureate, defines escape as estrangement from the social present. He argues that the need for escape was responsible for his generation's internal emigration into the realm of culture (it goes without saying that their vision of culture was ideologically incompatible with communist ideology). Andrei Bitov, in his novel *Pushkin House* (published abroad and distributed via *samizdat*), is highly critical of the intelligentsia, which claimed to carry on the values of pre-Soviet culture but in fact only simulated cultural continuity. For Bitov, the Soviet regime irretrievably severed all cultural links with the past; the intelligentsia's conformism and its dependence on the privileges granted by the regime weakened their ability to fill the cultural gap created by the aggressive monopoly of Soviet ideological production.

An extension of Bitov's thesis and a philosophic variant on the tragicomic existentialism of Vysotsky, Aleshkovsky, and Sapgir may be detected in Venedikt Erofeev's *Moscow–Petushki*. Its narrator—like the author himself (they share the same name)—performs a radical form of non-conformism as well as a constant state of living on the edge. Perpetually wasted, Erofeev's Venichka is indifferent to the values of those around him. This position allows him to generate an endless carnival around himself in which he seeks God and challenges all manner of cultural hierarchies. In this way he reenacts the traditional role of the holy fool (as Olga Sedakova and Mikhail Epshtein point out), addressing his social critique to the world and to God rather than against political authorities. Additional forms of escape can be found in the works of Evgeny Kharitonov, an openly gay writer whose works could only circulate in *samizdat*, as homosexuality was a punishable crime. Yurii Dombrovsky's short story "Little Arm, Leg, Cucumber" demonstrates that forms of non-belonging in the Soviet cultural context that may be considered a form of escapism in fact required active engagement on the part of the subject through constant confrontation with covert and overt "representatives" of social normativity. This confrontation could even lead to death, as happened to Dombrovsky himself.

A more lighthearted variant of Erofeev's and Kharitonov's artistic strategies can be found in the lifestyle and writings of the Mit'ki. As represented in this reader in the excerpt from Vladimir Shinkarev's book *Mit'ki*, the Mit'ki emerged as a quasi-monastic order, albeit totally agnostic, that practiced drunken relaxation and indifference to social, political, and consumerist values. Unlike hippies, to whom they have been compared, the Mit'ki poked fun at themselves and their movement as well as at conventional social norms. They mocked *any* form of idealism. This attitude is manifested in their work as a cheerful cynicism not unlike the irreverent *kynicism* that Peter Sloterdijk opposes to pragmatic cynicism.[1]

A new phase of the strategy of escape emerged with the Moscow Conceptualists, a circle of artists and writers who, in the mid-seventies, developed new artistic languages that were distinct from both Socialist Realism and the suppressed avant-garde tradition. The Conceptualist method, as represented by Dmitry Prigov, merges *kynicism* with analysis of the stagnant and disintegrating language and icons of Soviet culture, which often appear in their works in the form of ruins and fragments. The Conceptualists' work does not manifest any signs of despair, however; they perceive this as an opportunity for the creation of new languages or to explore new, or previously unnoticed, cultural and existential realms.

Certainly, this brief survey does not cover the entire spectrum of the cultural strategies explored by writers of unofficial and official literature of the Stagnation period. It bears noting, however, that by the end of the seventies, the borders between the literary underground and the liberal wing of published literature blurred, making way for new cultural communities. Furthermore, the sphere of culture situated "beyond" Soviet culture had grown so significantly that it even seemed that the authorities might allow non-conformist literature to enter official Soviet culture. This was the driving force behind the creation of *Metropol'* (1979), an almanac of uncensored texts, the story of which is vividly described in Viktor Erofeev's essay.

The authorities' assault on those who contributed to the almanac showed that the writers' optimistic hopes were premature. However, they were not entirely groundless, as the later development of Soviet cultural politics subsequently proved. Gorbachev's perestroika accomplished exactly what the Metropol' contributors hoped for. The inclusion of non-conformist literature into the context of official culture proved to be fatal for the latter, and for the entire Soviet ideological (and consequently, political and social) order as well.

---

[1]   See Peter Sloterdijk, *Critique of Cynical Reason*, trans. Michael Eldred (London and Minneapolis: University of Minnesota Press, 1987).

Alexei Yurchak
LIVING "VNYE": DETERRITORIALIZED MILIEUS[1]

> Like everyone else I have an angel
> Behind my back she dances away
> In the Saigon she orders me coffee
> It's all the same to her, come what may
> —*Boris Grebenshchikov*[2]

Brodsky's Model

Writer Sergei Dovlatov wrote about the passions of the "sixtiers" (shestidesiatniki) generation[3]: "Neils Bohr used to say, 'There are clear truths and deep truths. A clear truth is opposed by a lie. A deep truth is opposed by another equally deep truth.' . . . My friends were preoccupied with clear truths. We spoke about the freedom of art, the right for information, the respect for human dignity."[4] This preoccupation with clear truths has also been called

---

[1] From: Alexei Yurchak, *Everything Was Forever, Until It Was No More: The Last Soviet Generation* (Princeton and Oxford: Princeton University Press, 2006), 126–155.

[2] Boris Grebenshikov and his group Aquarium, from their 1981 album *Elektrichestvo* (trans. Melanie Feakins and Alexei Yurchak).

[3] The "sixtiers" generation is ten to twenty years older than the last Soviet generation. They came of age during Khrushchev's liberating reforms of the late 1950s to mid-1960s and identified with these reforms. Many of them started as young supporters of the Party in what they saw as its sincere attempt to regain the original purity of Communist ideals distorted under Stalin. They later became disillusioned by the retreat from the reforms under Brezhnev. As a result, many of them developed a mixture of an affinity to Communist ideals with a critical outlook on the shortcomings of the Soviet system.

[4] Sergei Dovlatov, *Remeslo: Selected Prose in Three Vols. Vol. 2.* (St. Petersburg: Limbus Press, 1993), 23

"the honesty psychosis" and "the active obsession with categorizing life choices as honest and dishonest."[5] Dovlatov compares this concern with clear truths to an attitude that he first encountered in the mid-1960s, in which people did not evaluate Soviet life as moral or immoral, because they considered the events and facts of Soviet life around them to be relatively irrelevant compared to "deep truths." An extreme manifestation of this attitude was that of Leningrad poet Joseph Brodsky:

> Next to Brodsky, young nonconformists seemed like people of a different profession. Brodsky created an unheard-of model of behavior. He lived not in a proletarian state, but in a monastery of his own spirit. He did not struggle with the regime. He simply did not notice it. He was not really aware of its existence. His lack of knowledge in the sphere of Soviet life could appear feigned. For example, he was certain that Dzerzhinskii[6] was alive. And that Comintern[7] was the name of a musical group. He could not identify members of the politburo of the Central Committee. When the facade of the building where he lived was decorated with a six-meter portrait of Mzhavanadze,[8] Brodsky asked: "Who is this? He looks like William Blake."[9]

Perhaps Brodsky's poetic intuition made him acutely aware that Soviet authoritative discourse had been distilled to what Jakobson called the "poetic function of language," which allowed him to read authoritative signifiers through his own universe of meaning. So profound was Brodsky's lack of involvement with the authoritative forms of everyday life that the Soviet state persecuted him for being a "loafer." But in the following decade, Brodsky's way of

---

[5]   Masha Gessen, *Dead Again* (London: Verso, 1997), 114.

[6]   Dzerzhinskii was a Bolshevik leader, Lenin's comrade, and the founder of the ChK (the precursor to the KGB); he was well known as a legend of Soviet history.

[7]   "Comintern" refers to the Communist International.

[8]   Mzhavanadze was a member of the Politburo in the mid-1960s.

[9]   Dovlatov, *Remeslo*, 23.

being became increasingly widespread among urbanites a decade younger than him—the last Soviet generation.

The previous chapter focused on the contexts and processes of the ideological production within the Komsomol, arguing that in addition to authoritative texts, reports, and rituals, it also produced new meanings and forms of temporality, spatiality, relations, discourses, and publics. This chapter takes this discussion outside that context of ideological production, focusing on the contexts that were in a peculiar relationship to the authoritative discursive regime—they were "suspended" simultaneously inside and outside of it, occupying the border zones between here and elsewhere. The above description of Brodsky's profound lack of concern with and ignorance of the facts and events of Soviet reality renders well this peculiar relationship. I refer to this relationship to reality by the term *vnye*. To be *vnye* usually translates as "outside." However, the meaning of this term, at least in many cases, is closer to a condition of being simultaneously inside and outside of some context—such as, being within a context while remaining oblivious of it, imagining yourself elsewhere, or being inside your own mind. It may also mean being simultaneously a part of the system and yet not following certain of its parameters. For example, the phrase *vnye polia zreniia* (not within one's field of vision) is used when something is known to be here, but is invisible or obstructed from view by another object. This chapter argues that late socialism became marked by an explosion of various styles of living that were simultaneously inside and outside the system and can be characterized as "being *vnye*." These styles of living generated multiple new temporalities, spatialities, social relations, and meanings that were not necessarily anticipated or controlled by the state, although they were fully made possible by it.

I begin by concentrating on more "extreme" examples of such living, describing several milieus in Leningrad, from the 1960s to the early 1980s, where young people related to the Soviet system in this way. The chapter also describes more widespread examples, and ultimately argues that being *vnye* was not an exception to the dominant style of living in late socialism but, on the contrary, a central and widespread principle of living in that system. It created a major *deterritorialization* of late Soviet culture, which was not a form of opposition to the system. It was enabled by the Soviet state itself, without being determined by or even visible to it.

Inna and Her Friends

Inna (born in 1958) was a student in the history department of Leningrad University. The move from secondary school to the university, in the mid-1970s, was a big shift for her:

> When I was in school everything was still clear, of course. . . . I joined the Komsomol with great enthusiasm in the eighth grade [age fourteen, 1972–73] . . . I also wanted to make a difference. I was the first person from my class to join . . . But at home, even then, we heard a little bit of Galich and Vysotskii . . . By the ninth or tenth grade [ages sixteen to seventeen] I had lost that [enthusiasm] . . . although I was still law-abiding, because I knew I had to be. But when I finished school I simply stopped participating in that life. I never went to the Komsomol meetings. I simply knew that I could avoid them without too many repercussions.

At the university, Inna met a group of friends who also lived this way, avoiding the system's ideological symbolism: "We never went to vote. We simply ignored elections and parades . . . My only connection with Soviet life was through work and also through the university, which I rarely attended since I had no time." However, Inna stresses, their life was not colored by any anti-system discourse. They were equally uninterested in overt support of, or resistance to, the Soviet system: "None of my friends was any kind of *antisovetchik* [a person with an active anti-Soviet agenda]"; and, "We simply did not speak with each other about work or studies or politics. Not at all, which is obvious since we did not watch television, listen to the radio, or read newspapers, until about 1986 [the beginning of *perestroika*]." The discourse of the dissidents (before 1986) left them indifferent: "We never spoke about the dissidents. Everyone understood everything, so why speak about that. It was *not interesting* [*neinteresno*]."[10] This comment refers to the performative shift of authoritative discourse, suggesting that the meanings of authoritative symbols, acts, and rituals were not supposed to be read literally, as constative statements. Therefore discussing them made no sense and was considered a mistake and a waste of time. Instead, one could use the possibility afforded by their performative reproduction to be engaged with other meanings, including creating one's own. And so Inna and her friends quietly differentiated themselves from the dissidents, and the activists:

> We had no attitude toward them. We were not them [*oni*]. We were here and they were there. We were different from them. We were different, because for us they were simply a change from plus to minus [*znaki meniaiutsia*]—the pro-system and anti-system types—they were all just Soviet people. And I never thought of myself as a Soviet person. We were organically different [*my organicheski otlichalis'*]. This is true. We were simply *vnye*.

Inna's use of language is revealing of her position: when she uses the pronoun *oni* (them), she does not limit it to the party or state bureaucrats, but also includes the party's self-styled opponents. Inna's position is different from those who describe Soviet society in the terms of an us-them dichotomy. From the perspective of Inna and her friends, the voice of the dissidents belonged to the same authoritative discursive regime, even though the dissidents confronted that discourse. Serguei Oushakine argues that dissident discourse related to authoritative discourse of the state "intradiscursively rather than interdiscursively" and calls this form of dissident resistance "mimetic resistance." Although the dominant and dominated were differently positioned within the discursive field, they drew on "the same vocabulary of symbolic means and

---

[10]   Emphasis added. Recollect also the words of Olesya in chapter 3, about being "uninterested" in the discourse of a dissident-like person who "is expecting some response from you, but you have nothing to say to him. Not because you are unable to analyze like him, but because you don't want to."

rhetorical devices. And neither the dominant nor the dominated could situate themselves 'outside' this vocabulary."[11]

Oushakine is right that most dissident and the activist discourses shared the same discursive field and rhetorical devices and that their relationship was intradiscursive. However, his conclusion that within that "'regime of truth' the dissident discourse that mimetically replicated . . . the discourse of the dominant was probably the only one that could be accepted in that society as truthful," is inaccurate.[12] It is wrong to extend the argument about "truth" to the Soviet discursive regime as a whole, precisely because, as we have seen, the concept of truth became decentered and no longer anchored to constative meanings of the authoritative discursive field. For people like Inna and her friends, the location of "truth" was displaced into a realm that related to that discursive field neither "intradiscursively" nor "interdiscursively." Rather, it occupied a peculiar position in between. Recollect again Dovlatov's distinction between different types of truth: as in "clear truths" were constructed within the authoritative discursive regime (and related to its constative meanings), but "deep truths," with which people like Brodsky, Inna, and many of her peers became increasingly preoccupied, were articulated in a different vocabulary and a different discursive and ethical "dimension"—not the constative dimension of this discourse.

This dimension and vocabulary were neither "inside" nor "outside" authoritative regime, but in a peculiarly deterritorialized relation to it—that is, while the forms, acts and rituals of authoritative discourse were immutable and ubiquitous, the constative meanings of these forms were irrelevant to Inna and her friends. Instead, they injected their lives with new meanings, forms of sociality, and relations, adding a "surplus value of code" and making them something else, deterritorializing them.[13] It is not by

[11]   Serguei Oushakine, "The Terrifying Mimicry of Samizdat," *Public Culture* 12:2 (2001): 207–8.

[12]   Ibid.

[13]   Gilles Deleuze and Felix Guattari, *A Thousand Plateaus: Capitalism and Schizophrenia* (London: Continuum, 2002), 10

chance that Inna and her friends talked about being "organically" different from Soviet people. They were *becoming*-different, as the orchid in Deleuze and Guattari's discussion above was becoming wasp-like.

Inna further elaborated this position: "We were strongly *vnye* any social status." She used the terms "Soviet person" (*sovetskii chelovek*) and "Soviet people" (*sovetskie liudi*) pejoratively to refer to any "organic" adherence to the authoritative discursive field, whether pro-Soviet or anti-Soviet. This distancing of herself and her friends from pro- and anti-positions parallels the feelings of dislike that many Komsomol secretaries and members had toward activists and dissidents . . . Like the Komsomol members, Inna employed the term *svoi*. For example, she explained: "We did not consider Solzhenitsyn *svoi* [*ne schitali ego svoim*]. This was important. No, no, we were not anti-system like him." Inna's *svoi* encompassed neither anti-system nor pro-system people. Even when Inna and her friends paid attention to the dissident discourse (for example, she read *samizdat* and foreign publications of Solzhenitsyn), this literature helped them to position themselves in relation to both dissident and authoritative discourses. In her own words, these publications helped her to "understand where we in fact stood — *not in relation to power but in general.*"[14]

Being *Vnye*

Inna and her friends, like the other groups and milieus described below, thought and spoke of everyone in their group as being *svoi*. As mentioned in the previous chapter, *svoi* was not a concept within a binary opposition between "us" (*svoi*, common people) and "them" (the state). This public, *svoi*, related to authoritative discourse neither supporting nor opposing it. Its location vis-à-vis that discourse was deterritorialized. This location was not invented by the last Soviet generation. [. . .] However, it became a constitutive part of the subjectivity of these younger persons.

[14]   Emphasis added.

These publics of *svoi* were often organized in tightly knit networks of friends and strangers who shared some interest, occupation, or discourse. Such networks can be described as tight milieus that were never completely bounded and isolated, and were always in the process of emergence and change, with an open-ended and somewhat shifting membership. Within these milieus, individual identities, collectivities, relations, and pursuits were shaped and normalized. To understand the nature of these milieus, consider again Inna's words: "We were very strongly *vnye* any social status"; "[w]e were organically different" from Soviet people, "We were simply *vnye*." Inna's use of the concept *vnye* suggests a particular relation to the system, where one lives within it but remains relatively "invisible." One employs discursive means that do not quite fit the pro/anti dichotomy in relation to authoritative discourse and cannot be quite articulated within the parameters of that discourse.

Instead of being explicitly involved with authoritative rituals and texts [. . .] Inna and her friends found involvement with that discourse *neinteresno* (uninteresting). Considering something uninteresting and being *vnye* are related categories. Both refer to something that is irrelevant, because the person, although living within the system, is not tuned into a certain semantic field of meaning. In this sense it may be "uninteresting" to have to choose whom to support in a match between Juventus and Ajax if you never pay attention to European football, even if it sometimes plays on the television. This lack of preoccupation with certain parameters within the discursive field meant that instead of Havel's appeal "to live in truth" and Solzhenitsyn's appeal "to live not by lies" (*zhit' ne po lzhi*), Inna and her friends spoke of "living lightly" (*zhili legko*), "leading a very fun life" (*veli ochen' veseluiu zhizn'*), and "making merry in general" (*voobshche veselilis'*). These words are not about the nonseriousness of existence but about a replacement of Soviet political and social concerns with a quite different set of concerns that allowed one to lead a creative and imaginative life.

In Russia the more extreme examples of this type of living are sometimes described as "internal emigration" (*vnutrenniaia emigratsiia*).[15] This powerful metaphor, however, should not be read as suggesting complete withdrawal from Soviet reality into isolated, bounded, autonomous spaces of freedom and authenticity. In fact, unlike emigration, internal emigration captures precisely the state of being inside and outside at the same time, the inherent ambivalence of this oscillating position. Although uninterested in the Soviet system, these milieus heavily drew on that system's possibilities, financial subsidies, cultural values, collectivist ethics, forms of prestige, and so on. [. . .]

Saigon

In the previous examples, the style of living by being *vnye* authoritative discourse was illustrated in the contexts that were strongly affiliated with state institutions. This however, was not the only possibility. Many similar collectivities emerged in various contexts with much looser connections to state institutions. Examples were various *tusovki*, a slang term referring to non-institutionalized milieus of people with some shared interest based on "hanging out" and interacting within such milieus.[16] These sprang up in the cities between the 1960s and the 1970s.

In the early 1960s, during Khrushchev's liberating reforms, many large Soviet cities, including Leningrad, experienced a cultural transformation that was minute in quantitative terms but enormous in cultural significance. The poet Viktor Krivulin called it "the Great Coffee Revolution" (*velikaia kofeinaia revoliutsiia*).[17] The revolution amounted to the creation of a few modest cafes in city centers that sold strong coffee and pastries and enabled new spatial

---

[15]   For example, Lev Gudkov and Boris Dubin, "Ideologiia besstrukturnosti: Intelligentsiia i konets sovetskoi epokhi" [Ideology of Unstructuredness: The Intelligentsia and the End of the Soviet Epoch], *Znamia* 11 (1994): 170.

[16]   *Tusovki* (plural of *tusovka*) is from the verb *tosovat'*—"to shuffle."

[17]   This is a play on the ubiquitous Soviet authoritative signifier, "The Great October Socialist Revolution," which referred to the Bolshevik Revolution of 1917 (Viktor Krivulin, *Nevskii do i posle Velikoi Kofeinoi Revoliutsii* [Interview with Viktor Krivulin], *Pchela* 6 [1996]: 4–9).

and temporal contexts for interaction among large groups of young people. This interaction was similar to the interaction enabled by the previously discussed clubs but without their limited thematic focus, state institutional organization, and registered membership.

Although most of these cafes had no official names (the signs on the doors simply said *"kafe"*), many quickly acquired slang names, often based on "Western" locations (e.g., Evropa, London, Liverpul', Tel'-Aviv, Rim, Olster). By the late 1960s, one cafe known as Saigon,[18] emerged as a particularly important context for interaction. It opened on September 18, 1964, (its former regulars still celebrate the date) in an ideal central location in Leningrad.[19] The slang name Saigon symbolized the existence of a different dimension of discourse, *vnye* in a location. The name's strength was in its ubiquity and recognizability, created by the critical discourse in the Soviet media against the American "imperialist war" in Vietnam. In the new context the name was completely reinterpreted, losing its negative political connotations while preserving a recognizable reference to an exotic and decadent "Western" locale. Perhaps the negativity surrounding the name in the Soviet press made it particularly attractive to the cafe patrons as a gesture of jocular defiance; this possible meaning, however, was never explicitly discussed, consistent with the cafe-goers' "uninterestedness" in political topics.

Saigon soon acquired regulars who would stop in to talk to acquaintances and drink strong coffee and sometimes port wine clandestinely brought in from the outside.[20] These regulars differed from random visitors off the street in that for them Saigon became not just a cafe but "a source of information, books and ideas; a territory where you established contacts with the opposite sex,

---

[18]   Today, memoirs and stories about Saigon are regularly published in St. Petersburg journals and newspapers, and in scholarly works [...] and although the original cafe has ceased to exist, its name lives on in clones in St. Petersburg and other Russian cities.

[19]   On the corner of Nevsky and Vladimirsky Prospekts.

[20]   Krivulin, *Nevskii do i posle Velikoi Kofeinoi Revoliutsii*, 4–5.

a shelter from parents' moralizing, and a cover from the nasty Leningrad weather."[21] The regulars tended to form groups that did not mix with each other. Because of this diversity, one patron observed that "Saigon was reminiscent of an aristocratic English club through which alcoholics walked."[22] The poet Viktor Toporov, a graduate of the club Derzanie and a Saigon regular, describes the crowd as follows: "There was our group of poets, then a group of artists that were connected to us, then a group of drug addicts, then a group of blackmarketers and *fartsovshchiki* [blackmarketers buying clothes from Western tourists and reselling them to Soviet citizens] selling shoes."[23] The nearby Palace of Pioneers fed Saigon's groups of literature lovers. For them the main attraction was the possibility of socializing in an atmosphere similar to that of the palace but even more mixed, open-ended, and unpredictable:

> I still do not like going to private dinner parties or inviting people to my place precisely because of the predictability [*predskazuemost'*] of the whole situation. But in Saigon the situation was open [*otkrytaia situatsiia*]. When I went there I never knew whether that evening would be extremely tedious or remarkably entertaining, who I would meet there, and whether I would end it in the police station or in the bar at the Hotel Evropeiskaia. I knew very well that if you came to Saigon around 2 P.M. you would definitely meet the person you were looking for, because he would also stop by. These were free people who were drinking and having conversations. Some of them wrote poetry, others drew pictures.[24]

The centrality of open-ended and temporally unconstrained interaction, and the unpredictable and changing milieu of

21   Gennadii Zaitsev, "Rok-klub," *Pchela* 6 (1996), http://www.pchela.ru/podshiv/6/rokclub.htm.

22   Boris Grebenshikov, "Saigon," *Pchela* 6 (1996), http://www.pchela.ru/podshiv/6/saigon.htm.

23   Viktor Toporov, "My vypivali kazhdyi den'," *Pchela* 6 (1996), http://www.pchela.ru/podshiv/6/krishna.htm.

24   Ibid.

participants that it involved, became reflected in slang expressions. One could meet *v Saigone* ("in Saigon," that is, in its physical space) or *na Saigone* ("at Saigon," within the milieu of its regulars).[25] Like Inna's friends, Toporov's circle was more interested in talking, socializing, drinking, and reading early twentieth-century poetry than discussing politics. Their relationship to political dissidents was also one of quiet distancing; according to Toporov, "there were occasional dissidents there . . . but for us this was uninteresting [*neinteresno*] . . . In our circle no one got involved in dissident activities."[26]

Even though "the dissidents" did not constitute a sizable group at the Saigon, their general presence, as well as the activities of others who were having long conversations and exchanging books, made the cafe an ideal place for KGB operatives to keep an eye on the general atmosphere among such milieus in the city. Partly because of the usefulness of the cafe for KGB monitoring, the place never closed down and remained relatively unbothered by the police, which allowed its milieus to thrive and grow. Viktor Krivulin claimed that most people at the Saigon did not worry too much about the KGB precisely because political concerns were for them relatively irrelevant. At the same time, he and his friends were occasionally summoned "to the organs" for questioning. Krivulin recollected that in the late 1960s, he recognized a man drinking coffee next to him at the Saigon as a KGB operative. The commonly understood presence of clandestine figures and potential threat, "added some feeling of romanticism and adventure."[27] This relationship between the milieu and the state "security organs" illustrates how the state enabled such milieus, which is why the KGB was not a profound concern for most members of these milieus.

Inna, whom we encountered above, began frequenting Saigon in the late 1970s. She and her friends "sat on the windowsills, drank

25   A. Fain and V. L. Lur'e, *Vse v kaif!* (Leningrad, 1991), 171.

26   Quoted in Gennadii Zaitsev, "Rok-klub," *Pchela* 6 (1996), http://www.pchela.ru/podshiv/6/rokclub.htm, 51.

27   Krivulin, *Nevskii do i posle Velikoi Kofeinoi Revoliutsii*, 7–8.

coffee, and talked about various things . . . Here one could always find someone to talk to. If you came to Saigon you would definitely find someone. *Obshchenie* [interaction, chatting, being together] was the most important thing." They read "various books which one could not buy anywhere . . . We read a lot of poetry from the turn of the century . . . We also read French poetry . . . We read works in classical physics [foundational texts in mechanics and thermodynamics]. We read Beckett and Ionesco."[28] Although this reading list may seem an incoherent mix, all these texts in fact shared the important feature of being temporally, spatially, and thematically *vnye* to the "uninteresting" social and political issues of the Soviet discourse.

In the early 1980s, many of the works of poetry and fiction read by these people had not been published for decades, and some of their authors had either been repressed or were out of favor with the party. However, in line with the cultural paradox of socialism, many of these works had never been made fully "illegal," so that students and people with contacts could still access their earlier Russian and limited Soviet editions, say, in research libraries. Inna's part-time job at the university library provided such access: "We could come to the reading room and read the kind of books that we could not get anywhere else. For example, we read [old Russian editions of] Gumilev, who was no longer published or sold in shops." Despite their reading, discussing, and exchanging of these books, Inna and her friends were also not particularly worried about the KGB:

> We always had bags full of literature. So we were taking little risks. But we also understood perfectly well that no one was terribly interested in us. Why would they be? At most, we had a typed song by Galich or a poem by Brodsky. And, of course, we exchanged this stuff. But as far as arresting us for this—who would do that? This was not serious stuff. As for signing dissident letters or getting involved in other [dissident] activities, we never believed in that.

---

[28] Author interview.

According to St. Petersburg cultural historian Lev Lur'e, himself once a frequenter of several literary milieus and the cafe Saigon, the authors that circulated among their members also included Andrei Platonov, Mikhail Bulgakov, Marcel Proust, James Joyce, and Arthur Miller.[29] As a result, "in the 1970s you could receive a better literary and philosophical education in the Saigon than in the departments of philology or history of Leningrad University," which is why the cafe's milieus played an important role in educating and preparing the future post-Soviet founders of private publishing houses, as well as their editors, translators, and readers.[30]

The venue of cafes naturally begs some comparison with Habermas's "public sphere," which emerged during early capitalism, when individuals constituted themselves as a "public" through critical and rational debate about political and social issues in bourgeois cafes and salons.[31] Drawing a parallel with this discussion of "public sphere" in the bourgeois context, Russian sociologist Elena Zdravomyslova argues that the phenomenon of Saigon "can be interpreted as a certain form of collective protest . . . a neverending strike of young Soviet intelligentsia against the regime [and] . . . a political protest."[32] However, the problem with using the concept of "public sphere" is precisely in the unfortunate binary models and metaphors of protest and political opposition that it drags out. Describing the cultural logic of milieus in this way obscures the crucial fact that they explicitly distanced themselves from dissident discourses or political protests. Like other milieus of the 1960s and 70s, Saigon did indeed breed certain kinds of publics of *svoi*. However, as we saw in the previous chapter, within these

29   Lev Lur'e, *Zanimatel'naia istoriia Peterburga*, a series of programs on Radio Ekho Peterburga, August 7, 2003.

30   Ibid.

31   Jurgen Habermas, *The Structural Transformation of the Public Sphere: An Inquiry into a Category of Bourgeois Society* (Cambridge, MA: MIT Press, 1991).

32   Elena Zdravomyslova, "Kafe Saigon kak obshchestvennoe mesto," in *Materials of the International Seminar Civil Society in the European North* (St. Petersburg: Center for Independent Social Research, 1996), 39–40.

publics Soviet reality was not resisted but deterritorialized. Not surprisingly, for members of these milieus critical debates about Soviet political and social issues were considered "uninteresting." The relation of these publics to authoritative discourse was one of neither opposition nor support, but of being *vnye*. As part of this relationship, one could avoid authoritative rituals and texts of the system but continue to be involved in many of the system's cultural ideals and pursuits. The latter were especially strengthened by the presence in the milieu of people of the sixtiers generation (poets, literary club teachers, etc.), with their more idealist relationship to the promises of socialism. It is not by chance that the discourse of "fun living" played a dominant role in that circle. The poet Krivulin summarized the atmosphere at Saigon: "We lived a fun life" (*my veselo zhili*).[33] The reference to "fun life" — like Inna's references (quoted earlier) to "living lightly" (*zhili legko*) and "leading a very fun life" (*veli ochen' veseluiu zhizn'*) — refers to a kind of "normal life" in everyday socialism, a life that had become invested with creative forms of living that the system enabled but did not fully determine. [. . .]

Boiler Rooms

During late socialism, especially in the 1970s and early 80s, it became increasingly common among some groups of the last Soviet generation, especially children of intelligentsia families, but also some from working-class backgrounds, to give up more sophisticated professional careers for occupations that offered more free time. The more extreme and telling examples of such jobs included boiler room technician (*kochegar*), warehouse watchman (*storozh*), freight train loader (*gruzchik*), and street sweeper (*dvornik*).[34] These jobs kept them busy for only two to three night shifts a week, leaving them plenty of free time for *obshchenie* and for pursuing

---

[33]   Krivulin, *Nevskii do i posle Velikoi Kofeinoi Revoliutsii*, 7–8.

[34]   Havel describes a similar tendency in Czechoslovakia (Joseph Brodsky and Vaclav Havel, "The Post-Communist Nightmare: An Exchange," *New York Review of Books* 41:4 [1994]: 28–30).

other interests. One's obligations were minimized because the work was undemanding, because it was organized in long shifts with breaks in between, and because one was spared the need to attend meetings, parades, and other public events (since only people with stronger institutional affiliations were required to attend such events through their jobs).

"Boiler rooms" (*kochegarka* or *kotel'naia*) were local technical hubs of the centralized heating system in the district: rooms with valves and control mechanisms for the district's hot water pipes. The jobs of boiler room technicians amounted to keeping track of the pressure in the pipes, turning on and off hot water and cold water, calling a repairperson in case of trouble, and so on. The technicians were required to be present in the room during their shifts, but they rarely had to do much work. They usually worked one twenty-four-hour shift every four days (*sutki cherez troe*). Although the salary was very low (sixty to seventy rubles a month, the lowest official wage), the job allowed a large amount of free time.

These jobs became attractive for some individuals because of the performative shift of authoritative discourse. The state's law of mandatory employment was reproduced purely performatively, at the level of form (its constative meaning of having a job became shifted almost beyond recognition), and this performative reproduction enabled new meanings, temporalities, communities, pursuits, interests, forms of aesthetics and expertise—in short, a whole universe of meaning. The state again enabled it, without quite being able to control or account for it. Such occupations allowed the person to pursue various interests and amateur careers, from scholar of ancient languages to rock musician. One could be a writer who was unrecognized by the state's union of writers and therefore unpublished and in need of official "employment" (Brodsky was a case in point). Many "amateur" rock musicians were employed in such occupations; they came to be referred to in slang as "boiler room rockers" (*kochegary-rokery*).[35] Having no professional status as mu-

---

[35]   Thomas Cushman, *Notes from Underground: Rock Music Counterculture in Russia* (Albany: State University of New York, 1995), 57–58.

sicians, they could not make a living playing music and so sought out employment that would provide some money, satisfy the law of mandatory employment, and allow as much free time for music as possible.

These occupations became so commonplace that the famous band Akvarium sang about their peers as "the generation of yard sweepers and night watchers" (*Pokolenie dvornikov i storozhei*).[36] By the early 1980s, it became difficult to find a vacancy in such jobs. Milieus of *svoi* that emerged in these contexts tried to hire only those who belonged. This allowed them to concentrate on joint pursuits in art and philosophy[37] and to guarantee a system of substitution at work since many were in fact busy with vocations outside of their employment. In the early 1980s in Leningrad, one often needed connections within these milieus to be hired at such jobs. Inna's friend, who was trying to get a position in a boiler room, was asked what she "also" did. When she said she was a medieval historian, they replied: "What? A medievalist? Oh, no, no. Here everyone is a legal scholar. Two PhDs [*kandidaty*] and the third is defending soon."[38] These legal scholars needed free time to engage in research that was unconstrained by work in law institutions and that allowed one to spend time reading and writing, often on topics that went beyond those accepted in Soviet publications. Essentially, their boiler room wages functioned as academic research grants that enabled scholarly pursuits and did not constrain the topics they pursued. However, they operated as such primarily in the world of *vnye* (one could not necessarily publish in the state owned journals). As a context for research that did not require teaching (like the theoretical physicists above), such employment was a *vnye* imitation of employment in academic institutions.

---

[36] From the song "Pokolenie dvornikov i storozhei" by Boris Grebenshikov.

[37] For example, in one Leningrad boiler room in the 1970s and early 1980s, Boris Ostanin and Boris Ivanov worked on a multivolume history of St. Petersburg cemeteries and churches that was eventually published during the post-Soviet period (Lur'e, *Zanimatel'naia istoriia Peterburga*).

[38] Author interview.

Such employment also allowed for engagement with cultural, philosophical, or religious topics that one could not pursue at all in Soviet institutions such as, Buddhism, Western jazz, existential philosophy, and so on. Although the salaries for boiler room jobs were lower than for most other occupations, one could easily survive because meeting one's basic needs in the Soviet Union was inexpensive. According to one rock musician, "before the advent of *glasnost* and *perestroika* he could live on three rubles per week, or roughly, at official exchange rates of the time, for about $1.80."[39] Rent, food, transportation, clothes, books, theater, cinema, and museums were all very cheap; medical care and education were free. In addition, the socialist state in fact subsidized these occupations. Therefore, a vibrant culture of artistic and philosophical milieus came about through the support of the state, pursuing many forms of knowledge that the state had never anticipated. Boiler rooms were literally *vnye*—inside and outside—the system. Their valves and heat pipes reached like arteries into thousands of apartments in the district embedding these boiler rooms inside the very entrails of the system, simultaneously providing utopian amounts of time, space, and intellectual freedom from its constraints. These were temporal, spatial, and thematic zones of *vnye* par excellence.

[39]   Cushman, *Notes from Underground*, 57.

Joseph Brodsky
(1940, Leningrad — 1996, New York)

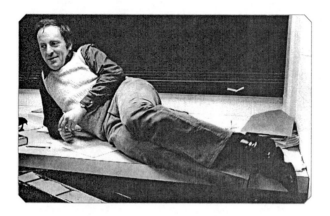

Born to the Leningrad family of a Naval officer/photographer, Brodsky started writing verse in the 1960s, when he was part of Anna Akhmatova's circle of Leningrad poets. In 1964 Brodsky was arrested and sentenced to five years of forced labor for "parasitism" (lack of officially recognized employment). His trial prompted letters of protest from prominent figures in Soviet arts and literature, contributing substantially to the rise of the dissident movement in the USSR. After one and a half years, he was released, and in 1972, he emigrated to the United States. Only a handful of his poems and translations were published while he was in the Soviet Union, although large collections of his poetry circulated in *samizdat*. In the United States Brodsky taught at a number of colleges and universities. Numerous collections of his poetry were published in America and throughout the world, but his reputation also rested on his highly intellectual and ironic essays, collected in *Less Than One* and *On Grief and Reason*. Brodsky is also the author of two plays, *Democracy* and *Marble*. After *perestroika*, most of his work was republished in Russia. In 1992–94 the first five-volume collection of his poetry appeared in St. Petersburg. Many critics consider his poetry to be a return to the tradition of Russian modernism, especially in its Neoclassical (Acmeist) version. Brodsky continually insisted that the poet is an instrument of language, whose metaphysical power is the only guarantee of the poet's freedom. Brodsky is a metaphysical poet *sui generis*, and his poetry and essays demonstrate how modernist conceptions of such categories as death, eternity, time, empire, solicitude, and language are transformed in the postmodern context. Brodsky was awarded the Nobel Prize in Literature in 1987 and became American Poet Laureate in 1991.

Less Than One (1976) [1]

1

As failures go, attempting to recall the past is like trying to grasp the meaning of existence. Both make one feel like a baby clutching at a basketball: one's palms keep sliding off.

I remember rather little of my life and what I do remember is of small consequence. Most of the thoughts I now recall as having been interesting to me owe their significance to the time when they occurred. If any do not, they have no doubt been expressed much better by someone else. A writer's biography is in his twists of language. I remember, for instance, that when I was about ten or eleven it occurred to me that Marx's dictum that "existence conditions consciousness" was true only for as long as it takes consciousness to acquire the art of estrangement; thereafter, consciousness is on its own and can both condition and ignore existence. At that age, this was surely a discovery—but one hardly worth recording, and surely it had been better stated by others. And does it really matter who first cracked the mental cuneiform of which "existence conditions consciousness" is a perfect example?

So I am writing all this not in order to set the record straight (there is no such record, and even if there is, it is an insignificant

[1]   From: Joseph Brodsky, *Less Than One: Selected Essays* (New York: Farrar, Straus, and Giroux, 1987), 3–33. Copyright © 1986 by Joseph Brodsky. Reprinted by permission of Farrar, Straus and Giroux, LLC.

one and thus not yet distorted), but mostly for the usual reason why a writer writes—to give or to get a boost from the language, this time from a foreign one. The little I remember becomes even more diminished by being recollected in English.

For the beginning I had better trust my birth certificate, which states that I was born on May 24, 1940, in Leningrad, Russia, much as I abhor this name for the city which long ago the ordinary people nicknamed Simply "Peter"—from Petersburg. There is an old two-liner:

> *The sides of people*
> *Are rubbed by Old Peter.*

In the national experience, the city is definitely Leningrad; in the growing vulgarity of its content, it becomes Leningrad more and more. Besides, as a word, "Leningrad" to a Russian ear already sounds as neutral as the word "construction" or "sausage." And yet I'd rather call it "Peter," for I remember this city at a time when it didn't look like "Leningrad"—right after the war. Gray, pale-green façades with bullet and shrapnel cavities; endless, empty streets, with few passersby and light traffic; almost a starved look with, as a result, more definite and, if you wish, nobler features. A lean, hard face with the abstract glitter of its river reflected in the eyes of its hollow windows. A survivor cannot be named after Lenin.

Those magnificent pockmarked façades behind which—among old pianos, worn-out rugs, dusty paintings in heavy bronze frames, leftovers of furniture (chairs least of all) consumed by the iron stoves during the siege—a faint life was beginning to glimmer. And I remember, as I passed these façades on my way to school, being completely absorbed in imagining what was going on in those rooms with the old, billowy wallpaper. I must say that from these façades and porticoes—classical, modern, eclectic, with their columns, pilasters, and plastered heads of mythic animals or people—from their ornaments and caryatids holding up the balconies, from the torsos in the niches of their entrances, I have learned more about the history of our world than I subsequently have from any book.

Greece, Rome, Egypt—all of them were there, and all were chipped by artillery shells during the bombardments. And from the gray, reflecting river flowing down to the Baltic, with an occasional tugboat in the midst of it struggling against the current, I have learned more about infinity and stoicism than from mathematics and Zeno.

All that had very little to do with Lenin, whom, I suppose, I began to despise even when I was in the first grade—not so much because of his political philosophy or practice, about which at the age of seven I knew very little, but because of his omnipresent images which plagued almost every textbook, every class wall, postage stamps, money, and what not, depicting the man at various ages and stages of his life. There was baby Lenin, looking like a cherub in his blond curls. Then Lenin in his twenties and thirties, bald and uptight, with that meaningless expression on his face which could be mistaken for anything, preferably a sense of purpose. This face in some way haunts every Russian and suggests some sort of standard for human appearance because it is utterly lacking in character. (Perhaps because there is nothing specific in that face it suggests many possibilities.) Then there was an oldish Lenin, balder, with his wedge-like beard, in his three-piece dark suit, sometimes smiling, but most often addressing the "masses" from the top of an armored car or from the podium of some party congress, with a hand outstretched in the air.

There were also variants: Lenin in his worker's cap, with a carnation pinned to his lapel; in a vest, sitting in his study, writing or reading; on a lakeside stump, scribbling his April Theses, or some other nonsense, al fresco. Ultimately, Lenin in a paramilitary jacket on a garden bench next to Stalin, who was the only one to surpass Lenin in the ubiquitousness of his printed images. But Stalin was then alive, while Lenin was dead and, if only because of that, "good" because he belonged to the past—i.e., was sponsored by both history and nature. Whereas Stalin was sponsored only by nature, or the other way around.

I think that coming to ignore those pictures was my first lesson in switching off, my first attempt at estrangement. There were more to follow; in fact, the rest of my life can be viewed as a nonstop avoidance of its most importunate aspects. I must say, I went quite far in that direction; perhaps too far. Anything that bore a suggestion of repetitiveness became compromised and subject to removal. That included phrases, trees, certain types of people, sometimes even physical pain; it affected many of my relationships. In a way, I am grateful to Lenin. Whatever there was in plenitude I immediately regarded as some sort of propaganda. This attitude, I think, made for an awful acceleration through the thicket of events, with an accompanying superficiality.

I don't believe for a moment that all the clues to character are to be found in childhood. For about three generations Russians have been living in communal apartments and cramped rooms, and our parents made love while we pretended to be asleep. Then there was a war, starvation, absent or mutilated fathers, horny mothers, official lies at school and unofficial ones at home. Hard winters, ugly clothes, public expose of our wet sheets in summer camps, and citations of such matters in front of others. Then the red flag would flutter on the mast of the camp. So what? All this militarization of childhood, all the menacing idiocy, erotic tension (at ten we all lusted for our female teachers) had not affected our ethics much, or our aesthetics—or our ability to love and suffer. I recall these things not because I think that they are the keys to the subconscious, or certainly not out of nostalgia for my childhood. I recall them because I have never done so before, because I want some of those things to stay—at least on paper. Also, because looking backward is more rewarding than its opposite. Tomorrow is just less attractive than yesterday. For some reason, the past doesn't radiate such immense monotony as the future does. Because of its plenitude, the future is propaganda. So is grass.

The real history of consciousness starts with one's first lie. I happen to remember mine: It was in a school library when I had to fill out an application for membership. The fifth blank was of course "nationality." I was seven years old and knew very well that I was a Jew, but I told the attendant that I didn't know. With dubious glee she suggested that I go home and ask my parents. I never returned to that library, although I did become a member of many others which had the same application forms. I wasn't ashamed of being a Jew, nor was I scared of admitting it. In the class ledger our names, the names of our parents, home addresses, and nationalities were registered in full detail, and from time to time a teacher would "forget" the ledger on the desk in the classroom during breaks. Then, like vultures, we would fall upon those pages; everyone in my class knew that I was a Jew. But seven-year-old boys don't make good anti-Semites. Besides, I was fairly strong for my age, and the fists were what mattered most then. I was ashamed of the word "Jew" itself—in Russian, *"yevrei"*—regardless of its connotations.

A word's fate depends on the variety of its contexts, on the frequency of its usage. In printed Russian *"yevrei"* appears nearly as seldom as, say, "mediastinum" or "gennel" in American English. In fact, it also has something like the status of a four-letter word or like a name for VD. When one is seven one's vocabulary proves sufficient to acknowledge this word's rarity, and it is utterly unpleasant to identify oneself with it; somehow it goes against one's sense of prosody. I remember that I always felt a lot easier with a Russian equivalent of "kike"—*"zhyd"* (pronounced like Andre Gide): it was clearly offensive and thereby meaningless, not loaded with allusions. A one-syllable word can't do much in Russian. But when suffixes are applied, or endings, or prefixes, then feathers fly. All this is not to say that I suffered as a Jew at that tender age; it's simply to say that my first lie had to do with my identity.

Not a bad start. As for anti-Semitism as such, I didn't care much about it because it came mostly from teachers: it seemed innate to their negative part in our lives; it had to be coped with like low marks. If I had been a Roman Catholic, I would have wished most of them in Hell. True, some teachers were better than others; but since all were masters of our immediate lives, we didn't bother to distinguish. Nor did they try to distinguish among their little slaves, and even the most ardent anti-Semitic remarks bore an air of impersonal inertia. Somehow, I never was capable of taking seriously any verbal assault on me, especially from people of such a disparate age group. I guess the diatribes my parents used to deliver against me tempered me very well. Besides, some teachers were Jews themselves, and I dreaded them no less than I did the pure-blooded Russians.

This is just one example of the trimming of the self that— along with the language itself, where verbs and nouns change places as freely as one dares to have them do so—bred in us such an overpowering sense of ambivalence that in ten years we ended up with a willpower in no way superior to a seaweed's. Four years in the army (into which men were drafted at the age of nineteen) completed the process of total surrender to the state. Obedience would become both first and second nature.

If one had brains, one would certainly try to outsmart the system by devising all kinds of detours, arranging shady deals with one's superiors, piling up lies and pulling the strings of one's semi-nepotic connections. This would become a full-time job. Yet one was constantly aware that the web one had woven was a web of lies, and in spite of the degree of success or your sense of humor, you'd despise yourself. That is the ultimate triumph of the system: whether you beat it or join it, you feel equally guilty. The national belief is—as the proverb has it—that there is no Evil without a grain of Good in it and presumably vice versa.

Ambivalence, I think, is the chief characteristic of my nation. There isn't a Russian executioner who isn't scared of turning victim one day, nor is there the sorriest victim who would not acknowledge (if only to himself) a mental ability to become an executioner. Our immediate history has provided well for both. There is some wisdom in this. One might even think that this ambivalence is wisdom, that life itself is neither good nor bad, but arbitrary. Perhaps our literature stresses the good cause so remarkably because this cause is challenged so well. If this emphasis were simply doublethink, that would be fine; but it grates on the instincts. This kind of ambivalence, I think, is precisely that "blessed news" which the East, having little else to offer, is about to impose on the rest of the world. And the world looks ripe for it.

The world's destiny aside, the only way for a boy to fight his imminent lot would be to go off the track. This was hard to do because of your parents, and because you yourself were quite frightened of the unknown. Most of all, because it made you different from the majority, and you got it with your mother's milk that the majority is right. A certain lack of concern is required, and unconcerned I was. As I remember my quitting school at the age of fifteen, it wasn't so much a conscious choice as a gut reaction. I simply couldn't stand certain faces in my class—of some of my classmates, but mostly of teachers. And so one winter morning, for no apparent reason, I rose up in the middle of the session and made my melodramatic exit through the school gate, knowing clearly that I'd never be back. Of the emotions overpowering me at that moment, I remember only a general disgust with myself for being too young and letting so many things boss me around. Also, there was that vague but happy sensation of escape, of a sunny street without end.

The main thing, I suppose, was the change of exterior. In a centralized state all rooms look alike: the office of my school's principal was an exact replica of the interrogation chambers I began to frequent some five years later. The same wooden panels, desks, chairs—a paradise for carpenters. The same portraits of our founders, Lenin, Stalin, members of the Politburo, and Maxim Gorky (the founder of Soviet literature) if it was a school, or Felix Dzerzhinsky (the founder of the Soviet Secret Police) if it was an interrogation chamber.

Often, though, Dzerzhinsky—"Iron Felix" or "Knight of the Revolution," as propaganda has it—would decorate the principal's wall as well, because the man had glided into the system of education from the heights of the KGB. And those stuccoed walls of my classrooms, with their blue horizontal stripe at eye level, running unfailingly across the whole country, like the line of an infinite common denominator: in halls, hospitals, factories, prisons, corridors of communal apartments. The only place I didn't encounter it was in wooden peasant huts.

This decor was as maddening as it was omnipresent, and how many times in my life would I catch myself peering mindlessly at this blue two-inch-wide stripe, taking it sometimes for a sea horizon, sometimes for an embodiment of nothingness itself. It was too abstract to mean anything. From the floor up to the level of your eyes a wall covered with rat-gray or greenish paint, and this blue stripe topping it off; above it would be the virginally white stucco. Nobody ever asked why it was there. Nobody could have answered. It was just there, a border line, a divider between gray and white, below and above. They were not colors themselves but hints of colors, which might be interrupted only by alternating patches of brown: doors. Closed, half open. And through the half-open door you could see another room with the same distribution of gray and white marked by the blue stripe. Plus a portrait of Lenin and a world map.

It was nice to leave that Kafkaesque cosmos, although even then—or so it seems—I sort of knew that I was trading six for half a dozen. I knew that any other building I was going to enter would look the same, for buildings are where we are doomed to carry on anyhow. Still, I felt that I had to go. The financial situation in our family was grim: we existed mostly on my mother's salary, because my father, after being discharged from the navy in accordance with some seraphic ruling that Jews should not hold substantial military ranks, had a hard time finding a job. Of course, my parents would have managed without my contribution; they would have preferred that I finish school. I knew that, and yet I told myself that I had to help my family. It was almost a lie, but this way it looked better, and by that time I had already learned to like lies for precisely this "almost-ness" which sharpens the outline of truth: after all, truth ends where lies start. That's what a boy learned in school and it proved to be more useful than algebra.

2

Whatever it was—a lie, the truth, or, most likely, their mixture—that caused me to make such a decision, I am immensely grateful to it for what appears to have been my first free act. It was an instinctive act, a walkout. Reason had very little to do with it. I know that, because I've been walking out ever since, with increasing frequency. And not necessarily on account of boredom or of feeling a trap gaping; I've been walking out of perfect setups no less often than out of dreadful ones. However modest the place you happen to occupy, if it has the slightest mark of decency, you can be sure that someday somebody will walk in and claim it for himself or, what is worse, suggest that you share it. Then you either have to fight for that place or leave it. I happened to prefer the latter. Not at all because I couldn't fight, but rather out of sheer disgust with myself: managing to pick something that attracts others denotes a certain vulgarity in your choice. It doesn't matter at all that you came across the place first. It is even worse to get somewhere first, for those who follow will always have a stronger appetite than your partially satisfied one.

Afterward I often regretted that move, especially when I saw my former classmates getting on so well inside the system. And yet I knew something that they didn't. In fact, I was getting on too, but in the opposite direction, going somewhat further. One thing I am especially pleased with is that I managed to catch the "working class" in its truly proletarian stage, before it began to undergo a middle-class conversion in the late fifties. It was a real "proletariat" that I dealt with at the factory where, at the age of fifteen, I began to work as a milling machine operator. Marx would recognize them instantly. They—or rather "we"—all lived in communal apartments, four or more people in one room, often with three generations all together, sleeping in shifts, drinking like sharks, brawling with each other or with neighbors in the communal kitchen or in a morning line before the communal john, beating their women with a moribund determination, crying openly when Stalin dropped dead, or at the movies, and cursing with such frequency that a normal word, like "airplane," would strike a passerby as something elaborately obscene—becoming a gray, indifferent ocean of heads or a forest of raised hands at public meetings on behalf of some Egypt or other.

The factory was all brick, huge, straight out of the industrial revolution. It had been built at the end of the nineteenth century, and the population of "Peter" referred to it as "the Arsenal": the factory produced cannons. At the time I began to work there, it was also producing agricultural machinery and air compressors. Still, according to the seven veils of secrecy which blanket almost everything in Russia that has to do with heavy industry, the factory had its code name, "Post Office Box 671." I think, though, that secrecy was imposed not so much to fool some foreign intelligence service as to maintain a kind of paramilitary discipline, which was the only device for guaranteeing any stability in production. In either case, failure was evident.

The machinery was obsolete; 90 percent of it had been taken from Germany as reparations after World War II. I remember that whole cast-iron zoo full of exotic creatures bearing the names Cincinnati, Karlton, Fritz Werner, Siemens & Schuckert. Planning was hideous; every once in a while a rush order to produce some item would mess up your flickering attempt to establish some kind of working rhythm, a procedure. By the end of a quarter (i.e., every third month), when the plan was going up in smoke, the administration would issue the war cry mobilizing all hands on one job, and the plan would be subjected to a storm attack. Whenever something broke down, there were no spare parts, and a bunch of usually semi-drunk tinkers would be called in to exercise their sorcery. The metal would arrive full of craters. Virtually everyone would have a hangover on Mondays, not to mention the mornings after paydays.

Production would decline sharply the day after a loss by the city or national soccer team. Nobody would work, and everybody discussed the details and the players, for along with all the complexes of a superior nation, Russia has the great inferiority complex of a small country. This is mostly the consequence of the centralization of national life. Hence the positive, "life-affirming" drivel of the official newspapers and radio even when describing an earthquake; they never give you any information about victims but only sing of other cities' and republics' brotherly care in supplying the stricken area with tents and sleeping bags. Or if there is a cholera epidemic, you may happen to learn of it only while reading about the latest success of our wondrous medicine as manifested in the invention of a new vaccine.

The whole thing would have looked absurd if it were not for those very early mornings when, having washed my breakfast down with pale tea, I would run to catch the streetcar and, adding my berry to the dark-gray bunch of human grapes hanging on the footboard, would sail through the pinkish-blue, watercolor-like city to the wooden dog-house of my factory's entrance. It had two guards checking our badges and its façade was decorated with classical veneered pilasters. I've noticed that the entrances of prisons, mental hospitals, and concentration camps are done in the same style: they all bear a hint of classicistic or baroque porticoes. Quite an echo. Inside my shop, nuances of gray were interwoven under the ceiling, and the pneumatic hoses hissed quietly on the floor among the mazout puddles glittering with all the colors of the rainbow. By ten o'clock this metal jungle was in full swing, screeching and roaring, and the steel barrel of a would-be antiaircraft gun soared in the air like the disjointed neck of a giraffe.

I have always envied those nineteenth-century characters who were able to look back and distinguish the landmarks of their lives, of their development. Some event would mark a point of transition, a different stage. I am talking about writers; but what I really have in mind is the capacity of certain types of people to rationalize their lives, to see things separately, if not clearly. And I understand that this phenomenon shouldn't be limited to the nineteenth century. Yet in my life it has been represented mostly by literature. Either because of some basic flaw of my mind or because of the fluid, amorphous nature of life itself, I have never been capable of distinguishing any landmark, let alone a buoy. If there is anything like a landmark, it is that which I won't be able to acknowledge myself—i.e., death. In a sense, there never was such a thing as childhood. These categories— childhood, adulthood, maturity—seem to me very odd, and if I use them occasionally in conversation I always regard them mutely, for myself, as borrowed.

I guess there was always some "me" inside that small and, later, somewhat bigger shell around which "everything" was happening. Inside that shell the entity which one calls "I" never changed and never stopped watching what was going on outside. I am not trying to hint at pearls inside. What I am saying is that the passage of time does not much affect that entity. To get a low grade, to operate a milling machine, to be beaten up at an interrogation, or to lecture on Callimachus in a classroom is essentially the same. This is what makes one, feel a bit astonished when one grows up and finds oneself tackling the tasks that are supposed to be handled by grownups. The dissatisfaction of a child with his parents' control over him and the panic of an adult confronting a responsibility are of the same nature. One is neither of these figures; one is perhaps less than "one."

Certainly this is partly an outgrowth of your profession. If you are in banking or if you fly an aircraft, you know that after you gain a substantial amount of expertise you are more or less guaranteed a profit or a safe landing. Whereas in the business of writing what one accumulates is not expertise but uncertainties. Which is but another name for craft. In this field, where expertise invites doom, the notions of adolescence and maturity get mixed up, and panic is the most frequent state of mind. So I would be lying if I resorted to chronology or to anything that suggests a linear process. A school is a factory is a poem is a prison is academia is boredom, with flashes of panic.

Except that the factory was next to a hospital, and the hospital was next to the most famous prison in all of Russia, called the Crosses.[2] And the morgue of that hospital was where I went to work after quitting the Arsenal, for I had the idea of becoming a doctor. The Crosses opened its cell doors to me soon after I changed my mind and started to write poems. When I worked at the factory, I could see the hospital over the wall. When I cut and sewed up corpses at the hospital, I would see prisoners walking in the courtyard of the Crosses; sometimes they managed to throw their letters over the wall, and I'd pick them up and mail them. Because of this tight topography and because of the shell's enclosure, all these places, jobs, convicts, workers, guards, and doctors have merged into one another; and I don't know any longer whether I recall somebody walking back and forth in the flatiron-shaped courtyard of the Crosses or whether it is me walking there. Besides, both the factory and the prison were built at approximately the same time, and on the surface they were indistinguishable; one looked like a wing of the other.

---

2   The Crosses has 999 cells.

So it doesn't make sense to me to try to be consecutive here. Life never looked to me like a set of clearly marked transitions; rather, it snowballs, and the more it does, the, more one place (or one time) looks like another. I remember, for instance, how in 1945 my mother and I were waiting for a train at some railway station near Leningrad. The war was just over, twenty million Russians were decaying in makeshift graves across the continent, and the rest, dispersed by war, were returning to their homes or what was left of their homes. The railway station was a picture of primeval chaos. People were besieging the cattle trains like mad insects; they were climbing on the roofs of cars; squeezing between them, and so on. For some reason, my eye caught sight of an old, bald, crippled man with a wooden leg, who was trying to get into car after car, but each time was pushed away by the people who were already hanging on the footboards. The train started to move and the old man hopped along. At one point he managed to grab a handle of one of the cars, and then I saw a woman in the doorway lift a kettle and pour boiling water straight on the old man's bald crown. The man fell— the Brownian movement of a thousand legs swallowed him and I lost sight of him.

It was cruel, yes, but this instance of cruelty, in its own turn, merges in my mind with a story that took place twenty years later when a bunch of former collaborators with the German occupation forces, the so-called *Polizei*, were caught. It was in the papers. There were six or seven old men. The name of their leader was naturally Gurewicz or Ginzburg—i.e., he was a Jew, however unthinkable it is to imagine a Jew collaborating with Nazis. They all got various sentences. The Jew, naturally, got capital punishment. I was told that on the morning of the execution he was taken from the cell, and while being led into the courtyard of the prison where the firing squad was waiting, he was asked by the officer in charge of the prison guard: "Ah, by the way, Gurewicz [or Ginzburg], what's your last wish?" "Last wish?" said the man. "I don't know . . . I'd like to take a leak . . ." To which the officer replied: "Well, you'll take a leak later." Now, to me both stories are the same; yet it is even worse if the second story is pure folklore, although I don't think it is. I know hundreds of similar tales, perhaps more than hundreds. Yet they merge.

What made my factory different from my school wasn't what I'd been doing inside each, not what I'd been thinking in the respective periods, but the way their façades looked, what I saw on my way to class or to the shop. In the last analysis, appearances are all there is. The same idiotic lot befell millions and millions. Existence as such, monotonous in itself, has been reduced to uniform rigidity by the centralized state. What was left to watch were faces, weather, buildings; also, the language people used.

I had an uncle who was a member of the Party and who was, as I realize now, an awfully good engineer. During the war he built bomb shelters for the Party *Genossen*; before and after it he built bridges. Both still stand. My father always ridiculed him while quarreling about money with my mother, who would cite her engineer-brother as an example of solid and steady living, and I disdained him more or less automatically. Still, he had a magnificent library. He didn't read much, I think; but it was—and still is—a mark of chic for the Soviet middle class to subscribe to new editions of encyclopedias, classics, and so on. I envied him madly. I remember once standing behind his chair, peering at the back of his head and thinking that if I killed him all his books would become mine, since he was then unmarried and had no children. I used to take books from his shelves, and even fashioned a key to a tall bookcase behind whose glass sat four huge volumes of a pre-revolutionary edition of *Man and Woman*.

This was a copiously illustrated encyclopedia, to which I still consider myself indebted for my basic knowledge of how the forbidden fruit tastes. If, in general, pornography is an inanimate object that causes an erection, it is worth noting that in the puritanical atmosphere of Stalin's Russia, one could get turned on by the one hundred percent innocent Socialist Realist painting called *Admission to the Komsomol*, which was widely reproduced and which decorated almost every classroom. Among the characters depicted in this painting was a young blond woman sitting on a chair with her legs crossed in such a way that two or three inches of her thigh were visible. It wasn't so much that bit of her thigh as its contrast to the dark brown dress she wore that drove me crazy and pursued me in my dreams.

It was then that I learned to disbelieve all the noise about the subconscious. I think that I never dreamed in symbols—I always saw the real thing: bosom, hips, female underwear. As to the latter, it had an odd significance for us boys at that time. I remember how during a class, somebody would crawl under a row of desks all the way up to the teacher's desk, with a single purpose—to look under her dress to check what color underpants she was wearing that day. Upon completing his expedition, he would announce in a dramatic whisper to the rest of the class, "Lilac."

In short, we were not troubled much by our fantasies—we had too much reality to deal with. I've said somewhere else that Russians—at least my generation—never resort to shrinks. In the first place, there are not so many of them. Besides, psychiatry is the state's property. One knows that to have a psychiatric record isn't such a great thing. It might backfire at any moment. But in any case, we used to handle our problems ourselves, to keep track of what went on inside our heads without help from the outside. A certain advantage of totalitarianism is that it suggests to an individual a kind of vertical hierarchy of his own, with consciousness at the top. So we oversee what's going on inside ourselves; we almost report to our consciousness on our instincts. And then we punish ourselves. When we realize that this punishment is not commensurate with the swine we have discovered inside, we resort to alcohol and drink our wits out.

I think this system is efficient and consumes less cash. It is not that I think suppression is better than freedom; I just believe that the mechanism of suppression is as innate to the human psyche as the mechanism of release. Besides, to think that you are a swine is humbler and eventually more accurate than to perceive yourself as a fallen angel. I have every reason to think so because in the country where I spent thirty-two years, adultery and moviegoing are the only forms of free enterprise. Plus Art.

All the same, I felt patriotic. This was the normal patriotism of a child, a patriotism with a strong militaristic flavor. I admired planes and warships, and nothing was more beautiful to me than the yellow and blue banner of the air force, which looked like an open parachute canopy with a propeller in the center. I loved planes rand until quite recently followed developments in aviation closely. With the arrival of rockets I gave up, and my love became a nostalgia for propjets. (I know I am not the only one: my nine-year-old son once said that when he grew up he would destroy all turbojets and reintroduce biplanes.) As for the navy, I was a true child of my father and at the age of fourteen applied for admission to a submarine academy. I passed all the exams, but because of the fifth paragraph—nationality—didn't get in, and my irrational love for navy overcoats with their double rows of gold buttons, resembling a night street with receding lights, remained unrequited.

Visual aspects of life, I am afraid, always mattered to me more than its content. For instance, I fell in love with a photograph of Samuel Beckett long before I'd read page of his. As for the military, prisons spared me the draft, so that my affair with the uniform forever remained platonic. In my view, prison is a lot better than the army. In the first place, in prison nobody teaches you to hate that distant "potential" enemy. Your enemy in prison isn't an abstraction; he is concrete and palpable. That is, you are always palpable to your enemy. Perhaps "enemy" is too strong a word. In prison you are dealing with an extremely domesticated notion of enemy, which makes the whole thing quite earthly, mortal. After all, my guards or neighbors were not any different from my teachers or those workers who humiliated me during my apprenticeship at the factory.

My hatred's center of gravity, in other words, wasn't dispersed into some foreign capitalist nowhere; it wasn't even hatred. The damned trait of understanding and thus forgiving everybody, which started while I was in school, fully blossomed in prison. I don't think I hated even my KGB interrogators: I tended to absolve even them (good-for-nothing, has a family to feed, etc.). The ones I couldn't justify at all were those who ran the country, perhaps because I'd never got close to any of them. As enemies go, in a cell you have a most immediate one: lack of space. The formula for prison is a lack of space counterbalanced by a surplus of time. This is what really bothers you, that you can't win. Prison is a lack of alternatives, and the telescopic predictability of the future is what drives you crazy. Even so, it is a hell of a lot better than the solemnity with which the army sics you on people on the other side of the globe, or nearer.

Service in the Soviet Army takes from three to four years, and I never met a person whose psyche wasn't mutilated by its mental straitjacket of obedience. With the exception, perhaps, of musicians who play in military bands and two distant acquaintances of mine who shot themselves in 1956, in Hungary, where both were tank commanders. It is the army that finally makes a citizen of you; without it you still have a chance, however slim, to remain a human being. If there is any reason for pride in my past, it is that I became a convict, not a soldier. Even for having missed out on the military lingo—the thing that worried me most—I was generously reimbursed with the criminal argot.

Still, warships and planes were beautiful, and every year there were more of them. In 1945, the streets were full of "Studebekker" trucks and jeeps with a white star on their doors and hoods—the American hardware we had got on lend-lease. In 1972, we were selling this kind of thing *urbi et orbi* ourselves. If the standard of living during that period improved 15 to 20 percent, the improvement in weaponry production could be expressed in tens of thousands of percent. It will continue to go up, because it is about the only real thing we have in that country, the only tangible field for advancement. Also because military blackmail, i.e., a constant increase in the production of armaments which is perfectly tolerable in the totalitarian setup, may cripple the economy of any democratic adversary that tries to maintain a balance. Military buildup isn't insanity: it's the best tool available to condition the economy of your opposite number, and in the Kremlin they've realized that full well. Anyone seeking world domination would do the same. The alternatives are either unworkable (economic competition) or too scary (actually using military devices).

Besides, the army is a peasant's idea of order. There is nothing more reassuring for an average man than the sight of his cohorts parading in front of Politburo members standing on top of the Mausoleum. I guess it never occurred to any of them that there is an element of blasphemy in standing on top of a holy relic's tomb. The idea, I guess, is that of a continuum, and the sad thing about these figures on top of the Mausoleum is that they really join the mummy in defying time. You either see it live on TV or as a poor-quality photograph multiplied in millions of copies of the official newspapers. Like the ancient Romans who related themselves to the center of the Empire by making the main street in their settlements always run north-south, so the Russians check the stability and predictability of their existence by those pictures.

When I was working at the factory, we would go for lunch breaks into the factory yard; some would sit down and unwrap their sandwiches, others would smoke or play volleyball. There was a little flower bed surrounded by the standard wooden fence. This was a row of twenty-inch-high planks with two-inch spaces between them, held together by a transverse lath made of the same material, painted green. It was covered with dust and soot, just like the shrunken, withered flowers inside the square-shaped bed. Wherever you went in that empire, you would always find this fence. It comes prefabricated, but even when people make it with their own hands, they always follow the prescribed design. Once I went to Central Asia, to Samarkand; I was all warmed up for those turquoise cupolas and the inscrutable ornaments of madrasahs and minarets. They were there. And then I saw that fence, with its idiotic rhythm, and my heart sank, the Orient vanished. The small-scale, comb-like repetitiveness of the narrow palings immediately annihilated the space—as well as the time—between the factory yard and Kubla Khan's ancient seat.

There is nothing more remote from these planks than nature, whose green color their paint idiotically suggests. These planks, the governmental iron of railings, the inevitable khaki of the military uniform in every passing crowd on every street in every city, the eternal photographs of steel foundries in every morning paper and the continuous Tchaikovsky on the radio—these things would drive you crazy unless you learned to switch yourself off. There are no commercials on Soviet TV; there are pictures of Lenin, or so-called photo-études of "spring," "autumn," etc., in the intervals between the programs. Plus "light" bubbling music which never had a composer and is a product of the amplifier itself.

At that time I didn't know yet that all this was a result of the age of reason and progress, of the age of mass production; I ascribed it to the state and partly to the nation itself, which would go for anything that does not require imagination. Still, I think I wasn't completely wrong. Should it not be easier to exercise and distribute enlightenment and culture in a centralized state? A ruler, theoretically, has better access to perfection (which he claims anyhow) than a representative. Rousseau argued this. Too bad it never worked in Russia. This country, with its magnificently inflected language capable of expressing the subtlest nuances of the human psyche, with an incredible ethical sensitivity (a good result of its otherwise tragic history), had all the makings of a cultural, spiritual paradise, a real vessel of civilization. Instead, it became a drab hell, with a shabby materialist dogma and pathetic consumerist gropings.

My generation, however, was somewhat spared. We emerged from under the postwar rubble when the state was too busy patching its own skin and couldn't look after us very well. We entered schools, and whatever elevated rubbish we were taught there, the suffering and poverty were visible all around. You cannot cover a ruin with a page of *Pravda*. The empty windows gaped at us like skulls' orbits, and as little as we were, we sensed tragedy. True, we couldn't connect ourselves to the ruins, but that wasn't necessary: they emanated enough to interrupt laughter. Then we would resume laughing, quite mindlessly—and yet it would be a resumption. In those postwar years we sensed a strange intensity in the air; something immaterial, almost ghostly. And we were young, we were kids. The amount of goods was very limited, but not having known otherwise, we didn't mind it. Bikes were old, of prewar make, and the owner of a soccer ball was considered a bourgeois. The coats and underwear that we wore were cut out by our mothers from our fathers' uniforms and patched drawers: exit Sigmund Freud. So we didn't develop a taste for possessions. Things that we could possess later were badly made and looked ugly. Somehow, we preferred ideas of things to the things themselves, though when we looked in mirrors we didn't much like what we saw there.

We never had a room of our own to lure our girls into, nor did our girls have rooms. Our love affairs were mostly walking and talking affairs; it would make an astronomical sum if we were charged for mileage. Old warehouses, embankments of the river in industrial quarters, stiff benches in wet public gardens, and cold entrances of public buildings—these were the standard backdrops of our first pneumatic blisses. We never had what are called "material stimuli." Ideological ones were a laughable matter even for kindergarten kids. If somebody sold himself out, it wasn't for the sake of goods or comfort: there were none. He was selling out because of inner want and he knew that himself. There were no supplies, there was sheer demand.

If we made ethical choices, they were based not so much on immediate reality as on moral standards derived from fiction. We were avid readers and we fell into a dependence on what we read. Books, perhaps because of their formal element of finality, held us in their absolute power. Dickens was more real than Stalin or Beria. More than anything else, novels would affect our modes of behavior and conversations, and 90 percent of our conversations were about novels. It tended to become a vicious circle, but we didn't want to break it.

In its ethics, this generation was among the most bookish in the history of Russia, and thank God for that. A relationship could have been broken for good over a preference for Hemingway over Faulkner; the hierarchy in that pantheon was our real Central Committee. It started as an ordinary accumulation of knowledge but soon became our most important occupation, to which everything could be sacrificed. Books became the first and only reality, whereas reality itself was regarded as either nonsense or nuisance. Compared to others, we were ostensibly flunking or faking our lives. But come to think of it, existence which ignores the standards professed in literature is inferior and unworthy of effort. So we thought, and I think we were right.

The instinctive preference was to read rather than to act. No wonder our actual lives were more or less a shambles. Even those of us who managed to make it through the very thick woods of "higher education," with all its unavoidable lip—and other members'—service to the system, finally fell victim to literature-imposed scruples and couldn't manage any longer. We ended up doing odd jobs, menial or editorial—or something mindless, like carving tombstone inscriptions, drafting blueprints, translating technical texts, accounting, bookbinding, developing X-rays. From time to time we would pop up on the threshold of one another's apartment, with a bottle in one hand, sweets or flowers or snacks in the other, and spend the evening talking, gossiping, bitching about the idiocy of the officials upstairs, guessing which one of us would be the first to die. And now I must drop the pronoun "we."

Nobody knew literature and history better than these people, nobody could write in Russian better than they, nobody despised our times more profoundly. For these characters civilization meant more than daily bread and a nightly hug. This wasn't, as it might seem, another lost generation. This was the only generation of Russians that had found itself, for whom Giotto and Mandelstam were more imperative than their own personal destinies. Poorly dressed but somehow still elegant, shuffled by the dumb hands of their immediate masters, running like rabbits from the ubiquitous state hounds and the even more ubiquitous foxes, broken, growing old, they still retained their love for the non-existent (or existing only in their balding heads) thing called "civilization." Hopelessly cut off from the rest of the world, they thought that at least that world was like themselves; now they know that it is like others, only better dressed. As I write this, I close my eyes and almost see them standing in their dilapidated kitchens, holding glasses in their hands, with ironic grimaces across their faces. "There, there . . ." They grin. "*Liberté, Egalité, Fraternité* . . . Why does nobody add Culture?"

Memory, I think, is a substitute for the tail that we lost for good in the happy process of evolution. It directs our movements, including migration. Apart from that there is something clearly atavistic in the very process of recollection, if only because such a process never is linear. Also, the more one remembers, the closer perhaps one is to dying.

If this is so, it is a good thing when your memory stumbles. More often, however, it coils, recoils, digresses to all sides, just as a tail does; so should one's narrative, even at the risk of sounding inconsequential and boring. Boredom, after all, is the most frequent feature of existence, and one wonders why it fared so poorly in the nineteenth-century prose that strived so much for realism.

But even if a writer is fully equipped to imitate on paper the subtlest fluctuations of the mind, the effort to reproduce the tail in all its spiral splendor is still doomed, for evolution wasn't for nothing. The perspective of years straightens things to the point of complete obliteration. Nothing brings them back, not even handwritten words with their coiled letters. Such an effort is doomed all the more if this tail happens to lag behind somewhere in Russia.

But if the printed words were only a mark of forgetfulness, that would be fine. The sad truth is that words fail reality as well. At least it's been my impression that any experience coming from the Russian realm, even when depicted with photographic precision, simply bounces off the English language; leaving no visible imprint on its surface. Of course the memory of one civilization cannot, perhaps should not, become a memory of another. But when language fails to reproduce the negative realities of another culture, the worst kind of tautologies result.

History, no doubt, is bound to repeat itself: after all, like men, history doesn't have many choices. But at least one should have the comfort of being aware of what one is falling a victim to when dealing with the peculiar semantics prevailing in a foreign realm such as Russia. One gets done in by one's own conceptual and analytic habits—e.g., using language to dissect experience, and so robbing one's mind of the benefits of intuition. Because, for all its beauty, a distinct concept always means a shrinkage of meaning, cutting off loose ends. While the loose ends are what matter most in the phenomenal world, for they interweave.

These words themselves bear witness that I am far from accusing the English language of insufficiency; nor do I lament the dormant state of its native speakers' psyche. I merely regret the fact that such an advanced notion of Evil as happens to be in the possession of Russians has been denied entry into consciousness on the grounds of having a convoluted syntax. One wonders how many of us can recall a plain-speaking Evil that crosses the threshold, saying: "Hi, I'm Evil. How are you?"

If all this, nonetheless, has an elegiac air, it is owing rather to the genre of the piece than to its content, for which rage would be more appropriate. Neither, of course, yields the meaning of the past; elegy at least doesn't create a new reality. No matter how elaborate a structure anyone may devise for catching his own tail, he'll end up with a net full of fish but without water. Which lulls his boat. And which is enough to cause dizziness or to make him resort to an elegiac tone. Or to throw the fish back.

* * *

Once upon a time there was a little boy. He lived in the most unjust country in the world. Which was ruled by creatures who by all human accounts should be considered degenerates. Which never happened.

And there was a city. The most beautiful city on the face of the earth. With an immense gray river that hung over its distant bottom like the immense gray sky over that river. Along that river there stood magnificent palaces with such beautifully elaborated façades that if the little boy was standing on the right bank, the left bank looked like the imprint of a giant mollusk called civilization. Which ceased to exist.

Early in the morning when the sky was still full of stars the little boy would rise and, after having a cup of tea and an egg, accompanied by a radio announcement of a new record in smelted steel, followed by the army choir singing a hymn to the Leader, whose picture was pinned to the wall over the little boy's still warm bed, he would run along the snow-covered granite embankment to school.

The wide river lay white and frozen like a continent's tongue lapsed into silence, and the big bridge arched against the dark blue sky like an iron palate. If the little boy had two extra minutes, he would slide down on the ice and take twenty or thirty steps to the middle. All this time he would be thinking about what the fish were doing under such heavy ice. Then he would stop, turn 180 degrees, and run back, nonstop, right up to the entrance of the school. He would burst into the hall, throw his hat and coat off onto a hook, and fly up the staircase and into his classroom.

It is a big room with three rows of desks, a portrait of the Leader on the wall behind the teacher's chair, a map with two hemispheres, of which only one is legal. The little boy takes his seat, opens his briefcase, puts his pen and notebook on the desk, lifts his face, and prepares himself to hear drivel.

Selected poems[3]

Letters to a Roman Friend (1972)

I.
Now it's windy and the waves are running crisscross.
　　Soon it will be fall, and nature's face will alter.
Shifts in these bright colors stir me more profoundly,
　　Postumus, than changes in my lady's wardrobe.

To a certain point a girl can satisfy you—
　　if you don't go farther than her knees or elbows.
But how much more joyous the unbodied beauty
　　of an autumn wood: no kisses, no betrayals!

II.
Postumus, I'm sending books, I hope you'll like them.
　　How's Imperial Rome?—A soft bed, hard to sleep on?
How fares Caesar? What's he up to? Still intriguing?
　　—Still intriguing, probably, and overeating.

In the garden where I sit a torch is burning.
　　I'm alone—no lady, servant, or acquaintance.
Not the humble of this world, nor yet its mighty—
　　nothing but the buzzing of an insect chorus.

[3] Joseph Brodsky, *Selected Poems in English*, trans. by or with the author, ed. Ann Kjellberg (New York: Farrar, Straus and Giroux, 2002), 58–60, 211, 49–52.

III.

In this graveyard lies a merchant out of Asia.
   He was clever, able, yet he passed unnoticed.
He died suddenly, of fever. Not to this end
   did he sail here, but to make a profit.

Underneath unpolished quartz there lies beside him
   an Imperial legionnaire, renowned in battle.
Target of a thousand thrusts, he lived till eighty.
   Rules here, Postumus, are proved by their exceptions.

IV.

Birds aren't very bright, my Postumus, that's certain;
   but there's misery enough even for bird-brains.
If one's fated to be born in Caesar's Empire
   let him live aloof, provincial, by the seashore.

One who lives remote from snowstorms, and from Caesar,
   has no need to hurry, flatter, play the coward.
You may say that local governors are vultures.
   I, for one, prefer a vulture to a vampire.

V.

I'm prepared, hetaera, to wait out this downpour
   in your company. But let us have no haggling.
Snatching silver coins from this, my covering body,
   is like ripping shingles from the roof above you.

This roof's sprung a leak, you say? But where's the puddle?
   I have never left a wet spot; no, not ever.
Better go and find yourself a proper husband:
   he will do it to your sheets and pay the laundry.

VI.

Here we've spent—I swear it—more than half our lifetimes.
   As a slave—now white-haired—
         told me near the tavern:

"When we look around us, all we see is ruins."
        A barbarian perspective, though a true one.

I'm back from the mountains carrying fresh wildflowers.
        I'll get out a jug and fill it with cool water.
What's the latest from that Libya or wherever?
        Are we still engaged in all that desert fighting?

VII.

Friend, do you remember our Proconsul's sister—
        rather skinny, though her calves were heavy?
You had slept with her . . . Well, she became a priestess—
        priestess, Postumus, with gods for her companions.

Come and visit me, and we'll drink wine together.
        Plums are ripe and bread is good.
                        You'll bring the gossip.
I shall make your couch up in the star-swept garden
        and teach you to name our local constellations.

VIII.

Soon, dear Postumus, your friend who loves addition
        will pay off his debt, his old debt, to subtraction.
Take my savings, then, from underneath my pillow—
        though not much, they'll pay the cost of my interment.

Post on your black mare to the House of Hetaeras
        hard against the wall of our provincial city.
Give each girl the sum for which she once embraced me:
        let them mourn me for the same amount of money.

IX.

Dark green laurels on the verge of trembling.
        Doors ajar. The windowpane is dusty.
Idle chairs and the abandoned sofa.
        Linen blinded by the sun of noonday.

Pontus drones past a black fence of pine trees.
　　　　Someone's boat braves gusts out by the promontory.
On the garden bench a book of Pliny rustles.
　　　　Thrushes chirp within the hairdo of the cypress.

Translated by the author

May 24, 1980 (1980)

I have braved, for want of wild beasts, steel cages,
carved my term and nickname on bunks and rafters,
lived by the sea, flashed aces in an oasis,
dined with the-devil-knows-whom, in tails, on truffles.
From the height of a glacier I beheld half a world, the earthly
width. Twice have drowned, thrice let knives rake my nitty-gritty.
Quit the country that bore and nursed me.
Those who forgot me would make a city.
I have waded the steppes that saw yelling Huns in saddles,
Worn the clothes nowadays back in fashion in every quarter,
planted rye, tarred the roofs of pigsties and stables,
guzzled everything save dry water.
I've admitted the sentries' third eye into my wet and foul
dreams. Munched the bread of exile: it's stale and warty.
Granted my lungs all sounds except the howl;
switched to a whisper. Now I am forty.
What should I say about life? That it's long and abhors transparence.
Broken eggs make me grieve; the omelette, though, makes me vomit.
Yet until brown clay has been crammed down my larynx,
only gratitude will be gushing from it.

Translated by the author

The Hawk's Cry in Autumn (1975)

Wind from the northwestern quarter is lifting him
                                           high above
the dove-gray, crimson, umber, brown
Connecticut Valley. Far beneath,
chickens daintily pause and move
unseen in the yard of the tumbledown
farmstead, chipmunks blend with the heath.

Now adrift on the airflow, unfurled, alone,
all that he glimpses—the hills' lofty, ragged
ridges, the silver stream that threads
quivering like a living bone
of steel, badly notched with rapids,
the townships like strings of beads

strewn across New England. Having slid down to nil
thermometers—those household gods in niches—
freeze, inhibiting thus the fire
of leaves and churches' spires. Still,
no churches for him. In the windy reaches,
undreamt of by the most righteous choir,

he soars in a cobalt-blue ocean, his beak clamped shut,
his talons clutched tight into his belly
—claws balled up like a sunken fist—
sensing in each wisp of down the thrust
from below, glinting back the berry
of his eyeball, heading south-southeast

to the Rio Grande, the Delta, the beech groves and farther still:
to a nest hidden in the mighty groundswell
of grass whose edges no fingers trust,
sunk amid forest's odors, filled
with splinters of red-speckled eggshell,
with a brother or a sister's ghost.

The heart overgrown with flesh, down, feather, wing,
pulsing at feverish rate, nonstopping,
propelled by internal heat and sense,
the bird goes slashing and scissoring
the autumnal blue, yet by the same swift token,
enlarging it at the expense

of its brownish speck, barely registering on the eye,
a dot, sliding far above the lofty
pine tree; at the expense of the empty look
of that child, arching up at the sky,
that couple that left the car and lifted
their heads, that woman on the stoop.

But the uprush of air is still lifting him
higher and higher. His belly feathers
feel the nibbling cold. Casting a downward gaze,
he sees the horizon growing dim,
he sees, as it were, the features
of the first thirteen colonies whose

chimneys all puff out smoke. Yet it's their total within his sight
that tells the bird of his elevation,
of what altitude he's reached this trip.
What am I doing at such a height?
He senses a mixture of trepidation
and pride. Heeling over a tip

of wing, he plummets down. But the resilient air
bounces him back, winging up to glory,
to the colorless icy plane.
His yellow pupil darts a sudden glare
of rage, that is, a mix of fury
and terror. So once again

he turns and plunges down. But as walls return
rubber balls, as sins send a sinner to faith, or near,

he's driven upward this time as well!
He! whose innards are still so warm!
Still higher! Into some blasted ionosphere!
That astronomically objective hell

of birds that lacks oxygen, and where the milling stars
play millet served from a plate or a crescent.
What, for the bipeds, has always meant
height, for the feathered is the reverse.
Not with his puny brain but with shriveled air sacs
he guesses the truth of it: it's the end.

And at this point he screams. From the hooklike beak
there tears free of him and flies *ad luminem*
the sound Erinyes make to rend
souls: a mechanical, intolerable shriek,
the shriek of steel that devours aluminum;
"mechanical," for it's meant

for nobody; for no living ears:
not man's, not yelping foxes',
not squirrels' hurrying to the ground
from branches; not for tiny field mice whose tears
can't be avenged this way, which forces
them into their burrows. And only hounds

lift up their muzzles. A piercing, high-pitched squeal,
more nightmarish than the D-sharp grinding
of the diamond cutting glass,
slashes the whole sky across. And the world seems to reel
for an instant, shuddering from this rending.
For the warmth burns space in the highest as

badly as some iron fence down here
brands incautious gloveless fingers.
We, standing where we are, exclaim
"There!" and see far above the tear

that is a hawk, and hear the sound that lingers
in wavelets, a spider skein

swelling notes in ripples across the blue vault of space
whose lack of echo spells, especially in October,
an apotheosis of pure sound.
And caught in this heavenly patterned lace,
starlike, spangled with hoarfrost powder,
silver-clad, crystal-bound,

the bird sails to the zenith, to the dark-blue high
of azure. Through binoculars we foretoken
him, a glittering dot, a pearl.
We hear something ring out in the sky,
like some family crockery being broken,
slowly falling aswirl,

yet its shards, as they reach our palms, don't hurt
but melt when handled. And in a twinkling
once more one makes out curls, eyelets, strings,
rainbowlike, multicolored, blurred
commas, ellipses, spirals, linking
heads of barley, concentric rings—

the bright doodling pattern the feather once possessed,
a map, now a mere heap of flying
pale flakes that make a green slope appear
white. And the children, laughing and brightly dressed,
swarm out of doors to catch them, crying
with a loud shout in English, "Winter's here!"

Translated by Alan Myers and the author

Andrei Bitov
(b. 1937, Leningrad)

Before embarking on his career as a writer, Bitov studied at the Leningrad Mining Institute, served in the army, took part in geological expeditions, and attended advanced screenwriting courses at the Moscow Film Institute. His first short stories were published in the late 1950s. He was acclaimed by critics as a profound and innovative psychological writer who provided refined cultural and intellectual analyses of his generation. The place of the Thaw generation in the vast context of the Russian intelligentsia's cultural legacy became the theme of his masterwork, *Pushkin House*. Before 1988 the novel was published in the USSR only in fragments; the first full edition of *Pushkin House* appeared in the United States in 1978 (Ann Arbor: Ardis). Bitov considers the Russian intelligentsia to be an inseparable part of the Russo-Soviet empire: the intelligentsia can play its sacred role of moral judge of the authorities only when the empire is strong and pitiless; but the decline and collapse of the empire meant, according to Bitov, the death of the Russian intelligentsia. In 1979 he participated in the almanac *Metropol'*, after which his works were not published in the Soviet Union for seven years. Bitov was the first chairperson of the Russian Pen Club. Lives in Moscow.

From *Pushkin House* (1978)[1]

The Sphinx[2]
(Pages Foisted on Us by the Hero in Parting)

. . . saying, and didn't hear my own words. Didn't even immediately realize that by now I was silent, I had said it *all*. Everyone else was silent, too. Oh, how long and rapidly I walked toward the exit in that silence!

I came out on the embankment—what a deep breath! By now I had no hatred left. Freedom! Well, that about does it. They won't coddle me any longer. "Got away, the scoundrel! Hey! / Tomorrow you'll get yours, just wait!"[3] By all means . . . Senior Lecturer N., glancing fearfully over his shoulder, darted out after me. Reproached and chided me. "You didn't even need to recant anything. You *knew* that Z. himself would be at the commission meeting! You should have said it was first and foremost a great literary monument, Ecclesiastes was the world's first materialist and dialectician. They'd

---

[1]   Andrei Bitov, *Pushkin House*, trans. Susan Brownsberger (New York: Farrar, Straus, and Giroux, 1987), 351–55. Translation copyright © 1987 by Susan Brownsberger. Reprinted by the permission of Farrar, Straus and Giroux, LLC.

[2]   From the chapter "God Is." M. P. Odoevtsev's last return to his Notes may be dated, by Blok's poem, as no earlier than 1921. —L. O. (Lyova's note. —A. B.)

[3]   A famous quotation from Pushkin's *The Bronze Horseman* (editors' note).

have calmed down. They had absolutely no desire to destroy you, Modest Platonovich. But you yourself . . ." I comforted the yellow-belly as best I could. We walked as far as the Academy of Arts and said goodbye. He ran back to "put in his time" at the meeting.

I went down to the water by the sphinxes. It was strangely quiet. The Neva was floating, and colorful sharp clouds—as does happen, precisely in gray Petersburg—were drifting across the sky. Drifting above, drifting below . . . and I stood motionless between the sphinxes, in the windlessness and quiet—a sort of farewell feeling . . . as in childhood, when you don't know which train has started, yours or the one opposite. Or perhaps Vasily Island had torn loose and floated away? . . . If we've got sphinxes in Petersburg, what can surprise us? They were identically indifferent to this: they stared with the same gaze—as if into desert wilderness. And truly: didn't the forests grow right up to them in the wilderness, wasn't there a swamp under Petersburg? Strange Petersburg—like a dream . . . As if it no longer existed. A stage set . . . No, it's not the one opposite—it's my train departing.

I'm a riddle to N., you see. Why me, if even these sphinxes are no mystery! Or Petersburg, either! Or Peter, or Pushkin, or Russia . . . They're mysterious only by virtue of their loss of function. The ties have been broken, the secret forever lost . . . a mystery is born! Culture remains only in the form of monuments contoured by destruction. A monument is doomed to eternal life, it is immortal merely because all that surrounded it has perished. In this sense, I'm not worried about our culture—it has already *been.* It's gone. It will exist in my absence, as a meaningless thing, for a good while longer. They will preserve it. Either so that nothing succeeds it, or just on the inexplicable off chance. N. will preserve it. N.—there's the riddle!

Insane liberal! You lament that culture is insufficiently understood, you being the main peddler of misunderstanding. Misunderstanding is your sole cultural role. I kiss you for this on your high little brow! Thanks be to God! After all, to be misunderstood is the sole condition for the existence of culture. You think the goal is recognition, and recognition is confirmation that you've been understood? Blockhead. The goal of life is to fulfill one's function. To be misunderstood, or understood not at all—that is, to go unrecognized—can only protect culture from outright destruction and murder. What has perished in our lifetime has perished forever. But the temple stands! It's still fit to store potatoes—that's a blessing! The great cunning of the alive.

You talk endlessly about the death of Russian culture. On the contrary! It has just emerged. The Revolution won't destroy the past, she'll stop it at her back. All has perished—and in this very hour the great Russian culture has been born, this time forever, because it will not develop in its sequel. And only yesterday we thought it was just barely beginning . . . Now it's hurtling into the past like a rock. Let a short time go by and it will acquire a legendary flavor, like egg yolk in a fresco, lead in brick, silver in glass, the soul of a slave in balsam—a secret! To our descendants, Russian culture will be a sphinx, just as Pushkin was the sphinx of Russian culture. Death is the glory of the alive! It's the boundary between culture and life. It's the genius and keeper of man's history. The People's Artist d'Anthès sculpted Pushkin from his bullet. And now, when we no longer have anyone to shoot at, we sculpt our last bullet in the form of a monument. A million academicians will try to guess its riddle— and fail. Pushkin, how you bamboozled everyone! After you, everyone thought that if you could, he could . . . But you were the only one.

Never mind about Pushkin . . . they don't understand Blok! This same N., full of delight, winking and frothing, slipped me Blok's last poem.

Pushkin! We have walked together
And have secret freedom sung . . .
Give us your hand in this bad weather,
Our mute struggle is not done.

N.'s so subtle, all he can grasp is the hint. The words he doesn't understand. He's inflamed by the sounds of "secret freedom—bad weather—mute struggle," understanding them as forbidden and yet pronounced aloud. Here again, "We have sung"—that means him, too. The only reason he's not Pushkin, you see, is that they've stopped his mouth. For one thing, nobody's stopped it, and for another, pull out the gag and there'll be an empty hole. Lord forgive me this sorry rage! So these are poems after all, if one can fall as far short of understanding them as N. So these poems will live on, in the manuscript copies of N. and his kind.

This inspires the hope—and precisely nowadays (Blok is king after all, if he can call this merely "bad weather")—that the ties have been chopped forever. Were there a last little thread—what despair!—a bullet through the head. But here: behind is the abyss, ahead is non-existence, on the left and right they've got you by the elbows . . . and yet the sky overhead is free! *They* won't look at it. They live on the surface, they're not likely to miss anything here, they'll flood every crack with blood . . . And yet, under other conditions, I might never have looked up and learned that I was *free.* I would have roved in all free directions, around Freedom Square, in the freely milling crowd . . .

> *You are king, live alone. Walk the free road*
> *Wherever your free mind shall draw you . . .*

It's not "the road of freedom." But the road is free! The free road—walk it! Walk it—alone! Walk the road that is always free—walk the free road. That is how I understand it, and it's what Blok meant, and Pushkin . . . Far more. Understanding is possible. We have been guaranteed muteness. Its very purpose is that we should have time to understand. Silence—that, too, is a word . . . It is time to keep silence.

Unreality is a condition of life. Everything is shifted and exists a step away, with a purpose other than it was named for. On the level of reality, only God is alive. He is reality. All else is divided, multiplied, canceled out, factored—annihilated. To exist on the honesty of authentic reasons is beyond a man's strength now. It voids his life, since his life exists only through error.

Level judges level. Men ponder God, Pushkinologists Pushkin. Popular experts in nothing *understand* life . . . What a mess! What luck, that it's all so far off the mark!

No need to explain oneself—no one to explain to. Words, too, have lost their function. And no use prophesying—it will come true . . . The last words will fall mute because they knew how to name things with themselves. They jinxed themselves. Only when the thing they fully matched has sunk into oblivion may they have meaning again. Who can say whether they are good enough to survive their own meanings? And especially—recognition. Recognition is retribution, whether for dishonesty or for inaccuracy. That is the "mute struggle." What must a Word be, in order not to wear away its own sound in incorrect use? In order to make all the missiles of false meanings land a step away from its bewitched true sense! . . . But even if a word is accurately pronounced and can survive its own muteness right up to the rebirth of its Phoenix sense, does this mean that anyone will find it in the papery dust, that anyone will even try to find it in a former meaning, let alone its true one—and not simply pronounce it a new way? . . .

Translated by Susan Brownsberger

Yurii Dombrovsky
(1909, Moscow — 1978, Moscow)

Born in Moscow into an educated Jewish family. Soon after graduating from the Higher Literary Courses he was arrested and sent
to exile in Alma-Ata (Kazakhstan). While in exile, he worked at
the local museum and became well-versed in ancient history and
archaeology. He was arrested again in 1937, but released after
a few months in prison. In 1938, Dombrovsky published his first
novel, *Derzhavin*. In 1939 he was arrested again, and this time sent
to the Kolyma Gulag. Released in 1943, he returned to Alma-Ata,
where he wrote his second novel, *The Ape Returns for its Skull*
(*Obez'iana prikhodit za svoim cherepom*, published in 1959). In 1949
arrested a fourth time, and released from prison in 1955. In 1956
he was fully rehabilitated and returned to Moscow, where he
lived until his death. Dombrovsky described his life in exile and
the story of his struggle against the regime in the major novels
The Keeper of Antiques (*Khranitel' drevnostei*) and *The Department of
Unnecessary Things* (*Fakul'tet nenuzhnykh veshchei*, 1978). While the
publication of *The Keeper of Antiques* in 1964 brought him fame,
The Department of the Unnecessary Things could not be published in
the USSR and appeared only in *tamizdat* in Paris. Having studied
the life and works of Shakespeare, Dombrovsky published a cycle
of stories about the bard. References to *Hamlet* are detectable in

the story published in this volume. The story "Little Arm, Leg, Cucumber . . ." ("Palka, palka, ogurechik . . .") is Dombrovsky's last. It describes how KGB agents disguised as thugs persecuted a writer following his publication abroad of a politically charged novel. The story parallels the events of Dombrovsky's own life and even accurately predicted the writer's death: Dombrovsky died in the hospital after an attack by thugs, not at a remote rail station as in the story, however, but in the Central House of Writers in Moscow.

Little Arm, Leg, Cucumber . . . (1977)[1]

On a very stuffy June evening he was lying on the couch, perhaps sleeping or simply dozing fitfully, and through his delirium it seemed to him that they were talking to him on the phone again. The conversation was rough, along the lines of blackmail; they were threatening him, promising to break his bones, or do something even worse than that—to lie in wait for him somewhere in an entryway and bash his head with a hammer. Such a thing had actually happened not long ago, except that the killer didn't use a hammer but a heavy bottle. He struck the man on the back of the head from behind. The man was in the hospital for a week without regaining consciousness and died. And he hadn't even turned thirty yet, and he had just published his first book of poetry.[2]

These thoughts woke him up and he heard someone really calling him.

He went to the phone and glanced out the window. It was dark already. "Once again I'll arrive at night," he thought and picked up the receiver.

---

[1]   This translation was first published in *50 Writers: An Anthology of 20th Century Russian Short Stories* (Boston: Academic Studies Press, 2011), 505–522. Translated and annotated by Valentina Brougher and Frank Miller.

[2]   Reference to what actually happened to the poet Konstantin Bogatyryov (1925–1976).

"Hello," he said.

A young, ringing, slightly brazen voice responded, "And who's this?"

"That's another one already," he realized. "What is this, has a whole bunch of them gathered over there?" He asked, "Well, and who do you want?"

"Who's this?"

"Who is it you want?"

"Maybe I got the wrong number. Who . . ."

"The right number, the right number, exactly the right number. Four of you guys have called me today already. So go ahead."

"So it's you, damned son-of-a-bitch, lousy writer. Just keep in mind: we're warning you for the last time. If you, bastard, don't stop your hateful . . ."

"Wait. I'll get a chair. Listen, do they hand out cue cards to you over there or something? Why do you all rattle off the same thing? I don't see any free creativity or flights of fancy from you. Have at least a few words of your own instead of everything from 'uncle.'"

"From what uncle?"

"From Uncle Zick.[3] No, seriously. Don't you have minds of your own? Only 'damned son-of-a-bitch,' only 'we'll bash your head,' only 'vile activities.' By the way, one of your freaking guys simply says 'activities.' Hey, men! Tell him I said hi!"

"Fine, cut the smooth talk—there's no need to put a spell on my teeth. They're healthy."[4]

"Oh! And all the better to knock them out!"

"Hey, you!" the voice in the receiver was even totally taken aback for a second. "I'll chew you up alive."

"And are you far from here?"

<hr />

[3]   In Russian the name is *Zuy*, which rhymes with the word for the male organ, *khuy*. We've rendered the name as "Zick" (to rhyme with "dick").

[4]   The phrase the speaker uses (*zuby zagovarivat'*) carries two meanings. The first is idiomatic, "meaning to engage in smooth talk." But when the speaker goes on to say, "they're healthy," it becomes quickly clear that he is simultaneously referring to the literal meaning of the phrase, "to cast a spell on teeth." Such spells, believed to cure tooth pain, were part of Russian folk belief.

"No matter where I am, we'll get you. So we're warning you, and for the last time . . ."

"Hang on! Someone's at the door. Just don't hang up."

He went to the door, looked through the peep-hole and saw her standing there, the one for whom he had been waiting for three days now, the one he had desperately needed this morning. She was supposed to play a role in his movie, and the whole country knew and loved her. Her portraits—young, beautiful, smiling—hung in the lobby of almost every movie theater, and the newspaper stands were full of her pictures. She was always recognized when she appeared on the street with him. He had been really, really waiting for her these three damned days, but now she was simply of no use to him.

"Here's something else for me to worry about," he thought. "Why has everything started crashing down on me at the same time?"

He opened the door. She didn't walk in but flew in, and immediately rushed toward him. Actually more at him than toward him. She had such an expression on her face and was breathing so hard and gasping for air that for several seconds she couldn't get a single word out.

"What's the matter with you?" he asked a bit roughly. "Has something happened, God forbid! Just look at you! Look at you!" He shook her lightly by the shoulders. "Well?"

She licked her dry lips. "Oh, I'm so happy to see you're all right. Your phone is always busy."

"Well, yes. I was taking a nap and took the phone off the hook. All kinds of riff-raff keep calling."

"And they called my brother too, asking for you and threatening to lie in wait for you in the entryway. I just got back from the set and he told me that. I rushed here right away. As you can see, I haven't even changed."

True, she was wearing her work outfit—a blouse, slacks, and big sunglasses.

"Well, sit down and catch your breath. I'll finish my phone conversation. Are you listening, buddy?" he asked the receiver. "Good boy. So, are you far from here?"

"And why do you need to know that?" he could suddenly hear real confusion in the voice. He seemed to hear other voices in the background as well. "You want to track us down, you son-of-a-bitch, is that it?"

"No, I want to propose a business deal. You've been to my neighborhood many times and know it well. How can it be otherwise? If you're planning to kill me, then you know everything over here. So look, there's an empty lot diagonally from my place. There used to be a shack there before, but it's been torn down. And drunks guzzle vodka there until eleven. You know it?"

"And just what are you leading up to, you dumb ass?

"Well, here's a proposition. There's no one there now. The drunks are all at home. In fifteen minutes I'll head there and wait for you. Do come. Be it with a hammer, a bottle, alone or with a gang—I'll be waiting for you. That's the deal . . ."

"What do you mean, you son-of-a-bitch? I'll . . . you . . ."

"Stop, no swearing! I'm sick of all this, you blockhead." He lightly pushed away the actress, who had rushed to him and was squeezing his fingers.

"For God's sake," she said, "you know it's . . ." He waved her away.

"So, do come. We'll have a talk. But remember, come prepared. If you miss, they'll take you away in an ambulance, that I can guarantee you. I know how to do it. You know where I've been, and what I've seen, and what crap I've been through."[5]

"Don't try scaring me, you son-of-bitch. We'll lie in wait for you and get you even in an empty lot. Just you wait!"

"Why do you need to lie in wait for me? I'm going on my own. I'm sick to death of you—you blockheads, damn babblers, well-fed bastards."

"One of your nice guys, a crappy painter—has already been shot. A drive-by . . ."

"You see, you ignorant bastard, how they treat you over there. They didn't even tell you who was killed, and how and why. That

---

[5]   · Dombrovsky himself spent seventeen years in labor camps.

wasn't a crappy painter or a doctor, but an artist. And he was shot accidentally by some piece of trash—a money collector. He got scared to death and fired from the car. But the poet was killed in an entryway."

"Like I was saying . . ."

"And it wasn't you who killed him, but someone more powerful. You only bark like sons-of-bitches from phone booths for two kopecks. You're morons and nothing else. When someone really wants to kill somebody, they don't call. So then, be there in fifteen minutes on the dot. Got it?"

"Are you going to get some police volunteers?"

"Don't shit in your pants just yet. I'll come alone. You can see everything from a distance. Everything. I'm hanging up."

The actress was sitting on the couch and looking at him. Her face wasn't even the color of chalk but of cocaine, which has that deathly crystalline sparkle.

"What's all this about?" she asked quietly.

"What do you mean, 'what'? A very business-like conversation."

"And you're going to go?"

"Absolutely . . ."

He went over to the table, opened the drawer, rummaged through the papers, and took out a hunting knife. A year or so ago a dark figure had jumped him on the stairs with it. It happened on the ninth floor around eleven at night, and the light bulbs had been unscrewed. He had wrenched open the dark figure's hand and the knife fell out. In parting he gave him a couple more blows across his whitish, grayish-red face and said calmly, "Leave, you idiot." If nothing else, they had taught him how to fight properly over there. The knife was homemade, beautiful, with inlaid work and all, and he prized it. He grasped it in his fist, took a swing, and admired his fighting arm. It really looked great. The knife was shiny and had a blood-red, coral handle.

"Just like this, madam," he said.

The actress stood there and stared at him, looking wild-eyed.

"I won't let you go anywhere. It's suicide. Right in front of me . . . No, no!" she shouted.

He frowned and tossed the knife on the table.

"Just like in my stupid screenplay! Listen here, silly," he said affectionately, "they can't do a damn thing to me. I swear to you on my honor. On my honor and yours. They're bull-shitters, hoodlums, drunks, ordinary wretches up to no good. They used to steal rations from us in the North[6] and we dunked them in the latrines for that. Not to kill, but just so they'd swallow some. And I'll teach them a lesson today, I will."

"There'll be at least a dozen of them. They won't even let you turn around. There's nothing but bushes over there."

"But I'm not blind either. I'll see them. And with that type of crowd it's like this: you punch one in the mug, knock another off his feet, and they'll all run away. But look how they've terrified you. How can I not teach those dimwits a lesson after that?"

He spoke easily, confidently, convincingly, and she gradually calmed down. He could always make her believe whatever he wanted. So now, too, she looked at him—calm, collected, and composed, as he was not in his personal life—and she almost believed that nothing terrible would happen. They'd just have a talk man to man, and that's all. He, too, realized that she had calmed down, and so he laughed and patted her on the shoulder.

"C'mon. Be a good girl. Sit here and wait . . . Then you can take me to the train station. I'll go to the dacha. I've been stuck around here for three days, drinking with all sorts of riff-raff, but my work is waiting for me. Take your cosmetics bag, powder your nose, and wipe your eyes. Right now they're redder than a grouper's, and your mascara is running. Take a look in the mirror. Isn't Masha a beauty?"

"And there's no other way?" she asked, taking out her cosmetics bag.

"No. Don't you understand, no other way! They're getting more brazen. And if they realize that I've lost my nerve, then they might really sneak up on me from behind a corner and clobber me with something, or lie in wait for me in an entryway like they did to that poor guy. But here—it's all out in the open!"

---

6   The North: reference to the camps of the Gulag.

"Oh!" And she jumped up again.

"Sit tight! I'll be right back. You can look out the kitchen window—you can see everything from there."

"Then I'll go with you too . . ."

"That'll do me a real favor! Are we putting on a show for them or something? A four-part film by Yulian Semyonov?[7] Sit tight and that's it."

And he took her by the shoulders again and nudged her towards the couch.

However, less than five minutes had passed since the phone conversation. And it was only a couple of steps to the empty lot, just a matter of crossing the street. So what was there to do—hang out in plain sight?

He sat down at the table again, propped up his head with his hand, and fell into thought. The phone rang. He picked up the receiver reluctantly, listened, became animated and said, "Yes, hello. But of course I recognized you." He listened some more and responded, "I'll be there the whole day. Please. No, it's not too early. I get up at six. So I'll be expecting you." He hung up the receiver and grinned. "This meeting on the empty lot—that's nothing! Tomorrow morning the editor is coming to see me, out of the blue . . ."

She understood at once whom he was talking about and sympathized. "You dislike him that much?" He frowned.

"No, it's not that I dislike him, it's just . . ."

She got up from the couch, went over to the mirror, then got a chair and sat down at the table next to him.

". . . it's just that you don't like him." And suddenly, on green paper, her finger began to trace something elongated, rounded, curling, with lots of flourishes and indentations going here and there, in and out.

"What's that? A snake?"

<hr>

[7] Julian Semyonov (1931–1993): writer of popular spy and detective novels, some of which were turned into television serials.

"Close. A French curve—a ruler for drawing curved lines. That's him. And here's you!" And quickly—one-two-three—she traced an oval, and on the oval two lines on the bottom, two lines on the top, and a small circle above them, and on the circle lots and lots of little lines sticking out above, below and to the sides—a head, messy hair, arms and legs.

He laughed. "I learned that as a child too. Little arm, leg, cucumber—and you've got a little man . . ."

"Yes, you've got a little man," she smiled right into his eyes.

"Hmm! So that's what I look like—little arm, leg, tufts of hair—not very flattering, you know."

"Not very, of course, but the French curve is much worse."

"Worse? Even though it's so elegant?"

"I hate it. It's sly, winds around everything, hugs everything and slithers up to everything. It doesn't have any straight lines—it's all curves, twists and turns."

"And do you know many like that?"

"They're all like that where I work. And I take first place."

"Terrific! And here's what I'm like . . ." He pointed at the spot where she had done the invisible drawing.

"Yes, you're like that." She used the informal form of "you" to him for the first time.[8]

He thought a bit and got up.

"Well, I think it's time. I'm going. Stay put. I'll be quick."

But he was gone a long time. She was now sitting calmly, because she saw that no one had approached him or stopped at the empty lot. He just sat around for half an hour for no reason on an empty crate that used to hold Moroccan oranges.

"Damned sons-of-bitches, bullshit artists," he said forcefully. "Oh, just try messing with me again!" And he slammed a cut-glass tumbler—a drunkard's salvation—on the table. He had a whole cupboard full of them; someone had told him that they brought good luck to a home. "Here, I made a dandelion wreath for you while I was sitting there. Look, it's like the sun. Smell it. And there

---

[8]   Russian has "thou" (*ty*) and "you" (*vy*).

are so many bumblebees over there that all you hear is buzzing. Is your car here? Your hands aren't shaking? Show me. Excellent. Can you drop me off at the train station?"

"Today I can drive you wherever you're going."

"No, there's no need today to drive me all the way. It's the weekend. There'll be traffic checkpoints everywhere. It'll be faster by train."

"Maybe you'll stay here? Couldn't you go tomorrow?"

"I can't. My wife has lost all track of me. The cats are yowling. They love me. Let's go!"

There was a good half hour left until the last commuter train for the dachas, and there weren't many people. It was now completely dark. The streetlights were lit. After an oppressive, sultry day, the air was still and somewhat stagnant. The dusty poplars looked weary in the purplish light from the street lamps. A man came up and sat down next to him.

"Would you happen to know what time it is?" he asked the man.

"The train will be here in five minutes," the man replied. "But don't you recognize me, my friend?" And the man addressed him by his first name and patronymic.

"Good Lord!" he exclaimed. "Fancy meeting you here! Do you live on this line now?"

"No, I don't live here, I'm just staying with a friend. You know him." And he named a rather prominent essayist. "I set him up in a dacha out there and so sometimes I come to spend the weekend with him. In the morning we hike, swim, and drink vodka. It's great."

"I bet!" he said with a smile, looking closely at his neighbor.

This was the former employee of a district newspaper and these days the chairman of the regional bibliophile society. Once, a couple of years ago, he called and asked him to speak at one of their evening events. Just to give a talk or read an excerpt. The evening was a great success. There was lots of applause, and people picked a bunch of gorgeous carnations and presented them to him, walked him back in a big group, and begged him to come again. From then on, he and the bibliophile became not quite close friends, but certainly good acquaintances. The bibliophile had an attractive appearance: such a robust fellow, with a round face, brown eyes with little specks in them, and a funny turned-up nose. A real tractor driver or foreman. The bibliophile would often invite him here and there—to read a story or give a speech on the occasion of some anniversary, or just talk about writers and the writer's craft. He was very courteous, direct, and always paid well, which the writer also appreciated. The writer was always short of money. His work wasn't published much and never republished. A year ago he had finished his big novel[9] and it began to make the rounds. That was when all kinds of unpleasantness began to rain down upon him, beginning with the phone calls and ending with rejections by editors. But he had anticipated it all and was not too upset.

"And where do you get off now?" he asked the bibliophile.

He named a station, one not very close but not terribly far either, about a half hour away from where the writer lived now.

"Well, that means we'll have plenty of time to talk. You know, I was starting to miss you already."

The train pulled in. The cars were practically empty. The electricity was working at half-power.

"By the way, how's it going with the novel? Any prospects?"

"Fat chance. It's a real dead season for me, my friend!"

"They say you've been writing it for eleven years?"

"And even a bit more."

"Ah!" the bibliophile sighed again and even shook his head. "And now, they say, you're starting to have some unpleasantness? Some thugs are threatening you . . ."

"Exactly, thugs. But no, it's nothing serious. You know, the usual nonsense."

"Don't worry. If something happens, we won't let them hurt you. See?" And he held up his small, not strong looking fist.

"Oh, I'm not afraid," the writer smiled, "but thanks anyway."

---

9 Reference to Dombrovsky's novel *The Department of Unnecessary Things*, which describes the events of the Great Terror.

"Listen!" the bibliophile suddenly grabbed him by the sleeve. "Why don't you get off with me? We still have a bottle left of the stuff that will put hair on your chest. How about it?"

"It's tempting!" the writer smiled. "You're a serpent! A green serpent[10] from paradise, that's what you are!"

"No, seriously! And tomorrow morning you could head on home. Why drag yourself all the way there in such darkness? Your wife has probably been sound asleep for hours by now. And I could introduce you to one of your ardent readers. He lives there too. A young guy. He's writing a historical novel. He'd be so happy! Let's get off together. How about it?"

"It's very, very tempting. Half a liter, you say? And what sort of novel is that guy writing?"

"You know, I haven't read it. But I know it's historical."

"Our history or some foreign country's?"

"Foreign."

"Which country?"

"Denmark."

"Wow! So he knows Danish history that well? That's pretty rare. And what's his name?"

"Name? Damn! I forgot it too. I usually call him, you know, by his first name—Sasha, Sasha. I used to know his last name too, of course. Damned if I know what's going on with my memory."

"That's exactly it. Who in the hell knows what's going on in the world," the writer thought. "Everyone's going crazy for some reason. Everyone's memory is going."

"So, maybe you'll make up your mind and we'll get off!" the bibliophile said again. "It's a ten-minute walk from the station. We'd have such a good time."

"You see, I'm afraid my wife will run off. Why in the blazes does she need a husband like that? He drinks, disappears hell knows where and with whom. But otherwise it would have been such a pleasure . . ."

---

[10]   The idiom *do zelyonogo zmiya* literally means to get drunk to the point of having hallucinations, seeing a "green snake," i.e., being dead drunk.

"You have a wonderful woman," the bibliophile said with heartfelt emotion. "The only thing is, she doesn't really like me very much."

"Where did you get that idea?" The writer was very surprised and remembered that his wife had seen the bibliophile only once and that, indeed, she had disliked him from the start. To be precise, something about him made her wary.

"For some reason she thought I was . . ." And he tapped the bench with his finger.[11]

The writer said nothing because that was in fact true. They had discussed it—where did he come from so to say, such a nice guy, and in these uneasy times no less—but she shared her doubts with only one male acquaintance. His name had been mentioned both by the bibliophile and the woman he had brought with him at that time. So it turned out that they had mutual acquaintances. And it was this mutual acquaintance that his wife had called, but she didn't find out anything specific. "No, that woman is very nice," the mutual acquaintance said. "Only she doesn't act very prudently. She has some undesirable acquaintances. She reads all sorts of literature and passes it around. She has a bit of a loose tongue. Maybe she's involved in something even more serious, so it's possible he's keeping an eye on her. Though it's unlikely, or I'd know about it."

And that was their entire conversation. So how had the bibliophile found out about it? There was no way the mutual acquaintance could have let something slip, and suddenly it came to him in a flash! They had been talking on the phone. So . . .

The train began to slow down. Station buildings and brick towers began to flash by.

"Well, I'm here!" the bibliophile said and got up. "So then, shall we get off?"

"No, I'll go home to my wife!" the writer cut him off firmly. "I'm beginning to get the chills."

"Well then, I guess it's bye-bye!" the bibliophile said, throwing up his hands.

---

[11] Tapping a finger or knocking on a surface signaled that an informer was present.

"All the best," the writer said, nodding and thinking to himself, "No, I'm clearly sick. All kinds of crazy ideas are creeping into my head. I should run and see a psychiatrist!"

His eyes absent-mindedly followed the bibliophile. He was walking along the platform and suddenly stopped and waved to someone outside the writer's field of vision. And then the writer saw that it was not at all the station that the bibliophile had mentioned earlier. That one was still a few stops away. "It's the oddest thing!" And he did not even have time to think when the bibliophile came back quickly, almost at a run, and plopped down in the seat he had occupied earlier.

"Got it mixed up!" he said. "What a head! By the way, I remembered that writer's last name. Virmashev. And the book is from Hamlet's time, the seventeenth century."

"It's Shakespeare who wrote his *Hamlet* in the seventeenth century, but Hamlet lived much earlier, in the eleventh century! At least that's what Saxo Grammaticus[12] says. There are no other sources, so maybe there wasn't even any Hamlet at all!"

"You know everything," the bibliophile said with some emotion and took out a notepad.

"So Varmishev?" the writer said and interchanged two letters on purpose. The bibliophile nodded. "You say he has half a liter?"

"Yes, maybe even more. They made some moonshine for a wedding over there."

"Hey, I'll get off," the writer decided quickly to himself, "it's the only way to get well, otherwise you can really lose your mind. And what have I got to be scared of? The novel's written and in a week I'll be sixty-eight! That's enough! And he's a swell guy. I'm the blockhead—damned if I know what I'm inventing. I'm scaring myself."

"All right," the writer said. "Let's get off."

"That's just great!" The bibliophile was happy and even rubbed his hands.

---

[12]   Saxo Grammaticus (c. 1150–1220): Danish historian who wrote the first important history of Denmark. The first mention of Hamlet is found in his book.

The writer automatically stuck his hand in his pocket. But the knife was not there. "To hell with it," he thought, "you don't cure fear with fear, you cure it by being fearless . . ."

. . . They got off two stops later. It was a way station in the woods, not even a way station—just a platform. It had gotten quite dark. A lone, yellow light illuminated the cool semi-darkness. There was probably a pond somewhere nearby, because the smell of scum and stagnant water was coming from somewhere, and frogs were out in full force. There were large, warm, still puddles on the pavement and in the potholes. Tiny, brown baby frogs were jumping around. The writer bent down and ran his hand affectionately along the tall grass.

"There was a nice rain here," he said, inhaling and filling his chest with the resinous smell of pine trees.

The bibliophile gently took the writer's arm, and the writer could feel the bibliophile's pocket against his hip, that is, the flat, smooth and massive thing that was in his pocket. "A Browning, not too big, probably Belgian," the writer realized and asked, "What's that you've got there?"

"A Browning," the bibliophile smiled. "Look!" He pulled out the Browning in a flash and aimed it at the writer. "Now then," he said and, putting the revolver to his own temple, clicked something. A tall, blue, transparent flame popped out.

They both laughed.

"I got it from some drunk for a fiver," the bibliophile said and put away the lighter. "Made in Germany. Burnished steel. Could scare someone if need be. Well, like the guys who call you."

"To hell with them! Will we be there soon?"

They went into the woods and right away the smell of resin and pine needles intensified. The bibliophile was still holding the writer by his arm, lightly pressing him to his side, and the writer felt his strong, hard muscles that seemed to have been cast from a mold.

"We're almost there. And you, are you really tired?"

"I am tired," the writer sighed. "I'm very tired, my dear friend. Things have been so difficult lately."

"You've been writing for eleven years . . . Well, it's all right, now you'll have a break from all your work," the bibliophile seemed to be smirking about something.

"A deadly grip," the thought pierced the writer's mind. "More like pistons than muscles. Like the ones in a locomotive. Can't break loose from someone like that. The woods, and in the woods a little hut on chicken legs . . ."[13]

Suddenly the bibliophile turned on a flashlight. Why hadn't he taken it out earlier? It illuminated a door. This was apparently a forest ranger's hut. It was in a remote place, and only a very brave or well-armed man could live in it. The bibliophile touched the door and it sprung back as if it were automatic. They entered and the door shut behind them with a wolfish, steely clank.

"That's it," the writer thought growing cold, but also relieved in a way. "And no one will know where my grave is to be found. Simply got on a train and never got off. Vanished into thin air. No one to blame. No traces. Complete annihilation."

A second door opened. Two strapping fellows were sitting at a table covered with oilcloth, and there was oilcloth also on the floor. White, slippery, and spine-chilling. A lamp with a green glass lampshade was turned on. "Father had one like that in his study," he thought. One of the guys was somewhat round, with a neatly trimmed head of hair, ruddy like a winter apple, and tanned. The other resembled a horse with a white mane. The guys looked at him silently. The ruddy one was smiling. The white-maned one just kept silent. The bibliophile stood in the back. No one said anything. There was simply no point in talking anymore.

"So, in the empty lot on the crate?" the white-maned one asked. "And just look at where we invited you—to a nice dacha, with a breeze." And he smiled, revealing flat and horsey teeth. He didn't move at all, but was somehow frighteningly, deathly tense, and this tension of his seemed to create an invisible but oppressive force field in the room covered with the white oilcloth.

"Yes, that one will crush your bones instantly," the writer thought.

---

[13]   "Hut on chicken legs" immediately brings to mind Baba Yaga, a witch who lives deep in the woods. Descriptions of her appearance and powers vary, but she is often portrayed as an old crone who eats the children who stray into her domain.

"Now he'll get a small box with a lid," the ruddy one smiled. "He's about to kick the bucket. Enough—he's caused trouble, slandered, drunk our blood, the slime-bucket."

The writer wanted to move away but couldn't; even though his legs were still holding him up, they didn't move, as if in a force field. At that moment something iron and unyielding squeezed his neck and crushed his throat. He didn't even have time to let out a scream; he only choked on his own blood. Evidently the bibliophile was a distinguished master of his craft. A blinding, hot, crimson light, an entire shroud of it remained before him for a fraction of a second not in his eyes but in his brain; his body, which over the long years had gotten used to everything, even to death, was still alive and answered evil with evil. The bibliophile doubled over from a powerful kick in the groin area. His grip loosened. "Well," the body said, instantly jumping away and pressing against the wall. It was a terrifying sight—all bloody, covered in something sticky and vile, crimson, with eyes hanging out of their sockets. All this had happened in mere seconds. The ruddy one jumped up, grabbed at his pocket, but sat back down right away. And then the horsey one, screaming "you lie, you bastard!" hurled himself at the man pressed against the wall who was still frightening and ready to fight to the death. He hurled a flat paperweight at him, and its sharp corner struck him right in the temple. The body collapsed to its knees. But when the horsey one ran up to strike again, it—the body—grabbed him by a leg and brought him down. They rolled on the floor. The horsey one immediately ended up on the bottom. And then the ruddy one came up and with a precise, well-calculated movement, struck the one on top with a lancet. The blow landed right in the hollow at the back of the head. The body's hands unclenched. The two lumped together came apart. The ruddy one struck the same spot again. The horsey one got up. He was dripping. He went into a fit of coughing. And the ruddy one bent down and felt his pulse like a professional—the medical pin he was wearing suddenly flashed crimson as he turned—and then glanced into the quickly fading eyes.

"It's all over," he determined.

"Thanks guys, you really hammered him," the bibliophile said in a hoarse voice, straightening himself up and catching his breath.

"Just step back, step back! As you can see, everything's spattered here! Oh, hell! That's what it means not to be prepared. He could've easily killed me, the bastard! The car will be here any moment. It wasn't far behind us. I went out and signaled them."

The horsey one stood and watched. He had taken a good beating. His breathing made a kind of whistling, sobbing sound.

"Whew!" the bibliophile said with hatred and kicked the corpse in the temple with the tip of his shoe. "Whew, the bastard!" He struck again and again, but the head just rolled gently on the oilcloth.

The horsey one stood; his mouth was half-open and his teeth gleamed.

"A strong one!" he said. "I never would've thought he'd go with you. 'Come on over, guy.'" It was hard to tell what in particular there was in the tone of his voice and in those words. But it was definitely there. That's why the bibliophile looked at him.

"And you, sit down, sit down, you're shaking all over," he said. "Where did he get you? Too bad we couldn't shoot him."

"He talked to me on the phone, swore, called me a muzhik. That woman came running to him, tried to convince him not to go, cried—I heard everything—but no, he went. He even picked a bouquet for her—dandelions. How can you convince someone like that?"

"What's this? You feel sorry for him?" the bibliophile became angry right away. "He didn't punch you hard enough? Here, have some water."

The one with the white mane was shaking; his face became wet right away and not because he was crying, but because all of him began to turn inside out.

"Do it, go ahead, all over him," the bibliophile yelled mockingly. "What a cry-baby I have . . . If you start crying over every bastard . . ."

The car horn sounded.

"Coming, coming," the bibliophile said and walked out.

"Now there's someone I'd do in," said the white-haired one, "right away . . ."

"What's he got to do with it?" the ruddy one with the medical pin responded in surprise. "He got an order, and he gave us an order. That's all."

The white-haired one sat down on the table, opened a crate, took out a bottle, bit off the metal cap, poured a full glass, and gulped it down all at once. Then he sat around for a while, gnashed his teeth, and suddenly hit the pedestal of the table with his foot. The table made a groaning, vibrating sound—it was made of plywood. Everything here was fake—made of plywood and oilcloth, except for the locks; those, it's true, were steel and automatic.

"I'd just crush his bones," the horsey one said. "I heard that order. When I radioed him that he was coming to see me, he said 'Oh, no, that's no good. Go and wait in the guardroom. Since he's not afraid, no more warnings—just get on with the job.'"

"So what? That was right," the ruddy one said. "And we did our job."

"And then after a while he radios me, 'Go to the guardhouse in the woods. You're not needed. He went to the dacha.'"

"He sent a car with three guys to the dacha too. He would've met his end one way or another," the ruddy one said, "so don't take it so hard."

"And that doll couldn't stop him. She even gave him a ride, that brainless broad."

"Quiet! They're coming. Stop carrying on."

***

"So Varmishev?" the writer asked and interchanged two letters on purpose, "And you say he's got half a liter?"

"Even more, probably. They made some moonshine over there. So maybe we'll get off?"

"No," the writer smiled. "Looks like I'll be going home, to my abode." But suddenly, when the bibliophile was already in the exit area of the train car, the writer shouted: "Just a second! A counter invitation. Let's go to my place. So what if they're asleep? We'll sit in the hallway. I've got a nice secret stash there. For God's sake, just don't say no! Because I'm going out of my mind! Here I am, just sitting with you, fully awake, but I keep seeing all kinds of crazy things."

And then the bibliophile returned obediently and sat down in his seat.

"With you, anywhere."

And he, an old man, an engineer of human souls, as someone put it once,[14] sadly, with deep self-deprecation, thought to himself: "What cowardly creatures we are after all! Let them call us like that a couple more times and we'll be running away from everyone. Those snakes know perfectly well what they're doing. Here I got all brave, went to meet them and came back all proud, not scared of anything, so to say, and then I was dying of fear the whole way home." He felt so awful that he didn't even know what to say or do. A normal, ordinary guy who was sincerely fond of him was now sitting in front of him, and he came to regard even that affection as hypocrisy or some kind of set-up. So then did he ever deserve real love? He thought about it while they were on the train, and then walking, and for that reason jabbered about something insignificant and nonsensical the whole time just to stifle the shame he was feeling. No, he wasn't even ashamed anymore; he was simply hurting and feverish like an open, inflamed wound. Those babblers! Worthless nothings! Those shitheads, as they say in the North. Nothing's done directly, everything's done in a roundabout way. Nothing for others, everything for themselves. Coiled up like vipers in a swamp, at each other's throats like dogs in a cage at the dog pound. Little arm, leg, cucumber . . . If it were at least like that, but it's not like that at all.

"A French curve," he said loudly and stopped, "damn French curve."

"Why such a negative attitude?" the bibliophile became upset. "I was a draftsman myself. You can't get along without a French curve."

"Yes, but I'm not a drawing!" he shouted in despair. "No matter what, I'm still a man. I'm a little arm, leg, cucumber! Not some French curve."

Someone laughed in the dark, and a woman's voice said in explanation, "It's always people like that who come back on these commuter trains from Moscow. They get plastered back there . . ."

---

[14]   In 1932 Stalin called writers "engineers of human souls."

They walked another half a block or so, and at this point the bibliophile said, "Well, it looks like we're here. There's the 'House of Creativity' sign. Goodbye. And I, excuse me . . ." He started to run back. "Or else I won't be able to leave. And I have to be there without fail. Today."

"So you won't stop by?" the writer shouted after him with disappointment.

"Sorry. I can't! Another time! I was only seeing you home. I saw that you weren't quite yourself. I don't have a minute left. Bye!"

"And what about the pint?"

"But I don't drink," the bibliophile laughed. "Did you forget or something? Yes?"

Yes, yes, he had forgotten everything, everything.

Translated and annotated
by Valentina Brougher and Frank Miller

Neo-Classical Poetry

Aleksandr Kushner

Lev Losev

Elena Shvarts

Viktor Krivulin

Aleksandr Kushner
(b. 1936, Leningrad)

Born to the family of a military engineer, Kushner graduated from the School of Philology at the Leningrad Pedagogical Institute. Worked as a schoolteacher. He has been a professional writer since the 1960s. His poetry represents the development of the Acmeist tradition in Russian literature (Innokenty Annensky, Osip Mandelstam, Anna Akhmatova) with its focus on the materiality of culture as a medium for communication between everyday life and historical and cultural memory. Since 1992 he has edited the prestigious book series The Poet's Library. Was awarded the major literary prize "Poet" in 2005. Lives in St. Petersburg.[1]

[1] All poems are selected from Aleksandr Kushner, *Apollo in the Snow: Selected Poems*, trans. Paul Graves and Carol Ueland (New York: Farrar, Straus, and Giroux, 1992), 6, 21, 36–37, 41, 61–62, 80–81. Translation copyright © 1988, 1989, 1991 by Paul Graves and Carol Ueland. Reprinted by permission of Farrar, Straus and Giroux, LLC.

* * *

No, not one face, but two: the world
has two wings also, and two meanings.
Two fathers, not just one, occur
in Shakespeare, crying out for vengeance.

When Hamlet sees Laertes' pain,
his binoculars are backwards;
but if this boy's an insect, then
why is the insect's face tear-spattered?

The wrinkles at their mouths are the same;
the same domestic problems needle
both, caught in such a narrow frame
they can't even tum around completely.

You touched a shoulder and you stopped
the turning at a half-turn, matching
the turning of a key in a lock
that pushes someone into action.

Hastily one of you walks out;
one of you hides his hand in a hurry.
Then you look back, crying, distraught,
to see someone else weeping near you.

* * *

Someone's crying all night.
Just behind the wall someone's crying.
      If I could, I would try
to help, but the aggrieved won't invite me.

      It's stopped. No, there it is.
"Go to sleep," you say. "Sleep; you imagined . . ."
      I need rest, I need rest.
In the dark, though, my heart's contracted.
      People crying these days?
Where'd you hear any crying, I wonder.
      No age kept dryer eyes
than ours, raised under a tearless banner.

      Maybe children—but they,
hearing, "Shame on you!," will fall silent.
      So in darkness we lie;
only the watch on the table's unquiet.

      Someone's crying nearby.
"Sleep," you tell me again; "I don't hear it."
      If I asked, your reply
would give rain on the roof as your theory.

      It's stopped. Now it starts up,
as if there's still more, deeper grief, hiding.
      But I'm falling asleep.
"Wake up! Listen!" you say. "Someone's crying."

* * *

We don't get to choose our century,
and we exit after entering.
Nothing on this earth is cruder
than to beg for time or blame
the hour. No marketplace maneuver
can achieve a birth's exchange.

Though all ages are the iron age,
lovely gardens steam and varnished
cloudlets sparkle. I, at five,
should have died of scarlet fever;
live, avoiding grief and evil
—see how long you can survive.

Looking forward to good fortune?
Hoping for a better portion
than the Terrible's grim reign?
Leprosy and plagues in Florence
aren't your dream? The hold's dark storage
doesn't suit your first-class aims?

Though all ages are the iron age,
lovely gardens steam and varnished
cloudlets sparkle. I embrace
my age and my fated ending.
Time is an ordeal, and envying
anyone is out of place.

I embrace it firmly, knowing
time is flesh instead of clothing.
Deep in us its seal is set,
as if fingerprints were signals
of an age's lines and wrinkles.
In our hands our time is read.

* * *

As at every doorstep grow rowan and maple,
so also at ours rose Rastrelli and Rossi;
as children know fir trees from pines, we were able
to distinguish Empire from Baroque without pausing.

So what, if all those pseudo-classical classics
strike us as examples of some sort of bathos?
The toga, in dense smog and encircled by traffic,
wraps round the great general like a sheet in a bathhouse.

We take such conventions as this one for granted;
we're used to it, for one thing. And when we were children
and saw this droll oddity, grownups explained it
to us as we came here, our small hands in their big ones.

These folds that were mightily rendered in copper
and stuck to the body—that is, to his jacket—
arranged to appear irreproachably proper,
give children a faith in a world where they'll make it

to similar fame. And we have to confess it's
a beauty from every angle of vision,
especially when a stray leaf hangs, pirouetting
in air, and autumn, banner-like, stands in the distance.

Pan

With a lamb on his shoulders, the god
took in each hand two legs of the creature.
He, eternal, immortal, cannot
understand why the sheep suffers torture.

But the sheep's life nears its last stroke.
Perhaps he will just shear it, release it?
He bears it, like a child round his neck,
through his backwoods archaic region.

And the lamb cannot figure it out;
it hangs down from his shoulders, thinking
about why its waves haven't been cut
—after all, they, too, hang down in ringlets.

It's too bad: all these yeanlings and lambs
—their eyes widen and fill up with anguish.
But the victim himself, in our times,
we'll be told, comes to think his role standard.

How unencumbered and swift are the clouds!
Then a puff of smoke like wool or cotton.
And the victim would fall to a god's
hands, a grip that all four legs are caught in.

Memoirs

N. V., my girlfriend then, who laughed nonstop
in high school (an S. R., she died in '20),
was with me there; we'd gone out for a walk,
as I recall, through Petrograd in springtime

—this was in '17—and met K. M.
running off to his tutoring; I imagine
we liked him because he was so poor and seemed
grownup (in Taganrog he died by hanging);

and Nadya T. was waiting at the gate
on Kovensky Prospekt near Chiniselli
Circus, where all that year a crowd would meet
for rallies (a Trotskyite, she perished);

at the time, she and Kolya U. were close;
as he liked singing more than politicians
(he, wounded in Crimea in the throat,
went to Paris and died in the Resistance),

he said we should skip the rally and stroll
to his place, where what must have been the highest
window anywhere looked out on the canal;
his sister (who later was to die of typhus)
recited some Akhmatova by heart,
and Borya K., so funny that we almost
collapsed, betrayed a mournful glance (he'd starve
in the blockade), as if of dire foreknowledge;

and to this day I recall the fallen sun,
the pearly sheen spread over that drowsy quarter;
I was retrieved by my older brother (gunned
down in '37) toward morning . . .

Before the War: Recollections

There they sit backstage, the dressing room door open;
They're dressed in khaki shirts or wearing suits.
These are bosses. And this is a dream, probably an omen.
They're having beers together: the actors, too.

Through the blinds I can just see the stage over plywood boxes,
beyond the fabulous curtain's folds.
There, onstage, the plague in Florence, actors' tunic costumes
—and here, the beery, everyday world.

There, onstage, a wisp of smoke, a lavish feast, declamation . . .
From there, after they have suffered and died,
they run off backstage, where Central Planning and Aviation
sit with the youths in this plague-stricken crowd.

Friend, what is this? Doesn't history turn out fiery?
I, coincidental with that fateful time,
had, from childhood on, the feeling that this phantasmagory
of ruination was kin to me, was mine.

Now a sweaty actress takes her paper cap off, jingling
its bells, and says, "It sure is warm out here!"
That's the dream I'm dreaming. Did a brief shadow linger
over them, a shadow of what was near?

"Oh, Ivan Lukyanich, why am I an actress? Why not a flier?"
Her cheap cloth braid has fallen to one side.
And the disinfectant smoke drifts downward offstage, hiding
street life in veils and eating at the eyes.

Bottles fill the table. And the lighting is a glorious crimson.
I've been forbidden to watch this outdoor scene.
All of it is ending: dreams, the film, flirting, and refreshment.
And life. Life, too, has almost reached the end.

Lev Losev

(1937, Leningrad – 2009, Hannover, New Hampshire)

Born to the family of the poet Vladimir Livshits. Graduated from the Department of Journalism, School of Philology, Leningrad State University in 1962. Losev actively participated in the cultural life of the Leningrad underground in the 1960s–early 70s, and belonged to the "philological" poetic group (Vladimir Ufliand, Mikhail Eremin, Leonid Vinogradov, Aleksandr Kondratov, Sergei Kulle). Losev's poetry engages in dramatic, sometimes sarcastic dialogue with the tradition of Russian classical literature and modernism, testing it against contemporary, postmodern perceptions of reality and culture. In 1976, he immigrated to the United States. Defended his PhD dissertation on Aesopian language in Soviet literature at the University of Michigan, Ann Arbor. Since 1979 was a professor of Russian literature at Dartmouth College. Wrote the first critical biography of Joseph Brodsky.

* * *

"I know, the Mongol yoke, the years of famine,
that we haven't got a thousand years of democracy,
but I cannot stand the paltry
Russian spirit," a poet was telling me.
"The rain showers, the birches,
the sighs apropos of graves,"
and the poet curled his delicate lips
into a threatening gesture.
Getting fired up, he continued:
"I hate these drunken evenings,
the penitential sincerity of drunks,
the Dostoevskian psychodrama of informers,
the vodka shots and mushroom tops,
the pretty girls, the petty sins,
and, come morning, instead of a cold compress,
the sodden rhymes of Blok;
the cardboard lances of our bards
and their well-rehearsed rasp,
the flat-footedness of our empty iambs
and the lameness of our haggard trochees.
Our rites and sanctities are insulting,
all designed for idiots,
and the life-bearing waters of Latin
flowed right past us.
There you have it: a land of scoundrels:[1]
and there isn't even a proper WC." —
with that, raving almost like Chaadaev,
the poet suddenly broke off.
But with his most pliant Russian speech
he'd skirted something essential,
and gazed as if across a river,
where an archangel with a trumpet was dying.

---

[1]   "Land of scoundrels" is the title of a poem by Sergei Esenin.

* * *

I used to work for *Campfire*.[2] In that dreary place,
far from the hustle and the headlines,
I met a hundred, maybe two hundred
pale young men and extremely plain maidens.
Coughing and shoving their way through the doorway,
and not without a brazen coquetry they'd say,
"Here're a couple of texts for you."
In their eyes I was an editor and a brute.
Dressed in unthinkable tatters,
they judged a text, as Lotman[3] had taught them,
as if it were something solid,
like a cement pillar with metal reinforcement.
All this was only square circles[4]
of nonsense, multiplied by apathy,
but from time to time I actually managed
to get some of this rubbish printed.

There was a frost. In the Tavrichesky Garden
the sunset was yellow, and the snow beneath was rose.
The ever vigilant Morozov, that same Pavlik[5]
who wrought evil, overheard them chatting on their walk.
The cold had caused the veneer to flake off
of a lacquered portrait of the young pioneer,
but they were warm.

---

2   *Campfire*: illustrious Soviet magazine for children, where Lev Losev worked as an
    editor from 1962–1975.

3   Yurii Lotman (1922–1993), Soviet literary scholar and cultural historian, known for
    his structuralist and semiotic studies of Russian literature and culture.

4   "Square circles": literally "fish on fur," itself a play on the expression "fish-lined fur"
    (*na ryb'em mekhu*) meaning shabby clothing.

5   Pavlik Morozov (1918–1932): peasant boy who denounced his own father. Raised to
    cult status under Stalin and served as an ideological exemplar for Young Pioneers.
    "Moroz" is Russian for "frost."

And time passed.
And the first of the month kept coming.
And the secretary kept writing out checks.
And time passed, showing no favorites,
and scattered everyone across the tussocks.
Those in the camp barracks get high on *chifir*,[6]
those in the Bronx battle the cockroaches,
those in the mental wards caw and coo-coo,
and shake demons from their cuffs.

---

[6]   *Chifir*: very strong tea possessing narcotic qualities.

At a Geneva Watchmaker's

To S. Markish

In important Geneva, no, in tender Geneva,
in Switzerland impressive and ridiculous,
in Switzerland with all Europe contiguous,
in polite Geneva, in Switzerland with its purse
packed with gold, cows, mountains,
with slabs of cheese that have dew drops,
with reconnaissance agents and card-sharps,[7]
I suddenly decided, "I'll but myself a watch."

The crowd was seething. The operatives
of the KCGIBA had all switched sides.
But I couldn't care less about all those spies.
I'd like to know, which here are factory-made,
which have ruby bearings,
are waterproof and with leather bands.

Suddenly I hear, from beneath a moustache's bristles,
the plaintive voice of the local Jew:
"Ach, sir, all that one needs from watches
is that they tick and tell time."

"That they tick and tell time . . .
Hey, are you talking about verse?"[8]
"No, about watches, wrist-watches and pocket-watches . . ."
"No, that's about verses and novels,
about lyric poetry and other trifles."

---

[7]   "Card-sharp": Russian *shuler*, also a homonym of the German *Schüler*, "school-boy."

[8]   "Hey, are you talking about verse?": cf. Paul Valéry's dictum "Rhyme establishes a law independent of the poem's theme and might be compared to a clock outside it" (*Analects*, translated by Stuart Gilbert, Princeton University Press, 102).

Bakhtin in Saransk

The flashy rosaries of the Capuchins.
The languid dances of the Saracens.
The hoarse holler of the high and mighty.

"M. Bakhtin," said the Saranskens,
peering into the exam scores with revulsion,
"is not a particularly good teacher."

Although Bakhtin was not superstitious,
he did know that this was no student,
hissing in the grey suit, but a petty devil:

"Someone snitched on you at the dean's,
meanwhile here's your *alter ego*—
                    your dialogue with this city."

The world capital of trachoma.
Mansions habitable only by bedbugs.
Two or three factories. A chemical plant.

Here potbellied small fry and scum
manufacture acids and alkalis
and breed rachitic whelps.

Here only some detritus remains
from the temple of the crucified God,
tall weeds and couch grass in the sacristy.

Bored and drunk, the old church
warden rises, like a clitoris,
in the doorway that leads nowhere.

All over they'd left potatoes to rot,
torn up books, scorched icons,
and would come here at nature's call.

Thus more surely, from the filth and dust,
clumps of coal and mouldy clothes,
humus grows here.

A sacred place cannot be empty.
Disintegrating, the lips of the golden-lipped[9]
revert to pure compost.

And the dead and decaying grain
is miraculously reborn there,
and a sprout shoots forth.

An incomprehensible ecstasy overcame
Bakhtin, and the professor remembered
how in a silly dream of late,

Golosovker stood with a yoke and buckets.[10]
And suddenly an idea stirred
amid the bustle, flickerings and fussings.

Everything came together: this Mordavian city.
The silly penis, sticking out like a carrot.
The star. And the whole universe.

And wrinkles darted out from his eyes.
And Mordavians were jostling each other at the door,
asking to retake the exam.

---

[9]   "Golden-lipped": in Russian *zlatoust*, from the Greek *chrusostomos*, meaning
      an eloquent orator or sermonist, also the name of the early Church Father, John
      Chrysostom.

[10] Golosovker: Yakov Emmanuilovich Golosvker (1890–1967), Russian philosopher,
      writer and translator, known for his scholarly works on myth and logic.

* * *

Grammar is indeed the god of the mind.
It alone decides all things for us:
what we will yell and what we will whisper.
And the tenses one may write,
the future crawls backwards
and slowly potters into the past.

The throng of Russian verbs
tugs at me as my grip finally loosens,
and, opening my mouth suddenly,
I know I've lost the bridle,
and, not without doubt, I wait
to see how things turn out.

Language lives independently
on the compost of souls and books,
and it will survive centuries.
And our century is nothing more
than a sigh, an 'ah,' an 'oh,'
two or three incidental interjections.

Amphibronchic Night

Evening Paper

Andropov's[11] old lady
kissed the official granite
and already a new fly
blackens the Kremlin wall.
They're grandpas—who should be
steaming what's left of their bones in a bathhouse,
who should be shoving fistfuls of sweets
at their granddaughter, Tanka,
who at night should be lying, with creaking guts,
in their underclothes on the stove,
who in the Lord's church should
atone bitterly for their sins—
instead, they mutter something, tense with effort,
first rubbing paw on paw, then
their nervous feet betraying
the suffering of those minutes they count off.
There is something melancholy about these quondam men,
these timorous grandpas who speak through their noses
in their petty fly-like habits.
Forgive them, Lord, their omission points,
have mercy on their mouldering ranks.
Already they don't have their full wits anymore
and, strictly speaking, they don't do anything.

[11] Yurii Andropov (194-1984)—one of the last ruler of the Soviet Union. Head of the KGB for 15 years (1967-1982), he succeeded Brezhnev in November 1982 and died in February 1984. Buried by the Kremlin wall.

* * *

An elegant cruise for a fabulously low price.
The itinerary: Munich – Yalta – Helsinki.

From the newspapers

The house
is filled with heat.
Past the window
poor weather.
I don't know where we're sailing
but I feel the steamship's shudders.
It's probably eighteen-hundred
and some year
in the seventies.
We don't know where we're being taken,
mustachioed passengers
in waistcoats, watch-chains, well-mannered,
               with auspicious beginnings . . .
Sleet and hail.
Speckled rain.
The multi-tonned surf
hammers
into the cliffs.
But one can still make coffee,
open
a fat volume of Russian verse—
"A Feast in Time of Plague":[12] there is rapture . . .
The starched captain, at the head of our table d'hôte,
tells us an anecdote
(he lost control of the ship
long ago, but the mirrors still
obligingly burst into laughter
and the gloom and the abyss are
still separated by four millimeters of glass).

---

[12]   "A Feast in Time of Plague": one of Pushkin's *Little Tragedies* (1830).

* * *

A poet is compost, in him dead words
ooze out, bursting apart, sometimes alkaline,
                                       sometimes acidic,
Sound escapes from sense, and
the ABCs, letters, etc. are uncovered, like numbers,

a smile, prone to decay, united his lips,
and his final thought fell flat.
Then a maggot consumed the little *larva*,[13]
bacterium produced children.

A poet is compost.
In him all paths are grains,
moistened by showers, warmed by the sun.

Then winter comes,
and covers the empty field
with a white shroud.

---

[13]   *larva*: Latin term designating a vengeful spirit of the dead; also means a costume mask.

* * *

> And he, trembling from love
> And death at hand . . .
>
> *V. Zhukovsky*

Near the lake, where one can easily drown,
along the highway, where one can always take
                                    a curve too wide,
under a sky of intricate jet vapor trails,
I saw a horse before a rickety cart,
and realized, peering at the herbivore,
that this business could be put off.
It was just like my native parts,
where it smells of hay and the dogs bark,
where they drink to Russia and fish for carp,
where girls named Klava date boys named Nikolai,
and where it's crammed full of my friends.
I thought of one in particular.

It was freezing in Moscow like never before.
My friend was sober, pensive, and had just been paid.
He divided the bills into two piles.
Then, having thought a bit, he took both with him.
We went to the very best restaurant,
were admitted distrustfully,
and were seeking out the best table in the room,
and instantly all kinds of riffraff shot up.
Towards the conclusion of the feast everyone
                                    was sluggish,

only my friend was lighter.
It then became clear that he's a wondrous logician,
and he took it upon himself to explain everything.
He rose to his not inconsiderable height,
amid the clatter of forks and the kitchen stench,
and said, "Friends, once again we're destitute,
and this will be our farewell toast.
So let's drink to the harmonious course of the planets,
to Pushkin, to the Russians and the Jews,
and let us brighten the hearts of our servants[14]
with the news that there is no death and never was."

[14]   "brighten the hearts of our servants": possible allusion to the famous line from
Villers de l'Isle-Adam's play *Axël*: "Live? Our servants will do that for us" ("Vivre? Les
serviteurs feront cela pour nous!")

Cloth (doctoral dissertation)

1. *Text* means cloth.[1] The rag of text is to be unwoven
    thread by thread.
    One must analyze the colors, catching each nuance.
    Thereafter one must explain in what color each
    thread is stained.
    There then follows a discussion of the weave
    of the cloth:
    the operation of the spindle, the deftness of the old
    woman's fingers.   5
    Then onto the sheep in question. The weather
    on shearing day.
    (Sic) The name of the shepherd's wife.
    (NB) The color of her eyes.

2. But don't presume to unweave if you yourself are
    an unskilled weaver,
    if you're a lousy tailor. Sackcloth of entangled
    threads,
    the lint of libraries, the rags of universities[2]—   10
    who, Philosopher, needs them? Weave the old
    yarn.
    Return the old mackinaw to the girl who's
    shivering in the corner.

2.1 There are colleagues who lack skill (see above)
    in our profession.
    All they can do is exclaim: "Ah, what an elegant
    dress!
    English burlap! A stylish Russian cut!"[3]   15

2.2 Then there are others. They won't even glance
    at the dress.

All they can do is count millimeters, draw dotted lines.
Piles of patterns are more important to them than
the cloth.[4]

2.3 And there are others. They are in government
service.[4]
All they can do is check attire against the uniform.   20
They'll find extra scallops or a hidden pocket, and
grab the hack at once: reprimand, lock-up,
execution.

3.   *Cloth* is *life*. And weavers weave it. But the Reaper[5]
rushes in—
and it's unfinished. Or the cloth underwent the
influence
of sun, snow, wind, rain, radiation, malice, dry-cleaning, 25
time, i.e., "the days unravel the rag that You've
been given,"[6]
and a hole remains.

3.1 That is how, Philosopher, the shroud of finely-
woven culture wore thin.
Out of every hole crawls inguinal chaos and
shame.[7]

4.   Cloth is text is life. If you're a doctor, sew it up.   30

Notes (by the author)

1.   Vide Latin dictionary. Cf. name of Goethe's grandmother.
2.   Cf. what Nabokov called "the Lethean library."
3.   These I call "fools" (Cf. Archpriest Avvakum).
4.   Cf. Cf. Cf. Cf. Cf. Cf.
5.   (. . .) Ivanovich (1937 – ?).
6.   Brodsky. Cf. also Pushkin on "tatters" and "singer", which,
     probably goes back to Horace: *purpureus pannus*.
7.   Vide, vide, vide, vide, vide, vide.!

Additional notes by the translator

Fn. 5. "the Reaper": original *kondratii* is a folk idiom meaning
"apoplectic shock."

Fn 6. "the days unravel the rag that You've been given": quotation
of first line of a 1980 poem by Joseph Brodsky.

Translated and with commentaries
by Henry Pickford

Elena Shvarts
(1948, Leningrad — 2010, St. Petersburg)

One of the leaders of Leningrad non-conformist culture of the 1970s–80s, Elena Shvarts studied for a short period of time at the School of Philology, Leningrad State University, but then was transferred to the Department of Theater History at the Leningrad Institute of Theater, Music, and Cinematography, from which she graduated in 1971. From 1975 to 1985, her poetry was published exclusively in *samizdat* and émigré magazines. Her neo-baroque poems explore oxymoronic fusions of the corporeal and spiritual (even mystical), mythical and mundane, harmonious and chaotic. In this way, she transfers traditional images of high culture into the intimate zone of immediate contact and communication. In 1979, Shvarts was awarded the non-official Andrei Bely literary prize. Since the late 1980s, her poetry and essays have been broadly published in Russia. In 2002–2008 her four-volume collected works appeared in St. Petersburg.

The Dump

O glorious dump, how shall I sing your praise!
You lie in the flickering sunset, sprawling, disheveled;
The rotting backs and shattered glass of mirrors
Enclose a wormwood's straggling roots;
You are as grand as Venice! (No, far grander!)
The cat is your gondolier, and sings a serenade.
The ruined wreck of an ottoman
Lies cramped in a pool of lilac shade,
Whispering tales of hookahs by the Golden Horn
To lionizing clumps of willowherb.
July bobs to admire its face in shards of glass.
A crow dives slowly, then plumps down,
And struts upon you, stately as Sulla,
Holding doom, or mercy, gripped in each claw.
You're peaches' slimy shreds, and berries' slippery bubbles,
Lost lenses, torn book-covers, broken medals;
Your skin is leprous; you're pink and blistered
As a child inundated in scalding soup.
You're Dionysus ritually dismembered,
You're a microcosm in a make-up mirror.
But I say this to you: shake your sleepy limbs,
Get up on your feet, and walk. And then,
You monster, incubus of night,
Open your tattered mouth and speak.
O glorious dump, shake out your limbs and walk!
Sing of the days spent lying in the sun,
Your body warm, your giant's brain crackling, burning,
Yet unifying all that you survey.
May great thoughts bloom and rot in you
As you feast on vodka droplets, chicken bones.
O glorious dump, get to your feet and sing!
O Rosa mystica, the gods must hear your voice.

Translated by Catriona Kelly

The Invisible Hunter

Perhaps—to my good fortune or my shame—
My sole worth is nothing but designs
Of birthmarks peppering my skin,
Dark constellations that have forgotten the sky.
The whole thing is a snapshot of the northern night—
Auriga, Aquila, Andromeda, Cygnus,
Spikes and speckles and swarms of dots . . .
Ah, I dread the way they single me out!
No, it's not my gift, my soul, my voice—
My skin is my most precious attribute,
And a keen-eyed, invisible hunter
May already be on its track.
(Certain whales exist
And there are tortoises
With letters and signs across their backs,
They are slaughtered as curios.)
Perhaps a flautist, a celestial spirit
Had nowhere to write his music
When he woke in eternal night
And in the darkness seized the first white scrap
And scratched his notes into it, jabbed
Snowy, unborn, paper-pale skin . . .
Perhaps he's searching, will find it, slice it up.
Do sable, mink or squirrel guess
How many dollars their fur can fetch?
Though brain will rot and soul fly off,
But skin—no!—that won't give the worms a feast.
For behold, my pegged-out pelt
Will be preserved as a palimpsest
Or a photo of the infant heavens.
Where can I hide, where can I run to, what can I do?
I sense keen eyes, hot breath . . .
Ah, those designs are marked for death.

Translated by Michael Molnar

Elegy on an X-ray Photo of my Skull

The flautist boasts but God's enraged—
He stripped the living skin from Marsyas—
Such is the destiny of earthly flautists:
Grown jealous, He will say to each in turn:
"You've licked the honey of music but you're just muck,
You're still a lump of that same dirt
And lodged inside you is the stone of death."
Apollo was the god of light
But he grew dark
When round his hands, you Marsyas,
Twisted in pain.
And now he is a god of glimmer,
But eternal also are your groans.

And my God, growing dark,
Slipped me this photograph
In which my glowing skull,
Etched from the invisible,
Swam, blocking out the dusk
And the stripped naked park—
It was a mass of fog
Embraced in liquid dark.
In it shadow and cloud were blended
And my hand began to tremble.
This skull was my own
But it didn't know me,
Its intricate pattern
Like a damascene dagger
Is skillfully crafted,
How pure and how strong.
But the mouth is bared,
Still alive its grin.

Bone, you yellowed a long time,
Grew as heavy as sin,
Like a walnut you aged and you ripened,
A present for death.
Grown brazen inside me, this yellow bone
Has lapped itself in a sleigh-rug of skin.

Translated by Michael Molnar

"I was born with an unlined palm"

Fate spins nets with the smallest holes,
so children catch their feet and fall,
but I break the nets, burst free.

I was born with an unlined palm,
a palm smooth as a waxwork's
no gypsy will tell my fortune
whether riches or treachery;
she will not predict true love
or prophesy separation;
the sheds where blue pigment is heaped
had none to make rope
when they stitched up my hands,
no knife-cuts marked my palm
no stars were mapped on it,
and no lines drawn;
not for me love and death,
or sudden ominous meetings.
Fate visits me at night
bent by a heavy sack
crammed with hoarded events
and weakly scratches my palm;
my future, unseen yet voracious,
spins and drowns in blue light.

Translated by Catriona Kelly

Orpheus

On the return
He took fright—
There was a wheezing and whistling behind him,
A grunting and coughing.

EURYDICE: Don't dare to glance aside,
                This is a savage place.
ORPHEUS: I cannot recognize this hissing as the voice
                Of my Eurydice.
EURYDICE: Bear in mind, until I leave the darkness
                I am worse than a dragon.
                I will not become my former self until I see
                The blue horizon.
                I will not become my former self until
                My lungs breathe in the painful air.
                I think we're close, I seem to sense
                The wind and the sea.

The voice was a savage gasping,
There was the rustling of a beard.

ORPHEUS: I am terrified, what if it isn't you, Eurydice,
                I am leading back into the starlight, but . . .

Plagued by his doubts, he stopped and turned—
A snake with pleading eyes,
Fat as a log, was bustling in his wake;
Terrorstruck, he leapt aside.
From its disgusting belly
Two beloved slender arms with their familiar scar
Stretched out towards him.
Hesitantly he touched the rosy nails.

"No, your heart was blind,
You do not love me,"
Whispered the snake with a bitter smile:—
"Please leave me! please leave me!" —
And melted like smoke in the shadows of hell.

Translated by Michael Molnar [1]

[1] From Elena Shvarts, *"Paradise": Selected poems*, trans. Michael Molnar and Catriona Kelly (Newcastle upon Tyne: Bloodaxe Books, 1993), 25, 67, 69, 77, 87, 89. Reprinted by permission of Bloodaxe Books.

Viktor Krivulin
(1944, Kadievka, Voroshilovgrad Region — 2001, St. Petersburg)

In 1967 Krivulin graduated from the School of Philology, Leningrad State University, defending his thesis on Innokenty Annensky. Krivulin was one of the most prominent leaders of Leningrad non-conformist literature in the 1970s–80s. Editor of such significant *samizdat* magazines as *37* and *Northern Post*. His first books of poetry were published in Paris (1981, 1988). Krivulin was among the first laureates of the non-official Andrei Bely prize in 1978. Since 1990, his works have appeared in editions published in Russia. In the words of Krivulin's friend and colleague Boris Ivanov, Krivulin created a "culturological poetic paradigm": "He appeals to culture as a meta-historical and impersonal cosmos . . . Both symbolists who wanted to live outside of historical time, and Acmeists, who, according to Mandelstam, wanted to live within history, they all are equally important for Krivulin as culture's actors."

FROM THE CYCLE "ANNIVERSARY VERSES" (2000)

Trash

just yesterday the Russian flag seemed red
while today it's blue-red-white
but the hot meld of color doesn't command us
we're the same we who once to be shot
were led at dawn by the convoy guards
who unbuttoning the holster
tears by night into apartments
and with a bloody print on the carpet
stretches out of that literature
that disappeared completely from the book stands
by the metro station as soon as new winds
began to blow — weren't they the ones by whom
the red trash white trash blue trash swept away

Where Is Our New Tolstoy?

strange two wars have already
passed and the third's on the horizon
but there's no Tolstoy at all
either in life or in nature

his bicycle is there
his typewriter, wax cylinder
so many places living and wet
that same oak or buffet

but it's as if they drove away
the spiritual depths from us
to Rio or to Caracas
into the African raspberries

the ensign having passed could
the afghan really write something
he's squeezed out to death by life
and stoned if he's not drunk

or I see in a dreadful dream—
a senior lieutenant of the special forces
having labored in Chechnya
is tormented: *Can't build a phrase*
Thought doesn't walk on a string

The Millennium Changing Shifts

who has drunk from the skull of his father
who has eaten from someone else's plate
but also didn't lose face
didn't spoil the young folks' evenings

and even who didn't eat didn't drink
but was simply allowed in
to stand on the stirrup by the railings
and to bow to the people coming

to the feast or from the feast where aquavit
Esenin gnawed with a bandit
where the tested master of the house
sleeps with his mug in the salad—

where seeing off every year
into nonbeing to the monks
how we rejoiced that here
we're living under a new sign

the year went away but the century stuck around
with the newborn aspic
in a clinch and the freeze grew stronger
and the stamp knocked on the fates

it wrote up a pass for itself
into the third millennium
through connections, by dull craving
by a passion for small children

and you think after all that
that it danced as it groveled
they'll let it go still white
from the peace negotiations?

Translated by Sibelan Forrester

FROM *METROPOL'* (1979)

Vladimir Vysotsky

Yuz Aleshkovsky

Genrikh Sapgir

Viktor Erofeev

METROPOL'

An independent literary almanac compiled and edited in Moscow by Vassily Aksyonov, Viktor Erofeev, Evgeny Popov, Fazil Iskander, and Andrei Bitov (all of whom also contributed to the almanac) in 1979. Among other contributors were Yuz Aleshkovsky, Bella Akhmadulina, Vladimir Vysotsky, Friedrich Gorenshtein, Inna Lisnyanskaya, Semyon Lipkin, Andrei Voznesensky, and Genrikh Sapgir. Texts included in the almanac confronted Socialist Realism aesthetically rather than politically. Most of the works stylistically alluded to "antirealist" literary movements, from expressionism and the grotesque to surrealism and absurdism. Despite its eclectic character, *Metropol'* was the first organized act to demonstrate that modernist and avant-garde traditions had been reborn in the Soviet Union after more than fifty years of Socialist Realism. The almanac was published in eight copies and circulated in *samizdat*. Soon afterward, in 1979, it was published by Ardis Publishers in Ann Arbor, Michigan, whereupon the Union of Soviet Writers began to wage an all-out war against the co-editors and contributors to the almanac. In the immediate aftermath, Vassily Aksyonov and Friedrich Gorenshtein emigrated from the USSR, Viktor Erofeev and Evgeny Popov were expelled from the Union of Soviet Writers (which effectively banned their works from publication in the

USSR), Semyon Lipkin and Inna Lisnyanskaya expressed their protest by resigning their membership in the Writers' Union, and most of the other participants (with the exception of Andrei Voznesensky) were forbidden to publish in the Soviet Union for several years. The *Metropol'* affair provoked an international response: letters in support of *Metropol'* were signed by Kurt Vonnegut, John Updike (also a contributor to the almanac), William Styron, and other prominent American writers. *Metropol'* was finally published in Russia in 1992.[1]

---

[1]   All poetic translations in this section are published in the following edition: *Metropol: Literary Almanac*, ed. Vassily Aksyonov, Viktor Yerofeyev, Fazil Iskander, Andrei Bitov, Yevgeny Popov, foreword by Kevin Klose (New York and London: W. W. Norton, 1983).

Vladimir Vysotsky
(1938, Moscow — 1980, Moscow)

Not only a popular bard (poet-songwriter-performer), but also a famous actor, Vysotsky became a cult figure during his lifetime. He graduated from the School-Studio of the Moscow Art Theater in 1960 and later worked as an actor at the Taganka Theater, where he performed many prominent roles (including Hamlet). Vysotsky started writing songs in the early 1960s. To an even greater extent than Galich, Vysotsky introduced *skaz*—narration from the standpoint of a personage other than the author—to poetic songs. Many of his songs narrate from the point of view of a character: a criminal youth, incarcerated hooligan, mental asylum patient, WWII soldier, a wolf, an emigrating Jew, a military jet, etc. In this way, Vysotsky created a broad panorama of the psychological and social types found in Soviet society. At the same time, a unifying theme of his poetry is a desperate longing for internal and external freedom, the lack of which causes existential conflicts that are expressed through metaphors of borderline situations, flights over an abyss, and deadly challenges. Although his songs were unofficially distributed in *magnitizdat* (privately shared tape-recordings of songs and concerts) and some of his recordings were even put on vinyl disks produced in the USSR, Vysotsky's poems were never published in Soviet editions. He participated in the non-official almanac *Metropol'*. His death in 1980, precipitated by drug abuse, was mourned as a national tragedy. His funeral in Moscow was attended by thousands.

Wolf Hunt

I'm at my wits end, tendons taut.
But like yesterday, again today
They've surrounded me, surrounded me,
Driving me happily for the flags.

From the pines—double-barrel flashes.
Hunters lurk there in shadow.
Wolves somersault in the snow,
Living targets.

      It's a wolf hunt, a wolf hunt!
      The drivers yell at the gray beasts of prey,
      At old-timers and pups alike! And the dogs
                     bay until they vomit.
      Blood on the snow and the red spots of flags.

The hunters don't play fair with wolves,
And their hands never quiver!
Fencing off freedom with flags,
They blast away happily.

A wolf shouldn't break with tradition:
As blind pups we sucked our mother's milk,
And with our mother's milk we learned—
"Don't go beyond the flags!"

      It's a wolf hunt, etc.

We're fast of leg and jaw.
Leader, why not give us an answer—
We're being driven by their guns—
Let's break through the boundary!

A wolf should not, cannot do otherwise
So this is the end of my life:
The one I was destined for
Smiled and raised his gun

    It's a wolf hunt, etc.

I disobeyed, passed through the flags,
—The thirst for life is stronger!
Only afterwards did I hear the surprised
Cries of the people behind me.

I'm at my wit's end, tendons taut,
But today is not like yesterday!
They surrounded me, surrounded me,
But this time the hunters
Were left holding the bag!

    It's a wolf hunt, etc.

Bathhouse Blues

Make me a steambath and let out the smoke,
I need a world without smoke.
I'll pass out, I'll go out of my mind,
The steam will loosen my tongue.

Make me a steambath, lady,
I'll roast myself, I will.
On the very top bench,
I'll burn out the doubt in myself.

I'll get obscenely mellow,
A mug of cold water—and everything is in the past.
And the tattoo on my left breast,
From the days of the cult of personality, will glow blue.

Make me a steambath and let out the smoke,
I need a world without smoke.
I'll pass out, I'll go out of my mind,
The steam will loosen my tongue.

So many truths and forests have fallen!
There's been so much grief, so many roads!
And on my left breast—Stalin's profile,
On my right—Marinka *en face*.

Make me a steambath and let out the smoke,
I need a world without smoke.
I'll pass out, I'll go out of my mind,
The steam will loosen my tongue.

I remember how early one morning
I just managed to yell to my brother, Give me a hand!

And two pretty bodyguards . . .
Carried me out of Siberia into Siberia.

And then, in quarry, in swamp,
Choking on tears and the dust of the mines,
We tattooed that profile over our hearts
So that He would hear how they were being torn to pieces.

Don't end my smokeless steambath,
I need a world without smoke.
I'll pass out, I'll go out of my mind,
The steam will loosen my tongue.

Ay, you're shivering! Getting sick listening?
The steam has driven things out of my head.
Out of the cold fog of the past
I plunge into the hot fog.

Thoughts start beating in my skull.
It turns out that I branded myself with Him for nothing!
So I beat myself with a birch branch
On the legacy of these gloomy times.

Make me a steambath and let out the smoke,
I need a world without smoke.
I'll pass out, I'll go out of my mind,
The steam will loosen my tongue.

Parody of a Bad Detective Story

Fearing counterspies,
Shunning social life,
Under the English pseudonym
Of Mr. John Lancaster Peck,
Eternally in leather gloves—
No fingerprints, you know—
In the Sovietskaya Hotel
Lived a certain non-Soviet chap.

Usually at night and all alone
John Lancaster
Clicked whatever it was
That he hid
His infrared lens in.
And then in normal night
There appeared in black and white
"That which we value and love.
That in which the collective takes pride."

The club on Nagornaya Street
Looked like a public toilet.
Our own Central Market
Became a dirty warehouse.
Distorted by the microfilm,
GUM[1] resembled a little hut.
And it would be indelicate to say
What the Moscow Art Theater looked like.

But working without subordinates
Can be sad, can be boring.
The enemy thought about it. Diabolically clever,
He wrote a counterfeit check

---

[1]   GUM - most luxurious department store in Moscow, located by the Red Square.

And, somewhere in the bowels of a restaurant,
Good Citizen Epifan
Was led astray
By the non-Soviet chap.

Epifan turned out to be hungry,
Sly, smart, voracious.
He knew no bounds
In women and beer
And didn't want to know any.
So it turned out like this:
John's subordinate was a find
For the spy. It could happen to anyone
Who's drunk and wishy-washy.

The first assignment:
At three-fifteen, next to the public baths,
Maybe earlier, maybe later,
A taxi would drive up.
He'd get in, gag the driver,
Play a simple thief, then later,
Blare it over the BBC.

And then: change clothes
And go to an exhibition at the Manege,
Where a man with a suitcase
Would come up and say:
"Would you like some cherries?"
And you answer: "Of course!"
He'll give you a loaf of bread
With explosives.
Bring it back to me.

"And for that, my drunken friend,"
He said to Epifan,
"There'll be money, a house in Chicago
And lots of women and cars . . ."
The enemy didn't realize, the idiot,
That he was ordering around
A Chekist, a major in intelligence
And a fine family man.

Even that master of such tricks,
The very Mr. John Lancaster!
He really slipped up,
The notorious Mr. Peck.
He was neutralized and even
Clipped and thrown into jail.
Then a peaceful Greek arrived
At the Sovietskaya Hotel.

Dialogue

Oh, Vania, look at the clowns!
They're grinning from ear to ear.
And they're all painted up, Vania!
And they talk like drunks.
      And that one looks like—no really, Van,
      Like my brother—same sort of booziness!
      No, no, just take a look, take a look.
      No kidding, Van!

Listen, Zina, leave your brother alone.
No matter what—he's kin!
You're painted up yourself, smoking like crazy . . .
Look out, I'll show you!
      Instead of blabbing, Zin,
      You go get some booze at the store!
      What? You won't? OK, I'll go.
      Get out of my way, Zin!

Oh, Vania, look at the dwarfs!
They're dressed in jersey, too, not worsted.
In our clothing factory No. 5
There's nobody who could make the like.
      But all your friends, Van,
      They're such riff raff!
      And they start drinking such crap
      So early in the morning!

Even if they don't have fancy outfits
My friends care for their families.
And they drink garbage to save money,
Even if they do start in the morning.

But you've got such friends yourself, Zin,
That guy from the tire factory,
He actually used to drink gasoline.
Remember Zin!

Oh Vania, just look at the little parrots!
Honest to God, I've got to yell!
And who's that in the tee shirt?
Van, I want one just like it, myself.
      At the end of this quarter, right, Van,
      You'll make me one like it, won't you
      Whaddaya mean "shove off"? "Shove off" again?
      That's not nice, Van!

You'd just better shut up.
You can kiss the quarterly bonus goodbye.
Who sent complaints about me to work?
Whaddaya mean "no" —I read them.
      What do you need a tee shirt like that for, Zin?
      It would just be a shame, just a waste of cloth.
      Where's the money, Zin?

Oh, Vania, I'll die from the little acrobats!
Look at how that one spins, the imp!
Our Director of Entertainment
Jumped just like that in the shop . . .
      So you come home, Ivan,
      And have something to eat—then onto the sofa.
      Or you yell when you're not drunk.
      What's with you, Van?

Zin, you're asking for trouble.
You're always aiming to hurt someone.
I race around all day,
Then come home and there you sit.
      Well, then, Zin, the liquor store beckons.
      My friends are there, waiting for me.
      I don't drink alone, you know . . .

Oho, you gymnast!
Ouch, what are you doing, at your age!
In the "Swallow" milk bar at work
There's a waitress who likes to do that stuff.
      And you've got friends, Zin,
      Keep knitting caps for winter.
      I go out of my mind from just looking
      At their ugly mugs!

What, Van? What about Lilka Fedoseeva,
The cashier from CPCR[2]?
At the housewarming you kept making up to her.
She's not so bad, is she?
      But why fight, Van?
      Better let's take a vacation to Erivan.
      Whaddaya mean "shove off"?
      That's not nice, Van!

Translated by H. William Tjalsma

---

[2] The Central Park of Culture and Relaxation; such a park was in every large city.

Yuz Aleshkovsky
(b. 1929, Krasnoiarsk)

Raised in Moscow, Aleshkovsky was forced to interrupt his high-school education when he was drafted during WWII. He was imprisoned for four years in the labor camps (1950–53) for breach of military discipline. He returned to Moscow and started publishing children's fiction in the mid-1950s, while his "prison" songs and "obscene" novels (especially *Nikolai Nikolaevich*, 1968) were widely circulating on tapes and in *samizdat*. His "prison" songs imitate the popular genre, while at the same time presenting a postmodern play with official formulae, melodramatic clichés, obscenities, and their ironic subversions. Aleshkovsky contributed to the almanac *Metropol'* and emigrated to the United States soon afterward. In emigration, he has published the novels *The Mask* (1980), *The Hand* (1980), *A Plain Little Blue Scarf* (1982), *A Book of Last Words* (1986), and *Ring in a Case* (1995), among others. After *perestroika*, most of his books were republished in Russia. Lives in Middletown, Connecticut.

Lesbian Song

Let them frisk us all they can during watch.
When the warder goes into the barrack,
We'll cry our fill to a concertina
and set our wedding table.

My little mate is a good-looking lady,
he pours me a glass of thick tea,
and instead of red caviar spreads lipstick
on a hunk of gray bread.

He doesn't wear lipstick himself,
and he walks with a masculine gait,
he seems like a man to me,
only his whiskers don't grow.

The girls stamp "The Gypsy Girl" tap-tap,
the old gals cry out "Kiss the Bride,"
and one lesbian weeps in the arms
of the unmarried girls.

Oh, let's have a smoke of Siberian weed,
the girls will have another drink,
to the bitter kiss, the lesbian kiss,
to our first married night.

It's sweet in the zone here and unbothered,
I don't send my husband outside any mail,
and he shall never, never know
that I love Maruska Belova.

Cigarette Butt

We were walking back to the zone
from the white hell of Kolyma.
I spotted a cigarette butt smeared with red lipstick
and broke ranks to pick it up.

"Stop or I'll shoot," yelled the escort.
His damned mutt tore my pea jacket.
"Take it easy, chief, old boy,
I'm already back in line."

I haven't seen a lady for years.
Finally now I'm in luck. Probably
oh, cigarette butt, fierce wind
carried you from a TU-104[1] to me.

And all the way back to the zone
Kopalin, who strangled his wife,
and one active fag couldn't
tear their eyes from my cigarette butt.

With whom are you fooling around now, bitch,
sucking on a single cigarette with whom?
You get drunk, you don't buy a ticket at Vnukovo[2]
just to fly over me here.

I threw drinking parties in your honor,
gave everybody French cognac to drink.
I got drunk myself from the way you smoked a Troika,
the one with the golden rim at the end.

---

[1]   Soviet passenger air jet.

[2]   Airport in Moscow.

I lost that cigarette butt at cards,
though it was dearer to me than a thousand.
Even here I haven't any luck
from grieving for my queen of hearts.

I've lost all my clothes playing cards
and my sugar ration two years in advance.
So here I sit on my bunk hugging my knees
with nothing to wear to roll call.

That cigarette butt was my downfall,
cursing no one, blaming nobody.
The big guys here among the cons
were impressed with my style.

I went to the guard shack barefooted,
like Christ, calm, quiet.
For ten days I painted my hand-rolled cigs
with my bloody lips.

"Scoundrel, you blew a million
on fancy women on the outside,"
"That's right," I say, to the citizen warder.
"Only, no point, citizen warder,
Wiping my lips with your cuff!"

Personal Meeting

I was serving my time in Siberia,
was considered a hard working guy,
and broke my back to get
a personal meeting with my wife.

I wrote: "Show up, wife, I miss you,
living here three miles from the camp station."
I waited, then stopped waiting, worried myself to death,
kept climbing up on the roof to watch.

My heart started aching when I saw the poor thing
bent to the ground from her rucksack.
But the zeks looked at her, hungry, from the roof,
they looked at my plain-looking woman.

I stood there in front of the guard shack,
as the warder frisked my wife,
but my letters had told her clearly
how to hide homebrew under her skirt.

So they locked us in the room,
the silly fool neither alive nor dead,
while I'm like at my trial, red-faced
and mixing up my words.

She perched on a bench
and I lay down on an old mattress.
Yesterday, the embezzler Lavochkin slept here
                                        with his wife;
day before that, the pickpocket Monia Kats.

The gray wallpaper was pretty faded,
there was a peephole in the iron door.
In the corner the portrait of Comrade Kalinin[3]
was silent, like the icon in our shack.

We grabbed a bite, I drank the homebrew
and smoked a hand-rolled cigarette . . . Ah, life,
make the bed wife, the government bed,
then lie down beside me like you used to do.

The duty warders toss jokes through the peephole,
the zeks roar sorrowfully outside the window:
"Stepan, give us your spouse for a minute,
we'll stretch her out for the lot of us."

Oh, people, people, people, you're not serious,
you need your heads examined.
This is my wife here and it's not
kolkhoz bulls servicing your cows.

I'm mad at them all and sorry for 'em too,
you don't share your wife with everyone . . .
   . . . at dawn it was like the escort
beating an iron rail in my heart.

Pour me something, wife, it's goodbye.
Get into the greenish railroad car yourself.
Don't grieve, they'll give us a chance next winter,
Don't forget—no, not me, you dope—
Don't forget how to hide the home brew.

Translated by H. William Tjalsma

---

[3]   Mikhail Kalinin (1875-1946) - in Stalin's time, the Chairman of the Residuum of the
Supreme Soviet, a nominal head of the state.

Genrikh Sapgir
(1928, Biisk — 1999, Moscow)

Genrikh Sapgir belonged to a circle of non-conformist poets and artists called "The Lianozovo School," which included Oskar Rabin, Evgenii Kropivnitskii, Igor Kholin, and Vsevolod Nekrasov. In the Soviet era Sapgir mainly published as a children's writer and poet, and authored scripts for many popular animated films. His poetry combined experimental playfulness with social satire and the grotesque. Participated in the almanac *Metropol'*. In 1998 he edited poetry for the anthology *Samizdat of the Century*.

A Voice

They killed a man over there,
They killed a man over there,
They killed a man over there
Down there—they killed a man.

Let's take a look at him.
Let's take a look at him.
Let's take a look at him.
Let's take a look at him.

The corpse—and a look just like one.
Oh he's asleep, he's dead drunk!
Oh, he's not a corpse, he just looks dead . . .
What corpse—he's dead drunk—

Sprawling in vomit . . .
Sprawling in vomit . . .
Sprawling in vomit . . .
....

Grab his hands and feet,
Grab his hands and feet,
Grab his hands and feet,
Grab his hands and feet,

And carry him outside.
Drag him outside.
Toss him outside!
Throw him outside!

And lock the front door.
Lock the door tight!

Snap it up, get it shut!
Turn all the locks and bolts!

Is he yelling or is he quiet?
Is he yelling or is he quiet?
Is he yelling or is he quiet?
Is he yelling or is he quiet?

Radioblab

Lying down, moaning.
Nobody there.
Just a black speaker on the wall.
It's blaring a national chorus.
He reached up, jerked the cord!
The plug's here, the outlet's there.
He couldn't believe his ears:
Noise,
Crackle,
Clanging of metal.
The radio began to mutter:
"The latest news.
Special report!
. . . At the scene
Of the crime.
. . . The majority of votes.
. . . Degrees
Below zero.
Threat of
Atomic attack
Epidemic . . .
War . . .
The quota is overfulfilled!"
The chorus again. Against the background
Of the chorus,
An airplane motor solo.
Roar of jet planes.
Burst of applause!
The sick man stares glassy-eyed,
His hand
Squeezes the blanket
convulsively.

Through the door—far away
Somebody appeared.
—Doctor!
You must check my nuts and bolts!
Announcer:
"'Moonlight Sonata'
On the balalaika."

Monkey

"What are you complaining about, citizenness?"
She was a sharp lady, but at this she was tongue-tied.
She stood there. She cried. She couldn't say anything.
"Give her a new apartment and ten thousand in my name!"

—from popular folklore

She got married.
Ordinary sort of husband.
At night the lady,
Honestly speaking,
Didn't get much of a look.
In the morning she looks:
He's all furry.
The husband, Lord forgive us,
Was a real monkey.
He'd been pretending
To be a brunet
Just to cover up.
The monkey squeals
And leaps about,
Bowlegged and hairy.
The young thing, all but crying,
Appealed to the court.
They say: no grounds.
A case of atavism . . .
Better get used to it . . .
They won't grant her a divorce!
Marvelous deeds! —
She gave birth to a pair of marmosets.
The father, a steelworker,
Crawled up on the bell tower
Of Ivan the Great Church
And hung there on the gold cross

From his tail
For three days.
They gave him an award.
The prize: a tea service.
He doesn't begrudge his wife anything,
Carries out her smallest whim!
So if your husband's a good one,
Who cares if he's a monkey?

Translated by H. William Tjalsma[1]

[1]   "Bathhouse Blues" by Vladimir Vysotsky, "Cigarette Butt" by Yuz Aleshkovsky, "Dialogue" by Vladimir Vysotsky, "Lesbian Song" by Yuz Aleshkovsky, "Monkey" by Genrikh Sapgir, "Parody of A Bad Detective Story" by Vladimir Vysotsky, "Personal Meeting" by Yuz Aleshkovsky, "Radioblab" by Genrikh Sapgir, "A Voice" by Genrikh Sapgir, "Wolf Hunt" by Vladimir Vysotsky, translated by H. William Tjalsma, from *Metropol: A Literary Almanac*, edited by Vassily Aksyonov, Viktor Yerofeyev, Fazil Iskander, Andrei Bitov, and Yevgeny Popov. Copyright © 1982 by ARDIS/RLT. Copyright © 1979 by Metropol. Used by permission of W. W. Norton & Company, Inc.

Viktor Erofeev
(b. 1947, Moscow)

Born to the family of a high-ranking Soviet diplomat, Erofeev graduated from Moscow State University's School of Philology and completed his graduate study at the Moscow Institute of World Literature, where he defended his PhD dissertation on Dostoevsky and French existentialism. He started his literary career as a critic, gaining fame for his essays on Lev Shestov, Marquis de Sade, Celine, Camus, Rozanov, Nabokov, Sologub, and other authors who were either totally or partly prohibited in the USSR. In 1979 Erofeev took part in the compilation of the almanac *Metropol'* as a co-editor. Erofeev's first fiction publications, a novella and short stories, appeared in *Metropol'*. After the scandal surrounding the publication of *Metropol'*, he was expelled from the Union of Soviet Writers. During *perestroika*, he became one of the most active propagandists of literary postmodernism. His own short stories were published in Russia and abroad. His article "A Funeral Feast for Soviet Literature" (1990) was a provocative critique of all Soviet literature from a postmodern perspective, leading to heated discussion in the Russian literary press. His erotic and mystical novel *Russian Beauty* (written in 1980–82, first published in 1990) is narrated from the perspective of a high-class Russian prostitute who considers herself to be Russia's spiritual savior. *Russian Beauty* was translated into many languages. Erofeev compiled the influential collection *The Penguin Book of New Russian Writing: Russia's Fleurs du Mal* (1995). His short story "Life with an Idiot" became the libretto for Alfred Schnittke's eponymous opera. Hosts several television shows in Russia. Lives in Moscow.

THE *METROPOL'* AFFAIR

Metropol' was an attempt to fight stagnation in the conditions of stagnation. That's what I think, looking back on it today. In this lie its idea and significance. But no less importantly, thanks to *Metropol'* you can understand the subtle meaning of the pronoun we, freed from its Orwellian[1] connotations, all too well known to us, and understand the strength and weakness of artistic solidarity. I lived through and survived this story as a rare idealist; maybe that's why I survived.

On my writer's identification card there is a temporal absurdity: accepted into the Writer's Union in 1978, date of issue 1988.[2] The question of how for ten years I could be seditiously without a card is answered by the story of the almanac *Metropol'* and its panicked shutdown, for which the meanest of years bears the responsibility ("there were worse times, but not meaner times"[3]), as well as those who, literally yesterday, controlled the fate of our culture.

---

[1]   "Zamyatinian" in the original. Evgeny Zamyatin (1884–1937) is the author of *We* (1921), a dystopian novel critical of the Soviet state which in turn influenced George Orwell's *1984*.

[2]   Henceforth abbreviated as "WU," to reflect the abbreviation used in the original Russian.

[3]   From Nikolai Nekrasov's 1875 poem "Contemporaries."

From their perspective I was, of course, completely justifiably expelled from the WU, for the rules of literary life at that time stank so strongly (everything was stiff, fettered, crumpled, crushed, distorted), that one didn't have the strength to make peace with them, and I truly did try to bring a devilish plan into existence.

In December of 1977, when I rented an apartment across from Vagankovo Cemetery and funereal music discordantly flowed through my windows every day, the jolly idea came to mind to create a "bulldozer" of a literary exhibition, united around a home-made almanac of recognized and respectable young people of letters, along the model of the Moscow artists who were at that time fighting for at least the shadow of independence for themselves. The bomb consisted namely in the mix of dissidents and non-dissidents, of Vysotsky and Voznesensky. Without any trouble I infected my older celebrated friend Vassily Aksyonov with my idea (without whom nothing would have happened); Andrei Bitov and my contemporary Evgeny Popov[4] were drawn into the deal (Fazil Iskander[5] joined in significantly later), and so it was set in motion.

The words in the foreword to the almanac, that it all started with a toothache, are not a metaphor, but reality. Aksyonov and I were having our teeth treated on Vuchetich Street. They had seated us in neighboring chairs. The interior was strange: a hall with no partitions, filled with the grinding of teeth. Aksyonov immediately established the format of the publication: it would be an almanac of "cast-off literature" which we would publish here at home.

Over the course of 1978 we assembled a thick almanac. More than 20 people participated in it, no one by chance. Everyone, from Semyon Lipkin to the young Leningrader Petr Kozhevnikov,[6] was talented in his own way. We consciously developed the

---

4   Evgeny Popov (b. 1946): one of co-editors of the almanac.

5   Fazil Iskander (b. 1929): a famous satirical writer, one of the co-editors of almanac.

6   Semyon Lipkin (1911–2003): a prominent Soviet poet and translator, close friend of Vasily Grossman. Husband of Inna Lisnyanskaya. Petr Kozhevnikov (1953–2012): a non-conformist writer; after 1991 worked as a screenwriter and film director.

idea of aesthetic pluralism. *Metropol'* would not be a manifesto for any particular school. Discussions arose. There were steady opponents: the philosophers Leonid Batkin and Viktor Trostnikov.[7] Bella Akhmadulina and Inna Lisnyanskaya argued poisonously with each other.[8] Some people took their manuscripts back. Yury Trifonov[9] explained that it was better for him to fight the censors with his own books. Bulat Okudzhava[10] noted that he was the only member of the Communist party among us.

We put *Metropol'* together in a one-room apartment on Krasnoarmeyskaya Street that formerly belonged to the by-then deceased Evgenia Semyonova Ginzburg, the author of *Journey Into the Whirlwind*.[11] There is symbolism in the choice of location.

Vladimir Vysotsky rang at the door, and in answer to the question "Who's there?" he responded: "Is this where they're counterfeiting money?" We roared with laughter, knowing that we'd take it in the teeth for our work, but we didn't suppose that the higher-ups would fly into a rage, or that in their eyes genuine counterfeiters would be social compatriots, almost relatives, in comparison with us, literary traitors.

---

[7] Leonid Batkin (b. 1932): cultural historian, an expert on the Italian Renaissance. In 1979, a researcher at the Institute of the World History, Academy of Science of the USSR. Viktor Trostnikov (b. 1928): a religious philosopher, author of underground works about Russian Orthodoxy. In the 1990–2000s became affiliated with Russian nationalists.

[8] Bella Akhmadulina (1937–2010): one of the most prominent and popular poets of the generation of the 1960s. Inna Lisnyanskaya (1928–2014): poet and translator, wife of Semyon Lipkin.

[9] Yury Trifonov (1925–1981): one of the most prominent liberal writers of the 1970s; author of the cycle of *Moscow Tales* and the novels *House on the Embankment* (1976), *An Old Man* (1978).

[10] Bulat Okudzhava (1924–1997) one of the most famous poets of the generation of the Thaw, he was a song-writer and performer of his own songs.

[11] Evgenia Ginzburg (1896–1977) is the author of the memoir *Journey into the Whirlwind*, which details her arrest on false accusations and the eighteen years she served in a labor camp. The memoir, which could not be published in the Soviet Union, was smuggled into the west and published in Italy and Germany in 1967. She is the mother of Vassily Aksyonov.

Everyone brought something of their own. Vysotsky dedicated a song to *Metropol'* and sang a few couplets from it. Then it all disappeared somewhere, like a lot of other things. Like Friedrich Gorenshtein, who now lives in Berlin.[12] He showed up in winter, for some reason wearing long underwear. Aksyonov was a little surprised and said:

"Friedrich, it seems you forgot to put on your pants . . ."

"Vasya!" cried Friedrich, "I didn't forget. I was just warming up."

Metropol' had a lot of assistants. They helped us paste pages and check the proofs. The size of the almanac was about 40 folio sheets. So, taking into account 12 copies, we had to glue about 12,000 typed pages on Whatman paper. What did the "first" issue of the almanac look like? Four typed pages were pasted on Whatman paper. The layout was done by David Borovsky of the Taganka Theater.[13] It looked like 12 greenish gravestones. Again, the funeral theme . . . Boris Messerer thought up the almanac's frontispiece and trademark, the gramophone. At first we wanted to paste in photos of the authors. Gorenshtein had already brought two: full-face and in profile. We soon discovered that they quickly came unglued and we decided against it. Credit for the name of the almanac goes to Aksyonov. *Metropol'* is the literary process here, in the metropolis. In the foreword, also written mainly by Aksyonov (his style is felt there), it is said that the almanac is a lean-to atop the best metro in the world.

We didn't want to pile up a mountain of manuscripts so we made the almanac in the form of a ready-made book. We were going to offer one copy to The State Committee for Publishing and one to The All-Union Agency of Writers' Rights. For publication here and abroad. That is, we offered to reprint what we had already published. That's why in the foreword it is written: "May be published in typographical form only in its given condition. No

---

[12]   Friedrich Gorenshtein (1932–2002) is the author of several philosophical novels. He had only a few texts published in the USSR. Emigrated to Germany, where he died in 2002.

[13]   A theater famous for its politically charged productions in the 1960s–70s, its director was Yurii Liubimov. David Borovsky was its chief art director.

additions or deletions allowed." This demand especially enraged our opponents.

The campaign against *Metropol'* began in the offices of the secretariat of the Moscow Organization of the Writers' Union on January 20, 1979. In the first place, we didn't think there would be so many people. There were about 50 of them. In the second place, we received some sort of very agitated summons from them via courier: you are requested to appear . . . in the event you don't appear . . . Then there were the threats. Thirdly, this session of the "party committee" was on the eve of our proposed debut; this especially frightened them and became the dominant theme of their incantations. They were convinced that after the debut of *Metropol'* people would begin to speak "in tongues," and then the book would be published in the West. "I warn you," announced the chairman of the meeting, Felix Kuznetsov,[14] "if the almanac is published in the West, we will accept no repentance from you."

All of this had been choreographed beforehand. One figure after another stood up, yelled, became indignant, made threats. Someone even shed tears of hatred. Gribachev[15] told me in the corridor, with thief-like confidentiality, "No matter what you say it's all the same for you guys, you're dead meat." There were five of us, the compilers. Everything was so vile, so despicable, that there was nothing left for us to do other than conduct ourselves "heroically." Iskander said we live in our own country as if we were under occupation. They became angry with Popov because he had copied down their speeches. Aksyonov called the Writers' Union the kindergarten of a fortified regime.

Later they accused us of thinking up *Metropol'* with the aim of publishing it in the West. This is factually incorrect. We sent two copies to France and America through acquaintances who appeared out of nowhere and took the almanac abroad at great risk to themselves, not to publish, but to preserve it, and in this we turned out to have had foresight. When the big scandal occurred and our

[14] Literary critic, head of the Moscow Writers Union.

[15] Official Soviet poet Nikolai Gribachev, known for his political conservatism.

plans to publish *Metropol'* in-country collapsed, the authors agreed to publish the almanac in Russian through the American publishing house Ardis, at that time run by Carl Proffer, who had published many excellent Russian books and was a friend to many of us. He hastened to announce on Voice of America that he had the almanac in his hands. After that there was no backing down. The almanac was published a little while later in English and French.

Originally we had planned a launch for *Metropol'* to introduce it to the public. We rented a location. The celebration was to be held at the cafe "Rhythm" near Miusskaya Square. We invited around three hundred people. Then the detective story began.

The KGB reacted in military fashion: they cordoned off the block, closed the cafe, sealed it due to the discovery of cockroaches, and hung a sign on the door: "Closed for sanitation." They began to bring us in to the Writers' Union for questioning.

They tried to split us up in every possible way. They told us that Aksyonov was not one of us—that he had millions in the West. They vilely made fun of Lipkin's surname: Lipkin-Vlipkin.[16] Iskander "fought them" but he couldn't "fight them off" . . . Repressions began, hitting almost every one of the "Metropolitans": they banned our books (those already published were made unavailable for loan in libraries), our plays, and fired us from our jobs.

The then-heads of the WU and its organizations play the fool even more conspicuously now and even justify their behavior, now that they've lost their way in the abrupt changes in the climate; but in 1979 they were genuine executioners. One example: my father, who at that time occupied a prominent diplomatic post in Vienna, was immediately called back to Moscow. In the name of the Politburo, where they had decided that *Metropol'* was the start of a new Czechoslovakia, the secretary of the Central Committee Zimyanin gave him a truly Nazi-like ultimatum: either your son signs a renunciation of *Metropol'* or you will not return to Vienna . . . Zimyanin didn't want to speak with my father one-on-one, because he already took him for an enemy. Also present were Albert Belyaev,

---

[16]   A play on the verb *vlipat'*, to get into trouble, into a mess.

at that time the "central" persecutor of culture, and Shauro, the head of the Department of Culture, who had known my father since his student years. When Zimyanin pointed at my father and asked, "Do you know one another?" Shauro extended his hand and introduced himself: "Shauro." Such was the fear . . . Zimyanin read the most "pointed" pieces from the almanac, called Akhmadulina a prostitute and drug addict, and on my account noted:

"Tell your son that if he doesn't write the letter it'll be the end of him." I didn't write it, and they threw my father out of work . . . I never regretted my participation in *Metropol'*; it was a good life lesson, but I don't thank the executioners of the almanac for such a lesson.

On the eve of his death they declared Vysotsky's songs to be vulgar. They dealt with Aksyonov by depriving him of his Soviet citizenship in the end. Popov, who had been expelled from the Writers' Union, was not published for many years. They persecuted Lipkin and Lisnyanskaya, who left the Union in a sign of protest against the expulsions.

Felix Kuznetsov headed the campaign to persecute *Metropol'* with full determination, reflected in his unceasingly perspiring face. When he would get tired, the doors of the office were flung open, and pale-faced Lazar Karelin and ruddy-faced Oleg Poptsov,[17] in a leather Red Army jacket, flew in to continue the fight against us. In the article "Confusion with *Metropol'*," Kuznetsov wrote: "The aestheticization of criminal acts, vulgar 'criminal' language, this inside-out snobbism, and in essence all the contents of the almanac *Metropol'* contradict the roots of the humanitarian tradition of Russian Soviet literature . . . There's no need to create a propagandistic stone soup and present ordinary political provocation as concern for the expansion of the creative possibilities of Soviet literature."

By order from above a whole gang of the almanac's critics was unleashed, and their opinion of *Metropol'* was unanimous: "pornography of the spirit." Rimma Kazakova considered *Metropol'* to be "trash, not literature, something close to graphomania."

---

[17] Karelin and Poptsov were liberal-minded writers, members of the secretariat of the Moscow Writers Union.

Vladimir Gusev was torturously alarmed by the "fate of young writers, including those participating in this collection. It isn't all the same to us, whether a young writer writes about men's or women's restrooms, like Erofeev, or solely about drunkenness and sexual perversion, like Popov." Those famous champions of the ideological front, literary counterintelligence agents Tatyana Kudryavtseva and Tamara Motyleva, were also alarmed in print about the "clarity of ideas," and Nikolai Shundik[18] threatened: "You, as a participant in this endeavor, will become the object of the cheapest political football."

All this looks like nonsense now, and even in 1979 we laughed at such ravings; at the same time the ravings were not a joke but a verdict. Sergei Zalygin[19] found the stories of Popov to be "beyond the bounds of literature." Grigory Baklanov,[20] repeating Kuznetsov, having gently called my story "Humping Hannah" "an immoral scrawl," declared: "I will no longer speak, for example, of the stories of Erofeev, which have no relationship to literature whatsoever." Did these venerable writers really not understand that their pronouncements would lead to diabolical conclusions? If the changes had not occurred, we would still be sitting with gags in our mouths. Along with Popov we would have died as former writers, having existed in the WU for 7 months and 13 days. To hell with it, with the WU of the USSR; but no one has ever repented, not on our side or theirs.

How many did we lose? Boris Vakhtin died. Yury Kublanovsky, Yuz Aleshkovsky, and Vassily Rakitin found themselves in emigration along with Friedrich Gorenshtein, who published his unforgettable story "House with a Turret" in *Youth* at some point in time. Yury Karabchievsky recently passed from this world.

The shutdown of *Metropol'* on the one hand was the peak, the culmination of stagnation; on the other hand, everything was

---

[18]   Nikolai Shundik (1920–1995), literary functionary, editor-in-chief of the journal *Volga*, director of the nationalistic press *Sovremennik*.

[19]   Sergei Zalygin (1913–2000), a popular liberal writer.

[20]   Grigory Baklanov (1923–2009), a popular liberal writer.

already on a downward trajectory, drawing its last breath. Hence the particular spite and rage of our "blue-arsed flies." Rumors flew, of course, that we would be expelled, but we cheekily did not believe them. Having fired back, three of us went to the Crimea: Aksyonov, Popov, and I. At an exhibition of holographs in some little southern town we wrote in the visitors' book: "We, the editors of the almanac *Metropol'*, greet the birth of the new art of the holograph . . ." I was told later that the note has been preserved somewhere. In Koktebel we met Iskander and set off to drink some apple brandy. When we had already downed a couple of shots, Fazil suddenly remembered: "I received an anonymous letter! 'Rejoice, you bastard! They've finally expelled two of your sons of bitches from the Writers' Union.'"

The anonymous letter turned out to be correct. They expelled us in our absence. It was, in essence, literary death. Those who were expelled were no longer published. In an instant Popov and I became dissidents. The impressive logic of banditry: strike at the youth to frighten and divide everyone. Our comrades, Aksyonov, Bitov, Iskander, Lisnyanskaya, and Lipkin, wrote a letter of protest: if they didn't reinstate us, they would all leave the Union. Akhmadulina sent a similar letter. The Voice of America did not delay to report this. Passions flared.

On August 12, 1979 the *New York Times* published a telegram from American writers to the Writers' Union of the USSR. Kurt Vonnegut, William Styron, John Updike (who had contributed to the almanac at the invitation of Aksyonov), Arthur Miller, and Edward Albee came out on our behalf. They demanded that we be reinstated into the Writers' Union; if not, they would refuse to be published in the USSR. The WU, it seemed, chickened out. In any event, Yury Verchenko, who "worked" with more than one dissident, took up with us after this telegram. Good-natured and odious, Verchenko looked like a big Chicago gangster. Once Georgy Markov[21] stopped by his office to take a look at us. Verchenko pulled himself up

---

[21] Georgy Markov (1911–91): Chairman of the Board of the Union of Soviet Writers of the USSR from 1977 to 1986.

Part II. Literature of the Stagnation

and began to yell "And I say that your *Metropol'* is a pile of shit!" Markov paced a bit, sniffed the air, and left, saying neither hello or good-bye.

Generally the atmosphere of the WU surprised me. It was an atmosphere of universal servility and cringing. With us they behaved themselves quite politely; we were enemies. But with subordinates, with Kuznetsov and others, they conversed with extreme disdain. And not only were they not offended, but took it as a sign of kindness. Once when we were with Verchenko, Lazar Karelin came in. As the conversation progressed, we bonded with him. Verchenko delighted in this scene, and then said: "Enough, Karelin, don't play the beggar here . . ." and then begin to promise to reinstate us into the Union ("Wait a bit, we'll take you back, you'll become the top people, you'll know all the authorities"), but he demanded various concessions and compromises from us. He was very afraid of Popov's bag, supposing there was a tape-recorder hidden in it.

The *Literary Gazette* answered the Americans' telegram with Kuznetsov's article, with the criminal title "Why All the Fuss?" He assured his "dear colleagues" that the Writers' Union "no less than anyone else" is concerned about the creative destiny of its writers and believes that "the deep and organic ties that connect authentic writers with their native literature and native land are indissoluble." "These hopes," continued Kuznetsov, "circulate among our young authors Viktor Erofeev and Evgeny Popov . . . Acceptance into the Writers' Union is such an internal matter of our creative union that we ask that it be given the opportunity to determine on its own the degree of maturity and the creative potential of every writer."

Metropol' turned out to be the mother lode for Felix Kuznetsov. He began to fly into offices that formerly he had no hope of getting into. A big theorist of morality in literature, he loved to practice slander for a bit of variety. My father told me that in their meeting Zimyanin declared to him that I was preparing to emigrate. My father was much surprised. "Kuznetsov told me about it," explained Zimyanin, "your son himself confessed to him."

Our exclusion was communicated in a very strange, illiterate formulation (O, these scribblers!). The resolution of the secretariat of the Writers' Union of the RSFSR was printed in *Moscow Litterateur*: "Taking into account that the works of the writers E. Popov and V. Erofeev received unanimous negative marks at the meeting of the Moscow Literary Organization, the secretariat of the administration of the WU of the RSFSR withdraws its decision on the acceptance of E. Popov and V. Erofeev as members of the Writers' Union of the USSR . . ."

From this moment on the authorities, trying to confuse everything, began to work out a version in which it was as if we had never been accepted into the Union. Popov and I appeared before Kuznetsov to find out why we had been expelled. "No one expelled you, we just withdrew our decision." "But there is no such provision in the regulations!" Then he got the regulations and read to us how a Soviet writer must participate in the building of communism. We made some sort of objection. Kuznetsov exclaimed: "Next you'll be talking about human rights!"

The episode when we were almost accepted back into the Union was mysterious and vague. All the same they must have been frightened. The letters from six of our authors, the Americans' telegram and articles in many countries — all this was rather serious. Of course without this support Popov and I would have had a good chance of following in the footsteps of Sinyavsky and Daniel; not without reason did we talk about some sort of investigator on particularly important government business who allegedly occupied himself with us. We never saw him in person. But I sensed the chill of the Gulag for a long while. They insolently listened in on phone conversations, secretly dispatched people, summoned friends to the "authorities" and dissuaded them from being friends, stole into my car at night, and spread fantastic rumors: Aksyonov and Erofeev are homosexuals who decided to create *Metropol'* to test the strength of their male friendship. Finally the KGB "abducted" me: they took me away to the top floor of the Hotel Belgrade to some special room, spoke "gently," proposing I give them the manuscripts without a search. They wanted to "get to know my work better," they threatened me with "writing pornography." Later I found out that the KGB had nicknamed me Woland while working out a scheme to deport me which, for some reason, never came into being.[22] Well, for that, thanks.

Of course our misfortunes of that time were nothing in comparison with the torments that fell to the lot of Anatoly Marchenko or Sakharov.[23] We were not beaten in prison, we were not force fed during hunger strikes. But in that *"Metropol'itan"* year I understood the essence of the society we lived in, the meanness and cowardice of some and the nobility of others, in a way that I would not have understood over half of a lifetime.

And so on 6 September Kuznetsov once again invited Popov and myself to see him. He said that the secretariat of the Organization of Moscow Writers held a meeting where it was decided to reinstate us. Popov immediately said "Give us a certificate!" "No, we won't give you a certificate." "Are we members of the WU?" "No." "Then who are we?" "You are members of the Organization of Moscow Writers . . ." We turned out to be in the unique position of accepted-not-accepted. Kuznetsov said, write a declaration and they will fully reinstate you into the secretariat of the RSFSR. They meant that they wanted us to write about the "ballyhoo in the West." We refused. Sergei Mikhalkov, secretary of the Russian WU, stepped into the fray. In the silence of an enormous office on Komsomolsky Prospect he said that at minimum they demand political loyalty from us. A political declaration is needed for our comrades from the provinces who are not up to speed. We did not give in. We simply wrote a declaration about the reinstatement.

In December a summons to the Secretariat of the RSFSR followed. We decided not to go: let them reinstate us in absentia. But on the day beforehand Verchenko assured us that everything had been agreed to and we had to appear for formality's sake. We met Aksyonov that same day. This was important, as there was a version of the events that suggested he had made *Metropol'* in

---

[22]   Woland is the devil in Mikhail Bulgakov's classic novel *The Master and Margarita*. His arrival in Moscow sets in motion a series of chaotic events.

[23]   Both famous dissidents. Anatoly Marchenko (1938–1986) was imprisoned in 1979. Andrei Sakharov (1921–1989), was exiled in the same year.

order to leave for the West. Vassily said "If they reinstate you, we can live normally." He even prepared to attend some meeting of the Inspection Commission he belonged to the following day.

The next morning a complete debacle took place. We understood that a fight lay ahead. We thought that they would humiliate us, force us to repent, so that our "confession" could be printed in the *Literary Gazette*, that they would smear us with shit, but in the end they would accept us, and this meant that the Union was betraying its Soviet essence. We considered reinstatement to be a victory.

They made us wait for a long time and then let us in one by one. Popov went in first: it was thought that, being a Siberian, from the people, he could smooth out the situation in a certain sense. It's hard to say if the result was planned beforehand. It's possible that they received from above first one set of directions, then another. The episode happened literally on the eve of the occupation of Afghanistan, and the leadership did not need liberal games of "detente." In any event, someone had visited the "upper echelons." Perhaps it was Kuznetsov, because he began the meeting with an inflammatory speech against *Metropol'*.

The entire secretariat, from the lowliest to the highest, were in attendance. They sat behind a long table and irritatedly wriggled their hands: it looked like a bundle of writhing snakes. Sergei Mikhalkov and Yury Bondarev sat at the chairman's table.[24] Bondarev didn't say a word, but his indignation was expressed in his gestures: he would grab his forehead then throw up his hands. The chief speaker was Shundik. Valentin Rasputin left halfway through for another meeting. Mikhalkov expressed impartiality. When they began to yell "Enough of listening to them!" he objected: "No, comrades, we should look into everything . . ." That they had called us in separately meant nothing. We laughed afterwards: we had all given absolutely identical answers.

---

[24]   Sergei Mikhalkov (1913–2009) was a popular children's poet, the author of the Soviet anthem, father of film directors Nikita Mikhalkov and Andrei Konchalovsky. In 1979, Chair of the Board of the WU of Russian Federation. Yury Bondarev (b.1924) was prominent writer and author of many novels about WWII. In 1979, served as the first secretary of the Board of the WU of Russian Federation.

The questions were ordinary and vile: how did you come up with such a detestable plan? Do you understand the damage this has done to the nation? How do you feel about the fact that reactionary circles in the West use your names? Who put you up to this? They wanted to bring everything down on Aksyonov. Popov said that Aksyonov is thirty-three years old and that he can answer for his actions himself, and that no one "put him up," he isn't shelving to be put up.

We had agreed that as soon as Popov came out he would give me a sign: good, OK, or bad. Popov came out and just waved his hand: completely bad . . . They asked me right off: do you believe you have participated in anti-Soviet activity? I understood. They were setting me up: this wasn't acceptance into the Writers' Union; participation in anti-Soviet activity is the 70th statute of the criminal code. Kuznetsov said: "How is that, having written about Sartre and the like, you did not understand that you would be used like a pawn in a grand political game?" Rasul Gamzatov, Mustai Karim, and David Kugultinov behaved entirely differently.[25] At some moment Gamzatov stood up and told Popov: "You answer well! Accept them all, and get it over with!" When Popov came out, Karim followed him out and said: "You've said everything correctly, but look who you've said it to!"

After the session of the secretariat some of the participants in the debacle came up to us and shook our hands. We found out later that they had voted unanimously. There was a long break, they deliberated, and we hung about the hallways. Then they called us back in, and Shundik read out the decision (edited by Daniil Granin)[26]: we are expelled from the Writers' Union for an indefinite time. When everyone was already breaking up, Mikhalkov whispered to us: "Guys, I did everything I could, but 40 people were against me . . ." Maybe that time he truly wasn't the chief thug?

---

[25]   Poets representing republics within the USSR, respectively, Dagestan (Gamzatov), Bashkiria (Karim), and Kalmykia (Kugultinov).

[26]   Daniil Granin (b. 1919): a prominent Soviet writer with a questionable liberal reputation.

This was all two days before the 100th birthday of Stalin. When Craig Whitney, correspondent for the *New York Times*, approached us we told him that this is how they celebrate the birthday of The Leader. Lipkin and Lisnyanskaya left the Writers' Union. They got it worse than anyone else: they were deprived of almost all means of existence. We always treated them like heroic figures. Aksyonov also left the Union, but his "betting on departure" weakened our solidarity. Soon he received an invitation from an American university, left and gave up his citizenship. I must add that Popov and I wrote a letter to our friends with an appeal not to leave the Union, not leave the left flank of literature exposed. Bitov, Iskander and Akhmadulina cautiously heeded our advice.

Metropol' turned out to be an X-ray that exposed our whole society. We saw authority clearly: it was no longer pushing forward on its ideological bulldozer as before, it barely crawled—asinine, degraded, and collapsing—but nevertheless was ready to destroy anything that lives just so as not to disturb its decay.

At the same time the saga of *Metropol'* showed that it was possible to resist that power, and that it should be resisted. Moreover, it became clear how to resist it.

For us the year of *Metropol'* was a frightful and jolly year: amicably, trying not to lose our sense of humor, we (how ambiguously I valued the meaning of that pronoun that year!) went against the grain, against the stream of slop pouring down upon us. They shouted that we had sold out to the Special Service, that we should be lined up either against the wall or with our faces to the people. They didn't break us, they just spoiled our biographies. And now I think and talk not about revenge, but about memory: social amnesia leads to catastrophic repetitions.

Those "epic" times have passed. A new trial has arisen: what to do, when one can do anything?

From the muzzle to freedom of choice to the choice of freedom.

Translated by Brian R. Johnson

Sergei Dovlatov
(1941, Ufa — 1990, New York)

Born to the family of a theater director and literary editor, Dovlatov was raised in Leningrad and was closely acquainted with the main figures of the Leningrad literary underground (including Brodsky). He studied at Leningrad State University, first in the Philology School (Languages and Literatures), then in the School of Journalism. He was expelled from the university and drafted into the army, where he served as a guard in the northern labor camps. This experience would provide the basis of his book *The Zone*, from which the story "The Performance" is taken. In the seventies he worked as a journalist at various Leningrad and Estonian newspapers and magazines. Belonged to a group of Leningrad nonconformist writers known as "Gorozhane" ("City-Dwellers"). Some of his works were published in Soviet journals, but his major collections of short stories were rejected by multiple publishing houses. In 1979, Dovlatov left the Soviet Union for the United States, where he became one of the most popular writers of the emigration. His works were widely published in Russian and in translation (after Nabokov, he was the first Russian author whose works were published in *The New Yorker*). Dovlatov's short stories were highly praised by American writers such as Kurt Vonnegut and Joseph Heller. *Perestroika* brought Dovlatov fame and popularity in Russia; a five-volume collection of his works, letters, and memoirs was republished several times in St. Petersburg. In his prose Dovlatov used the facts of his own life as material for his "absurd quest," illustrating the paradoxically foundational role of absurdity in human existence. The absurd in his works functions as the only valid source of personal freedom and as a force uniting individuals with one another and with history.

THE PERFORMANCE

There were three of us sitting in the Command Patrol Station.

Security Officer Bortashevich was shuffling creased, worn cards. Gusev, on watch, was trying to get some sleep without taking a lighted cigarette out of his mouth. I was waiting for the kettle to boil and the dry bread propped against it to warm.

Bortashevich drawled limply, "Take broads as an example. Say you and her are getting on good: movies, sugar wafers, polite conversations . . . You quote her Gogol with Belinsky . . . Go hear some bloody opera . . . Then, naturally, it's into the bunk. But Madame tells you: Marry me, you bastard. First the registry office, then the baser instincts. The instincts, you see, don't suit her. But if they're holy to me, then what?"

"So again, it's those kikes," Gusev said.

"What do you mean, kikes?" Bortashevich said.

"They're everywhere," I said, "from Raikin to Karl Marx. Take the venereal disease clinic at Chebyu. The doctors are Jewish, the patients are Russian. Is that the Communist way?"

Just then the telephone from the main office rang. Bortashevich put the receiver to his ear, then said to me, "For you."

I heard Captain Tokar's voice. "Come over and see me, and right away."

"Comrade Captain," I said, "it's already nine o'clock, by the way."

"Oh?" the captain said. "You only serve your country till six?"

"Then why bother posting work schedules? I'm supposed to report out tomorrow morning."

"Tomorrow morning you will be in Ropcha. There's an assignment from the Chief of Staff—to bring one prisoner from the Ropcha transit camp. To make it short, I'm waiting."

"Where are you off to?" Bortashevich asked me.

"Someone has to escort a zek here from Ropcha."

"For retrial?"

"Don't know."

"By regulation there should be two of you."

"What in the guard section is ever done by regulation? By regulation all they do is lock you up in the guardhouse."

Gusev raised his eyebrows. "And did you ever see a Jew locked up in the guardhouse?"

"You've got Jews on the brain," Bortashevich said. "We're tired of it. You take a good look at Russians. One look and you turn to stone."

"I don't argue," Gusev replied. The teakettle suddenly came to a boil. I moved it onto a roofing tile next to the strongbox. "All right, I'm off."

Bortashevich pulled out a card, looked at it, and said, "Oho! The queen of spades awaits you. I envy you." Then he added, "Take handcuffs."

I took a pair.

I walked through the zone, even though I could have gone around it on the patrol footpath. For a year now I'd been intentionally going through the zone at night. I kept hoping I'd get used to the feeling of terror. The problem of personal courage was posed to us here in a rather severe way. The champions in this category were generally acknowledged to be the Lithuanians and the Tartars.

I slowed down a little near the machine shop. At night this was where the *chifir* drinkers gathered. They would fill a soldier's mug with water and empty a whole packet of loose tea into it. Then they would lower a razor blade attached to a long steel wire into the cup. The end of the wire was then thrown onto a high-voltage wire. The liquid in the cup boiled within two seconds. The brown beverage had an effect somewhat like alcohol. People began to gesticulate excitedly, to shout and laugh for no reason.

The *chifir* drinkers didn't inspire serious alarm in anyone. Serious alarm was inspired by people who could cut your throat without drinking *chifir*.

Shadows moved in the darkness. I came closer. Prisoners were sitting on potato cartons around a small tub of *chifir*. Once they saw me, they went quiet.

"Have a seat, boss," a voice said from the darkness. "The samovar's ready."

"Sitting it out," I said, "is your department."

"He's literate," the same voice commented.

"He'll go far," a second said.

"No farther than checkpoint," a third said wryly.

Everything normal, I thought. The usual blend of friendliness and hate. Though to think of all the stuff I'd brought for them, the tea, margarine, cans of fish . . .

I lit a cigarette, rounded Barrack Six, and came out by the camp transport depot. The rosy window of the administration office swam out of the darkness.

I knocked. An orderly let me in. In his hand was an apple.

Tokar glanced out of his office and said, "Chewing on post again, Barkovets?"

"Nothing of the kind, Comrade Captain," the orderly protested, turning away.

"Do you think I can't see? Your ears are moving. A day before yesterday you fell asleep entirely."

"I wasn't sleeping, Comrade Captain. I was thinking. But it won't happen again."

"Too bad," Tokar said, and then said to me, "Come in."

I entered, reported for duty according to regulation.

"Excellent," the captain said, tightening his belt. "Here are the documents, you can depart at once. Convey here a zek by the name of Gurin. He's serving eleven years. Fifth conviction. Follows the Thieves' Law. Be careful."

"Just who," I asked, "needs him in such a hurry? Don't we have enough of our own recidivists here?"

"There are enough," Tokar agreed.

"So what's this all about?"

"I don't know. The orders are from top command."

I unfolded the travel sheet. Under the heading marked "Purpose" was this order: "To convey to the Sixth Subdivision Gurin, Fyodor Emelyanovich, in the capacity of performer of the role of Lenin."

I asked, "What does this mean?"

"I haven't the slightest idea. Better ask the Political Instructor. Most likely they're staging a theatrical production for the sixtieth anniversary of Soviet power. So they're inviting a guest actor. Maybe he's got talent, or the appropriate mug . . . I don't know. Meanwhile, deliver him here, and then we'll find out what it's all about. If anything happens, use your weapon. Safe journey."

I took the papers, saluted, and withdrew.

We neared Ropcha close to midnight. The settlement seemed dead. The darkness muffled the dogs' barking.

The logging-truck driver who had given me a ride asked, "Where are they sending you in the middle of the night? You could have gone in the morning."

I had to explain. "This way I'll be returning in daylight. Otherwise I'd be coming back at night. What's more, in the company of a dangerous recidivist."

"Could be worse," the driver said. "We've got dispatchers in logging who are more terrible than the zeks."

"It happens," I said. We said goodbye.

I woke the orderly in the checkpoint cabin, showed him my papers, and asked where I could spend the night. The orderly thought about it.

"It's noisy in the barracks. The convoy brigades get back in the middle of the night. If you took someone's bunk, they might use their belt on you. And in the kennels the dogs bark."

"Dogs—that's already better."

"You can stay here with me. All the comforts. You can cover yourself with a sheepskin jacket. The next shift comes in at seven."

I lay down, put a tin can near the trestle bed, and lit a cigarette.

The main thing is not to think about home, to concentrate on some urgent daily problem. Here, for instance: I'm running out of cigarettes, and the orderly, it seems, doesn't smoke.

I asked, "You don't smoke, or what?"

"If you offer me one, I'll smoke."

Still no better.

The orderly tried to start a conversation with me. "Is it true that your soldiers in the Sixth do it with she-goats?"

"I don't know. Doubtful. The zeks, now, they might indulge."

"In my opinion, it's better in a fist."

"Matter of taste."

"Well, all right," the orderly said, taking pity on me, "sleep. It's quiet here."

As for quiet, he was wrong. The checkpoint cabin adjoined the penal isolator. In the middle of the night, a zek woke up inside it. He jangled his handcuffs and sang loudly: "And I go, walking about Moscow . . ."

"Tomcat's in the mood for Pussy," the orderly grumbled. He looked into the peephole and yelled, "Agayev, shut your trap and go to sleep! Otherwise you get a fist in the eye!"

In answer, we heard, "Chief, the horns you're wearing are getting awfully long!"

The orderly responded with a torrent of ornate obscenity.

"Suck me till you're good and full!" the zek yelled.

This concert lasted about two hours. On top of everything, I ran out of cigarettes.

I went up to the peephole and asked, "You wouldn't happen to have any cigarettes or tobacco?"

"Who are you?" Agayev asked, startled.

"I'm on assignment from the Sixth Camp Subdivision."

"And I thought you were a student. Is everyone so polite in the Sixth?"

"Yes," I said, "when they're out of cigarettes."

"There's a ton of tobacco here. I'll push it under the door. You wouldn't happen to be from Leningrad?"

"From Leningrad."

"A fellow countryman. I thought so."

The rest of the night was passed in conversation.

In the morning I went looking for Dolbenko, the officer in charge of operations. I presented my orders to him. He said, "Have breakfast and wait at the checkpoint. Do you have a weapon on you? . . . Good."

In the mess hall, they gave me tea and rolls. They had run out of hot cereal. To make up for it, they gave me a piece of lard and an onion for the road, and an instructor I knew shook out ten cigarettes for me.

I sat in the checkpoint cabin till the convoy brigades moved out. The orderly was relieved close to eight. It was quiet in the penal isolator. The zek was sleeping off the night of talk. Finally I heard, "Prisoner Gurin, with belongings!"

The bolts clicked in the transit corridor. A security officer entered the cabin with my ward.

"Sign out," he said. "You have a weapon?"

I unbuckled my holster.

The zek was in handcuffs.

We walked out onto the porch. The winter sun blinded me. The dawn had come up quickly. As always.

On the gently sloping hill before us, cabins stood out black. The smoke above their roofs lifted straight up.

I said to Gurin, "Well, let's go."

He was a man of medium height, well built. Under his hat there was probably a bald spot. His soiled quilted jacket was shiny in the sun.

I decided not to wait for a ride with a log-carrier but to walk to the railroad crossing right away. If a truck or tractor going our way happened to come along, fine. If not, we could make it on foot in three hours.

I didn't know that the road had been closed off near Koina. Later I learned that two zeks had stolen a car the night before. By daylight, military police had set up roadblocks at every crossing. So Gurin and I had to travel all the way back to the zone on foot. We only stopped once, to eat. I gave Gurin some bread and the lard—

no great sacrifice, since the lard had frozen and the bread was in crumbs.

Silent till then, the zek kept repeating, "What a feed—pure calorie bacillas! Chief, we can enjoy ourselves from the bottom of our souls!"

The handcuffs hampered him. He asked, "If you could take off my cuffs—or are you afraid I'll run off on you?"

All right, I thought. In daylight it's not dangerous. Where's he going to run to in the snow?

I took off the handcuffs, fastened them to my belt. Gurin immediately asked permission to go relieve himself. I said, "Go do it there."

Then he crouched behind some bushes, and I held the black Vorkuta rifle by its front sight.

About ten minutes went by. My hand got tired. Suddenly, behind my back, a foot crunched in the snow. At that moment, a hoarse voice called out, "Let's go, Chief."

I jumped up. Before me stood Gurin, smiling. Evidently he had hung his hat on the bush. "Don't shoot, fellow countryman."

It would have been silly to bawl him out.

Gurin had acted straight with me. He had shown me that he didn't want to run away, or maybe he wanted to but didn't choose to.

We took the forest path and reached the zone without incident. On the way there, I asked, "So what kind of production will this be?"

The zek didn't understand. I explained, "In the orders it says you're the one who will play the role of Lenin."

Gurin burst out laughing. "It's an old story, Chief. Even before the war, I had the nickname 'Actor.' In the sense of a man who was clever, who could, as they say, move his ears. So they wrote on my record: 'actor.' I remember I was tied up in the Criminal Investigation Section, and the investigator wrote it down just as a joke. In the 'Profession before Arrest' column. As if I had a profession! From the cradle, I'm an inveterate thief. I never worked a day in my life. But the way they wrote it down, that's how it stuck—'actor.' From one paper to another. All the political instructors sign me up for amateur productions: 'After all, you're an actor, an artist . . .' Ech, if I could only meet one of those political instructors at a kolkhoz market, I'd show him what an artist I am."

I asked, "So what are you going to do? You're supposed to play Lenin himself."

"What, read a piece of paper? Simple. I'll polish my bald spot with wax, and it's in the bag. I remember we were robbing a bank once in Kiev, and I got dressed up as a cop—and my own pals didn't recognize me. If it has to be Lenin, then let it be Lenin. As they say, a day off work is a month of life."

We walked up to the checkpoint. I turned Gurin over to the sergeant major. The zek waved his hand. "Be seeing you, Chief. *Merci* for the feed."

He said the last words softly, so the sergeant wouldn't hear.

Since I'd been taken off work duty, I loafed for the next twenty-four hours. I drank wine with the weapon repairmen, won four rubles from them at cards, wrote a letter to my parents and brother, even planned to go see a young lady I knew in the settlement. But just then an orderly came looking for me and told me to report to Political Instructor Khuriev.

I made my way to the Lenin Room. Khuriev was sitting under an enormous map of the Ust Vym camp. The escape points were marked with little flags.

"Have a seat," said the P.I. "We have something important to discuss. The October holidays are approaching. We are beginning rehearsal of a one-act play called *Kremlin Stars*. The author"—here Khuriev glanced at some papers lying in front of him—"is Chichelnitsky, Yakov Chichelnitsky. The play is ideologically mature, recommended by the cultural section of the Department of Internal Affairs. The events take place at the beginning of the twenties. There are four characters: Lenin, Dzerzhinsky, a Chekist named Timofey, and his fiancee, Polina. The young Chekist Timofey is yielding to the bourgeois manner of thinking. Polina, a merchant's daughter, is dragging him down into the maelstrom of the petite bourgeoisie. Dzerzhinsky engages in educational work with them. He himself is incurably ill. Lenin insistently urges him to take care of his health. 'Iron Felix' refuses, which makes a strong impression on Timofey. In the end, Timofey throws off the bonds of revisionism. The merchant's daughter, Polina, shyly follows after him. In the closing scene, Lenin addresses the public." Here Khuriev again rustled his papers. "'Who is this? Whose are these happy, young faces? Whose are these cheerful, sparkling eyes? Can this really be the youth of the seventies? I envy you, messengers of the future! It was for you that we lit the first lights of the housing structures! For your sake that we rooted out the dark forces of the bourgeoisie! So then let your way be lighted, children of the future, by our Kremlin stars.' And so on. And then afterward, everyone will sing the 'Internationale.' In one outburst, as the expression goes. What do you say to all this?"

"Nothing," I said. "What can I say? A serious play."

"You're a cultured person, educated. We decided to draw you into this undertaking."

"I have nothing to do with the theater."

"Do you think I do? But a Communist should always demonstrate his social commitment."

"I'm not a Party member."

"All the more reason to take part. Your indifference goes too far. You put yourself outside the collective. Political awareness is not for you, social activity is not for you. Don't think you're so much cleverer than everyone else."

"I don't think that."

"Good. You will help with this cultural initiative. I'm managing, casting is done and I've already given out scripts, but without an assistant it's hard. Our actors—well, you know yourself . . . Lenin is being played by a thief from the Ropcha transit camp. A lifelong pickpocket, with high standing under the Thieves' Law. It's the opinion of some here that he's actively planning to escape."

I kept quiet. How could I tell the P.I. what had happened in the forest?

Khuriev continued, "In the role of Dzerzhinsky—Tsurikov, nicknamed 'Stilts,' from the Fourth Brigade, in for perverting minors, term—six years. There is evidence he takes drugs. In the role of Timofey—Gesha, an administration flunky, works on the sanitation brigade, a passive homosexual. In the role of Polina—

Tomka Lebedyeva from the Division of Economic Administration, an incredible bitch, worse than the female zeks. In a word, the public is the same. The use of narcotics is possible, also illicit contacts with Lebedyeva. All that skirt wants is to flap around the zeks. Do you understand me?"

"What is there to understand? Our people."

"Well then, put your hand to it. There is a rehearsal today at six. You will be assistant director. Your duties in the logging sector are temporarily suspended. I will notify Captain Tokar."

"No protest," I said.

"Be there at ten minutes to six."

I wandered around the barracks till six. A few times, officers wanted to send me off somewhere to take part in security operations. I told them that I had been placed at the disposal of Senior Lieutenant Khuriev, and they left me in peace. Close to six, I sat waiting in the Lenin Room. A moment later, Khuriev appeared with a briefcase.

"And where are our personnel?"

"They'll come," I said. "Most likely they were delayed in the mess hall."

Just then, Gesha and Tsurikov walked in. Tsurikov I knew from work in the unmarked sector. He was a sullen, emaciated zek with a revolting habit—he scratched himself. Gesha worked as an orderly in the sanitation brigade, cleaning barracks, looking after the sick. He stole pills, vitamins, and any medications with alcoholic content for those in charge. He walked with a barely noticeable dance step. It was said that zek chieftains in the zone would not let him near the campfire.

"Six on the dot," Tsurikov said, and without bending down scratched his knee.

Gesha was rolling some paper to smoke.

Gurin appeared, wearing only a worn undershirt under his jacket. "Hot in here," he said. "Pure Tashkent! But in general, this isn't a zone, it's a Palace of Culture. Soldiers address you in the polite form. And the rations are quite handsome. Is it really possible there are escapes here?"

"There are escapes," Khuriev replied.

"To get in or to get out?"

"To get out," the P.I. answered without smiling.

"And I thought, maybe they come running to this cooler from the outside. Or right from the capitalist jungles."

"You made your joke, now that's enough," Khuriev said.

Just then, Lebedyeva appeared in a cloud of cheap cosmetics, her hair in a six-month permanent. She was a civilian, but she behaved like the inmates and spoke their slang. Generally, administration office workers started resembling the zeks after a month. Even contracted engineers fell into using camp argot. Not to speak of the soldiers.

"Let's get down to it," the P.I. said.

The actors took creased sheets of paper out of their pockets.

"Your roles must be learned by Wednesday." Then Khuriev raised his hand. "I will now present the basic idea. The central line of the play is the struggle between feeling and duty. Comrade Dzerzhinsky, scorning illness, gives himself totally to the Revolution. Comrade Lenin insistently recommends that he take a leave. Dzerzhinsky categorically refuses. Parallel to this, the story line of Timofey develops. Animal lust for Polina temporarily blocks him from world revolution. Polina is a typical representative of the petit bourgeois mind—"

"The black-marketeer type?" Lebedyeva asked loudly.

"Don't interrupt. Her ideal is petit bourgeois well-being. Timofey experiences a conflict between feeling and duty. The personal example of Dzerzhinsky has a strong moral effect on the youth. As a result, his sense of duty triumphs . . . I hope everything is clear? Let's begin. So then, we see Dzerzhinsky at work. Tsurikov, sit there, stage left . . . Enter Vladimir Ilych. In his hand he holds a suitcase. We haven't got the suitcase yet, we'll use an accordion case for now. Take it . . . So then, enter Lenin. Begin!"

Gurin grinned and said with spirit, "How are you, Felix Edmundovich!" (He said this, swallowing his r's like Lenin, "How ag you?")

Tsurikov scratched his neck and answered gloomily, "Hello."

"More respect," Khuriev said.

"Hello," Tsurikov said a little louder.

"Do you know, Felix Edmundovich, what I have here in my hand?"

"A suitcase, Vladimir Ilych."

"And just what it's for—can you guess?"

"As you were!" the P.I. shouted. "It says here, 'Lenin, with a tinge of irony.' Where's the tinge of irony? I don't see it."

"It's coming," Gurin assured him. He stretched out the arm with the case and winked insolently at Dzerzhinsky.

"Excellent," Khuriev said. "Continue. 'And just what it's for—can you guess?'"

"And just what it's for—can you guess?"

"I haven't the slightest idea," Tsurikov said.

"Not so churlish," the P.I. said, breaking in again. "Milder. Before you is Lenin himself. The leader of the world proletariat."

"I haven't the slightest idea," Tsurikov said as sullenly as before.

"That's better. Continue."

Gurin winked again with even more familiarity. "The suitcase is for you, Felix Edmundovich. So that you, dear fellow, can go off and take a rest at once."

Without special effort, Tsurikov scratched his shoulder blade. "I can't, Vladimir Ilychv—there is counterrevolution all around us. Mensheviks, Social Revolutionaries, bourgeois spouts—"

"Scouts," Khuriev said. "Go on."

"Your health, Felix Edmundovich, belongs to the Revolution. The comrades and I have discussed it and decided: you must take a rest. I say this to you as a member of the ruling body."

Suddenly we heard a female yowl. Lebedyeva was sobbing, her head against the tablecloth.

"What's the matter?" the P.I. asked nervously.

"I'm sorry for Felix," Tamara explained. "He's skinny as a tapeworm."

"Dystrophies happen to be hardier," Gesha said with hostility.

"Break," Khuriev announced. Then he turned to me. "Well, what do you think? I would say they've grasped the main thing."

"Och," Lebedyeva exclaimed, "it's so close to life! Like in a fairy tale."

Tsurikov was giving his belly a good scratch. While he did this, his eyes clouded over.

Gesha was studying the escape map. This was considered suspicious, even though the map was displayed openly.

"Let's continue," Khuriev said. The actors put out their cigarettes. "Next come Timofey and Polina. The scene is the reception room of the Cheka. Timofey is manning the switchboard. Polina enters. Begin!"

Gesha sat on a stool and grew pensive. Polina took a few steps toward him, fanning herself with a rose-colored handkerchief. "Timosha! Yoo-hoo, Timosha!"

Timofey: "Why have you come? Or is something wrong at home?"

"I can't live without you, my gray-winged dove."

Timofey: "Go home, Polya. This is no village reading room."

Lebedyeva pressed her fists to her temples and let out an oppressive, piercing howl: "You don't love me anymore, don't fancy me . . . You've ruined the best years of my life . . . I'm all alone now, like a mountain ash in a meadow."

Lebedyeva had trouble suppressing her sobs. Her eyes turned red. Mascara ran down her wet cheeks. Timofey, on the other hand, behaved almost mockingly. "That's the kind of work it is," he said through his teeth.

"Why can't we run off to the ends of the earth!" Polina wailed.

"To do in General Wrangel and the White Army, is that it?" Gesha said, tensing up suddenly.

"Excellent," Khuriev said. "Lebedyeva, don't stick out your behind. Chmykhalov, don't upstage the heroine." (This was how I learned Gesha's real name, Chmykhalov.) "Let's go. Enter Dzerzhinsky. 'Ah, the younger generation!'"

Tsurikov cleared his throat and said gloomily, "Ah, the whore; the younger generation!"

"What kind of parasitical words are those?" Khuriev broke in.

"Ah, the younger generation!"

"Good health, sir, Felix Edmundovich," Gesha said, rising a little.

"You're supposed to be flustered," Khuriev said.

"I think he should stand up." Gurin gave his opinion.

Gesha jumped up, overturning the stool. Then he saluted, touching his palm to his shaved head.

"Good health, sir!" he shouted.

Dzerzhinsky reached out and squeamishly shook his hand. Homosexuals were not liked in the zone, especially passive ones.

"More dynamic!" Khuriev urged.

Gesha started talking faster. Then even faster. He rushed on, swallowing words. "I don't know how to proceed, Felix Edmundovich. My Polinka has gone completely wild. She's jealous of my service, do you understand?" (Gesha pronounced it "un-stan.") "'I'm lonesome,' she says. And I really do love her, that Polinka. She's my beloved, un-stan? She's captured my heart, un-stan?"

"Again, parasite words," Khuriev shouted. "Be more careful!"

Lebedyeva, her back to us, was freshening her lipstick.

"Break!" the P.I. announced. "That's enough for today."

"Too bad," Gesha said. "I was just starting to get inspired."

"Let's sum up." Khuriev pulled out a note pad. "Lenin more or less resembles a human being. Timofey gets a B minus. Polina is better than I thought she'd be, to be honest. As for Dzerzhinsky— unconvincing. Manifestly unconvincing. Remember, Dzerzhinsky is the conscience of the Revolution. A knight without fear or blemish. But the way you do him, he looks like some kind of recidivist."

"I'll try to do better," Tsurikov assured him indifferently.

"Do you know what Stanislavsky said?" Khuriev continued. "Stanislavsky would say, 'I don't believe it!' If an actor read a line in a phony way, Stanislavsky would stop the rehearsal and say, 'I don't believe it!'"

"Like the cops," Tsurikov said.

"What?" The P.I. didn't understand.

"The cops, I said, give you the same line. 'I don't believe it, I don't believe it . . .' They nabbed me once in Rostov, and the investigator was a real pig—"

"Don't forget yourself!" the P.I. shouted.

"Especially with the weaker sex present," Gurin said.

"I'm an officer in the Regular Army," Khuriev said, raising his voice.

"I wasn't talking about you," Gurin said. "I meant Lebedyeva."

"Ah-h," Khuriev said. Then he turned to me. "Next time, be more active. Prepare your remarks. You're a person who's cultured, educated. And now you're all dismissed. We meet again on Wednesday. What's the matter with you, Lebedyeva?"

Tamara was quivering with little sobs, wringing her handkerchief.

"What is it?" Khuriev asked.

"I'm feeling it so deeply . . ."

"Excellent. That's what Stanislavsky called 'transformation.'"

We said goodbye and we separated. I walked with Gurin to Barrack Six. We were going the same way.

By this time, it had grown dark. The path was lighted by yellow light bulbs above the fences. In the open-fire corridor, German shepherds ran back and forth, rattling their chains.

Suddenly, Gurin asked, "So how many people did they really do in?"

"Who?" I didn't understand.

"Those dogs, of course—Lenin with Dzerzhinsky. 'Knights without fear or radish.'"

I kept quiet. How could I know whether to trust him? And anyway, why was he being so open with me?

The zek wouldn't let it go. "Now me, for example—I'm in for theft. Stilts, we assume, stuck it where he shouldn't have. Gesha's in for something on the order of black-marketeering. As you can see, not one rub-out between us. While those two flooded Russia with blood, but that's all right."

"Look," I said, "you're going too far."

"What's going too far about it? Those people were the bloodiest no-termers ever."

"Listen, let's end this conversation."

"Good enough," he said.

After that, there were three or four rehearsals. Khuriev would get worked up, mop his forehead with toilet paper, and shout, "I don't believe it! Lenin is overacting, Timofey is hysterical. Polina is wagging her behind. And Dzerzhinsky looks like a thug."

"Well, what am I supposed to look like?" Tsurikov asked sullenly. "What's there is there."

"Did you ever hear of transformation?" Khuriev asked him.

"I heard," the zek said uncertainly.

"What did you hear? Just out of curiosity, what?"

"Transformation," Gurin explained for Dzerzhinsky, "is when thieves in the Law sell out to work as stoolies. Or else, let's say there's a hundred-percent-known square, but he carries on like he's a criminal . . ."

"Some conversation," Khuriev said angrily. "Lebedyeva, don't push out your form. Think more about the content."

"My bosoms are shaking," Lebedyeva complained, "and my legs are swollen. I always gain weight when I'm nervous. And I eat so little, cottage cheese and maybe eggs."

"Not another word about bacilla-calories," Gurin said to silence her.

"Come on," Gesha fussed, "let's try it again. I have a feeling this time I'm going to transform all the way."

I made an effort to take an active part. Not for nothing had they crossed my name off the convoy schedules. Better to rehearse than to freeze out on the taiga.

I said something or other, using expressions like "mise-en-scene," "super-task," "public solitude" . . .

Tsurikov practically never joined in these discussions. Or if he did say something, it was always totally unexpected. I remember, once, we were talking about Lenin, and Tsurikov suddenly said, "It can happen that someone looks like the lowest of the low, but his prick is healthy. Type of A-one baloney."

Gurin grinned. "You think we still remember what it looks like? I mean, that baloney."

"Some conversation," the political instructor said angrily.

Rumors about our dramatic circle spread through the camp. Attitudes toward the play and the leaders of the Revolution were ambivalent. Lenin was generally respected, Dzerzhinsky not very much. In the mess hall, one kapo made a crack to Tsurikov in passing: "So, you found yourself a nice job, Stilts! Made yourself into a Chekist."

Tsurikov's response was to hit him over the head with a ladle. The kapo fell down. It became very quiet. Later the morose truck drivers from logging said to Tsurikov, "At least wash the ladle. You can't dip it in the slops now."

Gesha was always being asked, "Well, what about you, Cleanup? Who do you play Krupskaya?" To this, Gesha would answer evasively, "Well, just . . . a working lad . . . an insider."

And only Gurin walked around the camp with an air of importance, practicing his Lenin's r's. "You ag following the tgue goad, Comgade Gecidivists!"

"Looks like him," the zeks would say. "Pure cinema."

Khuriev got more nervous each day. Gesha waddled, spoke his lines jerkily, and kept adjusting a nonexistent Mauser. Lebedyeva sobbed almost without interruption, even at her regular daytime job. She put on so much weight that she no longer zipped up her brown imported boots. Even Tsurikov—he too was slightly transformed. He was overcome by a hoarse, tubercular cough, which distracted him from his scratching.

The day of the dress rehearsal arrived. They glued little beards and mustaches on Lenin and Dzerzhinsky. To assist with the makeup, they temporarily released a counterfeiter named Zhuravsky from solitary. He had a steady hand and professional, artistic taste.

At first, Gurin had wanted to let his beard grow, but the security officer said it was against regulations. Still, for a month before the performance, the actors were permitted to let their hair grow. Gurin remained with his historically authentic bald head, Gesha turned out to be a redhead, and Tsurikov sprouted an entirely appropriate skewbald crew cut.

For costumes they dressed Gurin in a tight civilian suit, which corresponded to Lenin's real-life attire. For Gesha, they borrowed a leather jacket from Lieutenant Rodichev. Lebedyeva shortened a velvet party dress. Tsurikov was allotted a khaki tunic.

And so the seventh of November finally came around. Four red flags hung on the fences from early morning. A fifth was fastened to the building of the penal isolator. The sounds of the "Varshavyanka" carried from all the metal loudspeakers.

The only ones to work that day were orderlies from the housekeeping services. The logging sector was closed. The production brigades all stayed in the zone.

Prisoners roamed aimlessly about the open yard. By one in the afternoon, some began to appear drunk. It was more or less the same in the barracks. Many had gone for liquor early in the morning. The rest wandered about the area in unbuttoned fatigue shirts.

The weapons room was guarded by six trusted reenlistees. A sergeant stood guard outside the provisions storeroom. On the announcement board, a memo had been posted, entitled "On the intensification of military alertness on the occasion of the Jubilee."

Toward three o'clock, they assembled the prisoners on the square by Barrack Six. The camp commander, Major Amosov, gave a short speech. He said, "Revolutionary holidays touch every Soviet citizen. Even those who have temporarily stumbled . . . killed someone, stolen, raped, in general made some kind of stir . . . The Party gives to these people the opportunity to reform, leads them through unrelenting physical labor toward socialism. In short, all hail the jubilee of our Soviet government. But as for drunkards and smokers, we will, as they say, call them to account . . . not to mention sodomists. As it is, half the she-goats in the area have been messed with, you no-good—"

"That's a funny one," a voice called out from the rows of men. "What's the big deal? I laid the daughter of Second Regional Party Secretary Zaporozhe, but you tell me it's hands off a she-goat?"

"Quiet, Gurin," said the commander. "You're showing off again! We entrust him with playing Comrade Lenin, and all he can think about is a she-goat . . . What kind of people are you?"

"People, like people," one of the prisoners shouted from the columns. "Thugs and no-termers."

"You're a hardened lot, as I see it," the major said.

Political Instructor Khuriev popped up behind his shoulder. "Just a second, you're not dismissed yet. At six-thirty there will be a general assembly. After the ceremonial, there will be a concert. Attendance is required. Those absent will be sent to the isolator. Are there any questions?"

"A ton of questions," came a voice out of the rows. "Want to hear? Where's all the cleaning soap gone to? Where are the warm leg-wrappings that were promised? Why is this the third month no films have been shown? Are they or are they not going to give work gloves to the branch-cutters? Want more? When is an outhouse going to be put up in the logging sector?"

"Quiet, quiet!" Khuriev shouted. "Complaints in the prescribed manner, through the brigadiers! And now, you're all dismissed!"

Everyone grumbled a little and went off.

Toward six o'clock, the prisoners began to gather near the library. Here, in what had been the shipping workshop, general assemblies were held. The windowless wooden barn could hold about five hundred people.

The prisoners had shaven and cleaned their shoes. The one who served as the zone's barber was the murderer Mamedov. Every time he opened his razor, Mamedov would say, "One little slit and there goes your soul!" It was his favorite professional joke.

The camp administrators had put on full-dress uniform. Political Instructor Khuriev's boots reflected the dim lights which twinkled above the open-fire corridor. The civilian women who worked in the Division of Economic Administration smelled of powerful eau de cologne. The male office workers wore their imported jackets.

The barn was still closed. Reenlistees crowded near the entrance. Inside, final preparations for the ceremonial were still going on. Brigadier Agoshin of the production brigade was fastening a banner above the door. Letters in yellow gouache had been painstakingly stenciled onto a crimson background: "The Party is our Helmsman!"

Khuriev was issuing his final directions. He was surrounded by Tsurikov, Gesha, and Tamara. I also drew near them.

Khuriev said, "If everything goes well, I will give each of you a week off. Besides that, a visiting performance is being planned for Ropcha."

"Where's that?" Lebedyeva asked with interest.

"In Switzerland," Gurin answered.

At six-thirty, the barn doors were thrown open. The prisoners noisily took places on the wooden benches. Three guards carried in chairs for members of the presidium. The highest officials moved in a stately line down the aisle toward the stage.

The hall became quiet. Someone clapped uncertainly. Others joined him.

Khuriev rose before the microphone. The P.I. smiled, showing his trusty silver crowns. Then he glanced at a piece of paper and began, "It is already three score years . . ."

As usual, the microphone wasn't working. Khuriev raised his voice. "It is already three score years . . . Can you hear me?" Instead of answering, someone called from the audience, "For sixty years we haven't seen freedom!"

Captain Tokar rose slightly, to identify the transgressor.

Khuriev now spoke even louder. He listed the main accomplishments of Soviet power, recalled the victory over Germany, shed light on the current political situation, then fleetingly touched on the problem of the all-out building of Communism.

After him, a major from Syktyvkar spoke. His speech was about escapes and camp discipline. The major spoke softly; no one listened.

Then Lieutenant Rodichev came onstage. He began his speech like this: "Among the people, a document was born . . ." What followed was something like a list of socialist resolutions. One phrase stuck in my mind: ". . . to reduce the number of camp murders by twenty-six percent . . ."

Close to an hour had gone by. Prisoners were conversing quietly, smoking. In the back rows they were already playing cards. Guards moved noiselessly along the walls.

Then Khuriev announced, "The concert!"

First on was a zek I didn't know, who read two of Krylov's fables. To portray the dragonfly, he rolled open a paper fan. Switching over to the ant, he dug and swung an imaginary shovel.

Then Tarasyuk, manager of the bathhouse, juggled electric light bulbs. The number of them kept increasing. For the finale, Tarasyuk tossed them all up in the air at once, then stretched out his elastic waistband, and all the light bulbs fell into his loose satin pants.

Then Lieutenant Rodichev read a poem by Mayakovsky. He stood with his feet wide apart and tried to speak in a bass voice.

He was succeeded by the recidivist Shumanya, who performed a tap dance called "The Little Gypsy Girl" with no accompaniment. As he was being applauded, he exclaimed, "Too bad—without patent-leather boots you don't get the full effect."

Then they announced a camp kapo, Loginov, "accompanied by a guitar." Loginov walked out, bowed, touched the strings, and sang:

> *"A gypsy reads my cards, her eyes cast down,*
> *An ancient necklace and a string of beads.*
> *I wanted to try Fate for a queen of diamonds*
> *But once again it was the ace of spades.*
>
> *Why is it, my unhappy fate,*
> *Again you lead me on a road of tears?*
> *The barbed wire is rusty, the iron bars close,*
> *A railway prison car, the noise of wheels . . ."*

They applauded Loginov for a long time and called for him to sing an encore. However, Khuriev was against it. He walked out and said, "As they say, the good in little doses."

Then he adjusted his chest strap, waited for silence, and shouted out, "The revolutionary play *Kremlin Stars*. The roles will be played by inmates of the Ust Vym camp complex. Vladimir Ilych Lenin—prisoner Gurin. Felix Edmundovich Dzerzhinsky—prisoner Tsurikov. Red Army soldier Timofey—prisoner Chmykhalov. The merchant's daughter Polina—Economic Administration worker Lebedyeva, Tamara Evgenievna . . . And so, Moscow, 1918."

Khuriev backed off the stage. A chair and a blue plywood stool were carried onto the proscenium. Then Tsurikov climbed up onstage wearing the khaki tunic. He scratched his leg, sat down, and fell into deep thought. Then he remembered that he was sick, and began to force a cough. He coughed so hard that the tunic came up out of his belt.

Meanwhile, there was still no sign of Lenin. From the wings, a stagehand belatedly brought out a telephone without a cord. Tsurikov stopped coughing, picked up the receiver, and fell into even greater thought.

A few emboldened prisoners in the audience started yelling, "Come on, Stilts, don't drag it out!"

At that moment, Lenin appeared, carrying an enormous yellow suitcase. "Greetings, Felix Edmundovich."

"Hello there," Dzerzhinsky answered without getting up.

Gurin set down the suitcase, squinted cunningly, and asked, "Do you know, Felix Edmundovich, what I have here in my hand?"

"A suitcase, Vladimir Ilych."

"And just what it's for—can you guess?"

"Haven't the slightest idea." Tsurikov even turned away slightly, showing complete indifference.

From the audience, some shouted again, "Get up, Stilts! What kind of a way is that to talk to the boss?"

"*Sha!*" Tsurikov answered. "We know about that . . . Too many of you here are overeducated." Reluctantly, he rose slightly.

Gurin waited for silence and continued. "The little suitcase is for you, Felix Edmundovich. So that you, dear fellow, can go off and take a rest at once."

"I can't, Vladimir Ilych. There's counterrevolution all around us. The Mensheviks, the Social Revolutionaries"—Tsurikov glanced angrily at the audience—"bourgeois . . . what do you call them?"

"Scouts?" Gurin prompted.

"'At's it, 'at's it . . ."

"Your health, Felix Edmundovich, belongs to the Revolution. The comrades and I have discussed it and decided: you must take a rest. I say this to you as a member of the ruling body."

Tsurikov was silent.

"Do you understand me, Felix Edmundovich?"

"I understand," Tsurikov replied, and grinned stupidly. It was blatantly obvious that he had forgotten his lines.

Khuriev came near the stage and whispered loudly, "'Do what you want . . .'"

"And what can I want to do," Tsurikov said in the same loud whisper, "if my memory's gone full of holes?"

"'Do what you want,'" the P.I. repeated louder, "'but I'm not leaving service.'"

"Everything's clear," Tsurikov said. "I'm not leaving—"

Lenin interrupted him. "The main asset of the Revolution is people. To care for them is our arch-important task. So get your things together, and to the Crimea, dear fellow, to the Crimea!"

"It's still early, Vladimir Ilych, it's still early. Let us first finish with the Mensheviks, decapitate the bourgeois cobra—"

"Not cobra, but hydra," Khuriev said.

"Same bugger," Dzerzhinsky said, and waved his hand.

Beyond that, everything went more or less smoothly. Lenin reasoned, Dzerzhinsky wouldn't give in. A few times, Tsurikov raised his voice shrilly.

Then Timofey came out onstage. Lieutenant Rodichev's leather jacket did remind one of the double-breasted Chekist *toujourka*. Polina asked him to go to the ends of the earth with her.

"To do in General Wrangel and the White Army, is that it?" Timofey asked, and grabbed his imaginary Mauser. From the audience, zeks yelled, "Play your hearts, Cleanup! Drag her to your berth! Show us something's still clucking in your pants!"

Lebedyeva stamped her foot wrathfully, straightened her velvet dress, and again drew near Timofey. "You've ruined the best years of my life! You've left me, I'm all alone now, like a mountain ash in a meadow."

But the sympathy of the audience was with Timofey. Their cries carried from the hall: "Look how she's laying it on, the bitch! You can see her candle's burning out!"

Others yelled back, "Don't frighten the actress, you goats! Let the séance continue!"

Then the barn door flew open and Security Officer Bortashevich cried, "Legal convoy, report for duty! Lopatin, Gusev, Koralis—get your weapons! Sergeant Lakhno, go for documents on the double!"

Four of the guards headed for the door. "Excuse me," Bortashevich said.

"Continue," Khuriev said, and waved his hand.

The performance moved to the final scene. The suitcase was stored away for better times. Felix Dzerzhinsky stayed at his battle post. The merchant's daughter Polina forgot her personal claims . . .

Khuriev sought me out with his eyes and nodded with satisfaction. In the first row, Major Amosov squinted contentedly. Finally, Vladimir Ilych stepped up to the microphone. For a few seconds he was silent. Then his face lit up with the light of historical prescience. "Who is this?" Gurin exclaimed. "Who is this?"

Out of the darkness, thin pale faces focused on the leader.

"Who is this? Whose are these happy, young faces? Whose are these cheerful, sparkling eyes? Can this really be the youth of the seventies?"

Romantic notes sounded in the voice of the actor. His speech was colored with unfeigned excitement. He gesticulated. His powerful palm, covered with tattoos, swept upward. "Can it really be the splendid grandchildren of the Revolution?"

At first, there were a few uncertain laughs from the front row. After a few seconds, everyone was laughing hard. You could hear Major Amosov's bass in the general chorus. Lebedyeva yelped in a reedy voice. Chmykhalov held his sides. Onstage, Tsurikov took off his beard and shyly laid it beside the telephone.

Vladimir Ilych tried to speak. "I envy you, messengers of the future! It was for you that we lit the first lights of the housing structures. It was for your sake . . . Hear me out, you dogs! There's just a sparrow's beak of this junk left!"

The hall answered Gurin with a terrible, irrepressible yell: "Die, Lisper, before the Rule of the No-Termers!"

"Hey, whoever's closest, give that Maupassant a good tickle!"

"Beat it, uncle, your pretzels are burning!"

Khuriev pushed through to the stage and tugged at the leader's pants. "Sing!"

"Already?" Gurin asked. "There are literally two lines left. About the bourgeoisie and the stars."

"Forget the bourgeoisie. Go on to the stars. And start the 'Internationale' right away."

"Whatever you say." Straining his voice to the utmost, Gurin yelled, "Cut the noise!" Then he added, in a vengeful tone, "So then let your way be lighted, children of the future, by our Kremlin stars!"

"Let's go!" Khuriev ordered, and then, lifting a rifle cleaning rod, he began to conduct.

The hall became a little quieter. Gurin broke into song in an unexpectedly beautiful, pure and ringing tenor:

"Arise, you prisoners of starvation . . ."

And further, in the silence that had fallen:

"Arise, you wretched of the earth . . ."

Suddenly he became strangely transformed. Now he was a country peasant, mysterious and cunning, like his recent ancestors. His face seemed aloof and coarse. His eyes were half closed.

All of a sudden, someone began to sing with him. At first, one uncertain voice, then a second and a third. And then a whole dissonant, unorganized chorus of voices:

"For justice thunders condemnation —
A better world's in birth.

'Tis the final conflict, let each stand in his place . . ."

The multitude of faces joined into one trembling spot. The actors onstage froze. Lebedyeva pressed her hands to her temples. Khuriev waved his cleaning rod. A strange, dreamy smile had set on the lips of the leader of the Revolution.

"No more shall chains of violence bind us,
Arise, you slaves, no more in thrall,
The earth shall rise on new foundations . . ."

Suddenly, my throat contracted painfully. For the first time, I was part of my unique, unprecedented country. I was entirely made of cruelty, hunger, memory, malice . . . Because of my tears, I couldn't see for a moment. I don't think anyone noticed.

And then the singing died down. The last stanza was finished out by a few isolated, embarrassed voices.

"The performance is over!" Khuriev said.

Overturning the benches, the prisoners headed for the door.

Translated by Anne Frydman[1]

Evgeny Kharitonov
(1941, Novosibirsk — 1981, Moscow)

Kharitonov is the founder of gay literature in post-Stalin culture (despite the criminalization of homosexuality in the Soviet Union from 1934 to 1993). He graduated from the State Institute of Cinema and defended a PhD dissertation on pantomime. Directed the Studio of Pantomime in Moscow. In his prose, one sees the marginalized position of the underground writer and criminalized homosexual. Kharitonov presents social marginalization as a foundation for cultural innovation. Stylistically his works resonate with Moscow Conceptualism and European modernism (Joyce and Proust in particular). His literary works were published exclusively in *samizdat*. He was awarded the Andrei Bely literary prize posthumously. His collected works and translations appeared in Russia only in the 1990s and afterward.

"How I Found Out": One Boy's Story

"It was when I went to Moscow [from Izhevsk] for the International Women's Day holiday on 8 March, that was when I found out all about it. No, before that there was the business with the famous artist. He came to our college and asked me to go to his studio and pose for him. Well, and then he started talking about stuff, but very tactfully, and the main thing was he was the teacher and I was the pupil. He opened my eyes to a lot of things about art, he said it should be the main thing in my life and those other distractions were a quagmire, and the main thing was to work hard and become an artist. It was all very proper with him, mostly, anyway it would have been disgusting, he was sixty, I just respected him as a person. He taught me a lot that was good, and in bed we mostly just lay there, he just liked stroking me, he was wild about me and my figure, he said I was everything in life to him, his son, his wife, his friend, and his pupil. He was married, actually, he had a wife and daughter. Then he sent me off for the Women's Day holiday to Moscow to go round the art galleries and exhibitions, he gave me the address of a friend of his, another painter, at least he had been, married, not musical. Well, and then in Moscow I found out: at Bykovo airport I went into the toilet, it was all written up on the wall, look through such and such a gap, and a guy there signaled to me and gave me a blow job through a hole in the partition."

"How did you find out about cruising in the city center?"

"Well, that guy told me and asked me to meet him there. I didn't meet him, but over the next few days I met other guys, that's how I know all this stuff. I only had to show up for them to approach me. I turned down this one, didn't fancy that one, I looked them over to see who I liked."

"But what about earlier on, when you were just a child, you probably did something of the kind in a childish way, with a school-friend, perhaps?"

"Yes, I did have one friend. We used to wank together."

"Often?"

"You bet, whenever no one was looking we were at it. But we only wanked, nothing more."

"And did you have girlfriends?"

"Yes, of course I did."

"Why don't you have a steady girlfriend now?"

"They all seem a bit stupid. I didn't have a steady girlfriend, and what's the point of just walking around with one, going out with her and trying to think of things to say, no thanks. They don't really want to sleep with you, really they just want you to like them and go out with them. I did get it now and then. Yes, I liked it a lot. One time on the collective farm, I timed it on my watch, I *ploughed* a girl for one hour ten minutes, as an experiment, controlling it, when I felt it coming I held back, she was streaming buckets."

"Right, and do you prefer it with girls or boys?"

"Girls, of course, inside them wraps all round you, I like that, and it stays wet."

But gradually he told me more, both about the days in Moscow and about all his other contacts.

"Actually, to tell the truth, Bykovo wasn't how it all started, or that artist. It was one time I was going through Kirov, I went into a toilet and someone had written on the wall, go to a different toilet on such and such street. And I did."

"You weren't frightened, it didn't put you off?"

"Nobody knew me in Kirov, I didn't know anyone there either. And I was leaving town that evening. There was this guy in there, really ugly, but young, he had glasses, and great blubbery lips. He invited me into a cubicle, two cubicles next to each other, he signaled me from there and took me in his mouth. Wow! It was miles better than cunt, even wetter. He had such a big mouth, he didn't scratch me with his teeth, everything was so soft; I was in ecstasies, and he was really thrilled, he said, 'You've got such a big one! Let's meet up again!' I said, 'No, I can't. I'm leaving today.' He said, 'Let's see each other next time you're here, I'll be thinking of you.' But he was so ugly with those great thick lips of his, and this kind of big mouth. Anyway, when I came to Izhevsk I started looking for other people like that."

"And where did you find them?"

"In the same sort of places, and at the station. But they were all so horrible, absolutely no young people you could like. They were always laughing at each other, they all had camp names, one would be called Juliet, another was Jacqueline, one was called the Nun because she used to work in a church corrupting everybody there. So then, the famous artist. When he came to the college I already knew all about it. I knew what was coming the minute he invited me back. When I was posing he started straight in about you know what. He touched me lightly and said, 'You really are hung like a pony.' That was in his studio. Then we went to another room where there was a side table with drinks next to a sofa. He asked me to lie down beside him on the sofa and touched my cock and said women would go crazy over it, and he cuddled me. Of course I didn't enjoy being in bed with him, he was old, but as a person it was a different matter. He gave me a lot, we were more just friends. I really respected him, of course. He said, 'Oh dear, I would be glad to let you have me, but the orifice is too tight, yours would never get in.' He did give me head, but mostly for me to enjoy it, just taking a little, in a way that blubber-lipped guy didn't know anything about. He said, 'Never in your whole life tell anyone you come to see me, or that you have posed for me.' He made me a present of my portrait, and asked me not to show that to anyone either, then he said, 'Some day, when you have finished your studies and become an artist yourself, then you can show it, I shall tell people you are my pupil myself, but for now you mustn't, if you did I should have to kill myself, I would lose all my positions,

I have so many enemies.' On 8 March I decided to make my first-ever trip to Moscow. He told me to visit the art galleries and gave me an address to stay at, and that's how I ended up in the city center, the main thing was knowing him. On my last evening this guy called Misha came up, he was nice and had a mustache, I liked him more than any of the others straight away and we went back to his place. He lived with his sister and her husband, but they weren't at home. We went into the bathroom and he lubed me up behind and fucked me. I liked him so much. It was the one time I have actually wanted to suck someone off myself, and I didn't! I so wanted to stay with him. Luckily his sister and her husband didn't come back from their dinner party and we got to sleep the whole night together. The next day I had to fly out, I couldn't tear myself away from him until the very last minute. I only just made it to the plane. I couldn't think about anything else, he was all I had in my mind. When I got back it was spring and I walked all over town trying to find someone who at least looked like him, but there was no one. We wrote to each other. I couldn't wait for the May Day holiday, to get back to Moscow. I told my teacher all about him, but he said it was no good at all, I needed to study and only think about that, and these adventures were a quagmire which would pull me down. He talked me out of it, he wouldn't allow me to go. I wrote to Misha to say I wasn't coming. After that I didn't get any more letters from him. I wrote another letter to Sasha, that friend I had wanked through my schooldays with, saying, 'I've got to see you. You'll never believe all I've got to tell you, what I got up to in Moscow. It'll take your breath away, for God's sake come and see me, I can't write about it all here.' So instead of going to Moscow on May Day to see Misha, I did as my artist told me and went home to the village to see Sasha, my schoolfriend. He listened and was completely bowled over, then he heated up the bathhouse and said, 'Do everything to me that you had done to you in Moscow.' But they had sucked me off in Moscow, did that mean I had to do the same for him? I had always thought his cock was really horrible, kind of bent, and it had a blue tip. Well I did what had to be done and sucked it, but it practically made me sick. That was it, the only time, never again! He's so soft, sitting at home all the time, he likes reading about history, but only ancient

Russian history, he's got no time for the West, a real patriot, and he only listens to classical music, no pop groups or light music, only recently he's started listening to it a bit. And what sort of friend is he anyway? You find out who your friends are when you're in trouble, but with him it's only while he's interested in something, one time while we were still at school we went to a dance, the girls there were all falling over themselves to dance with me and their boyfriends told me to push off. I didn't want it to look as if I was scared so I carried on dancing, and they took me outside and gave me a split lip. And there's Sasha saying to me too, 'Come on, let's clear off,' he was too scared to stay with me. That's the kind of friend he is."

For the October Revolution holiday I went to Izhevsk myself and saw them all, the famous artist and, a bit later, Sasha. Seryozha agreed to invite Sasha to visit him when I got there. The artist wasn't at all the little old man I had imagined from Seryozha's story. He would have been educated in the post-war years. His studio wasn't the basement I had expected either, but a roomy, spotless hall with a polished floor in a newly-built block of flats. His paintings were what you expect to see in a Palace of Culture. The famous artist himself was modest and polite, as if his name wasn't already in the history books. It would be the best thing for him if some pushy new gangster who wanted his position publicly destroyed his reputation with the big brass of the Union of Artists, wrote to *Krokodil* about him, wrecked everything he has and sent him begging. Then he might become a really famous artist.

Sasha turned up for Revolution Day. Seryozha and Sasha, side by side. Seryozha, a playful, pleasant airhead, a dancer whose friends in the student residence where he lives sense that he isn't quite the same as them, but like him for it, and even, without realizing, flirt with him a bit; and Sasha who is well used to sitting at home reading about Ancient Russia and the Church, and quite happy to carry on doing so until something comes to him of its own accord. Thus, when he knew for sure that Seryozha had one of his Moscow friends coming to see him, he came in from his village too, and there he now sits waiting to see what is going to happen. Of its own accord. I have a feeling he's on tenterhooks, although he doesn't show it. Later, in the old bed, he is so yielding and affectionate, so slim and warm and very young. He so much enjoys everything that is done to him. He hesitantly touches my dick, but only after I encourage his hand in the right direction. He would never have worked up the courage to do it himself.

So what future do I see for him? Certainly he should go into the church. Everything will come together nicely for him there. He didn't even manage to pass the entrance exam to study history at college because, although it's his favorite subject, he only more or less knows Russian antiquity. What marvelous narrowness! What a gift to love one thing only and look neither to left nor right. He has an obedient, uncreative mind. He can remember what happened when, who was called what, and who had which rank, and there's nothing wrong with that, in fact there's something delightful about it. At least he's never going to become a heretic theologian, a Pavel Florensky puffed up with intellectual pride. He will just be a good obedient parish priest. Seryozha says, "You can't mean it, he'd never go against the wishes of his mother and father." Sasha's father is a Party organizer on the collective farm and his mother a schoolteacher. "They would think it was a terrible disgrace." "Not a bit of it, Seryozha. Sasha would just have to be ready to endure all things and make sure he explained it to them properly. He could point out that for all the anti-religious propaganda the church is a perfectly respectable institution from a Soviet point of view, with ranks and career progression. He could point out that Brezhnev awarded medals to the Patriarch and metropolitans as part of the Revolution Day celebrations." The old women in their village have been saying for ages that Sasha is going to be a priest, with all those old books and crucifixes he collects. And what a priest he would make, with those soulful eyes and long dark eyebrows and vivid lips. A beard would really set him off. He should put his back into it and go to the seminary at Zagorsk. That is where he'll find his niche. Sodomy must, of course, be rampant among the seminarists and in the church generally, to say nothing of the monks. Oh yes, if a boy hides away in a corner from other boys, doesn't play rough games with them, if a boy spends his time dreaming not of wars or cars but of celibate saints resplendent in gorgeous vestments, then that boy is, in Vasily Rozanov's expression, a man-maiden. In the saints' aloofness from warrior virtues he perceives his own, and is glad to find there is a morality which values this so highly.

There is, however, an alternative path for Sasha outside the church.

Seryozha has told the famous artist about Sasha, just as he told me, and he too has been asking when Sasha will be coming to see him. "You must bring him to see me, I can pull strings, I can get him a place in the History Faculty." Sasha, indeed, has been lecturing Seryozha for not properly appreciating the famous artist: "He has amazing contacts, he could help you in your career."

In short, Sasha would be a real find for the famous artist. He so wants a discreet, non-scene, faithful boy, and Sasha would be perfectly satisfied with a one-to-one relationship with the old man. But he would qualify as a historian, and that would mean Marxist-Leninist social science and joining the Communist Party. The artist would get him married to conceal their liaison, and everything would be perfectly to the famous artist's mousy tastes. Better if Seryozha doesn't introduce them. Let Sasha go into the church, and we shall put a cross on the map of the USSR to show where a certain young priest of our acquaintance is ministering to his flock.

Flysheet

We are sterile, poisonous blooms, and as such we should be made up into flower arrangements and put in vases for purely decorative purposes. Our Question has points of similarity with The Jewish Question.

Just as, for example, in the opinion of most anti-Semites *their* genius most often flowers in commerce, mimicry, investigative journalism, art without pathos, in practical everyday discretion, the art of survival; just as certain spheres of activity may be thought to have been created on purpose by them and for them: so too *our* genius has flourished in, for example, that most ephemeral and flimsy of the arts: ballet. It is quite obvious that ballet is our creation, whether literally as dance, or as pop music, or indeed as any other art form based on delectation.

Just as Jewish people have to be ridiculed in jokes, and the image of the crafty yid firmly retained in the mind's eye by all non-Jewish humanity to ensure that anti-Semitism should not perish from the earth, since if it did what would there be to prevent Jews from getting all the jobs in the world? (and there are those who believe that this is precisely how the world will end) . . . so too our ethereal flower-like sport with its pollen flying who knows whither must be mocked and transformed by the coarse, direct common sense of common people into a term of abuse, so that immature silly boys should not take it into their heads before their masculine drive has finally become established in them to give in to the weakness of falling in love with themselves.

Because of course, and there can be no doubt about this (for us), although the very thought is highly subversive and must not be allowed to circulate freely (in order not to hasten the end of the world from the opposite direction), but for all that it is true: you are all repressed homosexuals; and it is quite right that you should for all time think of this activity as a pathetic and squalid perversion, or preferably not think about it all.

But that all of you are us is as clear as the light of day. If you were not, how do you explain why you are so taken with looking at yourself, a person of your own sex, in the mirror? Why do boys fall platonically in love with the leader of their gang? Why do people whose youth is past look sometimes at young people and sigh upon seeing themselves as they will never be again? Why do you exhibit the young and beautiful for the whole world to admire at the Olympic Games? Of course, to your straight way of thinking there is absolutely no hidden sexual agenda. Heaven forbid! If you admitted it the world would neatly polarize, the passions of the sexes would be directed inward on themselves, and Sodom and Gomorrah would have arrived.

We, as a chosen and predestined few, must be quarantined behind a *cordon sanitaire* of hostility so that our example should not prove infectious: our elect destiny is to live only for love, endless and insatiable.

You find yourselves a (heterosexual) partner for life when you are young, and even if your eyes do stray and you split up and find yourselves a new partner, the point is that you nevertheless live basically in your cozy family unit free from the daily love hunt, free for intellectual endeavor, honest artisanship or, at the very least, single-minded alcohol abuse.

The couplings of us flowers, however, are ephemeral, not tied to the rigors of fruit production, or any other strings. The emptiest of people, we live from hour to hour in the expectation of new encounters, playing records of love songs till the day we die, looking around us with nervous anticipation for more and more young you's.

The vocation of the very best of our empty brothers and sisters is to dance as no one else can the dance of impossible love, and to sing of it sweetly.

We are secret rulers of the world's tastes. What you are to find beautiful is often decided by us, although you do not always realize this (as Vasily Rozanov[1] did). Eschewing many of the things

---

[1] Vasily Rozanov (1856–1919) was an iconoclastic writer, philosopher, and critic who

in life which inflame you, we have expressed ourselves in various centuries and periods in signs of our own which you have taken for expressions of a lofty asceticism or the aesthetic of decay, trying to read a universal meaning into them.

Quite apart from the fact that it is we who as often as not dictate your fashions in clothing, it is even we who exhibit the women you admire, types which possibly, left to your direct inclinations, you might not have chosen. Were it not for us, your tastes would incline more strongly towards the literal, the carnal, and the bloody. Taking your cue from us, often unawares, you rate highly the playful and the non-utilitarian.

And it is also plain as the light of day that all who are vulnerable, or artful, all fallen angels, all who are clothed in spangles or artificial flowers or tears, are closest to God's heart. It is they who will sit at His right hand, they who will receive His kiss. The best of our doomed young creatures He will set closest to Himself, while all who are devout, and normal, and bearded, all who are held up on earth as an example, whom the Lord assures of His love—well, actually, in His heart of hearts He is not that bothered about them.

The laws in the West allow our flowers to meet openly, to be openly portrayed in works of art, to have clubs and festivals and declarations of rights. But what rights? Rights to what?

Behind the sluggish morality of our Soviet Russian Fatherland there is a point. Soviet Russia pretends we do not exist, and its Criminal Code decrees that our flower-like existence is against the Law, because the more visible we are, the nearer is the End of the World.

Translated by Arch Tait[2]

---

was known for his controversial views on religion and sex and occasional outbursts of anti-Semitism. He often championed different political views under different pseudonyms simultaneously.

[2]   From: Yevgeny Kharitonov, *Under House Arrest*, trans. Arch Tait (London: Serpent's Tail, 1997), 149–57; 184–7.

Venedikt Erofeev
(1938, Komi Peninsula — 1990, Moscow)

One of the most influential authors of Russian postmodernism. In addition to *Moskva–Petushki* (1970, translated variously as *Moscow to the End of the Line, Moscow Circles,* and *Moscow Stations*), he wrote the play *Walpurgisnacht, or The Commander's Steps,* several essays ("Vasily Rozanov through the Eyes of an Eccentric," "My Little Leniniana"), and the unfinished play "Fanny Kaplan." Although he never completed his university education (he was expelled from Moscow State University after three semesters and fared no better at Vladimir Pedagogical Institute), he was extraordinarily well read. Among his literary precursors he named Saltykov-Shchedrin, Gogol, the early Dostoevsky, and Sasha Cherny. After numerous odd jobs in various Russian towns, Erofeev settled down in Moscow in 1974 where he became the spiritual heart of the intellectual circle that included the translator and philologist Vladimir Muraviev, the poet Olga Sedakova, and other noteworthy writers and scholars. *Moskva–Petushki* was first published in 1973 in the Israel-based almanac *Ami* and widely circulated in *samizdat.* In the USSR it was published only during *perestroika* in 1988–89 by the newly founded journal *Sobriety and Culture.* At the same time, postmodernism was just becoming a topic of heated debates in Russian criticism, and Erofeev was acknowledged as a postmodernist classic. A notoriously heavy drinker, Erofeev foresaw his premature death, although he died of throat cancer, rather than the brutal beating that ended the life of his fictional counterpart. There is a monument to the hero of his novel in Moscow, on Ploshchad' Bor'by.

Recommended for discussion:
   Venedikt Erofeev, Moscow to the End of the Line,
   trans. H. William Tjalsma (Evanston: Northwestern University Press, 1992).

Olga Sedakova
(b. 1949, Moscow)

Poet, philologist, essayist, and translator. Graduated from the Department of Slavic Studies, Moscow State University. Defended her doctoral dissertation in 1993. Until 1989, her poetry was banned from publication in the USSR. Her first book of poetry appeared in 1986 in Paris. Since the 1990s she has published a large number of poetic books and essays, some of which are included in her *Collected Works in 4 Volumes* (2010). Has been awarded many literary prizes, including the Andrei Bely Prize (1983), the Pushkin Prize (1994), the Aleksandr Solzhenitsyn Prize (2003), and the Dante Alighieri Prize (2011), among many others.

Remembering Venedikt Erofeev

I think that for anyone who knew Venedikt Erofeev, a meeting with him constituted a life event. The farewell, however, was not as notable: Venia, having bid farewell, "remained" with his acquaintances. I can clarify: and remaining, he bid farewell. For many years—in fact, for all the years I knew him (twenty years, terrible as it is to say)—Venichka lived on the edge of life. And it wasn't a matter of his final illness or the usual dangers of being a drinker, but his way of life, and even the nature of his inner life, which he lived "in view of the end." Those who have passed always remain, but in Venia's case this is particularly true: he noticeably changed our consciousness, became a part of it, became some kind of organ of our perception and evaluation.

"Venichka would have liked that . . . Oh, and to that he would have said . . ."—so we, having known him, say to one another on various occasions. It's interesting that Venia's responses as imagined by us do not really diverge. No disagreements arise. His position, fanciful or simply outlandish—as he would often say, "from my otherworldly point of view"—is profoundly consistent. The fact that he might say contradictory things on one topic was also a part of this consistency. In light of all his eccentricity and extreme subjectivity, his otherworldly point of view is close to what is called a "voice of conscience." I do not know what attitudes he held toward himself, that is, whether he placed himself before the same judge as that to which he subjected everything around him. But for some reason his usually peremptory judgments were always accepted without objection. For some reason we ascribed to him the authority to judge so decisively. It was earned somehow, perhaps by his otherworldly state of living towards the end. In any case, it wasn't on account of his literary pursuits that he earned the right of "last judgment." I became acquainted with him before his famous *Moscow–Petushki* was written,[1] and even then I was struck by how it seemed as if everyone around him stood inwardly before him at attention, awaiting and accepting his words on any subject, without question. At first I thought that they were somehow bewitched, but very soon I, too, became just as bewitched. He judged—we felt—as an unengaged witness, as a person not distracted by the vanity of his own "interests." It is easy to say that he was distracted foremost by a different main interest—his passion for alcohol.

"That's all nonsense," he would interject during conversation. "Listen, I've got an idea . . ."

What the idea was everyone already knew: chip in or gather up the empty bottles and head to the nearest liquor store. I remember the idea of Alexander Pope (Venia at once would have rattled off the English classicist's date of birth, when he died, and all his works in chronological order; his enthusiasm for precise knowledge always astonished me—if he ever confused any dates, names, etc., it was a catastrophe)—the idea that the struggle with the passions consists not of their total abolishment as in stoic ataraxia, but of the advancement of a single guiding passion which occupies one's entire essence, leaving no strength or time for other passions. Alcohol was, in its own way, such an elevating passion for Venia. It seemed as if this way of life was not trivial drunkenness, but some kind of service. A service to the Tavern? There was incomparably more torture and labor in it than pleasure. The intrinsic pleasures of

---

[1] *Moscow–Petushki* was begun in 1969 and completed in 1970. Its title, which indicates the protagonist's departure point (Moscow) and desired destination (Petushki, a town located seventy miles east of Moscow), has been rendered in English as *Moscow to the End of the Line* (translated by H. William Tjalsma [Evanston: Northwestern UP, 1994]).

this activity such as "unwinding," "forgetting oneself," or "easing conversation"—not even to mention the pleasure of an alcoholic drink's taste (to whomever praised the taste of wine Venia would say "Faugh, vulgar man!")—these pleasures were, in his case, not spoken of. I have never met a more vehement enemy of any well-known "pleasure" than Venichka. For him, there was nothing more vile than experiencing or seeking pleasure. Things should be bad; "everything on earth should take place slowly and incorrectly so that man doesn't start feeling proud . . ." as readers of *Moscow–Petushki* remember.[2] Admittedly, Venia's list of those who were "vulgar" and "hateful" was vast, and I'm not certain that seekers of a good life occupied first place on it. There was a lot else on it: conceit, phrase-mongering (as phrase-mongering generally entailed lofty and undisguised words), submergence in "the everyday," thoughtless cruelty, over-enthusiasm, glibness, fussiness, prudence, worship of intellectual heroes—and non-recognition of them, as well—inquisitiveness—yet also intellectual laziness—"excessive propensity for generalization"—and the incapacity for generalization . . . the list goes on . . .

"Uncircumcised in the heart,"[3] he would quote on relevant and still many other occasions. It seems I would not be mistaken if I say that he loved meekness most. Any display of meekness crushed him.

"I meet a man, and he says, 'You probably don't remember me . . . We spent an entire evening together quite recently.'"

"And what's special about that?" I ask, surprised.

"What? Others say, 'Well, you must've been pretty smashed if you don't remember me!'"

Though one can say many things about our communist upbringing, it is well known that humility, modesty and meekness are things that were almost completely forgotten in our country, and

---

2   "Everything should take place slowly and incorrectly so that man doesn't get a chance to start feeling proud, so that man is sad and perplexed" (Venedikt Erofeev, *Moscow to the End of the Line*, 14).

3   See Jeremiah 9:25–26.

a person is not up for "gazing into some kind of frivolous distance" as Venichka would have wanted—much less looking at oneself from that frivolous distance. Everything is close by, everything is at hand; don't look away, or someone else will snatch it all up! Venia was nauseated by the ever-present "anxious halfwits" that surrounded us, by their beginnings, continuations, and achievements.

"Why do they do that?" he would ask with the pathos of an Old Testament prophet. "Why must a man go—no, *crawl* to his desk to compose such verse? Oh, they're hateful . . ."

He called himself "God's meekest creature," and that's not thoughtless bragging as it might seem to those who knew him less well. I can recall many examples of this meekness of his, which came from goodness knows where.

Once, having gotten offended by quite a nasty trick, I gathered up all of Venia's things that he'd left at our place, put them in his briefcase, which he had also left, and sent my husband to return it all to its owner and convey the end of our relations. Upon returning, my husband said:

"Venichka's laying there, not saying anything. He's down. I felt sorry for him, so I said, 'Don't be offended by Olga; she's not a saint. A saint would have forgiven you.' And at that Venia turned over: 'You're a great guy, but you don't understand a thing about saints. A saint would not have condemned me so harshly in the first place.'"

Or another time: once Venichka stayed to spend the night, so we put him up in our kitchen on a cot. Suddenly, in the middle of the night we were awoken by an incredible chill; as it turned out, the balcony door in the kitchen had swung wide open (and it was nearly negative 30 degrees Celsius outside). Wind was blowing in, snow swirling about, but Venia was just lying on the cot without a stir.

"Why didn't you close the door?"

"I thought you had it that way. To air the place out at night."

I cannot think of another person I know who, under those conditions, would have thought and acted like that (or, more precisely, who would have *not* acted: not closed the door without asking or not awakened the hosts in order to ask). It was Venia's way—something contrary to the usual fight for one's place in the sun, the plebeian "I have the right!" or "I need it!" and plebeian aggressive self-defensiveness. His deep humility before everything and his desire to protect all of it from himself enraptured me to no end. When he was sober for a long time, it was impossible not to feel one's own coarseness next to him: the contrast was striking.

Here is another example of Venia's meekness. Once three or four of us were having a long friendly discussion—it even led to some reciting of verse. Suddenly, near the end, I for some reason felt the need to brag about some perfume I had received as a gift.

"Well, show me," Venia said good-humoredly. But when I looked, the perfume wasn't in its place.

I gave Venia a glare that could have been straight out of a Red Army propaganda poster. "You drank it," I said. "And you're still mocking me. Give it back! That's mean and deceitful. And what did you drink my French perfume for when there was some Soviet stuff right next to it?"

"I didn't drink it," Venia assured me. "I didn't drink it. I'll swear to God, if you want." Without convincing me, Venia got up to leave and said:

"An excellent coda to a poetic evening. You will apologize when you find out it wasn't me."

Later my husband returned and informed me that, knowing of Venia's visit, he'd hidden the perfume beforehand, fearing Venia might drink it. I called Venia to apologize.

"Enough already," he laughed, "As soon as I left I thought: what have I reduced Olga to, for her to assume such things! So for that please forgive me."

Of course, I saw a lot that was incomprehensible and objectionable to me in Venia's life. Over the years I visited him less and less frequently, so as not to have to cross paths with any of his guests. These Walpurgis[4] guests of his and their parties that

---

4   This characterization of Erofeev's guests recalls the bacchanalian celebrations of the witches' sabbath, Walpurgis Night (Walpurgisnacht), depicted in Goethe's *Faust Part One* (1808) and Thomas Mann's *The Magic Mountain* (1924). It also recalls the title of Erofeev's play, *Walpurgis Night, or "The Steps of the Commander,"* written in 1985, about the time his throat cancer was diagnosed. A play of five acts, it tells the

were reminiscent of Tatyana's dream[5] drove me away from even Venichka himself, who with inexpressible suffering on his face, writhing as if on a frying pan, would sometimes—after remarks that were especially offensive to those gathered—let out soft moans while listening to everything his dubious admirers spouted and not interrupt.

It could be that these parties were isolated incidents of the general principle that "everything on earth should take place slowly and incorrectly . . ." Once, amongst some limericks I composed at one point, Venia pointed one out and said, "This one's about me."

> *Once over at Baudelaire's place*
> *Three officers got tanked.*
> *They were tossing empty bottles*
> *At one another's heads,*
> *But they all just fell on Baudelaire.*

And, in fact, all the rubbish and vulgar things exchanged by the guests did fall on Venichka. Usually while lying down, he would survey those who had gathered there from his lowly vantage point with a look I found described in Khlebnikov:

> *A needle of mad Russian eyes*
> *Pierced us, simple, light.*
> *In him was a wide open gaze*
> *Of some terrible villages.*
> *And the faces of the others after it—rhubarb.*[6]

story of Lev Isaakovich Gurevich, an alcoholic, half-Jewish poet, who is confined in a Soviet mental ward.

[5] In Alexander Pushkin's *Evgeny Onegin* (1823–31), Tatiana Larina, Onegin's love interest, dreams that she is walking alone in the woods and crosses paths with a menacing bear.

[6] These lines are from Velimir Khlebnikov's "Crane Fly #2nd" and describe the gaze of a "rustic" Christ.

Every so often, however, his otherworldly patience would reach the end of its rope. "Quiet, fool!" he'd growl. Twice in my presence he kicked out new acquaintances: one for a scabrous joke and another for blasphemy. Both had in fact been trying to please the host: after all, according to Venichka's widespread reputation, both things should have pleased him. But they failed to take into account one thing: when a man is facing his end, he cannot find those things pleasing. And Venia, like I said, lived facing the end. And his fatal disease did not change the terminally suffering character of his life—it only added torment. Which is why, upon learning of his death, the first thing everyone said was probably: "His torments are over now."

His funeral service was performed, and it seemed strange to me since Venia did not have a relationship—in a conventional sense—with the Church. No, he had his own extremely strained and painful relationship, which remained unclear for decades. Maybe he took it too seriously to just go and become a good churchgoer like many of his acquaintances did at the beginning of our "religious renaissance."[7] I cannot say anything about his Catholic baptism near the end of his life: it was too intimate a topic for him and never came up in conversation. Was it a political act? An act of love for Latin and Rome? (Venia said, "For me, Latin is a kind of music." And for him, it seems, there was nothing higher than music; perhaps only tragedy, from whose spirit music was born, as Nietzsche, well read by him, asserted.) The stylized piety of the Orthodox neophytes, their unbearable complacency, which they acquired at the speed of light, their "communalism" with which they began saving others,[8] their "truth" which they already seemed to have in their

---

[7]   By the late 1980s, under Mikhail Gorbachev, the new political and social freedoms introduced by *glasnost* resulted in many church buildings being returned to local parishioners to be restored. In 1988, on the millennial anniversary of the Baptism of Kievan Rus', many government-supported Russian Orthodox celebrations took place in the major cities, and church services were shown on live television for the first time in Soviet history. This signaled the end to the ban on religious propaganda on state television.

[8]   "Communalism" (*sobornost'*) is a term coined by the Slavophiles in the nineteenth

pockets—all of it, undoubtedly, contributed to Venia's doubts over ecclesiasticism. He said once:

"They'll get off of that tram. Mark my words."

"Tram?"

"Well, yeah. I wanted to find my way by foot. They all jumped on the tram."

Thus, the funeral in the Orthodox temple was in complete disaccord with Venichka, and it was "in the spirit of the moment" to the point of indecency: the funeral of the Russian writer, a dissident who had lived to see the "victory" of liberal ideas, a rehabilitated hero of the people, was held in the rehabilitated Church. "All is in order; there are no drunkards here."[9] And so, not without embarrassment, I watched the proceedings . . . Yet when we got to the Beatitudes, from the very first verse, I realized with full distinctness that if they are about anyone, they are about Venichka. Many, many people, undoubtedly respectable, will hardly dare to ask themselves: is it true that these terrible beatitudes are in fact (loftily speaking) the blessings, which their souls seek? Is it not true that if they then no longer ask for this blessing, that they will not object, should it come to pass? Venichka did not object; that is certain. "Everything on earth should take place slowly and incorrectly . . ."

Once I was reading him my translation of a story about Saint Francis, in which he, having learned from the doctor that his days are numbered, stretches out on his bed, falls silent for bit, and then says joyfully, "Welcome, death, our sister!" Tearing myself away from the reading, I looked up at Venia (expecting to see that it had lifted his spirits as well) but saw that he was gloomier than ever.

"What's wrong? Why are you displeased?" (I thought maybe it was my translation.)

"Because that's not how we are," Venia said with despair.

century to denote the spiritual unity experienced by people when they share the common beliefs and values of the Slavic Orthodox church (as opposed to following the cult of individualism of the West).

9   A Russian saying.

At first, when mentioning the idea of a "guiding passion," I had in mind an ideological "universal drunkenness," as in Blok:

But the poet partakes in a universal drinking bout
And for him constitutions are not enough.[10]

But that is superficial. Venia's real passion was grief. He proposed to write the word with a capital "G," like Tsvetaeva did: Grief.[11] What was this Grief about, this Grief that always seemed new, freshly caught? Venia described it in *Moscow–Petushki* (in the episode with the widow from *Inconsolable Grief*),[12] and spoke of it in this way. He compared it to that which anyone could understand: "When a person has just buried his father, does much really seem necessary or interesting to him? Well, that's how it is for me every day."

But what this Grief was about or whose daily burials these were—it does not seem as though he ever mentioned anything about it to any of his acquaintances. He certainly never mentioned anything about it to me . . .

Yet, insofar as his Grief was not an everyday grief, he was a rather happy person, and not at all gloomy. It was extraordinarily easy to make him laugh, and he would laugh until he fell over, to tears, repeating, "Mother Queen of Heaven!" Once someone remarked:

"You, Venichka, laugh as though you do not have a single mortal sin to your soul."

And then Vadia Tikhonov,[13] the "beloved first reader," hit the nail on its head:

---

[10]   These are lines from Alexander Blok's poem, "Poets," written in 1908.

[11]   Marina Tsvetaeva (1892–1941) was a Russian poet whose verse is known for its independence from any poetic movement of her time. Sedakova's characterization of Tsvetaeva as having written "Grief" ("Gore") with a capital "G" echoes Erofeev's characterization of Tsvetaeva in his 1973 essay, "Vasily Rozanov through the Eyes of an Eccentric," as having written "Misfortune" with a capital "M."

[12]   *Inconsolable Grief* (1884) is a painting by Ivan Kramskoy (1837–87), which depicts a grieving widow.

[13]   Vadim Tikhonov was the first person to read the manuscript of *Moscow–Petushki*

"His sins are all immortal."

Venia loved all the unloved heroes of history, literature, and politics. All the "Regimes of the Colonels,"[14] the Moshe Dayans, those African dictator-cannibals (Somosa, or something, was his name?)—were his favorites. In the Bible, King Saul was especially dear to him. He forgave David a lot for the incident with Bathsheba. He remembered Peter the Apostle in the episode of the renunciation by the fire with great fondness. He liked everything antiheroic, all antiheroic deeds, and an out-of-tune piano better than a tuned one. On his mad piano, unyielding to renovation, where not a single sound sounded like itself—and all the better if it was a single sound alone: from each seized key an entire loathsome chord was stirred—on that piano played distinguished pianists and composers alike, to the host's great pleasure. He loved all ugly ducklings—but not because he saw future swans in them. Swans downright repulsed him. Thus, knowing Russian poetry extremely well, he preferred Igor Severianin[15] to all its swans for his unabashed impropriety.

In anything that was perfect or that aspired to be perfect, Venia suspected inhumanity. "Human" for him meant that which is imperfect, and he demanded that imperfection be treated "with first love and last tenderness"; the more imperfect something was, the more it should thus be treated. In his opinion, he who deserves the most tenderness is (and I quote), "he who wet himself in front of everyone."

I cannot say that I fully understood this extreme humanism. "Well, yes," Venia replied, suddenly taking on a lofty tone, "leniency never did hold a place in your heart."

and was therefore the "beloved firstborn," or the "beloved first reader" to whom Erofeev dedicated his novel.

[14] "The Regime of the Colonels," or Greek military junta of 1967–1974, refers to a series of right-wing anti-communist military governments that ruled Greece following a coup d'état.

[15] Igor Severianin (1887–1941) was a poet, translator, playwright, and memoirist who attained widespread notoriety in 1910 when Lev Tolstoy publicly criticized his verse for its frivolity and excessive irony. His poetry was popular from 1913–14, but by the 1920s his art had gone out of fashion and become an object of ridicule.

Even more incomprehensible to me was the other side of this humanism: his hatred for heroes and heroic deeds. The champion of this hatred of his became the unfortunate Zoya Kosmodemyanskaya;[16] his worship of this Beautiful Lady,[17] however, cost him dearly (they say he was discharged from the Vladimir Pedagogical Institute for a tongue-and-cheek sonnet sequence dedicated to her). Even Gorky, "the Stormy Petrel,"[18] with his "Man—that sounds proud"[19] and other such aphorisms didn't rouse such rage in Venia: in the Stormy Petrel he found something comical. The Stormy Petrel was base and two-faced, and he had already reconciled himself with that. But the flawless Zoya, the martyr, Zoya! At the thought of Zoya, Venichka lost even his sense of humor.

"Don't you think," I asked once, "that the heroes of communist propaganda are just refashioned ascetic figures from the Church calendar? What do you say about the real martyrs? Have they also, in your opinion, perverted that which is human?"

Venia made a face and didn't answer.

He often spoke not only of forgiveness, but normalcy and even the praiseworthiness of cowardice, and about how man

---

[16]   Zoya Kosmodemyanskaya (1923–1941) was one of the most celebrated heroes of the Soviet Union. While still a schoolgirl, she volunteered for a partisan unit at the Soviet Western Front and in 1941 received an assignment to burn the village of Petrishchevo, where a German cavalry regiment was stationed. While attempting to execute the assignment, Zoya was caught by the Germans and, two days later, hanged. When Stalin learned of Zoya's execution and heroism, he declared her a "people's heroine" and initiated a propaganda campaign in her honor, posthumously awarding her the order of Hero of the Soviet Union.

[17]   Here Sedakova compares Erofeev's ironic worship of Zoya to Alexander Blok's worship of the "Beautiful Lady" in his *Verses on a Beautiful Lady* (1898–1904) in which the poet anticipates a new world illuminated by her essence—the Eternal Feminine.

[18]   Maxim Gorky (1868–1936) was a writer, playwright, newspaper columnist, and political activist whose works served as models for subsequent propagandistic literature written in the Soviet period. His "Song of the Stormy Petrel" (1901) is an allegorical romantic prose poem that celebrates revolutionary struggle. Thanks in part to this poem, Gorky became known as "The Stormy Petrel," in other words, "the harbinger of the stormy revolution" of 1917.

[19]   This aphorism is from Gorky's play *The Lower Depths* (1902).

should not be subjected to trials and tribulations. Was it a rebellion against communist stoicism, against the valor and "recklessness of the brave," for which we had to repay not only the reckless and courageous, but the millions of rational and uncourageous? (After all, we were taught to demonstrate such courage at other people's expense since our school years: "it's nothing, they'll endure it"; it's nothing that they'll execute all the people of Petrishchevo for the beautiful Zoya, or that, for the diligent Stakhanov,[20] make his colleagues' lives a living hell—the important thing is that there will always be a place on earth for heroic deeds!) Or was it that courage and self-sacrifice in their purest forms were intolerable for Venia? I still do not know . . .

Amongst the writings of Pascal (Venia's favorite) there reads: "As soon as you wish to make an angel of man, you get a brute."[21] One might add: "As soon as you wish to find in man an angel, you come across a brute." "Angelness" is an unfortunate fruit of the European idealism of the last century in relation to man. The brutality of the twentieth century—both the theoretical (the philosophy of "life") and the practical (the GULAGs, the Treblinka,[22] and even peaceful mass society)—got its revenge for this "angelization," for this attempt to represent man as that which was not at all in his virtues. And, having not encountered this desired angel in anyone, we, lovers of "ideals," already see in its place something unbearably base; having not found this angel in ourselves, we decide life is not worth living. Venia very much loved my irrevocable disappointments in people, authors, and works; he called them my "Cleopatra complex."

"It was alright," he would say after my unrestrained praise of somebody. "Soon 'the lucky man's head will fall off.'"[23]

---

20   Aleksei Stakhanov (1906–1977) was a miner and Hero of Socialist Labor. He became a symbol of worker productivity in 1935 when he reportedly mined a record amount of coal in less than six hours and exceeded his quota by fourteen times. He became a popular image in Soviet propaganda as a model for workers to emulate.

21   See Blaise Pascal's *Pensées* (1669).

22   Treblinka was an extermination camp in occupied Poland during World War II.

23   Erofeev here is quoting Pushkin's retelling of the Cleopatra myth in his *Egyptian Nights* (1836).

In Venia's emphasis on the "too human" as the "chiefly human" (and not something that is beastly or scurrilous), there was something therapeutic. I cannot say, however, that in my case this course of treatment for "angelness" turned out successfully. For example, I know that Venia would have loved Mandelstam more had he known of his last verses to Stalin. For me the discovery of the "Savelovo Notebooks" was a profound grief.[24] It would be better for it to have all ended as we knew it before that . . . Leniency still does not hold a place in my heart—though I suppose I can understand it rationally . . .

In this point—"Love us warts and all"—Venia found a kindred soul: Vasily Vasilievich Rozanov.[25] A sharp national self-consciousness drew him to Rozanov.

"After all, it's not me; it's us they're judging," he said after reading a foreign article about himself.

He generally had a very strong Russian identity. For him such categories remained real, like "we" and "them" ("them" being Europe). He in all seriousness said: "We taught them how to write novels (Dostoevsky), music (Mussorgsky) and everything else." But, like many very Russian people, he was drawn to "them." He did not like "ancient piety" and did not even take the trouble to get to know it better. Christian civilization for him was embodied in Dante, Pascal, Aquinas, and Chesterton—not in Russia. How many times he said, "I will never understand what they find in Rublev's

---

[24]   Osip Mandelstam (1891–1938), one of the most significant Russian poets of the twentieth century, was well respected by his peers, but not well known during his lifetime due to the suppression of his work and his arrest in 1934. The "Savelovo notebooks" to which Sedakova refers is a collection of ten or eleven poems Mandelstam wrote in Savelovo, where he and his wife, Nadezhda Mandelstam lived after his exile (1934–37). The discovery of these poems in the 1970s was controversial: they are not only addressed to another woman, Lilia Popova, but contain pro-Stalin sentiments. Although Mandelstam had already penned pro-Stalin verse (1937's "Ode to Stalin") in an attempt to ingratiate himself to the state, he later asked N. E. Shtempel', the keeper of the ode, to destroy it.

[25]   Vasily Rozanov (1856–1919) writer, philosopher, and critic known for his controversial views on religion and sex and occasional outbursts of anti-Semitism.

Trinity![26] (Though, he also said, "I'll never understand all the fuss over Bach!" Whenever I played Bach's preludes, however, he did not at all listen with indifference.) In his Russianness there was nothing of the soil, nothing of the old patriarchal tradition, nothing of what is *en vogue* now. He did not experience tenderness for "the people," and "Russian" did not mean "peasant" for him. Venichka never came across a Peasant Marey,[27] and, of that which is ascribed to "cultural heritage" —

> *Tall tales and bylini*[28]
> *Of Orthodox past*[29]

—he preferred tall tales. Actual concrete, historical people were something "completely different" for him: he professed that he did not even know how to communicate with them; and among the so-called "simple folk" he favored only extreme cases: those who had ruined themselves by drinking, little fools, and the like. To be Russian for him most likely meant something Dostoevskian: indeed, it is not difficult to imagine the protagonist of *Moscow–Petushki* amongst Dostoevsky's heroes. And in Venia himself there glimmered sometimes something of Versilov[30]—and sometimes

[26]   *Trinity* is a famous Russian Holy Trinity Icon, believed to be created by the Russian painter Andrei Rublev, in the fifteenth century. It depicts the three angels who visited Abraham at the oak of Mamre (Genesis 18:1–15).

[27]   "The Peasant Marey" (1876) is a reminiscence, frequently published as a work of fiction, from Fyodor Dostoevsky's *Writer's Diary*. It is about a young boy (Dostoevsky) who, while running away from what he thinks is a wolf, comes across the peasant Marey. Marey comforts the boy and assures him there are no wolves. In the story Marey comes to represent the strong empathy and culture of the peasantry.

[28]   A *bylina* is a traditional Russian oral epic song.

[29]   These lines are from Alexander Pushkin's poem, "Matchmaker Ivan, as soon as we begin to drink..." (1833).

[30]   Andrei Versilov is a character from Dostoevsky's *Adolescent* (1875). Though a privileged landowner, he is often surrounded by controversy due to his womanizing and rumored Catholicism; he is also the biological father of the protagonist, Arkady Dolgoruky (whose mother is a servant).

something of Stavrogin.[31] He sympathized very much with Dmitry Pisarev,[32] while he hated Chernyshevsky and Dobrolyubov[33] almost as much as he hated Zoya. Such was his paradoxical division of the *raznochinets* cohort[34] — and it was not an empty caprice.

I believe that Venia's Grief with good reason could be called a Russian Grief, and, more precisely: a New Russian Grief. The nightmare of the communist epoch was the Grief that he experienced daily. It was as if he did not divert his eyes from the entire avalanche of brutality, stupidity and sacrilege committed by his people. One could go mad more seriously than Hamlet at such a sight and, in the time remaining, "simulate sanity," as Venichka described his own behavior. And most terrible of all was that there was no end to it in sight.

"We'll die and they'll still have only one foot in the grave," he said whenever anyone said that the regime did not have much longer. Everything metamorphosed from one ugliness to another and promised to do so eternally, until full victory. A nonconformist of those years (which were slyly called the years of "stagnation") was surrounded by a terrible society. Venichka was to the highest degree a nonconformist — one who talks about rope, whether he is in the house of a hanged man or in the house of a hangman — and, as all nonconformists remember, the surrounding society was possibly

---

[31]   Nikolai Stavrogin is the central character in Dostoevsky's *Demons* (1872), who is characterized by pristine beauty and almost sociopathic indifference, both of which give him the upper hand in all of his relationships, whether personal, romantic, or political. He considers the powerful influence he holds over people, however, not to be an advantage or an honor, but an undeserved burden, and, eventually commits suicide.

[32]   Dmitrii Pisarev (1840–68) was a literary critic, materialist and positivist who believed that literature should influence real life.

[33]   Nikolai Chernyshevsky (1828–89) and Nikolai Dobroliubov (1836–61) were, like Pisarev, critics of the radical camp of literary critics in the mid-nineteenth century. Chernyshevsky authored the influential socialist utopian novel *What is to be Done?* (1863).

[34]   *Raznochintsy* (literally, "people of various ranks") were generally educated people who were not of noble birth. They comprised a significant portion of the Russian *intelligentsia* in the nineteenth century.

a bit more terrible than the legendary KGB. In its hatred of that which "isn't ours" and the "incomprehensible," in its readiness to condemn anyone who "wanted more," it surpassed the commands from above. And a loyal member of such a society was assured of his own rectitude with extraordinary force. Doubts were unknown to him.

Now that these strongholds of self-affirmation, this "faith," these "ideals" and "principles" have collapsed like a house of cards, I look around and I search: where are they? Where are our denouncers? Where are these "honest people"? (With heavy reproach they said, "I am an honest man." "I have lived a respectable life.") Are these "patriots"? Are these "wise men"? (They said, "You need to know life." "If you had my experience . . .") Are these "good family men"? "Humble and responsible workers"? Where are these individuals, openly dangerous and secretly fearful, ready to confront whomever necessary? The streets and stores were filled with them, educational institutions, bureaus . . . Where are their cordial and cheerful songs, films, and poetry? . . .

Confusion, misery, simple childish animosity (and not the former grownup, lordly animosity)—that is what is now in place of all that . . . Will something new really bring back their notorious "faith" and "ideals"—that is, the possibility to turn their backs on conscience and reality—for the sake of "spirituality," for the sake something else . . .

Venia's hatred of "virtue" ("You diamonds will sink, and we, the shit, will float on") can only be understood in this sequence of events. He hated the virtues of the collaborators (and the collaborators were, generally, all of society), because that was the most sinister parody of virtue one could imagine. It was only after Nuremberg that history learned how an active participant of a crime can consider himself, and be considered by all, to be "a personally respectable person"—and indeed *be* a respectable person in everything, except that which is essential. What it is like to live amongst such respectable people only a nonconformist can explain. And in a world where one must pay for everything by selling one's soul (incidentally, for a long time Venia was considering a plan for a *Russian Faust*, of which the sketches are now lost), by practicing

Satanism, or conniving with it, or, at the worst, keeping silent about it—what way of life would seem even a little bit acceptable to one's conscience? A slow perishing, if speaking in all seriousness.

> *We didn't promise to take the barrier,*
> *We will perish openly.*[35]

But, of course, that's not all about Venia's Grief. He once asked me:

"For you, it's as if some things are still serious. How is that possible?"

"Why not?"

"What can be serious when the main thing already happened . . . 194 . . . (I don't have Venia's memory for dates) years ago?"

"But that which you have in mind is not the end," I objected. "It's as if you didn't read past Good Friday."

"But you," Venia answered, "read about Christmas and then went straight to Easter, and skipped everything in between."

The Nietzschean phrase everyone is sick of—"God is dead"—in Venia's version would have gone something like this: "God is murdered."

But we generally had no concern for such topics and only touched on it that one time by accident. "Drink and hold your tongue," Venia, quoting Blok,[36] would usually interrupt any "conceptual" conversation. Or without Blok: "Better to eat your apple; eat, it's more becoming of you than talking about smart things . . ." He, by the way, very much loved to feed everyone; already from the doorway he would ask, "I suppose you're hungry?"

For me Venia was least of all a writer. That may seem strange, but everyone who knew him well enough, I think, would agree with me. Venia himself was more significant than his works. Rather, if they became significant, it was only thanks to the presence of his personality—in the text, behind the text, over the text (need one say that the personality of a writer *par excellence* can be completely

---

[35]   Here Sedakova quotes Boris Pasternak's poem, "Autumn" (1949).

[36]   This is a line from Alexander Blok's play *The Unknown Woman* (1906).

uninteresting to the reader? There operates a certain energy in his plots.) But, of course, not all of his personality is present there. Those who knew Venia saw what in principle cannot be in a work: his reactions to circumstances that came from without, his reactions to any encountered trifle. It wasn't necessarily in words (and with Venia, who shunned all lofty and straightforward words, it was most often not in words): it lay in a gesture, in an intonation, in a look, in silence. And all these life answers, which cannot be retold—alive, unprejudiced, strikingly delicate and precise—are what is unforgettable in Venia. And it's not something you can put into words.

And—what would Venia have said upon seeing these recollections?

"Better to keep quiet, stupid woman!"

Or:

"You didn't understand a thing."

Or:

"This is all nonsense, but I've got an idea . . ."

And we would have gone and tried to get a ration card for some vodka . . .

Translation and notes by Sarah H. Kapp

Mikhail Epshtein
(b. 1950, Moscow)

Prominent Russian-American literary and cultural scholar, critic, and philosopher. Graduated from the School of Philology, Moscow State University in 1972. Author of more than twenty books and six hundred articles, Epshtein is a leading theorist of Russian postmodernism. Since 1990, he has lived in the United States. A distinguished Professor of Russian Studies at Emory University, Epstein has been awarded numerous literary prizes, among them, the Andrei Bely Prize (1991) and the Liberty Award for his contributions to Russian-American culture (2000).

From "Charms of Entropy"[1]

3. The Myth of the Hangover

Although the myth of "Venia" has gradually taken on definite form, it nevertheless shares many of the attributes of the myths of Esenin, Vysotsky, and even the unsuccessful myth of Nikolai Rubtsov. All four burned themselves out, dissipated themselves, fell into darkness in order to behold the last saving light, as is recommended in Eastern "negative" theology, where God is represented as a "no" — as the negation of light, honor, cleanliness, dignity, wisdom and goodness, since all of these virtues have already been taken over by the Philistines and serve their abominable un-Christian prosperity in a Christian world. And only the holy fool makes his way to God, casting off all propriety, as well as his outer and sometimes even his under garments.

But "Venichka" had something that did not fit the framework of the widely respected myths of "Seriozha" (Esenin) and "Volodia" (Vysotsky). If nothing else, there was his name, "Venichka," which he himself immortalized. Who else would have dared to present himself under such an affectionate diminutive in our cynical times, in a circle of drunks and brawlers—and then to pass for a hero

[1]   Published in: Alexander Genis, Mikhail Epstein, and Slobodanka Vladiv-Glover, *Russian Postmodernism: New Perspectives on Post-Soviet Culture*, ed. and trans. Slobodanka Vladiv-Glover (Oxford and New York: Berghahn Books, 1999), 427–42.

among them? Later, another writer, following in Erofeev's footsteps, began to peddle a myth about himself by appropriating Erofeev's intonation: "It's me, Edichka." But the first one to refer to himself with such meek pathos was "Venichka" Erofeev.

He did not like hyperbole at all, preferring litotes and diminutives. Moreover, the relationship of an author to words begins with his relationship to his own name, which in this case represented a bashful attempt to disarm others and to negate himself. And so Venia writes: "there were little birdies," "there were two little chaps," or he affixes the epithets "a tiny little red," "a little cold one" to his favorite beverage. Although one might write off these litotes as drunken sentimentality, aimed at inspiring the same sort of worship for banquet glassware as for one's own children— "a little cup," "wa-wa," etc.—the fact remains that never before in Russian literature had revelry been expressed in such a sentimental, non-hyperbolic form.

The proverbial holy fool, including his poetic double, is often captured in the clichéd gesture of tearing the shirt from his chest to free his sincere, burning soul from all constrictions. By contrast, Venichka always held up his collar, out of embarrassment perhaps and so as not to bare his throat? ". . . Young and handsome, he always bashfully covered his throat, holding together the buttonless collar of his shirt," "And if his top button came off, Venia would hold his collar with his hand so that it would not come open. This was his trademark gesture." This is so unlike Seriozha (Esenin) and Volodia (Vysotsky); they would tear off their collars; they would drive their horses into a lather and tear the bridles off. In them was something of the jaunty spirit of revelry of the beginning of the twentieth century, the hysteria of the superhuman and the urgent desire to burn the candle at both ends in order to put out the light a little sooner. Only in his last years did Vysotsky start to recite: "Slow down, steeds, slow down." But his voice nevertheless broke into a back-breaking scream, as if with one hand he held the horses back and with the other lashed them forward.

But with Venichka one really gets an unambiguous sense of slowness. To be slow and to be incorrect was his credo. "Everything on earth should occur slowly and incorrectly so that a person would

be unable to grow proud, so that man would be sad and confused."
When someone is convinced of his righteousness, he usually tries
to set about things as quickly as possible: this is heroic success and
youthful vitality. But in Venia there was not a trace of heroism,
not even of that upside-down, decadent form that usually coexists
historically with the kind of straightforward heroism whose aim
is to teach. For Venichka, Maxim Gorky, whom he did not like,
was just as alien as Igor Severianin, whom he did like. He was as
far from the thrills of the summit as he was from the thrills of the
abyss; as far also from Blok and Esenin, who divided themselves
between heights and depths; far from righteous writers and rowdy
singers. Any regularity perturbed him deeply. He ran from sobriety
but did not fall into the opposite temptation, into the heroism of
decadence—of rowdy chaos, of fiery intoxication. He drank but was
not prone to drunken rage, or the exaltation of love-friendship or
dangerous, hoarse courage. He drank more than his predecessors
but he no longer got drunk. He was thus like a sober man, but one
who is sober from the other end, not before drinking, but after it.
Not a self-assured sober man, but one who has gone quiet, sad,
and timid.

This sort of meekness was the kind he most appreciated in
others, a meekness authentically known only to the drunk; or rather,
the drunk who is gradually coming out of his drunken delirium.
Venia's state of glory was not the drinking binge, but the *hangover*,
the delicate and over-scrupulous accounting for all previous binges,
his own and others'. Any revelry going on around him, drunken
ecstasies and the torn collar, thrilled him even less than the feats
of Zoya Kosmodemyanskaya. In the dialectic of sobriety and
drunkenness, the ultimate level is the hangover: the negation of
negation.

Let us investigate the stages of this dialectic that inexorably
leads from arrogance to meekness. Drinking is a means of driving
out the demon of arrogance from a sober man who stands firmly on
his own feet, who speaks clearly and deliberately, living as if he had
complete mastery over his body and soul. But he need only take
a drink and *voila*: our good man will soon realize that things are
not so obedient to him after all. Strut as he might with his worldly

privileges; boast as he will about trampling the earth underfoot and mastering the meaning of things: gone is the arrogance of sobriety.

But what remains in reserve is the arrogance of drunkenness. Now the old friend does not care a damn, his lips are on fire with his own wit, his gaze burning from his own seductive powers: again the whole world spreads itself before him, but this time on an undulating road. He now feels light and confident precisely by virtue of not being in control.

After which the sobering-up begins and, "with disgust reciting the story of my life . . ." There is not a trace left of those earlier witticisms and fiery glances! Only drunken hiccups and winks exchanged with some plastered lassie. At first drinking knocked the arrogance out of the sober man, then sobriety knocked the arrogance out of the drunk, and finally, through the torments of shame, the third stage of this great synthesis is ushered in—the *hangover*. The sorrowful and wise hangover, simultaneously boring and illuminating. All a man can do at this stage is sigh, cooling himself by imbibing fresh air without polluting the air around him with his own breath. ". . . I sighed, sighed so deeply, that I almost dislocated everything I had."

Such is this sly dialectic. Venia knocks out of himself, and out of those around him, first sober arrogance and then drunken arrogance. He dislodges both types of arrogance, sober and drunken, finally arriving at the hangover, a state of extreme meekness. The one who suffers from a hangover is fastidious towards himself and consequently totally forgiving towards his neighbor. The one who suffers from a hangover offends no one; on the contrary, like a child he is offended by everyone. He is so weakened that he begins to display something virginal—a ticklishness and nervous sensitivity toward the slightest touch.

Venia, for example, was horribly touchy and feared tickling more than anything else. "I have a lot of ankles and armpits. I have them everywhere. An honest man must have a lot of ankles and armpits and must fear tickling." Who before him in Russia was so ticklish, defending his honor laughing and kicking like a little girl? Not even Lermontov, Blok, or Gumilev, the most sublime of poets, was so ticklish. They created myths of the eternal feminine but had nothing of that kind of girlishness in them. Venia, afraid of the slightest touch, quivering and guffawing, was entirely virginal. It is with this quality that he partakes of that "eternal-womanly" (*vechno-bab'ie*) quality of the Russian soul. Through him, however, "womanliness" ceases to be a quality of the mature woman and becomes, once again, a quality of the young maiden. From the point of view of a being consisting entirely of ankles and armpits, the entire world now seems rude in the light of this "womanly" softness and delicacy. What other man could be so fragile and so sensitive just because of a hangover?

> "Why are they all so rude? Huh? And why so in particular, so emphatically rude, just at such a time when it is impossible to be rude, when a man with a hangover has all his nerves exposed, when he is faint-hearted and timid? Why is it so?"

It is strange: not only did Venia sense the rudeness of those around him, but those around him, even the most refined of them, such as the poet Olga Sedakova, sensed their own rudeness when they were in Venia's proximity. ". . . Next to him it was impossible not to sense one's own rudeness: the contrast was impressive."

It must be said that neither of Venia's typical states, namely that of being "drunk or with a hangover," led to a loss of sobriety. Essentially, it was a single prolonged state, comprised of three stages: drinking, sobering up, suffering a hangover. "I, having tasted so much in this world that I have lost count and track—I am more sober than anyone in this world; sobriety just has a troubling effect on me . . ." "Venia himself never got drunk. He did not permit himself to. He regarded the onset of dullheadedness, the drunken muttering and pestering as ill-mannered and boorish . . . . One of the virtues of our circle of friends was not getting drunk . . ."

This is where the myth of Venichka truly begins—the myth about his *non-inebriety*, which must not be confused with simple, unconcerned sobriety. Sobriety is before, and *non-inebriety* occurs afterwards. Sobriety is self-righteous and didactic, while *non-inebriety* is meek and depressed. Sobriety can be under delusion and still get drunk on itself: non-inebriety can no longer get drunk on anything. And this is the highest state of the soul: when it has the fewest possible worldly ambitions and altogether very little animation (which comes from *anima* — "spirit," "breath") left in it — the state of faint-heartedness or lack of spirit [*malodushie*]:

> Oh, if only the entire world, if everyone in the world were like me right now — timid and shy and unsure of everything: of himself, of the seriousness of his place under the heavens — how good it would be! No enthusiasts, no heroic feats, no obsessions! — a universal faint-heartedness. I would agree to live on earth for all eternity if they'd show me a little corner where there is not always room for a heroic feat. "Universal faint-heartedness" — this is really the salvation from all misfortunes, this is a panacea, the predicate of the greatest perfection!

Faint-heartedness is not as bad as it seems, and must not be confused with cowardliness. A coward is afraid for himself while one who is faint-hearted is afraid for everything on earth. His soul simply sinks to his boots when he touches a fragile vase or meets an intelligent person — as if he might somehow tear something, misplace something, injure something or someone. A faint-hearted person is delicate because more than anything else he fears offending someone. He does not have enough spirit to assume responsibility or to harbor a secret ambition.

4. Trans-irony

At the center of the Venia myth is just this delicacy, an extremely rare and still little noticed attribute of Russian culture. There is a lot of holiness and sin in it, much illumination and darkness, heights and depths, but little delicacy. Try to say that Tolstoy or Dostoevsky was delicate: it would sound funny applied to such prophetic giants. Although there may have been some delicacy in them, it rarely came into view. As for the delicacy of a Chekhov or Timiriazev, of a doctor or a scholar, they simply could not have been other than delicate in the delicate circumstances of their time and profession.

But Venia's kind of delicacy, when he eats and drinks in the hallway of a train car because he feels shy in front of other passengers, is of a totally different kind. When he sighs bitterly over the vulgar "uncircumcised hearts," when he conceals from his drinking buddies his *sorties* prompted "by the call of nature," not daring to put into words his secret desires, Venichka is delicate in all respects—so delicate that he does not announce to his friends his intention to go to the bathroom. And even more delicately, he agrees to go to the bathroom only in order not to oppress them with his delicacy.

Such delicacy in a person who by all indications ought not to and cannot be delicate, is something phenomenal and, at the same time, as Venia would say, something noumenal. This is a manifestation of a new kind of delicacy, turning Venia into the hero of an altogether indelicate milieu. If this delicacy had emanated from somewhere outside, from the realm of authority or high morality, it would be a simple object of ridicule. But here it emanates from the very heart of "plebeianism, of debauchery, and rebellion"—from Venichka himself, who is tasting both "A Komsomolka's Tear" and "Aunt Klava's Kiss," as well as other cocktails, some infused with shampoo, others with methyl alcohol, brake fluid, or something to prevent sweaty feet. Delicacy in such a creature is not a tribute to tradition or family, to upbringing or social norms. It cannot be obsolete. It cannot be edifying. It is other-worldly. "From my other-worldly point of view. . ." as Venia used to say.

Coming from Venia, even the words "infant," "angels," "sorrow" or "sigh," were not old-fashioned or pompous. He spoke often of ". . . immortal angels and dying children . . ." Who in the Soviet period would call his son an "infant" [*mladenets*], and his inner voices "angels"? Such words have not been in circulation since the time of the romantic and symbolist poets, such as Vasily Zhukovsky or Alexander Blok. These words reached Venia through a barrier of so much filth, verbal rot, and decay, that one involuntarily hears irony in them. Venia, however, does not use them ironically. To perceive irony in these pure words would be simply vulgar. What would be more appropriate here is the word "counter-irony" (*protivoironiia*) as suggested by Erofeev's friend, the philologist Muraviev. One might propose an even stronger term—"trans-irony"—indicating not just the opposition to irony, but rather a movement beyond irony, its sublation (to use Hegel's term). If irony inverts the sense of a straightforward, serious word, then trans-irony inverts the sense of irony itself, resurrecting seriousness—but now without its direct and monosemantic character. Trans-irony is not simply a denial of irony. Rather it is the metalevel of irony, which presupposes an irony toward irony itself and, therefore, a polysemantic play of literal and figurative meanings. Here, for example, is a dialogue between Venichka and the Lord:

> I took everything I had out of the suitcase and felt it: from a sandwich to the stout rosé at a ruble thirty-seven. Touched everything and began to languish. Again I touched it all—and I withered. . . . Lord, here you see what I possess. But do I really need *this*? Is *this* really what my soul is longing for? This is what people have given me instead of what my soul is longing for! And if they'd given me *that*, would I really have needed *this*? Look, Lord, here: the stout rosé for a ruble thirty-seven . . .
> And, all in blue flashes of lightning, the Lord answered me:
> "And what did Saint Theresa need stigmata for? She did not need them either, yet she desired them."
> "Yes, that's it!" I answered in delight. "Me too, me too—I desire it, but I do not need it in the least!"
> "Well, since it's desired, Venichka, go on and drink," I thought quietly, but was still slow to act. "Is the Lord going to say something more to me: or not?"
> The Lord was silent.

If one were so inclined, one could find a lot of irony in this passage. The stout rosé and the stigmata of Saint Theresa are so different that it would seem impossible to compare them without sinking into pathos. But at the same time: what exactly is being ridiculed? Where is the irony? In the stout rosé? That would be stupid. Saint Theresa? That would be even more stupid. It is as if the irony is implied, but only as a shade of trans-irony, as its expressive nuance. Trans-irony works with irony the same way that irony works with seriousness, lending it a different sense. The initially serious subtext can be read this way: "O, Saint Theresa! Ugh! Worthless Venichka!" Irony shifts the accents: everyone has his/her own pink spirits, one has stout rosé, another has stigmata. Trans-irony again shifts the accent: everyone has his/her own stigmata, one has holes in her hands and feet, another has stout rosé. It cannot be said that trans-irony restores the same level of seriousness as existed before the injection of irony. On the contrary, trans-irony immediately rejects both trivial seriousness and vulgar irony, establishing a new point of view—"God's point of view." What man does not need, he desires. Both holiness and drunkenness are located in this *gap* between need and desire. The greatest man is not too big for this gap, and the least worthy man is not too small for it.

Venia's entire style is made up of the kind of trans-irony that uses ready-made ironic clichés as its material. They have become just as ossified in social consciousness as have weighty, pathos-laden clichés. The two possible modes of receptions of the words "fatherland" or "Soviet power," for instance, have been frozen into clichéd gestures: either that of standing at attention or of sniggering behind one's hand. Venia, however, endows these words with a new intonation, which is neither serious nor ironic, but "otherworldly," so to speak, from beyond the grave:

> "Erofeev, as to the beloved Soviet government—to what extent did it fall in love with you when your fame became international?"
>
> "It decidedly paid no attention to me whatsoever. I love my government."
>
> "Why in particular do you love it?"
>
> "For everything."
>
> "Because it did not touch you and did not send you to prison?"
>
> "For that I especially love it. I am prepared to love my government for everything. [. . .]"
>
> "Where does this unrequited love of yours come from?"
>
> "In my opinion, it's requited, as far as I can see. I hope that it's requited, or else what's there for me to live for."

This is an excerpt from an interview in *Kontinent*, which at the time was still being published in Paris. The interviewer tries in every way to get Venia "to kid," but Venia does not succumb to the temptation of cheap irony, any more than to the temptation of patriotic pride or pain. He answers the interviewer's absurd questions in the manner of souls at a spiritistic séance. His intonation is unassailably flat, disengaged. This precisely is trans-irony, which leaves just enough room for irony in order to signal its inappropriateness.

5. The Carnival Transcended

Trans-irony is a new quality of the Venia myth—and of the ritual performance associated with it. Any myth, scholars assert, is the verbal record and ideological justification of a certain rite. In this sense the Venichka myth signifies a new rite of passage for the initiation of the young. Initiation is a dedication, a rite of entry into the social life and adulthood. Noble youths of the nineteenth century, leaving the cozy domestic realm and setting out on the path of masculine initiation, tried to be as coarse as possible. They swilled vodka and went visiting gypsy girls (think of Pierre Bezukhov in the first volume of *War and Peace).* Youths of the late Soviet period were also swilling vodka at a tender age. But they had no need to go visiting anywhere, everything was right next door in the dormitory: remember the way of life described by Venia and his friends!

Venichka's initiation began just where the initiation of the heroes of classic Russian literature left off, namely at the tavern-brothel, the dormitory-public house. While remaining within this familiar space, Venia however turned it inside-out, suddenly revealing the glimmering features of an aristocratic youth through the intoxicated and violent haze. It is almost as if we were going back to the sentimental era of Karamzin and Radishchev. Yes, ladies and gentlemen, reckless young people also know how to feel: "For if someone has an overscrupulous heart . . ."

In those days, at the end of the 1960s and throughout the 1970s, the typical initiation of the young was called "Rabelaisation." It was based on Bakhtin's carnival theory and its association with the corporeal and comic depths of folk culture. All the orifices of the body had to be opened up to ingest and expel the flow of the universal circulation of matter. Drunkenness is only a small metaphor for the gushing excess with which Bakhtin, in his book-myth on Rabelais, associates such things as puking, spitting, sweating, snot, sneezing, gluttony, copulation, defecation, farting, and so on.

All of this, however, Venia found terribly embarrassing. He was "unbelievably shy even in front of himself." And he used to say that the person who deserves the most tenderness is "the one who pees in his pants in front of everyone." What Venia did was turn the values, which had been turned upside down by a carnivalesque culture, the right way up again. The carnival appreciated this, as if it had not noticed that, around Venia, carnival ceased to be a carnival. Timidity that was expelled in a burst of obscenities is now extended to obscenity itself. "Tenderness toward the one who peed in his pants." Understandably, this is not the same as tenderness towards a sprig of lilac. It is tenderness that makes a detour around sentimentality, via the distance of carnival. However, this is no longer carnival either, but its afterlife. All former attributes, overturned by carnival, are now resurrected in a new, "noumenal" dimension. The tenderness and grief, weeping and timidity, loneliness and boredom are already transcendental, liberated from any attachment to their former objects.

Take, for example, sadness: what made Erofeev sad? He knew that every creature experiences post-coital sadness. This natural law was observed by Aristotle. But Venia, unlike Aristotle, "[was] constantly sad, before and after coitus." Or, for example, a person usually feels animated when thoughts rush to his head whereas Venia would break out with the following confession: "Thoughts were pressing in my head, pressing so hard that I got depressed . . ."

It is as if all the things for which people once had feelings had been torn away from Venia and placed at a distance of historic proportions. It is as if the necessary correspondence between feelings and objects had been abolished. Feelings are resurrected following the death of feelings, and the heart of man does not know to what to attach them. To what should grief be attached — to a child's tiny tear, as in Dostoevsky's *Brothers Karamazov*, or to "A Komsomolka's Tear," Venia's favorite cocktail? Venia, not wanting to miss the mark, grieves for everything simultaneously. Thus his sadness applies both to sad things and to things that are not sad at all, although his feeling is no less sad for it, perhaps now only otherworldly. It stands on the other side of former feelings, which have been dulled, cut off or torn out. What feelings are possible after the Holocaust, after the revolution, after Auschwitz and Kolyma: what kind of sadness is left? But then sadness opens "two enormous eyes" (O. Mandelstam) and searches for its object, about which it still knows nothing. Who said that there must be a strict correspondence between an object and a feeling, as in classicism?

Even ordinary language does not manifest such a correspondence. Every sign, according to the founder of contemporary linguistics, Ferdinand de Saussure, is arbitrary, and any word can signify any object. Why then can sadness not refer to a happy object, and to a mundane object, and to a funny object, and to an entirely indifferent one? Is it not a sad thing if it is so indifferent? And is it not sad if it is so funny? Why can sorrow not refer to wine and merriment to stigmata? There is nothing carnivalesque here. It is simply another level of feelings. Meta-emotions.

Perhaps Venia himself did not notice this new post-carnivalesque transformation of his feelings—but Mikhail Bakhtin, who had an extraordinarily keen sense for everything carnivalesque, did. He was delighted by Erofeev's long poem, finding in it support for his theories of carnival and an expression of pure pantagruelism. In the poem, Venia is frequently occupied with rinsing his throat. Is this not reminiscent of Pantagruel, both in the proper and dictionary definition of his name? For the word "pantagruel," before being given to Rabelais' hero, was the name of a throat disease—the loss of one's voice as a result of heavy drinking (a drunkard's disease). If only Bakhtin could have known to what degree the prophetic meaning of this name would be embodied in Erofeev's own destiny! The loss of voice towards the end, followed by several operations—which Erofeev survived—and finally death from cancer of the larynx. It was as if the essence of pantagruelism had been literally re-enacted down to the smallest detail of Erofeev's own life.

Nonetheless, despite being fatally doomed to the grotesque, Erofeev in a way escaped it. The phenomenon of Venichka, growing out of pantagruelism, outgrows it, contingent precisely its literal and concrete embodiment. The carnival itself becomes an object of the carnivalesque, and with this it moves into the realm of a strange new seriousness.

It is significant that Bakhtin, delighted by the poem, did not approve of its denouement, because the hero appears to die "for real," and "entropy" seems to enter "carnival." But what kind of seriousness can there be in carnival? What kind of entropy can there be in the midst of the carnivalesque splash of pent-up energies? Nevertheless, one can discern entropy and a fading of energy in

Venia himself long before the end of the poem. Venia's shyness amidst carnivalesque revelry: is that not entropy? What has become poeticized is not debauchery: it is the "man with a hangover . . . who is faint-hearted and quiet." And this poetics of "universal faint-heartedness" is, from the carnivalesque point of view, sheer entropy. The great Bakhtin sensed this, too, although he failed to appreciate its new value. He saw in Erofeev something kindred that was turning into something unfamiliar. He sensed that here carnival had ceased to be carnivalesque.

The critic Andrei Zorin has remarked that, contrary to the laws of carnival, "elements of folk laughter in the end deceive the hero and expel him. Such an ending is foreshadowed from the beginning." It is even more accurate to say that from beginning to end it is the author who deceives and expels the elements of folk culture. Insofar as the author and the hero are one, they do this together. The hero withdraws from the mob by escaping onto the platform of the train carriage. The author distances himself from the folk element [*narodnaia stikhiia*] by escaping into the space of artistic understatement (the litotes and diminutives). Together they alienate themselves from the masses through the name of "Venichka," as well as through flight into a private melancholy and a lyrical state of confusion and perplexity. Folk laughter [*smekh*], no less than folk diligence [*spekh*]—indeed the entire popular universe, filled with characters such as Vasily Terkin, Zoya Kosmodemyanskaya and Aleksei Stakhanov—are equally alien to Venichka, who loves slowness and irregularity. As for his entropy: is it really such a bad thing?

Translated by Slobodanka Vladiv-Glover

Dmitry A. Prigov
(1940, Moscow — 2007, Moscow)

One of the most important figures in the Russian underground culture of the 1970s–80s who effectively continued his artistic experiments into the post-Soviet period. Came to be seen by many as the leading practitioner and theoretician of Russian postmodernism. Prigov graduated from the Sculpture Department of the Moscow Art-Industrial Institute in 1966. After graduating he actively participated in the Moscow circle of nonconformist artists and poets. He is famous for the extraordinary number of literary texts he wrote: more than thirty thousand poems, dozens of plays and narrative poems, as well as four novels, and roughly a hundred theoretical essays and manifestoes. His poetry confronts and challenges expectations associated with the poet's mission, particularly as that mission is defined in Russian culture. Prigov's poetic texts are invariably written from the standpoint of an invented (often parodic or fantastic) subject: an official Soviet poet, a loyal Soviet citizen, a fanatical neo-Nazi, a pedophile, a victim of child abuse, a "Japanese poet" (as s/he is imagined in Russian culture), an avid news junkie, a lesbian, etc. In 1986 he was arrested and sent to a mental institution for posting his ironic, yet not political, *Appeals to Citizens* (*Obrashcheniia k grazhdanam*) in public spaces. Before the late 1980s, his works circulated exclusively in *samizdat*. Prigov's first book was published in the USSR in 1990. In the 1990s–2000s, he widely published his works, participated in many exhibits as a visual and performance artist, sang opera, collaborated with musicians, lectured at many European and American universities, and acted in films. After his death, The Prigov Readings conference has been held on an annual basis. In 2012, a collection of his visual works entered into the permanent exhibition of the State Hermitage Museum in St. Petersburg.

Selected poems from *Texts of Our Life*[1]

From *The Tears of the Heraldic Soul*

In Japan I'd be Catullus
In Rome I'd be a Hokusai
And here in Russia I'm the same
As a Catullus in Japan
Or a Hokusai in Rome
Would be

Translated by Robert Reid

* * *

I'm already tired on the first line
Of the first stanza
Now I've crawled to the third line
And now to the fourth

Now I've reached the first line
Of the second stanza
Now I've dragged myself to the third line
And now, O Lord, to the end

Translated by Stuart Norgate

---

[1]   Dmitry A. Prigov, *Texts of Our Life: Bilingual Selected Poems*, edited and introduced by Valentina Polukhina (Keele: Essays in Poetics Publications, 1995), 16–33.

* * *

It's raining outside. Me and a cockroach
Are sitting staring through the moist pane
Into space where our desired country
Arises from the fog
Like distant esoteric smoke.
"Well: my dear friend, what if we fly away right now?"
I say it gently. As he answers,
"Don't feel like flying. Can only run."
"Oh, really? Well, then run,
Run if you want"

Translated by Oleg Atbashian

* * *

When a Policeman stands here at his post
An expanse opens up for him as far as Vnukovo
To the West and the East looks the Policeman
And the void behind them opens up
And the center, where the Policeman stands
From everywhere a sight of him opens up
From everywhere can be seen the Policeman
From the East can be seen the Policeman
And from the South can be seen the Policeman
Also from the sea can be seen the Policeman
Also from the sky can be seen the Policeman
Also from under the earth . . .
But he isn't hiding, is he

Translated by Stuart Norgate

* * *

In the bar of the House of Writers
A policeman is drinking beer
Drinking in his usual manner
Not even seeing these men of letters

They though are looking at him
Around Him it's bright and empty
And all their various arts
In the presence of Him count as nothing

He represents Life
Manifested in the form of Duty
Life is short, but Art is long
Yet in the battle Life will win the day

Translated by Stuart Norgate

* * *

From one side, the people are understandable
From the other, they're inexplicable
It all depends which side you're on,
Whether you find them understandable or inexplicable

But you are understandable to them
From any side. And from any side inexplicable
You're surrounded, you have no sides
So you can't be understood — or otherwise

Translated by Carol Rumens,
Nik Abu-Haidar, and Jury Drobyshev

* * *

A woman in the metro kicked me
It wasn't just a case of elbowing
That one could take—but here she went too far
And so the whole thing passed into the realms
Of quite uncalled-for personal relations
I naturally kicked her back
But at that moment begged her pardon
Being, quite simply, a superior person

Translated by Sally Laird

From *An Image of Reagan in Soviet Literature*

In the United States
A new President has been elected
In the United States
The old President is discarded

What's in it for us?—a President
A President in States United
It is a curious Pre-cedent
In the United States

Translated by Maria Marquise

A Banal Discourse on the theme
"To Be Famous Isn't Beautiful"

When you're let's say famous
It's not beautiful to be famous
But if you're not famous
Then to be famous is not only
Desirable, but beautiful too
For beauty, after all, is not the result
Of your chance of fame
Rather fame is a result
Of being beautiful, and beauty will save!
But to be famous, of course, isn't beautiful
When you're already famous

Translated by Stuart Norgate

SELECTED POEMS
FROM *WRITTEN BETWEEN 1975 AND 1989*

I got a kilo of fish salad
As I went through the kitchen
There's nothing to offend in that—
I procured, so I procured it
Ate a little bit myself
My son from the same womb
I fed with a bit of this
And we sat there by the window
Beside the transparent glass
As if we were two male kittens
To let the life below flow past.

1975

* * *

Here, I'll fry up a chicken
It's a sin to complain
But really I'm really not complaining
What am I—better than everyone?
I even feel guilty, no strength
There, off you go—here
The country ruined a whole
Chicken for me

1975

* * *

The whisk is broken, doesn't cotton
I have nothing to sweep the floor
Yet think, dammit, how I used to
Sweep the floor, in old times
There, I used to, I would sweep
Everything light around, now I—
Everything's broken, doesn't work
Don't feel like living

I struggle with the household entropy
As a source of energie divine
Blind unnoticeable powers
I conquer in unelevated struggle

I'll wash the dishes thrice a day
I'll wash and wipe the floor ubiquitously
I'll erect a sense and structure of the world
On a place, see, that would seem empty

1974

* * *

We all face the threat of freedom
Freedom without end
With no way out, with no way in
Without mother or father

In the very middle of Rus'
For the whole past century
And I am terrified of it
As a decent man.

1976

Kulikovo Field

So here I've set them all out in their places
Those ones there I've put on the right
Those ones there I've put on the left
I've left all the rest to put there later
I've left the Poles to put there later
I've left the French to put there later
And the Germans to put there later
Here I've set out my angels
And I've put ravens overhead
And I've put other birds above
While below I hand the field over
For a battle I've handed the field over
I've surrounded it with trees
Surrounded it with oaks, with firs
I've put some bushes here and there
I've spread a bed on the ground with soft grass
I've settled it with various insects
Let it all be as I've imagined
Let them all live as I've imagined
Let them all die as I've imagined

Let the Russians be victors today
After all the Russian guys aren't bad
And the Russian gals aren't bad
They've suffered a lot, the Russians
They suffered non-Russians horrors,
So today the Russians will be victors
What will be here, if already now
The earth's crumbling up already now
And the sky is dusty already now
The underground species are collapsing
And the underground waters are rushing about
And underground beasts are rushing about
And the people who live on earth are running

They run here and there on earth close to the earth
And the birds above the earth have gathered
All the birds, the ravens above the earth

But still the Tatars are rather nicer
And to me their faces are rather nicer
And to me their voices are rather nicer
And their names are rather nicer
And their habits are rather nicer
Though the Russian ones are rather neater
But still the Tatars are rather nicer
So let the Tatars be the victors
From here I will see everything
The Tatars, that is, will be the victors
And anyway—tomorrow we'll see.

1976

* * *

To burn it all away to the last bird
And to run away into your lair—
That there's the partisan principle
And higher—the partisan logos
Not to say that everyone here is occupied
With the likes, but we are partisans
In part
All
In part
Except for those rare ones, who are entirely

2006

Translated by Sibelan Forrester

Vladimir Shinkarev
(b. 1954, Leningrad)

An artist and writer. In 1984 was one of organizers of the group Mit'ki, together with the artists Dmitry Shagin, Alexander Florensky, and Olga Florenskaya. In 1985, while working in a boiler room, Shinkarev wrote the book *Mit'ki*, which played an important role in shaping the anti-ideology of the Mit'ki movement. In 1984 and 1985 the Mit'ki held annual apartment exhibitions of artwork produced by the group's members. Since 1987 they have exhibited their work in various cities in Russia and abroad. In 2008, Shinkarev broke with Shagin due to the latter's participation in the presidential campaign for the election of Dmitry Medvedev. Now, Shinkarev claims that Mit'ki was an entirely fictional movement.

From *Mit'ki*[1]

Part One

Below you will find the beginnings of a vocabulary and rules of behavior for a new mass youth movement akin to the hippies or the punks.

I propose that the participants of the movement be called mit'ki, following the name and archetypal example of Dmitry SHAGIN (his image, however, is by no means thoroughly reproduced by the substance of the movement).

The mit'ki movement promises to be more organic than the movements named above: it is impossible to fake being a mityok if you are not one; outside attributes are almost nonexistent—mit'ki wear whatever is at hand, preferably in the beatnik style of the 50s, but nothing pop-related under any circumstances.

The mityok's face alternates between two affected submissive expressions: tenderness that borders on idiocy, and sentimental dejection. All his movements and intonations, although very tender, are also energetic, and therefore the mityok always appears to be a bit drunk.

---

[1]   From: Vladimir Shinkarev, "Mit'ki," in *Mit'ki: Vybrannoe*, compiled by P. V. Krusanov (St. Petersburg: Kanon, 1999), 11–16, 43–50.

In general, every sign of life that the mityok exudes is maximally pitched so that the word or utterance sounds like an undivided growl, while his face remains just as touching.

In theory, the mityok is a highly moral personality; his worldview leans toward the formula "Orthodoxy, Autocracy, Nation," but in practice he is so thoughtless that he might appear to lack any moral anchors. However, the mityok never resorts to force; he does not purposefully cause others pain and is utterly nonaggressive.

If the mityok's feelings are hurt, he will never express indignation or displeasure directly to his offender. More likely he will tenderly, but with sadness, exclaim: "How could you, brother?" However, once out of sight he will complain, almost with tears in his eyes, that, with every accusation that was levied against him, he was "made into a shit sandwich."

Here are the words and expressions used by the mit'ki, based on the vocabulary of Dmitry Shagin:

DYK: a word that can be used in place of practically any other word or expression. DYK pronounced with a questioning intonation replaces the words *how, who, why, what for*, etc., but most often it is a sign of reproach: *how come? Why did you treat the mityok this way?* DYK with an exclamatory intonation is more often a prideful self-assurance, or agreement with his conversation partner, or it can express caution. DYK with ellipsis is an apology, an acknowledgement of having made a mistake, or committed a dirty trick, etc.

BRICKS-STICKS (usually *eh, bricks-sticks*; or even more often *eh, brickies-stickies*): second-most-used expression. Expresses insult, regret, delight, apology, fear, joy, anger, and so on. Multiple repetitions are typical. For example, while the mityok searches for a misplaced item, he continually exclaims, in an extremely expressive fashion: *"eh, brickies-stickies!"* Very often, it is used in tandem with "DYK." Two mityoks can spend an indeterminably long time talking:
   —Dyk!
   —Eh, brickies-stickies!
   —Dyk!

—Eh, brickies-stickies!

Such a conversation can mean many things. For example, it can mean that the first mityok is trying to find out from the second: what time is it? The second answers that it's past nine and it's too late to run to the store; the first one then suggests going to a restaurant, while the second one complains about the lack of money. However, often this conversation does not express anything, but is simply there as a mode of self-affirmation and a way to kill time.

MAKE (someone into) A SHIT SANDWICH: to offend someone, reproach. Apparently constructed out of the expressions "to eat shit" and "make a sandwich."

KICK BACK: do something pleasant to forget about the difficulties of a mityok's life; most often means to get drunk.

KICKSTER: anyone that attracts the mityok's attention, for example, a cat that jumps up to a high place. (By the way, the mit'ki are very attentive to the animal world, and express their regard exuberantly.)

AT FULL LENGTH: very strongly. For example, to kick back at full length is to get very drunk.

CARNAGE, MURDER, SLAUGHTER, MASSACRE: praise, approval of any event; almost always used with the adjective "total." For example, "this bit of port is total carnage (murder, slaughter, massacre)."

CARDBOARD FOOL: a tender address to one's conversation partner.

CAN'T WE FOR ONCE (do something) IN PEACE?: a proposal to do something, or indignation about any obstruction in some endeavor. For example: "Can't I for once drink (smoke, pee, lace up boots) in peace?"

REEKS: an insult, often offense at inadequately attentive treatment of the mityok. For example: "It reeks that you're holding me up here."

FLUSH: overly meticulous. (An art historical term.)

A-A-A-A!!!!: an often used sound. With a tender or a sad intonation it is an expression of soft reproach; with a sharp intonation that turns into a croaking or a squeal, it is an expression of approval.

THAT'S HOW IT IS!: same as the exclamatory DYK, but more triumphant.

When deciding how to split something, for example when sharing a bottle between friends, three expressions are used that correspond to three ways to split a bottle of wine between the mityok and his drinking partners:

SPLIT EQUALLY: wine is shared equally.

BETWEEN BROTHERS: the mityok drinks the larger portion.

AS CHRIST WOULD HAVE: the mityok drinks everything himself.

This is how the mityok expresses the highest approval: he puts his hand on the stomach, thigh, or groin; having formed a fist, he rhythmically raises and lowers it. His face at this time expresses an indescribable joy. The mityok uses this gesture only in extreme situations, for example when listening to songs by Aquarium.

The mityok characteristically uses long quotations from movies; he prefers quotations that have a sorrowful or tender tone. For example, "Your Grace! Oh, Your Grace! Not in front of the boy! Oh dear, not in front of the boy! Your Grace!"

If the fellow mityok has not seen the movie that was quoted, he will likely not understand what idea the mityok wanted to convey, especially since the quote is seldom connected to the discussion that preceded it. An especially deep emotional disturbance is communicated by the use of the following quotation: "Mit'ka . . . brother . . . is dying . . . . Wants some fish stew . . ."

If the mityok is not the one speaking, he greets his conversation partner's every phrase with peals of laughter, slapping his knees or thighs and exclaiming "carnage!" "murder!" — or, by contrast, he uses sad expressions: "Dyk! How can that be?!" The choice of one type of reaction over the other is not motivated by what the mityok hears.

The mityok's way of relating to anyone he meets is characterized by extreme friendliness. He uses terms of endearment with everyone, calling them little brother, little sister, etc. (Sometimes this makes it difficult to understand who is being referred to, since the mityok will necessarily refer to Sergei Kurekhin as "Koreshok-Kureshok," and to Boris Grebenshchikov as "Grebeshochechok").[2]

Even when meeting people he does not know very well, the mityok is obliged to kiss their cheeks three times, and on leaving, he embraces the person, leans his head on his shoulder and stands in this pose, eyes closed, for a long time, as if in a trance.

The mityok's array of interests is rather varied; however, discussion of a topic that interests the mityok, for example a work of art, is almost entirely confined to the use of expressions "carnage," "murder," etc. To express the highest praise for a work of art, the mityok uses the exclamation "A-a-a-a!" while with his hand he makes a gesture that resembles throwing a fistful of dirt against a wall.

Such sensational events in the city's cultural life as the Tutankhamun or the Thyssen-Bornemisza exhibit elicit in the mityok only a studiedly indifferent reaction.

The mityok likes to engage in self-affirmation by interacting with people who are not part of the mityok movement. Here, for example, is a typical telephone conversation between Dmitry Shagin and Alexander Florensky.

FLORENSKY (lifting the receiver): Hello.

SHAGIN (sadly and tentatively, after a long pause and inarticulate groaning): Shurka? Shurochek?

---

2   Boris Grebenshchikov is a famous rock singer known for his solo work as well as his
     work with his group Aquarium.

FLORENSKY: Hello, Mitya.

SHAGIN (tenderly): Shurenochek . . . Shurka . . . A-a-a- . . . (after a pause, with alarm). How are you? Well, how are you over there?!!

FLORENSKY: Not bad, Kuzya's here, he dropped by.

SHAGIN (with an inexpressible tenderness toward Kuzya, whom he does not know very well): Kuzya! Kuzyunchik . . . Kuzyarushka's over at your house . . . (Pause). Kuzya's over?

FLORENSKY (with irritation): Yes.

SHAGIN: A-a-a . . . You're kicking back with Kuzya then, right? (Pause. Suddenly, with emotion) And my sister, where's my little sister?

FLORENSKY (with a bit of ill feeling, guessing that it is his wife, Olga Florensky, that is being referred to): What little sister?

SHAGIN: This sister that I have . . . Olen'ka.

FLORENSKY: Olya is at work.

SHAGIN: Olen'ka . . . (deeply and seriously, as if sharing a deep mystery). She's a sister to me . . .

FLORENSKY: Mitya, what are you calling about?

SHAGIN: Dyk! Brickies-stickies! Dyk! brickies-stickies! . . . Dyk . . . brickies-stickies!

FLORENSKY (irritated): Mitya, enough already.

SHAGIN (tenderly, reproachfully): Shurenok, bricks-sticks . . . You cardboard fool you . . .

FLORENSKY (with undisguised irritation): Enough!

SHAGIN (with feeling): Shurka! Little brother! You're a brother to me, a brother! How could you? . . . With your own brother?!

Florensky throws down the phone in a fit of anger. Dmitry Shagin is deeply pleased with the conversation.

Like the leading man of any mass youth movement, Dmitry Shagin experiences a conflict with society. Strange as it may seem, any mityok is, generally speaking, not satisfied with his life circumstances. To any positive fact in the lives of others he tenderly, but with sadness replies: "For some life is a caramel, for others it's only torture . . ." naturally putting himself in the role of the tortured.

It's true, the participant in the mityok movement should be forewarned that such participation entails certain inconveniences.

Decide for yourself: what stamina should the wife of the mityok have in order to refrain from nagging and chiding him when he evinces a lack of desire to get anything done; more precisely, the unpleasantness lies in the fact that the mityok readily accepts any task, but will compulsively sabotage it. In response to any reproaches addressed to him, the mityok smiles angelically, and softly whispers to his wife: "Little sister! My dear little sister! . . . Dyk! Bricks-sticks! Dyk!" In response to the strongest accusations, he objects, quite reasonably: "Where would you find another golden boy like me, and one who'll get things done, at that?"

At other times, the mityok will take on responsibilities in a de-cidedly adventuresome spirit—like deciding to remodel a room himself. In that case, he calls on several other mit'ki for help, and they hold a drinking binge in the room to be remodeled—in order to kick back from a life full of torture. If the persistent efforts of many people really force the mityok to begin the remodel, the room will in short order resemble a dark torture chamber; future efforts on the part of the mityok will have an impact on the room that is analogous to the detonation of a high-caliber missile.

Dmitry Shagin, having heard this essay, was more insulted than pleased, and announced that he'd been made into a shit sandwich enough times, bricks-sticks, isn't it time to say something good for a change; in particular, let's not forget to mention D. Shagin's wonderful painting. Well, we'll do just that: not only does D. Shagin produce wonderful paintings (which, actually, have no relation to the mit'ki movement), but everything we've already said creates the image of a highly positive hero who became the head of a movement not at all unknowingly.

The mit'ki movement develops and deepens the "likable good-for-nothing" type, which is perhaps our most charming national type—except for perhaps the saint. [. . .]

1984

Part Five

Mit'ki Ethics

> Nowadays you only have fun with your darn mit'ki!
>
> *From talks with my wife*

That's how it turns out! A mass youth movement, and all of a sudden: "The mit'ki are not sexual." What the hell, one might ask, do we need a mass youth movement like that for, who will join it?

Last winter, to expected acclaim, the movie "Dear friend," based on Maupassant, was shown on TV. The film had absolutely nothing of the mit'ki in it, not even one quotation could have been gleaned from it—it's even awkward to mention it as an example.

I was able (rather, I was lucky enough) to watch it with Dmitry Shagin. I won't hide it: Mitya watched the film without pretending indifference, without decrying its total lack of mityok qualities; instead he showed exaltation and a joyful wonderment. His comments were even more lively than when watching the classics of mityok cinema.

—Ho! Another chick! Look . . . Yeah, for sure! Now he'll land her! Look, look . . . . Look! Look! . . . Yeah, for sure! He landed her!

This fun contrasted sharply with the coldness and the badly masked envy of the rest of the audience, which could not relate to the characters in such a detached manner. Mitya took in the romantic adventures of the movie's plot as if they were the entertaining behavior of exotic animals (characteristic in connection with this is the use of the term "landed" from animal husbandry).

TO LAND (someone): . . .

With the same curiosity and joy, Mitya would have watched how, for example, an elephant could have eaten, incredibly, several quintals of cabbage at one sitting.

—Ho! He's picking up another head of cabbage! Now he's going to eat it! Look, look . . . Yeah, for sure! He ate it!

And who would not have shown a joyful interest in that ability! But even though I'm fond of cabbage I personally do not envy that elephant. A person who has a good life will not turn all his thoughts to cabbage or girls. Properly speaking, ethics has nothing to do with it.

—Yeah he's slick, this "dear friend." But I feel bad for him . . . Poor guy! He's bored, nothing interests him . . .

The mityok delivers himself from sin not by hysterically turning away, not with the foam of melancholy, but with laughter and compassion.

And let the movement's undecided neophytes get spooked by this, but not for nothing was Fil's chapter "Mit'ki and sex" so short: "The mit'ki are not sexual." This not a condemnation; it is simply a not very interesting fact.

What is there that's more interesting? Drinking cheap wine, while tearing the bottle out of each other's hands?

Yes, reader, of course I've exposed the mityok to criticism of the most severe sort—here, make him into a shit sandwich!—but it's one of the most charming aspects of the movement: the sin of the mityok is visible to all!

Somewhere I heard a wonderful thought about the ethics of Soviet punks: there's morality, and there's decency. To be moral is to refrain from swearing, whereas to be decent is to refrain from betraying your friends. The punks have no morality, but they do have decency. If that were really so, the mit'ki would be ready to befriend the punks (although if one were to take this proposition literally, it would turn out that mit'ki have not only decency but also morals—they never swear. What for? When one has such a large arsenal of expressive means, swear words are pale and primitive).

Morality is something artificial; it's a toll gate that warns of some possible unpleasantness. But dwarves easily slip under it, while giants jump over it without noticing—and is such a toll gate, one that's always closed, needed? Morality is necessary for those for whom everything needs to be tip-top, open-closed, clear eyes, pleasant conversations and, daily—a knife in the back.

No, the mityok wears his sin on his sleeve. Did not drop off the laundry at the laundromat, drank away two rubles, got home late—but in exchange, these and all his sins, are visible to the whole world. Everyone blames the mityok, and the first one to blame him is the mityok himself.

Would you, reader, go with the mityok on a reconnaissance mission? He won't betray you, but he'll come to the task with a tender submissive smile, that's the problem. In any case, not everyone can be a scout; reconnaissance—it's completely out of the mityok's character.

—We know, we know! In character for him is to rip the bottle of cheap wine out of his friend's hands!

Yes, reader, one can rip a bottle of cheap wine out of a friend's hands; there are times even when it's necessary. But what's to be said! Reconnaissance is reconnaissance, a bottle is a bottle, but if I need to defend myself against the whole world, I would like to lean my back against the dirty body of a mityok . . . .

Mityok culture has not as yet spread by leaps and bounds, and the frightening image of the bottle ripped from a friend's hands does not exhaust the complex image of the mityok.

There's a holiday—Day of the Mityok Equinox (this incomprehensible name came about in the course of history). The holiday is not celebrated on any particular date; it can be celebrated once a month, once a week, or every day. Often it coincides with the showing on TV of mityok TV favorites (however, these days also have their own, separate holidays. For example, "His Excellency's aide-de-camp is dry"—movie-watching without drinking; or "His Excellency's aide-de-camp is wet"—movie-watching while drinking).

Let's imagine the meeting of three mityok friends (A, B, and C), who've gotten together to celebrate the Day of the Mityok Equinox.

A: Now, to start I'm going to read you Pushkin.

B: Wait, dear. Today's the Day of the Mityok Equinox. Let me run to the store first. I even have money.

C: Can't be done! Each time you contribute more than the rest of us! I'll go.

A: No! You might as well cut me into pieces—I can't drink anymore on your dime! I'll go!

(A runs to the store. B and C during this time decorate the space with banners and posters with slogans like "THE MIT'KI DO NOT WANT TO TRIUMPH OVER ANYONE." "THE MIT'KI WILL ALWAYS BE IN SHIT." And "MIT'KI WILL CONQUER THE WORLD."
A returns and puts the bottles on the table. Usually here a short warm-up follows, during which the mit'ki circle the table like a cat circles a saucer of sour cream):

A: Uncle Zakhar, does it really happen, real love?

B: It happens, Nats . . . It's better to be in your own jacket in the camps at the logging place than in a feather-lined suit at Fox's. What is it, Abdullah, do your people want to scorch something?

C: This one guy got in here and won't leave! What to do, Ivan Petrovich? Will you call the KGB yourself or should I?

A: You were right to call, but you didn't count on one thing: Anya wouldn't have shot up on the Petrovka!

B: Wouldn't have, you say? Even the fellows that were with me behind bars, they would all shoot up! Dzhabded killed my father, wanted to bury me too!

C: Get up, you swine! Volodya! Open it, you shameful wolfskin!

(The warm-up over, the mit'ki open the bottles and sit down at the table.)

A: Now, to start I'm going to read you Pushkin!

B: No, dearie, to start with, drink!

A: You drink first.

B: No, brothers! I've had enough of drinking you dry! You drink to your heart's content—and I'll look on and be happy for you.

C: What are you being like that for? You always drink less than the rest of us and now you don't want to at all? Don't insult us, drink!

B: Does that offer come from the heart?

A and C (together): Drink, drink, dearie!

B: (drinks with tears of tenderness in his eyes).

A and C: Drink, drink some more!

B (offering the bottle to C): My heart breaks just to see how you can't even take a sip properly! Finish the bottle!

C (having just taken a sip, quickly offers the bottle to A): Here, brother, you drink! I've nearly walked all over God's image in myself in drinking you dry! Drink as much as is in you!

A (bowing to all four sides and making a movement toward kissing the earth): I'll drink a very little sip in order not to insult you, and I ask the earth and the heavens and my brothers for forgiveness for all the booze that I've poured into my maw, as if into a bottomless abyss, and never again . . . .

C (in a voice that breaks from emotion): Always! From now on you'll always drink your fill, we've hurt you enough!

A: (hitting the floor and choking on tenderness, drinks).

B and C (together): Finish it! Finish it!

And so on until the end of the get-together.

That's how good, how kind the mit'ki are! But how many absurd, mean rumors are spread about them—essentially because people cannot separate historical reality from the mit'ki's mythological symbolism.

There's talk even of the sexual libertinism of the mit'ki, but that is already beyond all measure. The mit'ki, as is well known, are so asexual that they pride themselves on it. Dmitry Shagin, for example, proudly asserts that he has never in his life known a woman. These discussions bring him both pride and pain; he pets his three daughters on the head and sorrowfully bites his lip. And it is all so high and so noble that the tongue does not dare ask—where did the three daughters come from, then? I once decided to ask: under the weight of facts D. Shagin admitted that after all yes, three times in his life he had known women (it's emblematic that in spite of their love of freedom, the mit'ki are as fertile as rabbits).

So, a question: where do the rumors that besmirch the public's estimation of the moral image of the mit'ki come from? Answer: from the mythology of the mit'ki. The consciousness of the undeveloped listener gathers from the myth not the suggestive layers, not even the moral of the story, but what the undeveloped consciousness takes as fact. Let's examine this and disprove it on the evidence of two myths formed in the mit'ki sphere at about the same time.

THE BRIDE: Fil's tale

Once Fil decided to show off his bride (named Olen'ka, of course) to Florenych: have a bride-show.

He spent a long time with her walking the streets, could not commit himself, doubt assailed him—will Florenych like the bride?

Frozen like a dog, poor, sick, hadn't eaten anything since morning. Finally buys a bottle of wine—comes over to Florenych's place.

Florenych sits there. Piss-drunk, red-faced, putting away scrambled eggs and ham. Fil sits down across from him on a stool, puts a bottle of wine on the table, worries, waits to find out what Florenych is going to say.

Florenych gobbles up the eggs and ham, drinks all the wine that Fil brought, then moves over to the bride and starts feeling her up: touches her breasts, gropes under her dress. Apparently, plans to use the right of the first wedding night.

USE THE RIGHT OF THE FIRST WEDDING NIGHT (mythological): A. Florensky's mode of conducting himself with his friends' girlfriends.

For Fil everything went dark; he lowered his head, clenched his teeth, only his little legs stick out.

But the heart is not a stone—he grabs a knife from the table, throws it at Florenych. But either Fil was shaking so badly, or Florenych was so unsteady on his feet—the knife hit the bride instead, just barely grazed her cheek—left a little scar. Small, white. Under the eye.

THE BRIDE: Florenych's tale

One time Florenych—poor, sick, cold—was sitting around. Came home from work, hadn't eaten all day, his back hurts, his head is about to explode; sits on his stool, only his little legs are sticking out.

Made himself eggs and ham—let me, he thinks, just once in my life eat in peace.

Fil comes over. Piss-drunk, red-faced, two chicks with him, one under each arm. One of these, Olen'ka, he says, jokingly, is his bride.

Fil sits down at the table, gobbles up Florenych's eggs and ham, drinks the bottle of wine that Florenych had hidden away. Puts down the glass, lays down the fork, and starts to feel up one of the chicks (not the bride, the other one). Touches her breasts, gropes under her dress.

Poor Florenych sits across from him on a stool, staring, while Fil's bride has only her poor little legs sticking out. Hangs her head low, shoulders start to shake, starts sniffling with her nose. Florenych moves closer to her: as if to say, don't cry, he's only like that when he's drunk, and pets her on the back.

Suddenly Fil jumps up, his face drunk, red, grabs a knife off the table and throws it at Florenych. Missed, of course, but it nicked the bride, just barely grazed her cheek—left a little scar. Small, white. Under the eye.

It's interesting that both these stories, from the first word to the last, are fantasy; more precisely, mit'ki myths with characteristic mythological markers. Both storytellers, for example, without prior discussion, use in their myths the luminous image of the "eggs and ham," which, as everyone can understand, was not, would not be and could not have been in A. Florensky's studio.

The myth is based on the fact that Florenych and Fil did drink together (and more than once) in the studio with sister Olya, who has under her eye a little white scar from falling off a slide when she was a child.

Why did Fil and Florenych need to sully each other in this way? Because, for the sake of the movement, they were creating a mityok mythology, with no regard to personal cost. Both stories carry one and same simple moral: if it's only the case that your little legs stick out, that's good; if life's a caramel, that's bad. The negative hero is full, drunk, content, successful; the positive hero is poor, sick, hungry.

So, does that mean that the mityok is necessarily poor, sick, hungry? No, that applies only to the particular myth in question.

It is hard to define what a mityok is. And in general I can no longer say what constitutes a mityok.

The crux of the matter is this: the first parts of *Mit'ki* were written with detachment; it's a view of the movement from the outside. But anyone who even for a short time stops to stare at the victory march of the mit'ki is himself drawn, as if by a magnet, into their ranks.

Every definition of the movement made by the mit'ki themselves is charming but incomplete (for example, one of the movement's pioneers, A. Goryaev, in his work "Mit'ki and Painting" proposed the following definition: "The mityok is a person who keenly feels beauty").

So, I can no longer be a dispassionate and objective observer of the movement and must put down the pen—I no longer think about what the mityok is.

In the same way that a person who lives a full life cannot explain why he lives. And a painter why he must paint paintings. And Grebenshchikov never answered the TV audience's question— why he sings.

What's a mityok? How many stars are in the sky? Why do flowers grow?

1986

Translated by Rebecca Pyatkevich

Recommended additional readings:

Alexei Yurchak, *Everything Was Forever Until It Was No More: The Last Soviet Generation* (Princeton: Princeton University Press, 2006), 237–243.

Alexandar Mihailovic, "'In the Heat of the Boiler Room': The Subculture of the Russian Navy in St. Peterburg's *Mit'ki* Group," *World Literature Today* (July–August 2006): 50–57.